risk management and
value creation
in financial
institutions

GERHARD SCHROECK

John Wiley & Sons, Inc.

Library of Congress Cataloging-in-Publication Data:

Schroeck, Gerhard.
    Risk management and value creation in financial institutions / Gerhard Schroeck.
      p. cm.
      ISBN 0-471-25476-2 (CLOTH : alk. paper)
    1. Banks and banking—Valuation. 2. Financial institutions—Valuation. 3. Risk management. 4. Asset-liability management. I. Title.

  HG1707.7 .S37 2002
  332.1'068'1—dc21

                                                                                    2002008564

Printed in the United States of America

10 9 8 7 6 5 4 3 2 1

To Tiger
For your invaluable support

My ventures are not in one bottom trusted,
Nor to one place; nor is my whole estate
Upon the fortune of this present year;
Therefore, my merchandise makes me not sad.

—Antonio, in: *The Merchant of Venice,*
Act I, Scene I
by William Shakespeare

From an empirical as well as a personal point of view, risk management in the financial industry has been one of the most exciting and most researched areas over the last decade. Depositors and regulators claim that risk management is necessary, and many banks argue that superior risk management can create (shareholder) value. However, from a theoretical point of view, it is not immediately clear if and how risk management at the corporate level can be useful. Very little research has been conducted as to why there is an economic rationale for risk management at the bank level.

This book provides a closer and a more differentiated view on the subject than previous research and is intended to describe both the theory and the practice of corporate risk management in financial institutions. It is different from other works on this subject in the following significant ways.

First, it addresses the question of under which circumstances risk management at the corporate level can help to maximize value. These conditions require a deviation from standard neoclassical finance theory because in (risk) efficient markets corporate risk management could destroy value, especially if it comes at a cost, and it is shown that risk management at the bank level is not restricted to hedging activities in such a world.

Second, the book agrees in principal with what other publications find are the correct building blocks on which risk-management decisions in banks should be based in such a world, namely economic capital and RAROC (risk-adjusted return on [economic] capital). It also explains, that in the circumstances under which corporate risk management can add value, the conclusions of classical finance theory are not valid in general, and that the Net Present Value (NPV) rule might not always be the correct measure to decide whether a (risk management) transaction adds or destroys value.

Third, this book, therefore, develops the foundations for a model that would allow banks to identify comparative advantages that, in turn, would enable them to select those risk-management strategies that really add value.

Fourth, the approach presented in this book is able to reconcile the debt holders' (who are averse to default risk) and the shareholders' (who prefer more volatility rather than less because they are option holders on the firm's value) perspectives and to identify those activities that are helpful to all constituents/stakeholders of a financial institution because they avoid the consequences of a bank run.

Even though the following Chinese proverb:

A smart man learns from his own mistakes,
A wise man learns from the mistakes of others,
And a fool never learns

applies to both risk management and writing a manuscript on this subject, I hope this book will be a valuable contribution to the ongoing discussion.

There are undoubtedly errors in the final product both orthographically and conceptually that remain my own responsibility, and certainly further research needs to be done. Thus, I encourage anybody with constructive comments to send them on to me.

All views presented in this book represent the author's views and do not necessarily reflect those of Oliver, Wyman & Company.

acknowledgments

No book is solely the effort of its author. Many people have played a crucial part in making this book happen and suffered from me writing it. I am indebted to both academics and practitioners who have made excellent and useful suggestions. Even though the following list is almost surely incomplete, many people deserve special thanks for their help:

First and foremost, I owe a great deal to my academic teacher and Ph.D. supervisor Prof. Dr. Manfred Steiner (University of Augsburg, Germany) for leaving both the necessary and sufficient degrees of freedom in my research.

I am grateful to John D. Stroughair (also for helping to coordinate the required time off from Oliver, Wyman & Company), Til Schuermann, Martin Wallmeier, and, last but not least, Victoria Sheppard for their helpful criticism when reviewing my manuscript.

From the bottom of my heart, I would like to thank my family and especially Bettina Klippel for the sacrifices they have made on behalf of this book. The loyal support and encouragement of my parents throughout my life—whichever way it took me—are truly appreciated. Heartfelt thanks to Bettina for enduring late nights and long weekends consumed to write this book; without her help and understanding, I would not have made it!

Gerhard Schröck
Bad Homburg, Germany

contents

Figures   xv

Tables   xvii

Symbols   xix

Abbreviations   xxiii

CHAPTER 1
Introduction   1

CHAPTER 2
**Foundations for Determining the Link between Risk Management
and Value Creation in Banks**   9

Value Maximization in Banks   10
Value Maximization as the Firm's Objective   10
Valuation Framework for Banks   14
Problems with the Valuation Framework for Banks   16
   Empirical Conundrum   16
   Other Stakeholders' Interests in Banks   21
Risk Management in Banks   23
Definition of Risk   24
Definition of Risk Management   25
Role and Importance of Risk and Its Management in Banks   28
Link between Risk Management and Value Creation in Banks   30

Goals of Risk Management in Banks   *31*
  Choice of the Goal Variable   31
  Choice of the Stakeholder Perspective   33
  Choice of the Risk Dimension   34
  Choice of the Risk-Management Strategy   38
Ways to Conduct Risk Management in Banks   *39*
  Eliminate/Avoid   40
  Transfer   41
  Absorb/Manage   41
Empirical Evidence   *43*
Summary   48
Appendix   48
Part A: Bank Performance   *48*
Part B: Systematic versus Specific Risk   *49*

CHAPTER 3
Rationales for Risk Management in Banks   **55**

Risk Management and Value Creation in
the Neoclassical Finance Theory   58
The Neoclassical Finance Theory   *58*
Corollaries from the Neoclassical Finance Theory
  with Regard to Risk Management   *61*
The Risk Management Irrelevance Proposition   *64*
Summary and Implications   *70*
Discrepancies Between Neoclassical Theory and Practice   *72*
Risk Management and Value Creation in
the Neoinstitutional Finance Theory   74
Classification of the Relaxation of the Assumptions
  of the Neoclassical World   *75*
The Central Role of the Likelihood of Default   *80*
Agency Costs as Rationale for Risk Management   *81*
  Agency Costs of Equity as a Rationale for Risk Management   82
  Agency Costs of Debt as a Rationale for Risk Management   91
  Coordination of Investment and Financing   97
Transaction Costs as a Rationale for Risk Management   *105*
  The Costs of Financial Distress   105
  The Costs of Implementing Risk Management   113
  The Costs of Issuance   114
  The Costs of a Stable Risk Profile   114
Taxes and Other Market Imperfections as Rationales
  for Risk Management   *116*
  Taxes   116

Other Market Imperfections 121
Additional Rationales for Risk Management in Banks 122
Summary and Conclusions 123
Appendix 127

CHAPTER 4
Implications of the Previous Theoretical Discussion for This Book **129**

CHAPTER 5
Capital Structure in Banks **137**

The Role of Capital in Banks 138
Capital as a Means for Achieving the Optimal Capital Structure 138
Capital as Substitute for Risk Management to
Ensure Bank Safety 140
The Various Stakeholders' Interests in Bank Safety 141
Available Capital 145
Required Capital from an Economic Perspective 150
Determining Capital Adequacy in the Economic Perspective 160
Summary and Consequences 162
Derivation of Economic Capital 164
Types of Risk 164
Economic Capital as an Adequate Risk Measure for Banks 166
Ways to Determine Economic Capital for
Various Risk Types in Banks (Bottom-Up) 170
Credit Risk 170
Market Risk 186
Operational Risk 196
Aggregation of Economic Capital across Risk Types 210
Concerns with the Suggested Bottom-Up Approach 212
Suggestion of an Approach to Determine Economic
Capital from the Top Down 219
Theoretical Foundations 221
Suggested Top-Down Approach 225
Assessment of the Suggested Approach 235
Evaluation of Using Economic Capital 236
Summary 237

CHAPTER 6
Capital Budgeting in Banks **239**

Evolution of Capital-Budgeting Tools in Banks 239
RAROC as a Capital-Budgeting Tool in Banks 242

Definition of RAROC   242
Advantages of RAROC   245
Assumptions of RAROC   247
Deficiencies of RAROC   253
   Deficiencies of the Generic RAROC Model   253
   Modifying RAROC to Address Its Pitfalls   259
   Fundamental Problems of RAROC   261
Evaluation of RAROC as a Single-Factor Model
*   for Capital Budgeting in Banks*   267
New Approaches to Capital Budgeting in Banks   268
Overview of the New Approaches   269
Evaluation of RAROC in the Light of the New Approaches   272
Implications of the New Approaches to Risk Management
*   and Value Creation in Banks*   273
   Implications for Risk-Management Decisions   274
   Implications for Capital-Budgeting Decisions   279
   Implications for Capital-Structure Decisions   279
New Approaches as Foundations for a Normative
*   Theory of Risk Management in Banks*   280
Areas for Further Research   282
Summary   285

CHAPTER 7
Conclusion   **287**

References   **293**

Index   **311**

figures

Figure 1.1   Integrated view of value creation in banks.

Figure 2.1   Average bank performance versus broad market index.
Figure 2.2   Deviations in bank performance.
Figure 2.3   Best bank performers.
Figure 2.4   Worst bank performers.
Figure 2.5   Systematic versus specific risk in the banking industry.
Figure 2.6   Overview of ways to conduct risk management.
Figure 2.7   Deutsche Bank.
Figure 2.8   Energy industry.
Figure 2.9   Consumer cyclical industry.
Figure 2.10   Utility industry.

Figure 3.1   The Wheel of Misfortune.
Figure 3.2   Overview of risk-management rationales in the neoinstitutional world.
Figure 3.3   Variations in firm value and default point.
Figure 3.4   Ownership concentration in European banks.
Figure 3.5   The underinvestment problem and risk management.
Figure 3.6   Over- and Underhedging.
Figure 3.7   Influence of bankruptcy costs on firm value.
Figure 3.8   Tax schedules.
Figure 3.9   Effects of convex tax schedules on tax liabilities.
Figure 3.10   Effects of convex tax schedules on after-tax income.

Figure 4.1   The interdependency of capital budgeting, capital structure, and risk management when risk management can create value.

Figure 5.1   Capital ratios in U.S. banks over time.
Figure 5.2   Stakeholder tranches and risk capital.
Figure 5.3   Economic capital.
Figure 5.4   Types of risk in banks.

Figure 5.5   Value at risk.

Figure 5.6   Deriving expected losses.

Figure 5.7   Economic capital for credit risk.

Figure 5.8   Typical distribution for market risk.

Figure 5.9   Distribution for deriving economic capital for event risk.

Figure 5.10 Distribution for deriving economic capital for business risk.

Figure 5.11 Distribution of asset values and default probability.

Figure 5.12 Input and output variables for suggested top-down approach.

Figure 6.1   Return on equity and changing capital structure.

Figure 6.2   Changes in RAROC for changes in riskiness and correlation.

Figure 6.3   RAROC and nonzero NPV projects.

Figure 6.4   Problem areas applying the RAROC decision rule—Zero NPV projects.

Figure 6.5   Problem areas applying the RAROC decision rule—Negative NPV projects.

Figure 6.6   Problem areas applying the RAROC decision rule—Positive NPV projects.

Figure 6.7   Fundamental problems with RAROC.

Figure 6.8   Economic balance sheet including economic capital.

Figure 6.9   Overview of the components of a normative theory for risk management.

tables

Table 2.1   Industry Control Sample
Table 2.2   Bank Performance

Table 3.1   Overview of Corporate Risk-Management Scenarios
Table 3.2   Financial Risk Management by the Firm
Table 3.3   Sample of European Banks Selected for Testing Ownership
             Concentration

Table 4.1   Summary Table for Comparison

Table 5.1   Bank Book Capital Ratios
Table 5.2   Overview of Capital Concepts in Banks
Table 5.3   Split of Economic Capital
Table 5.4   Input Data from Publicly Available Sources
Table 5.5   Iterative Procedure
Table 5.6   Approximate S&P Default Probabilities
Table 5.7   Distance to Default
Table 5.8   Weighted Average Asset Return
Table 5.9   Final Results

Table 6.1   Effects of Keeping the Default Probability Constant
Table 6.2   Split of Economic Capital among Types of Risk
Table 6.3   CAPM Hurdle Rate and Economic Capital

↑	Increase in the respective measure
↓	Decrease in the respective measure
α	Confidence level or α-quantile of a cumulative probability distribution or constant
β_i	Stock market beta of asset i as derived in the market model version of the CAPM or constant
Δ	Change in value or option delta $N(d_1)$
ε	Random change in return
λ	Unit cost for volatility of the bank's portfolio of nonhedgable cash flows
μ_i	Expected rate of return of transaction i
μ	Drift rate or expected return on a bank's assets or expected value of a distribution
Φ^{-1}	Inverse standard normal cumulative density function
$\rho_{i,j}$	Correlation between the rate of return of transaction i and j or default correlation between loan i and j
σ_A	Constant asset volatility
σ_i	Standard deviation (volatility) of the rate of return of transaction or index i
$\sigma_{i,j}$	Covariance between i and j
$\sigma^2_{E,W}$	Variance of weekly stock returns
$\sigma^2_{specific}$	Specific risk
Σ	Correlation matrix of value changes in the portfolio positions
ω_i	Portfolio weight of the i-th credit asset
'	Indicator for a first proxy
A	Asset(s)
a_j	Number of years of data history in the event database in category j

B	Stock market index for the banking industry
BV_A	Book value of total assets or asset A
BV_D	Book value of debt D
BV_E	Book value of equity E
BV_{OBS}	Book value of off-balance sheet liabilities
c	$(1 - \alpha)$-quantile of the standard normal distribution or (convex) cost of external funds or call option or constant
CF_t	Cash flow in period t
CM	Capital multiplier
$cov_{i,j}$	Covariance of losses
CR_r	Concentration ratio for r largest shareholders
D	Debt
DP	Default point
DTD	Distance to default
E	Equity
e	External funds
$e(\cdot)$	Function of after-tax income
$E(\cdot)$	Expected value of $\cdot$
$E(R_H)$	Expected (or mean) return R of the portfolio over time horizon H
$E(R_i)$	Expected rate of return of transaction i
EA_H	Exposure amount at time H
EC_i	Economic capital transaction i
E_j	Total number of observed events in category j
$EL_{ER,j}$	Expected losses due to event risk in category j
EL_H	Expected loss (experienced at time H)
EL_P	Expected Loss of a portfolio of n credits
$f(\cdot)$	Function of $\cdot$, also convex tax function
$f(R_H)$	Assumed distribution of the portfolio returns R over time horizon H
F	Cumulative probability distribution or face value of debt D
F^{-1}	Inverse function of F
F^{-1}	Inverse of the cumulative probability function
FDC	(Proportional) financial distress costs of the bank
$g(\cdot)$	Function of $\cdot$, also linear tax function
H	End of the measurement period (horizon) or time in the end of the predetermined measurement period
I	Initial cash investment or cost of an investment

ln	Natural logarithm
$LPM_n(t)$	Lower partial moment n with target return t
LR_H	Loss rate (experienced at time H)
M	Broad stock market index market or Market Portfolio
n	Moment of the distribution (see LPM)
n_j	Overall number of banks in the event database in category j
$N(\cdot)$	Cumulative standard normal probability distribution function
Other%	Other (long-term) liabilities as percentage of total assets
p	Probability density function of the returns X (see LPM) or put option
$p(\cdot)$	Probability
P	Portfolio P
ΔP	Change in the price of a risk factor P
PD_H	Probability of default (up to time H)
PE_j	Probability of an event occurring in category j
r	Risk-free rate
R_D	Return on debt (also R_D)
R_D	Promised yield to maturity of the debt D
R_E	Return on equity (also R_E)
R_E^h	Hurdle rate of return on equity capital
$R_{E,i}$	Required rate of return for transaction i on the invested shareholder capital E
R_f	Risk-free rate of return (also r)
$R_{i,t}$	Return of transaction or index i at time t
R_M	Return on the market portfolio M
$R_M - r$	Market risk premium
r_t	Discount rate for period t
s	Spread above the risk-free rate commensurate with the bank's rating
S_i	Sharpe ratio for transaction i
$S_{i,t}$	Index value S for index i at time t
S_t	Stock price at time t
ST%	Customer and short-term liabilities as percent of total assets
t	Time or target (minimum) return (see LPM)
T	Time of maturity
τ	Transposed vector of
UL	Unexpected loss
ULC	Unexpected loss contribution
$UL_{ER,P}$	Unexpected loss due to event risk at the portfolio level P

UL_i Unexpected Loss of the i-th credit asset

$ULMC_i$ Marginal contribution of loan i to the overall portfolio unexpected loss

V Firm value or value of the portfolio

ΔV_H Change in the portfolio value V over period H

$V_{A,t}$ Market value of the firm's assets or of asset A at time t

VaR Vector of single transaction VaR

VaR_α Value at risk at the $(1 - \alpha)$ confidence level

VaR_H Value at risk for period H

var_i Variance of losses

$V_{D,t}$ Market value of debt D at time t

$V_{E,i}$ Invested shareholder capital E of transaction i

$V_{E,t}$ Market value of equity E at time t

w Internal sources stemming from the bank's existing assets or internal wealth stemming from existing assets at the end of the investment horizon

x Total firm (market) value (for calculation in concentration ratio CR)

x_i Share of overall firm (market) value held by shareholder group i

X Random variable or also pretax income or realized return (see LPM)

X_H Return that accumulates until the end of the measurement period H

z Wiener process

Z_t Normally distributed random variable with zero mean and variance t

APT	Arbitrage Pricing Theory
BIS	Bank for International Settlements
bn	Billion
bps	basis point(s)
CAPM	Capital Asset Pricing Model
CML	Capital Market Line
CSV	costly state verification
DCF	discounted cash flow(s)
e.g.	for example
EVA®	economic value added
EXIM	Export-Import Bank
FDIC	Federal Deposit Insurance Corporation
i.e.	that is
M&A	mergers and acquisitions
M&M	Modigliani and Miller
NPV	net present value
OPT	Option Pricing Theory
P&L	profit and loss statement
PV	present value
RAPM	risk-adjusted performance (or profitability) measures
RAROC	risk-adjusted return on capital
RARORAC	risk-adjusted return on risk-adjusted capital
ROA	return on assets
ROE	return on equity
RORAC	return on risk-adjusted capital
S&P	Standard and Poor's
SML	Security Market Line
TQM	Total Quality Management
VaR	value at risk
WACC	weighted average cost of capital

CHAPTER 1

Introduction

Increased (global) competition among banks[1] and the threat of (hostile) takeovers, as well as the increased pressure from shareholders for superior returns has forced banks—like many other companies—to focus on managing their value. It is now universally accepted that a bank's ultimate objective function is value maximization. In general, banks can achieve this either by restructuring from the inside, by divesting genuinely value-destroying businesses,[2] or by being forced into a restructuring from the outside.[3]

The approach typically applied to decide whether a firm creates value is a variant of the traditional discounted cash flow (DCF) analysis of financial theory, with which the value of any asset can be determined.[4] In principle, this multiperiod valuation framework estimates a firm's (free) cash flows[5] and discounts them at the appropriate rate of return[6] to determine the overall firm value from a purely economic perspective. However, since a bank's liability management does not only have a simple financing function—as in industrial corporations—but is rather a part of a bank's business

---

[1]Even though many other financial (and nonfinancial) institutions face the same fundamental problems described in this book, its focus will be exclusively on the banking industry.

[2]These business units or transactions could be of more value to other firms or their shareholders.

[3]Takeovers are a reflection of the market for corporate control, see, for example, Jensen (1986).

[4]See e.g., Brealey and Myers (1991), pp. 63–67.

[5]To both equity holders and debt holders.

[6]The so-called weighted average costs of capital that reflect both the riskiness and timing of the cash flows and the firm's leverage.

operations,[7] it can create value by itself.[8] Therefore,[9] the common valuation framework is slightly adjusted for banks. It estimates the bank's (free) cash flows to its shareholders and then discounts these at the cost of equity capital,[10] to derive the present value (PV) of the bank's equity[11]—which should equal (ideally[12]) the capitalization of its equity in the stock market.

This valuation approach is based on neoclassical finance theory and, therefore, on very restrictive assumptions.[13] Taken to the extreme, in this world—since only the covariance (i.e., so-called systematic) risk with a broad market portfolio counts[14]—the value of a (new) transaction or business line would be the same for all banks, and the capital-budgeting decision could be made independently from the capital-structure decision.[15] Additionally, any risk-management action at the bank level would be irrelevant for value creation[16], because it could be replicated/reversed by the investors in efficient and perfect markets at the same terms and, therefore, would have no impact on the bank's value.

However, in practice, broadly categorized, banks do two things:

- They offer (financial) products and provide services to their clients.
- They engage in financial intermediation and the management of risk.

Therefore, a bank's economic performance, and hence value, depends on the quality of the provided services and the "efficiency" of its risk management.[17] However, even when offering products and services, banks deal

---

[7]See Copeland et al. (1994), p. 479.

[8]A spread can be earned by accepting deposits at lower rates than the market opportunity cost.

[9]There are a number of other reasons described, for example, in Copeland et al. (1994), pp. 477–479, and discussed below.

[10]As, for example, derived via the Capital Asset Pricing Model (CAPM).

[11]So-called Equity Approach or Flows-to-Equity Approach as described by Copeland et al. (1994), Strutz (1993), Kümmel (1993), and many others.

[12]When considering and pricing all real options, see e.g., Dixit and Pindyck (1994).

[13]This theory assumes perfect and complete markets.

[14]See, for example, the CAPM, which is one of the most famous representatives of the neoclassical finance theory.

[15]Note that banks and all other companies would be able to recapitalize at no extra cost.

[16]Risk management can be useful, even in the neoclassical world, for other purposes. For instance, risk management can ensure that a company stays within a certain risk class as defined in the Modigliani and Miller (M&M) world.

[17]See Harker and Stavros (1998), pp. 7–8.

in financial assets[18] and are, therefore, by definition in the financial risk business.[19]

Additionally, risk management is also perceived in practice to be necessary and critically important to ensure the long-term survival of banks. Not only is a regulatory minimum capital-structure and risk-management approach required,[20] but also the customers,[21] who are also liability holders, should and want to be protected against default risk, because they deposit substantial stakes of their personal wealth, for the most part with only one bank. The same argument is used from an economy-wide perspective to avoid bank runs and systemic repercussions of a globally intertwined and fragile banking system.

Therefore, we find plenty of evidence that banks do run sophisticated[22] risk-management functions[23] in practice (positive theory for risk management). They perceive risk management to be a critical (success) factor that is both used with the intention to create value and because of the bank's concern with "lower tail outcomes",[24] that is, the concern with bankruptcy risk.

Moreover, banks evaluate (new) transactions and projects in the light of their existing portfolio[25] rather than (only) in the light of the covariance risk with an overall market portfolio. In practice, banks care about the contribution of these transactions to the total risk of the bank when they make capital-budgeting decisions, because of their concern with lower tail outcomes. Additionally, we can also observe in practice that banks do care

---

[18]In order to offer products that are tailored to their clients' needs, banks need to transform their "resources" along the following dimensions: term, scale, location, liquidity, and/or risk itself by originating, trading, or servicing financial assets; see Allen and Santomero (1996), p. 19.

[19]They enable most of the market participants to cope with economic uncertainty by hedging, pooling, sharing, transferring, and pricing risks. See Harker and Stavros (1998), p. 2.

[20]See, for example, the Basle Accord from 1988 (Basle I), the European Capital Adequacy Directive (CAD), and the recent discussion on the newly proposed Basle Accord (Basle II).

[21]And many other stakeholders.

[22]Over the last ten years, we have seen dramatic improvements in risk measurement tools to make the risk management in banks more effective.

[23]Managing risks has been one of the hottest topics in banking and finance over the last decade. For instance, *Risk Magazine* devoted a whole special issue, under the topic "The Decade of Risk," to this phenomenon; see *Risk Magazine* (1997).

[24]See Stulz (1996), p. 8.

[25]For instance, the concern with credit concentrations to one borrower, region, or industry is a well-established banking guideline and is also reflected in regulatory rules (e.g., the "Grosskredit-Richtlinie" in Germany).

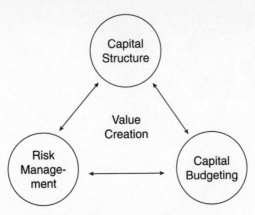

Figure 1.1 Integrated view of value creation in banks.

about their capital structure[26]—when making capital-budgeting and risk-management decisions[27]—and that they perceive holding capital as both costly and a substitute for conducting risk management.

Therefore, banks do not (completely[28]) separate risk-management, capital-budgeting, and capital-structure decisions, but rather determine the three components jointly and endogenously[29] (as depicted in Figure 1.1).

However, this integrated decision-making process in banks is not reflected in the traditional valuation framework as determined by the restrictive assumptions of the neoclassical world. And therefore it appears that some fundamental links to and concerns about value creation in banks are neglected.

Apparently, banks have already recognized this deficiency. Because the traditional valuation framework is also often cumbersome to apply in a banking context,[30] many institutions employ a return on equity (ROE) measure[31] (based on book or regulatory capital) instead. However, banks

---

[26]They also have to do so due to regulatory requirements.

[27]For instance, when banks have capital constraints, they decide either to not take additional risks on their books (which would increase the bankruptcy risk) or to hedge/sell other risks instead.

[28]As is assumed in the neoclassical world.

[29]See Froot and Stein (1998a), p. 58.

[30]This is especially true for outsiders. Even though they are heavily regulated, banks are opaque institutions. Therefore, even bank analysts, who closely follow these organizations, have—according to anecdotal evidence—difficulties in estimating the necessary input parameters.

[31]This already reflects the evolution of bank performance measures from a pure earnings focus in banks to a return on assets (ROA) focus. Realizing that capital is the limiting factor in banking, which is also related to risk, banks introduced ROE numbers.

have also realized that such ROE numbers do not have the economic focus of a valuation framework for judging whether a transaction or the bank as a whole contributes to value creation. They are too accounting-driven, the capital requirement is not closely enough linked to the actual riskiness of the institution, and, additionally, they do not adequately reflect the linkage between capital-budgeting, capital-structure, and risk-management decisions.

To fill this gap, some of the leading banks have developed a set of practical heuristics called Risk-Adjusted Performance Measures (RAPM[32]) or also better known, named after their most famous representative, as RAROC (risk-adjusted return on capital[33]). These measures can be viewed as modified return on equity ratios and take a purely economic perspective.[34] Since banks are concerned about unexpected losses[35] and how they will affect their own credit rating, they estimate[36] the required amount of (economic or) risk capital[37] that they optimally need to hold and that is commensurate with the (overall) riskiness of their (risk) positions. To do that, banks employ a risk measure called value at risk (VaR), which has evolved as the industry's standard measure for lower tail outcomes (by choice or by regulation). VaR measures the (unexpected) risk contribution of a transaction to the total risk of a bank's existing portfolio. The numerator of this modified ROE ratio is also based on economic rather than accounting numbers and is, therefore, adjusted, for example, for provisions made for credit losses (so-called expected losses). Consequently, "normal" credit losses do not affect a bank's "performance," whereas unexpected credit losses do.

In order to judge whether a transaction creates or destroys value for the bank, the current practice is to compare the (single-period) RAPM to a hurdle rate or benchmark return.[38] Following the traditional valuation framework of neoclassical finance theory, this opportunity cost is usually determined by the covariance or systematic risk with a broad market portfolio.

However, the development and usage of RAROC, the practical evidence for the existence of risk management in banks (positive theory), and the fact that risk management is also used with the intention to enhance value are phenomena unexplained by and unconsidered in neoclassical finance theory.

---

[32]See Reyniers (1991).

[33]See, for example, Zaik et al. (1996). We will use the acronyms RAPM and RAROC interchangeably in this book.

[34]See, for example, Schröck (1997), pp. 93+.

[35]This is because (and as we have seen) they are concerned with the risk of default.

[36]This is done at a certain level of confidence that corresponds to their target credit rating.

[37]This fictional capital measure is proportional to the risk taken and is often called *economic capital*. It forms the denominator of the modified ROE ratio.

[38]See, for example, Schröck (1997), pp. 96+.

It is, therefore, not surprising that there has been little consensus in academia[39] on whether there is also a normative theory for risk management and as to whether risk management is useful for banks, and why and how it can enhance value.[40]

Therefore, the objective of this book is to diminish this discrepancy between theory and practice by:

- Deriving circumstances under which risk management at the corporate level can create value in banks
- Laying the theoretical foundations for a normative approach to risk management in banks
- Evaluating the practical heuristics RAROC and economic capital as they are currently applied in banks in the light of the results of the prior theoretical discussion
- Developing—based on the theoretical foundations and the implications from discussing the practical approaches—more detailed instructions on how to conduct risk management and how to measure value creation in banks in practice

In order to achieve these goals, we will proceed in the following way: We will first lay the foundations for the further investigation of the link between risk management and value creation by defining and discussing value maximization as well as risk and its management in a banking context, and establishing whether there is empirical evidence of a link between the two.

We will then explore both the neoclassical and the neoinstitutional finance theories[41] on whether we can find rationales for risk management at the corporate level in order to create value. Based on the results of this discussion, we will try to deduce general implications for a framework that encompasses both risk management and value maximization in banks.

Using these results, we will outline the fundamentals for an appropriate (total) risk measure that consistently determines the adequate and economically driven capital amount a bank should hold as well as its implications for the real capital structure in banks. We will then discuss and evaluate the currently applied measure economic capital and how it can be consistently determined in the context of a valuation framework for the various types of risk a bank faces.

Subsequently, we will investigate whether RAROC is an adequate capital-budgeting tool to measure the economic performance of and to iden-

---

[39]For an overview see Smithson (1998).
[40]See Harker and Stavros (1998), p. 8.
[41]This theory introduces agency and transaction costs and other market imperfections to explain real-life phenomena.

tify value creation in banks. We do so because, on the one hand, RAROC uses economic capital as the denominator and, on the other hand, it is similar to the traditional valuation framework in that it uses a comparison to a hurdle rate. When exploring RAROC, we take a purely economic view and neglect regulatory restrictions that undeniably have an impact on the economic performance of banks.[42] Moreover, we will focus on the usage of RAPM in the context of value creation. We will not evaluate its appropriateness for other uses such as limit setting and capital allocation.[43]

We close by evaluating the derived results with respect to their ability to provide more detailed answers on whether and where banks should restructure, concentrate on their competitive advantages or divest, and whether they provide more detailed instructions on why and when banks should conduct risk management from a value creation perspective (normative theory).

---

[42]However, regulation more and more adopts the economic perspective outlined in this book (see, for example, the recently suggested Basle II Accord, which is not covered in detail in this book). Therefore, the discrepancy between the results of this book and the regulated reality should diminish over time.

[43]RAPMs have been found extremely useful for these purposes, see, for example, Matten (1996) and Schröck (1997). For a differing opinion see Johanning (1998).

CHAPTER 2

Foundations for Determining the Link between Risk Management and Value Creation in Banks

Risk management in banking and insurance is not a new phenomenon. Dealing with risk has always been the raison d'être of financial intermediation and its underlying principle.[1] However, risk analysis—although well established from an individual investor's perspective in the context of modern portfolio theory[2]—was not well determined and rigorously analyzed on an industry or bank level until very recently.

This is also true for viewing risk-management activities in banks from a risk-return perspective and, hence, in the context of value creation—which should be for banks, as for any other company, the firm's ultimate objective. Given the central role of risk in banks, in order to use risk management the right way, it is crucial to understand its impact on and the relationship of risk management to the overall firm value.

We are going to lay the theoretical foundations for the detailed analysis of this link between risk management and value creation in banks in this chapter. We will first discuss value maximization in a banking context. Second, we will define risk and its management and will then discuss its importance in banks. Third, we will evaluate which goals risk management can have and which instruments are available to conduct risk management in banks. We will close this chapter by briefly reviewing the empirical evidence on the link between risk management and value creation.

---

[1]See Scholtens and van Wensveen (2000), p. 1247.
[2]As first introduced by Markowitz (1952) and (1959).

VALUE MAXIMIZATION IN BANKS

In this section, we will investigate if and how value maximization should be the ultimate objective of banks, how value creation is currently measured, and what problems can be related to this approach.

Value Maximization as the Firm's Objective

The last decade has witnessed a revolution in the relationship of corporations to their owners. It is now almost universally[3] recognized that a firm's general objective is to create value for its shareholders by maximizing the firm's value.[4] If companies underperform (i.e., do not maximize shareholder value), hostile takeovers[5] and corporate raiders[6] frequently force out underperforming management. Investor activism, especially from activist shareholder groups and institutional investors, is on the rise.[7] This so-called "market for corporate control"[8] is becoming more and more efficient and has forced corporations and banks to focus on economic rather than accounting measures. This is due to the fact that many studies[9] provide empirical evidence that cash-flow-based, that is, economic measures, seem to show a higher correlation with stock price performance, companies' market values, and, hence, shareholder value than traditional accounting measures.[10]

This development assumes that firms (including banks) should also do what shareholders would do in their own interest: maximize their end-of-period wealth.[11] However, from an economic point of view, this general firm objective is not immediately obvious, because firms are only a means rather than an end in modern finance theory.

The ultimate goal of any economic activity is to maximize an individual's

---

[3]At least in the Anglo-American countries.

[4]See, for example, Damodaran (1997), p. 5.

[5]With the Mannesmann-Vodafone deal, a new cross-border dimension of hostile takeovers was reached in Europe.

[6]As first described by Burrough and Helyar (1990) as "barbarians at the gate."

[7]This development can be summarized as either being able to restructure the business from the inside or being forced to restructure from the outside. As a recent example, "Cobra" and its role in the Commerzbank merger talks can be mentioned. See, for example, FAZ (2000), p. 23.

[8]See Jensen (1993), pp. 850–852.

[9]See, for example, Stewart (1991), pp. 72 and 217, and Copeland et al. (1994), p. 83.

[10]See Friedrich et al. (2000), p. 31. However, this result is little surprising since these methods are used by almost the entire analyst and investment community, which "makes" the markets.

[11]See Brealey and Myers (1991), p. 22.

utility, as described in the Arrow-Debreu neoclassical market theory. In this world, an investor's utility is determined by the stream of income available for consumption, which is characterized by three dimensions:[12]

- Its absolute value(s)
- The time of occurrence (time structure)
- Its uncertainty (risk characteristics)

Any investment is an economic activity that gives up some of this stream of consumption in order to increase consumption in the future, which is uncertain. Therefore, the decision rule for any economic activity should be whether an investment increases the utility that the investor hopes to extract in the form of consumption from the investment's future income stream, while considering preferences with regard to the time structure and uncertainty of this income stream.[13]

However, as Fisher has already shown in 1930,[14] the capital-investment decision can be separated from the individual's preferences with respect to current versus future consumption.[15] The optimal investment decision, therefore, only needs to maximize the expected utility over the planning horizon of the decision maker.[16] This in turn is equivalent to the maximization of the net present value of wealth, because shareholders can transform that wealth into their preferred time pattern of consumption with their desired risk characteristics as long as they have frictionless access to capital markets. Hence—at least in the classical world, with no agency or transaction costs and perfectly efficient markets—it is correct that the objective of the firm is to maximize the wealth of its shareholders by trying to maximize the stock price.[17]

In this world, the net present value (NPV)[18] criterion for capital-budgeting decisions is consistent with shareholder wealth maximization, and managers should—on behalf of the firm[19]—pursue all investment opportu-

---

[12]See Schmidt and Terberger (1997), p. 49.
[13]See Schmidt and Terberger (1997), pp. 48–49.
[14]See Fisher (1965).
[15]See, for example, Brealey and Myers (1991), p. 22, also commonly referred to as Fisher separation.
[16]See Copeland and Weston (1988), p. 17. In many cases this means to maximize the present value of the shareholder's lifetime consumption.
[17]See Copeland and Weston (1988), pp. 17–18. Strictly speaking shareholders try to maximize total return, that is, stock price plus dividends.
[18]As long as the discount rate is chosen appropriately and any real options are valued correctly.
[19]While neglecting their own preferences.

nities that have a positive NPV. In turn, the discounted cash flow of the firm[20] can be used to estimate the value of a firm:

$$\text{Firm Value} = \sum_{t}^{\infty} \frac{E(CF_t)}{(1+r_t)^t} \qquad (2.1)$$

According to Equation (2.1), the value of a firm is the present value of its expected (future) cash flows $E(CF_t)$[21] in each period t, discounted at the appropriate rate r_t reflecting the riskiness and the timing of the cash flows as well as the financing mix,[22] that consequently can affect the discount rate and the expected cash flows.[23]

However, there is some disagreement as to whether the firm's objective should be to maximize the wealth of shareholders or that of the firm.[24] If the objective is to maximize shareholder value, this can potentially lead to conflicts of interest between shareholders and debt holders as well as between shareholders and managers.[25] It is especially this last point that relaxes the assumption that all decisions by the firm are always made in the best interest of the shareholders, because in most of the cases these decisions are made by managers who are pursuing their own goals instead. These problems,[26] however, can only occur in less than perfect markets—which

---

[20]See Copeland and Weston (1988), p. 24.

[21]These are cash flows available for redistribution to the firm's stakeholders and are, therefore, called free cash flows. See, for example, Copeland et al. (1994), p. 135.

[22]Modigliani and Miller (1958) distinguish between business risk and risk stemming from financing decisions for firms within the same risk class. See, for example, Perridon and Steiner (1995), p. 457.

[23]Expected cash flows can also be influenced by dividend decisions.

[24]Including the wealth of all claimholders (or stakeholders), especially debt holders.

[25]Shareholders can take, for example, actions that expropriate wealth from the bond holders. Even though shareholders maximize the value of their stake in the firm, their actions may not be in the best interest of the firm and might reduce the value of the stakes that belong to other stakeholders. See Damodaran (1997), pp. 6, 13, and 822.

[26]Value maximization is often viewed as "unethical," but as self-correcting with respect to its problems. For example, if the manager–shareholder conflict becomes too great, proxy battles and hostile takeovers will occur. If the shareholder–bond holder conflict becomes too great, bond holders will use more covenants. If markets are inefficient (and short-term focused), long-term investors will step in to take advantage of these inefficiencies. Or, if social costs become too high, governments will restrict and regulate firms. See Damodaran (1997), p. 822.

brings us to the next problem: Even if one agrees to maximize shareholder value, the question is whether this translates into maximizing stock prices. Markets may be less than perfect, and stock prices may not reflect the long-term value of the firm, but rather myopic market assessments and poor information. Shareholder value could be—provocatively—viewed as only a theoretical concept. It is perception of value that drives share prices, which, at best, is correlated with "true"[27] value.[28] Therefore, the general firm objective should be to maximize firm value and only in special cases the maximization of the stock price.[29]

Likewise, there is some discussion on whether other objectives[30] would be better suited for maximizing an individual's utility than (shareholder) value maximization.[31] However, the firm's objective should be consistent with economic theory, that is, it should try to maximize utility from consumption. Besides, it should have—according to Damodaran[32]—the following characteristics in order to lead to meaningful decision rules:

- Be clear and unambiguous
- Be operational (measurable)
- Have as few social costs associated as possible
- Enable and ensure long-term survival of the firm

---

[27]One would have to define, though, what "true" value is.

[28]Inefficiencies in the financial markets may lead to a misallocation of resources and incorrect decisions so that "true" firm value is not reflected in the stock prices. See Shimko and Humphreys (1998), p. 33.

[29]See Damodaran (1997), p. 822.

[30]Alternate objectives could be the maximization of other financial goals (e.g., profits, income, etc.). However, when evaluated in the light of whether they maximize the utility that can be extracted from their consumption by the individual investor, these are measures that do not reflect what can be distributed to investors so that they can use it for consumption. Likewise, turnover, market share, company growth, and company survival are only means of trying to maximize the stream of consumption and can, therefore, only be viewed as interim objectives. Nonfinancial goals (e.g., power, prestige, etc.) are difficult to measure and, hence, operationalize. See Schmidt and Terberger (1997), pp. 44–47.

[31]See, for example, Schmidt and Terberger (1997), pp. 41–47, Copeland (1994), pp. 101–107, and Copeland et al. (1994), pp. 4–29 and the references to the literature provided there.

[32]See Damodaran (1997), p. 11.

When benchmarking the alternatives against these criteria, we can conclude that value maximization is the objective that best suits these postulated characteristics.[33]

All of the preceding is also true for banks. However, as indicated by Equation (2.1), investment, financing, and dividend decisions are essentially all linked to firm value in that they can affect current cash flows, expected growth, and risk.[34] The challenge for bank management is to maximize Equation (2.1) by trying to increase current and future cash flows (especially by exploiting growth opportunities), while keeping the (perceived) riskiness of the bank relatively unchanged. Since risk taking is an integral part of a financial institution's business, it is obvious that the relationships between risk, the objective to manage it, and the overall objective of (firm) value maximization need to be closely scrutinized.

Before we enter this discussion, we will first address in the next two sections how the value of a bank can be determined and the problems that are associated with this approach.

Valuation Framework for Banks

The approach that is typically applied to decide whether a firm creates value is a variant of the traditional discounted cash flow (DCF) analysis of financial theory, with which the value of any asset can be determined.[35] This (shareholder value) approach estimates the value of the entire firm (therefore, it is also called "entity" approach[36]) using a multiperiod framework. It estimates a firm's (free) cash flows, which are available for distribution to both shareholders and debt holders, and discounts them at the appropriate rate, which is the so-called weighted average[37] costs of capital (WACC) and reflects both the riskiness and timing of the cash flows and the firm's leverage. The (market) value of the firm's equity is then determined by

---

[33](Shareholder) Value maximization provides a clear and unambiguous goal of using the NPV criterion (using cash flows and not accounting numbers) as focus for corporate financial decisions. Shareholder wealth is also an operational goal because welfare is measurable. Since, in its idealized form, it assumes the existence of perfect and efficient markets with no agency or transaction costs, all social costs associated with value maximization can be priced and will be charged to the firm. Even though value calculated as discounted cash flows (DCF) can have its difficulties when one is trying to estimate the input factors, it seems to be nonetheless a superior metric (see Copeland [1994], p. 104), because it uses a long-term perspective, the most complete information, and is well correlated with a company's market value.

[34]See Damodaran (1997), p. 826.

[35]See, for example, Brealey and Myers (1991), pp. 63–67.

[36]See Copeland et al. (1994), p. 478.

[37]The weights are determined using the market values of debt and equity.

subtracting the (market) value of the firm's liabilities from the determined entity value.

As an exception to the rule, a different approach is often chosen for banks—even though the results are mathematically equivalent. This so-called "equity" approach[38] estimates the bank's (free) cash flows to its shareholders and then discounts these at the cost of equity capital[39] to derive the value of the bank's equity directly. Besides being easier to apply, this approach also has the following practical and conceptual advantages in the financial industry:[40]

- Determining the equity value by first determining the entity's value and then subtracting the value of the liabilities is much more difficult for banks than for industrial companies, because a bank's debt is, to a large extent, not traded in the capital markets. For instance, savings and current account deposits have either no interest rate or an interest rate far below their fair market return—and an unknown maturity. Hence, it is very difficult to determine the fair overall market value of debt because of the simple practical inability to determine the appropriate cost of capital for these liabilities.
- Additionally, the fact that taking in deposits may allow the bank to generate value (because it pays interest rates below their market opportunity costs) makes liability management a part of the bank's business operations and not just a pure financing function. This potential for value creation needs to be adequately reflected in the applied valuation methodology, which is not the case in the entity approach.
- Given the narrow margins of the banking business, small errors in the estimation of the appropriate interest rates can lead to huge swings in the value of the equity when applying the entity approach.

Even though we will not discuss the details[41] of the determination of (free) cash flows and the application of this framework at the business unit or even the transaction level[42] here, some authors[43] and—by anecdotal evidence—many bank analysts point out that this valuation framework is

---

[38]See Copeland et al. (1994), p. 478. For a detailed discussion, see, for example, Strutz (1993) or Kümmel (1993).
[39]As, for example, derived via the Capital Asset Pricing Model (CAPM).
[40]See Copeland et al. (1994), p. 479.
[41]For these details, see, for example, Benninga and Sarig (1998) or Schröck (1997), pp. 81–89, and the list of references to the literature provided there.
[42]The results of such an analysis could be the basis for restructuring and value-based management of the bank, see Copeland et al. (1994), pp. 502+.
[43]See, for example, Copeland et al. (1994), p. 482.

notoriously difficult and cumbersome to apply to banks. This observation is true for bank insiders, but especially for bank outsiders and is mostly due to the fact that banks are opaque[44] institutions.[45] However, these informational problems[46] may be only one reason for the scarce application of the valuation approach in banks. We will discuss potential other problems in the following section.

Problems with the Valuation Framework for Banks

Empirical Conundrum   For an initial sample of ninety European banks from fifteen different countries, whose (equity) market capitalization was larger than Euro 1 billion on December 31, 1999, we collected time series of quoted equity prices denoted in or transposed into Euro available on Datastream. Comprehensive time series between January 1, 1992 and December 31, 1999 were available for forty-seven of these banks. Additionally, we collected, for the same time period, the two price indices DJ EURO STOXX 50 (broad market portfolio) and DJ EURO STOXX BANK (index for banks).

We could make the following observations, shown in Figure 2.1, when comparing the relative performance (Index = 100% on January 1, 1992): A broad index for European banks underperformed compared to the broad market index by roughly 35% (320.90% versus 490.45%) over the eight-year period (see Figure 2.1).

There were big deviations in the performance of the forty-seven banks. Sorting their individual performance (measured by the index value as of December 31, 1999) in ascending order, we can draw the chart shown in Figure 2.2.

Plotting the performance of the two indices as horizontal (benchmark) lines, Figure 2.2 reveals that roughly 77% (or thirty-six) of the forty-seven banks performed worse and only eleven better than the broad market index. Note that twenty-three banks performed better and twenty-four banks worse than the bank index, indicating that our final sample of forty-seven banks represents the broad market fairly well (the [simple] average performance for this sample was 357.20%[47] versus 320.90%). The results for the individual banks range from 76.29% to 797.98%, making some banks value destroyers even on an absolute level and some others value creators on a

---

[44]See Merton and Perold (1993), p. 16.

[45]Even insiders will face similar difficulties, because of the problems associated with transfer pricing and (cost) allocation.

[46]For instance, it is also difficult to determine the appropriate cost of capital for illiquid credit transactions.

[47]Its standard deviation: 198.13%.

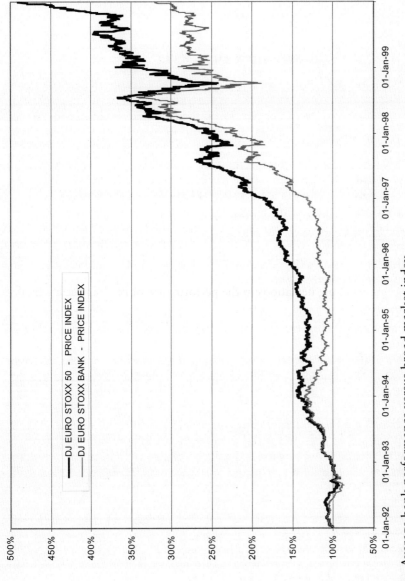

Figure 2.1 Average bank performance versus broad market index.
Source: Datastream and author's analysis.

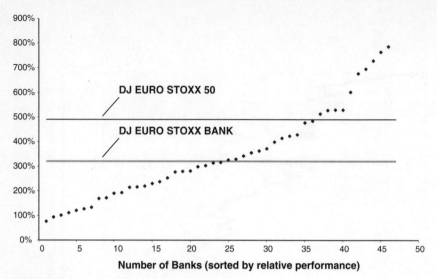

Figure 2.2   Deviations in bank performance.
Source: Datastream and author's analysis.

relative level vis-à-vis the broad market. The best and worst performers are depicted in Figures 2.3 and 2.4.

It is worthwhile to note the sharp decrease in value for all banks following the Russian and Southeast Asian crises in the fall of 1998, reflecting the extreme sensitivity of the market capitalization of banks to financial crisis situations.

Of course these results are only a snapshot and will deviate for different time windows. But, despite the influence of numerous merger and acquisition (M&A) activities[48] and the broad consolidation in the banking industry,[49] which do also influence these results,[50] we can observe a general trend that banks tend to underperform compared to the overall market.[51]

What are the reasons for this phenomenon and how can the differences in performance between various banks be explained? Given the preceding results, one could ask the provocative question: "Is value maximization really

---

[48]For instance, The Securities Data Company, Inc., reports 744 completed (no self-tendered) merger & acquisition deals exceeding $100 million in the financial services sector worldwide for the time period from January 1, 1993 to January 18, 1999.
[49]The *Journal of Banking & Finance* devotes an entire issue to this topic: February 1999, Volume 23, Numbers 2–4, pp. 135–700.
[50]Practically all of the banks in the final sample were influenced by one or the other event.
[51]Matten (1996), p. xiii, and Dermine (1998), p. 21, make the same observation.

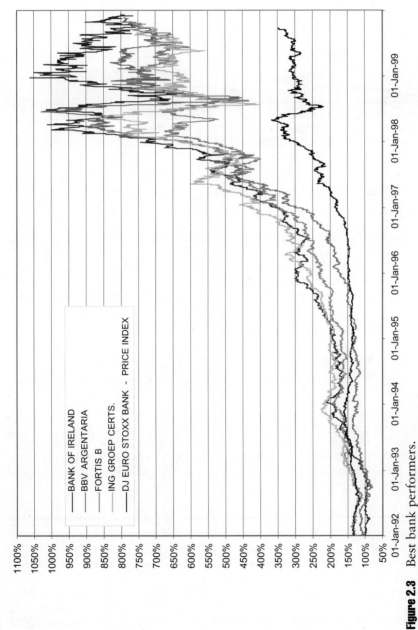

Figure 2.3 Best bank performers.
Source: Datastream and author's analysis.

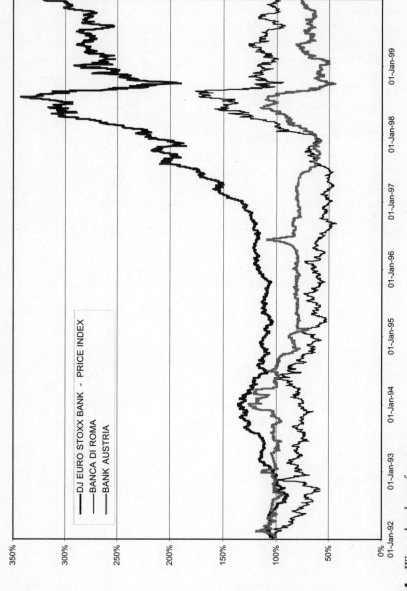

Figure 2.4 Worst bank performers.
Source: Datastream and author's analysis.

the ultimate objective in banking, or do regulatory constraints limit the overall performance by a certain degree?"[52] However, this book is not intended to address these questions.

Rather, we will assume that value maximization is the ultimate goal in banking. However, we then need to ask whether the valuation framework (as introduced above) is the right tool for banks or whether it is simply not applied.[53] Or, if it is applied, whether it does not (properly) work for banks, because an important component might be missing (because this model is largely based on the assumptions of the neoclassical finance theory).[54] Additionally, we will have to clarify whether and how risk and its management are major influencing factors in this process.

Other Stakeholders' Interests in Banks   As discussed previously, (firm) value maximization is—from a theoretical point of view—the ultimate objective of any corporation. And, as we have concluded, banks are no different from industrial companies in this respect,[55] because they should only invest in projects with a positive NPV or a return above the appropriate hurdle rate of return that is commensurate with the risk profile of the project.[56]

In reality though, the stakeholders of a company require[57] that the management of a corporation needs to make decisions that balance their own interests and the interests of the shareholders as well as those of other stakeholders.[58] These other stakeholders (besides shareholders and manage-

---

[52]For a discussion of this point see Kim and Santomero (1988).

[53]Note that bank stock prices are mostly dependent on risk factors such as changes in exchange rates and interest rates; see, for example, Choi et al. (1996).

[54]We will address this question mainly in Chapter 6.

[55]Banks are different in many other respects. For a description of these differences, see, for example, Merton and Perold (1993), p. 16.

[56]See Damodaran (1997), p. 824. Note that—as we will see later—this is equivalent to the application of the "equity" approach at the transaction level.

[57]We have seen above that value maximization for shareholders may mean that other stakeholders lose out.

[58]Therefore, besides the focus on shareholders, there are many valid arguments that other stakeholders' interests should be included in the process. Even though it is true that without economic success there will not be any opportunity to satisfy the wants and needs of employees, customers, and so on, it is also true that, for example, unhappy customers will not buy products as may occur if efficiency is more highly valued than customer satisfaction, which then reduces (shareholder) value (see Friedrich et al. [2000], p. 31). Many authors consequently suggest a "balanced stakeholders" approach; see, for example, Copeland (1994), p. 97 and Copeland et al. (1994), pp. 4–29.

ment) are, for example,[59] debt holders (such as bondholders, lenders/depositors, and other creditors), employees, customers, suppliers, society, the government, and, especially, regulatory bodies in the banking industry.

Still, since management can always apply the NPV criterion[60] to find out how much a particular decision benefits or harms the shareholders,[61] any decision made under the value maximization proposition—as long as all "externalities" are priced and included—automatically reflects the optimal choice for all involved constituents.[62]

However, this might not function so automatically for banks. The various stakeholders' interests are much more relevant and have a more far-reaching impact on banks. Banking is a heavily regulated industry in many countries—for good reasons.[63] Regulators on behalf of society at large and bank depositors in specific try to avoid systemic risks[64] and to protect customer savings.[65] As indicated by Equation (2.1), if banks try to (naïvely) maximize value (for example, in the interest of the shareholders), they can often only increase cash flows by exploiting growth opportunities, which are in turn usually associated with increased risk taking. Risk is therefore a necessary but manageable complication in the effort to increase a bank's returns.[66]

Nonetheless, all bank stakeholders are extremely concerned with this increased risk taking, because they are particularly sensitive to any increase in the likelihood of bank default. This is true because:

---

[59]It seems rather difficult to generate a complete list of stakeholders in a company. Schmidt and Terberger (1997), pp. 41–42, generate the list that is used in the main text and which is in line with other references [e.g., Copeland (1994), p. 97].

[60]See Brealey and Myers (1991), p. 23.

[61]According to Copeland (1994), pp. 106–107, shareholders are the only stakeholders who, in seeking to maximize the value of their claim, simultaneously maximize the value of everyone else's claim. As residual claimants of a company's cash flows, they are the only stakeholders who need full information of all other claims in trying to maximize the value of their claim. By that, they implicitly maximize the value of all other claims. And they have the incentive to use this information to align other stakeholders' interests and make their company successful in competitive markets.

[62]There is (at least anecdotal) evidence that in many cases, decisions that increase shareholder value also benefit other stakeholders and, therefore, do not seem to conflict with their long-term interests, because successful companies create greater value for all stakeholders. See Copeland (1994), pp. 101–103.

[63]For a discussion of the theory of regulation, see Hartmann-Wendels et al. (1998), pp. 321–337, who also provide an extensive list of references to the literature.

[64]This argument is also often used by economists who want to ensure a safe and sound financial system and the avoidance of so-called domino effects.

[65]See Mason (1995), p. 37.

[66]See Shimko and Humphreys (1998), p. 33.

■ The existing banking business might immediately vanish[67] as soon as there is the slightest indication of problems.[68] This is mostly relevant to shareholders who would consequently lose most of the residual cash flows of the bank.

■ The bank debt holders[69] are extremely credit sensitive[70] because they cannot diversify the bankruptcy risk of the bank[71] and therefore are very focused on the lower-tail outcomes of the net asset value distribution[72] of a bank. This is especially true for depositors, who want their savings and deposits to be safe and do not want to worry about default risk at all.

This means that banks and their stakeholders are much more concerned with bankruptcy risk than industrial companies,[73] which is also particularly reflected in the regulatory point of view.

As can be easily seen, the bank stakeholder and shareholder views of risk (and risk taking by the bank) differ, but are still related.[74] The difficulty for a bank (and its management) is how to strike the right balance to address these various interests.

RISK MANAGEMENT IN BANKS

Before we shed some more light on the problems discussed in the previous section, we need to define the terms risk and risk management and then discuss if and why risk and risk taking are so important for banks, making risk management a significant means of influencing value.

---

[67]The derivatives business is extremely sensitive to the credit standing of the intermediary.

[68]Deposit insurance is often used to try and avoid this problem. It is also used to avoid "bank runs" (see discussion below).

[69]Mostly customers (depositors), but also any other suppliers of funds (e.g., other banks).

[70]Not only on an absolute level, but also from a relative change in the likelihood of default.

[71]See Stulz (2000), p. 4-5.

[72]See Drzik et al. (1998a), p. 24.

[73]We will discuss the reasons for this in more detail in the next chapter.

[74]The fact that the shareholder perspective tends to dominate all others is often neglected in the discussion on risk management, which is only focused on the regulators' and bond holders' point of view; see Drzik et al. (1998a), pp. 22–23. Trying to avoid the occurrence of bank default and to minimize the variability of returns (i.e., to limit downside risk) is very different from the shareholders' interest of exploiting the upside potential.

Definition of Risk

Risk is defined as uncertainty, that is, as the deviation from an expected outcome.[75] We can differentiate uncertainty into:[76]

- **General uncertainty:** Complete ignorance about any potential outcome makes both rational decision making and any quantification impossible.
- **Specific uncertainty:** Objective, or at least subjective, probabilities can be assigned to the potential outcomes[77] and hence allow for quantification.

The term *risk* is usually used synonymously with *specific uncertainty*, because statistics allows us to quantify this specific uncertainty by using so-called measures of dispersion. The variability around the expected or average value is usually measured by calculating the variance or (its square root) the standard deviation,[78] which is also often called *volatility* in a finance context, because we can usually observe positive and negative deviations from the mean.[79] In a business context, risk usually expresses only the negative deviations from expected or "aimed at" values and is therefore associated with the potential for loss,[80] whereas positive deviations are considered to represent opportunities.

Other classifications of risk encompass:

- (Firm-) Specific versus market (-wide) risks:[81]
  - Specific risks are risks that are specific to the firm or the industry in which a firm operates.
  - Market-wide (also often called systematic) risk is risk that cannot be diversified away and expresses the covariance of the de-

---

[75]See Johanning (1998), p. 47.
[76]See, for example, Steiner and Bruns (1995), pp. 49–50, and Perridon and Steiner (1995), pp. 95–98.
[77]These outcomes are therefore stochastic.
[78]For a discussion of other measures of dispersion (such as, for example, range, semi-interquartile range, semi-variance, mean absolute deviation), see Copeland and Weston (1988), pp. 149–153.
[79]See Steiner and Bruns (1995), p. 53.
[80]See Glaum and Förschle (2000), p. 13.
[81]The distinction between firm-specific and market-wide risk can be fuzzy, because of different investor clientele: Widely held firms with well-diversified investors may categorize more risks as firm-specific, whereas firms whose investors hold significant portions in the firm may look at the same risks as being market-wide risks. See Damodaran (1997), pp. 776–777.

viations with the changes in the broad economic development. Only market risk is reflected in the expected returns as derived, for example, by the CAPM.

- Continuous versus event risk:[82]
  - Continuous risk is caused by a source or factor that can change continuously (e.g., interest and foreign exchange rates).
  - Event risk is created by a specific (discontinuous) event (e.g., an earthquake, a fire, etc.).

Risk in a banking context arises from any transaction or business decision that contains uncertainty concerning the result. Because virtually every bank transaction is associated with some level of uncertainty, nearly every transaction contributes to the overall risk of a bank. Some examples of the risks faced by banks are:

- Will all payments on a loan be made according to the expectations/schedule?
- Will interest rates fluctuate more than expected in the near future?
- Will demand for new mortgages fall short of the expectations in the next year?

All of these risks lead to possible fluctuations in the bank's income stream or profitability[83] and hence the value of the bank. In general, event risk has a much larger impact on a firm's cash flows and value than continuous risk.[84]

Definition of Risk Management

In this section, we are going to define the term *risk management*. On the one hand, risk management is often associated with an organizational unit,[85] which is ideally an independent staff function reporting directly to the board of directors, making risk management a board responsibility, function, and

---

[82]See Damodaran (1997), p. 777.

[83]Assuming that all risk is eventually fed through the bank's profit and loss (P&L) account.

[84]See Damodaran (1997), p. 777.

[85]Such an organizational unit is also mandated for banks by regulatory requirement. See, for example, in Germany the "Mindestanforderungen an das Betreiben von Handelsgeschäften," which require written guidelines, the organizational separation of trading, settlements, and control (minimum critical size necessary); regular marking-to-market of the positions' regular quantification of loss potential of open positions; regular performance measurement; regular reporting of results; and open positions to the board.

task.[86] However, the board cannot conduct risk management on its own. It has to set strategic targets and ensure, via strict controls, that the delegated goals are actually achieved within the centrally mandated guidelines. Running a risk-management function in a centralized manner has the following advantage: it allows for an independent, integrated view of all types of risk,[87] so that only the net positions need to be managed[88] and specialized staff can achieve better pricing in the capital markets. However, firms rarely measure and manage the entirety of their risk exposures. They rather micromanage single-risk exposures[89] because of the high cost of running the risk management centrally[90] or because of legal restrictions.[91]

On the other hand, risk management can be defined as a distinct process, that is, as a set of activities.[92] This process is divided into the following steps:

1. Definition, identification, and classification[93] of a firm's risk exposure and the source of risk (risk factors).
2. Analysis and quantification of the risk exposure, that is, the understanding of the relationship between and the measurement of how much the cash flows and the value of a firm are affected by a specific source (risk factor). An exposure profile relates unexpected changes in a risk factor to unexpected changes in the firm's value (including correlations between the risk factors), which is the foundation for being able to analyze the impact of risk management on the firm's value.[94] So far, many banks concentrate on this (passive) risk measurement step, which is only a requirement for being able to actively influence firm value.
3. Allocation of (risk) capital[95] to the business units as a common currency of risk that is comparable across business units and risk

---

[86]Shimko and Humphreys (1998), p. 33, see an independent and senior risk-management function as an important part of the overall management quality of a bank.

[87]We will define and discuss the typical types of risk in banks in Chapter 5.

[88]This also allows the recognition of compensating effects in the portfolio.

[89]See Pritsch and Hommel (1997), p. 685.

[90]For instance, process-related costs (expensive political fights with the subsidiaries, etc.) and IT-related costs (unless adequate IT-systems are available, many functions cannot be provided on a timely basis).

[91]For internationally operating organizations, there might be, for example, capital transfer restrictions between various countries in which they operate, and so on.

[92]See Damodaran (1997), pp. 795–796, Schröck (1997), pp. 23–25, Glaum and Förschle (2000), p. 13.

[93]For instance, firm-specific versus market risks or continuous versus event risk.

[94]See Smith (1995), p. 20.

[95]See Froot and Stein (1998a), pp. 59+.

types and that is commensurate with the risk taken—as measured in Step 2^{96}—and the allocation of a charge reflecting the cost of capital.

4. (*Ex ante*) decision of whether a new transaction should be accepted from a portfolio perspective and consideration of whether the risk taking is compensated appropriately from a risk-return perspective.[97]

5. Limitation of risk taking to ensure a constant risk profile by "mitigating" risk. This step is the actual and active management of risk and, therefore, what people commonly refer to when they use the term risk management. In order to "mitigate" risk, various (hedge) instruments and policies can be applied, such as, for example, (1) complete avoidance of risk, (2) reduction of risk, (3) transfer of risk to third parties, and (4) limitation of risk.[98]

6. Risk controlling usually encompasses the documentation and controlling of risk-management actions to ensure the achievement of the goals that have been set. Deviations between targets and actual performance are analyzed to identify causes, which in turn lead to changes in either the planning or the implementation process. Additionally, risk control also covers controlling the involved people and business units by checking whether methods and instruments are applied properly in order to avoid abuse, manipulation, and other misconduct (process controlling).

7. (*Ex post*) performance evaluation in order to link risk-management actions to the overall corporate goals. Management has to develop strategic goals for the various risk areas (risk strategy) that are commensurate with the ultimate firm objective to maximize firm value. The goal of risk management should, therefore, be to identify any uneconomic risk taking, that is, to ensure that any risk-management activity is consistent with value maximization. The goal, however, cannot and should not be to avoid or minimize all risk taking. Rather, it should be to find the optimal balance between risks and expected returns by concentrating on the competitive and compara-

---

[96]This step provides an immediate link to the required capital structure in banks, which we will discuss in Chapter 5.

[97]This step provides an immediate link to the capital-budgeting decision in banks, which we will discuss in Chapter 6.

[98]Note that all of these actions are usually associated with costs—even avoidance in the form of lost profit opportunities.

tive advantages of the firm,[99] redefining the role of risk management from pure "hedging" to a more differentiated activity in light of the goal of value maximization.

All of these steps are dependent on each other. For example, a goal-oriented active management of risks is not sensible without accurate quantification, and so on.[100]

In this book, we will refer to risk management as an active, strategic, and integrated process[101] that encompasses both the measurement[102] and the "mitigation"[103] of risk, with the ultimate goal of maximizing the value of a bank, while minimizing the risk of bankruptcy.[104]

Role and Importance of Risk and Its Management in Banks

The traditional role of banks can be seen in the transformation of cash flows with respect to (1) scale, location, and liquidity, (2) term (maturity), and (3) risk, in order to reduce frictions from both asymmetric information as well as transaction costs in (less than perfect[105]) markets.[106] By specializing in

---

[99]As we will see in the section "Empirical Evidence," many firms choose "selective" hedging strategies, that is, that they leave ca. 70% of their risk exposure open (only ca. 30% are therefore hedged), if they believe markets move in their favor. On the contrary, almost 100% are hedged when the firms believe that markets will move in the opposite direction. However, decision makers, in the belief that they can generate superior cash flows by leaving positions unhedged, are running the risk of substantial losses. It seems very difficult that someone can consistently earn superior returns in highly liquid and (information) efficient markets. Even banks do not appear to have a comparative (information) advantage in these markets that they could consistently exploit.

[100]However, given anecdotal evidence, some market players conduct risk management without any measurement.

[101]And hence not the organizational unit.

[102]That is the quantification of the overall risk exposure, that is, aggregation of the effects of all risk factors on the firm value, including the derivation of the causative relationship between risk and a change in value.

[103]We do not restrict ourselves to only hedging transactions, but rather include all possible risk-management actions like, for example, diversification (see the later section "Ways to Conduct Risk Management in Banks").

[104]We control for risk of being caught short of funds, as described by Froot and Stein (1998a), p. 58. However, this depends on the portfolio composition and the amount of capital backing it as well as the quality of the risk-management team, the risk-management systems, the liquidity of the positions, and so on.

[105]In perfect markets banks would not even exist, because there would be no reason for intermediation between market participants.

[106]See, for example, Scholtens and van Wensveen (2000), pp. 1249–1250, and Hartmann-Wendels et al. (1998), pp. 5–10.

information production and processing, banks fulfill an origination and servicing function[107] as well as a distribution function in financial markets.[108]

While basically taking deposits from savers and lending them to borrowers with risky businesses, banks can exploit the effects of the diversification of individual credit and term risks, which allows them to absorb risks within. But banks are also able to transfer risks and thereby distribute them across different market participants. Here lies the key value-added feature of banks: the ability to allocate risk efficiently at minimum cost through the trading of[109] and the bundling and unbundling of the risks of various financial contracts.[110] Additionally, banks can and do create products with relatively stable distributions of returns, and hence constant risk profiles, which can lower the participation cost of other market players.[111]

Since banks deal in financial assets, they are, by definition, in the financial risk business. Because of the simple fact that they originate, trade, or service financial assets, banks transform, manage, and underwrite risk.[112] Even though it may not be immediately obvious that risk management is the core capability of banking, the increased concentration by banks (and other financial institutions) in the business of asset trading and risk transfer reveals the importance of risk management. Thus, risk management plays a central role in intermediation, and is therefore an integral part and a key area of the business of banking,[113] and is viewed as one of the most important corporate objectives.[114]

Risk management, therefore, also appears to be one of the most likely sources of value creation in banks and "value maximizing banks should have a well-founded concern with risk management".[115] The question is how risk management can be linked to the overall objective of value maximization. It is essential to know how risk management can contribute to this overall goal, because, in order to use risk management the right way, one has to have a clear objective function for it and needs to know its impact on the firm's overall objective. Since positive NPV projects are the result of good

---

[107]Disintermediation (as indicated by securities issued directly by firms) is reflecting the changing nature of the information set available to market participants.

[108]See Allen and Santomero (1996), p. 7.

[109]See Allen and Santomero (1996), p. 7.

[110]See Merton (1995b), p. 25.

[111]See Allen and Santomero (1996), p. 24.

[112]See Allen and Santomero (1996), p. 19, and Scholtens and van Wensveen (2000), p. 1247.

[113]See Merton (1989).

[114]According to Meridian Research, the 400 largest banks and security firms worldwide spent US$2,063 million on enterprise-level risk technology. See Williams (1999), p. 1, Table 1.

[115]See Froot and Stein (1998a), p. 55.

strategic decisions and the firm's ability to create comparative advantages over their competitors,[116] conducting risk management without a clear strategy will not automatically increase (shareholder) value.

However, so far, the most important rationale for risk management has typically been seen as the prevention of the bankruptcy[117] of a bank. This rationale is also reflected in the regulatory constraints for financial institutions. On the one hand, merely to ensure a bank's long-term survival by avoiding lower-tail outcomes[118] (i.e., extreme losses) will not completely satisfy the shareholders of a bank. On the other hand, treating risk management as a subobjective to value maximization or optimizing value subject to risk-management[119] constraints will neglect the questions of why, how, and when risk management can contribute to value creation. Since many bank stakeholders are so concerned with the survival of the bank, the framework of simple value maximization needs to be expanded and adjusted in regard to banks and their risks to reflect a stakeholder approach that incorporates a risk-management orientation.

LINK BETWEEN RISK MANAGEMENT AND VALUE CREATION IN BANKS

Accepting that risk and its management plays a central role in banks, we now need to address the "logic of links"[120] between risk management and value creation. As described by Smith (1995), we have to answer the following questions:

- Why practice risk management?
- How should we measure risk?
- What should we do about the risks? What instruments should we use?

We have already agreed that the objective of risk management in banks should be to contribute to the firm's overall objective of value maximization. However, the choice of the objective has a direct impact on how risk

---

[116]See Damodaran (1997), p. 824.

[117]Or in the avoidance of any financial distress situation.

[118]See Stulz (1996), p. 8.

[119]As indicated above, this is meant in the sense of simply avoiding lower-tail outcomes.

[120]This means the development of an understanding of the benefits of a well-structured risk management program and how its mechanisms increase the value of the firm in designing an effective risk-management program. See Smith (1995), p. 20.

should be measured[121] and, what is equally important, what the goals of risk management should then be and which one of the various ways to conduct risk management should be applied. We will describe the various options in the subsequent sections and return to the question of what should be done in detail in Chapter 6.

Goals of Risk Management in Banks

The choices related to the risk-management goal can be differentiated along the following dimensions:[122]

- The goal variable
- The (dominant) stakeholder perspective
- The risk dimension
- The risk-management strategy

We will discuss each of these dimensions in turn below.

Choice of the Goal Variable According to survey evidence,[123] firms view the primary goal of their risk-management efforts as the reduction of the volatility of the company's cash flows and its earnings. Typically, firms name the following subdimensions:

- **Reduction of the volatility of (near-term) operating income[124]/(reported or accounting) earnings.**[125]
- **Simple reduction of the volatility of (free) cash flows:**[126] Risk management aims to protect the bank's balance sheet against severe losses of a monetary nature (e.g., shocks in foreign exchange rates) and the

---

[121]We will address this question in detail in Chapter 5.

[122]We neglect here how risk management ranks against other financial objectives in banks.

[123]See Glaum and Förschle (2000), pp. 19+; also see Bodnar et al. (1996) and (1998) for the U.S. market. Note that these surveys exclude financial institutions. We will discuss this problem in more detail in the section "Empirical Evidence."

[124]See Fenn et al. (1997), p. 23, who refer to Dolde (1993) who finds that the probability of using derivative increases with the volatility of firms' operating income. Even though this is consistent with hedging motives for using derivatives, this assumes that the volatility of operating income is itself not affected by the use of derivatives (which is usually, although not always, the case).

[125]See Smith (1995), p. 20, Glaum and Förschle (2000), pp. 19+.

[126]See Smith (1995), p. 20, Fenn et al. (1997), p. 13, Glaum and Förschle (2000), pp. 19+.

bank's (operational) cash flows against serious financial uncertainties (interest and foreign exchange rate fluctuations, or credit risk).[127]

■ **Strategic (sophisticated) reduction of the volatility of cash flows:** Following Froot et al. (1993), firms should ensure via risk management that they have the cash available that is required in order to make value-enhancing investments. This goal is based on the M&M-observation that the key to creating corporate value is making good investments. According to the pecking order theory,[128] internally generated cash flows are the cheapest source of funds. However, sophisticated risk management should ensure that the cash flow volatility translates into the changes in the company's required funds for lucrative investment opportunities, which are dependent on the general economic conditions.[129]

■ **Reduction of the volatility in the firm's market value**[130] **and hence share return volatility:**[131] The goal of risk management in this area is the insulation of the stock price from shocks in economic and financial variables.[132]

■ **Stabilization of the return on equity.**

■ **Increase in (accounting/reported) earnings:** This is mostly associated with using risk-management tools as a means for speculation (see also, below, risk-management strategy).

■ **Minimization of borrowing costs (especially important for banks).**

It is important to note that using risk management in order to address each of these subdimensions (in isolation) can have very different effects on the other subdimensions. For instance, hedging value and hedging earnings are simply not the same thing.

---

[127]See Scholtens and van Wensveen (2000), p. 1249.

[128]See Brealey and Myers (1991), pp. 446+.

[129]The starting point of Froot et al.'s model is that, when external finance is more costly than internally generated sources of funds, it can make sense for firms to hedge. However, the optimal hedging strategy does not generally involve complete insulation of firm value from marketable sources of risk: (1) firms want to hedge less, the more closely correlated their cash flows are with future investment opportunities; (2) firms will want to hedge more, the more closely correlated their cash flows are with collateral values (and hence with their ability to raise external finance). See Froot et al. (1993), p. 1655.

[130]See Smith (1995), p. 20.

[131]See Stulz (2000), p. 2-36.

[132]See Fenn et al. (1997), p. 13.

Choice of the Stakeholder Perspective   As we have already identified above, there are various stakeholder interests in a bank. The different perspectives with regard to the goal of risk management are:

- **Firm value maximization:** For obvious reasons, the shareholders' interests mostly drive this perspective. Some authors express the opinion that in order to increase firm value, the goal of risk management should be to reduce the volatility of the firm's value[133] (also see above). However, since shareholders have an option on the upside potential,[134] they could have a valid interest in using risk management in order to increase the volatility in firm value, while increasing the value of their option.

- **Elimination of costly lower-tail outcomes:**[135] This view is driven mostly by the regulators'[136] and debt holders' interest in ensuring the survival of the bank.[137] This narrows down the focus of the goal of applying risk management, because this interest does not play any role in neoclassical finance theory, where the right to exist is a simple matter of profitability (see value-orientation above) and where there are no costs associated with default.

- **Maintenance of a certain financial risk profile:** This goal of risk management is a form of signaling to all stakeholder groups.

- **Reduction of the tax burden.**[138]

- **Tool for achieving a certain accounting policy:**[139] The goal of risk management could also be the protection of (cash-flow-irrelevant) balance sheet numbers with cash-flow-relevant transactions, which can lead to real losses. Even though this is a value-destroying proposition, managers could have an incentive to hedge the negative consequences of some balance sheet positions (because they are evaluated and compensated on the basis of those numbers).[140]

---

[133]See Smith (1995), p. 20.

[134]Meaning that an increase in the firm value benefits them more than all other stakeholders.

[135]See Stulz (1996), p. 8.

[136]Of course, risk management can also be used to arbitrage out the deficiencies in the regulatory requirements.

[137]Glaum and Förschle (2000), pp. 19+, report that the concern with the long-term survival of a company is especially a concern in continental Europe.

[138]See Glaum and Förschle (2000), pp. 19+.

[139]See Glaum and Förschle (2000), pp. 19+.

[140]See Tufano (1998).

■ **Motivation of employee and subsidiary behavior:**[141] The goal of risk management is to remove certain risk factors that cannot be influenced by these stakeholder groups in order to motivate their appropriate behavior in the areas that they can influence.

As already observed, the difficulty is to strike the right balance among these various stakeholder views and to find out which view (should) dominate(s) the others.[142]

Choice of the Risk Dimension   Another dimension for the choice of the goal for risk management is which type of risk should be managed—systematic (market-wide) or (firm-) specific risk.[143] From a theoretical point of view, the answer to this question would be fairly clear. If one assumes that one is in a neoclassical finance world and that financial risks are mostly unsystematic, then transferring these specific risks to efficient capital markets does not influence the firm's value. It only shifts the firm along the Security Market Line (SML).[144] Therefore, a bank should only manage its systematic risks. However, in practice, we can observe that most of the risk-management actions within a bank try to address specific issues at the individual transaction level, that is, banks try to focus on specific risks and mostly neglect the overall portfolio perspective (systematic risks).

Yet, if we look at stock market data, we can observe for banks that over time specific risk tends to increase (measured as percentage of overall risk) and systematic risk tends to decrease (see Figure 2.5).

We have derived these results in the following way: In order to avoid the effects of idiosyncratic influences at the individual bank level, we selected a banking industry level index (DJ EURO STOXX BANK) and a broad market index (DJ EURO STOXX 50) for the time period January 1, 1992 to December 31, 1999 and obtained respective data from Datastream. We then calculated daily returns on the banking industry (B) as well as the broad market index (M):

$$R_{i,t} = \ln\left(\frac{S_{i,t}}{S_{i,t-1}}\right) \qquad (2.2)$$

---

[141]See Glaum and Förschle (2000), pp. 19+.

[142]See Smith (1995), p. 20.

[143]For a definition see above.

[144]See Copeland and Weston (1988), pp. 197+, for a discussion of the security market line in the context of the CAPM.

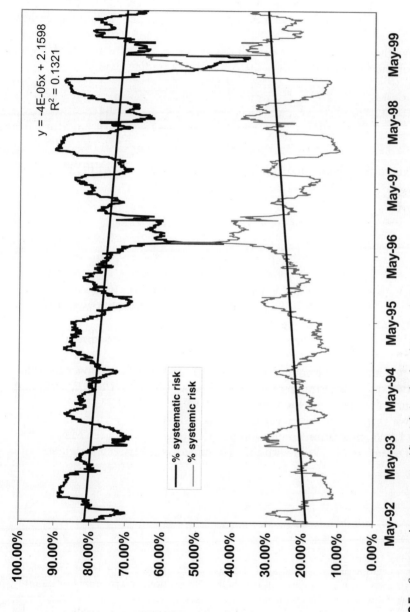

Figure 2.5 Systematic versus specific risk in the banking industry.
Source: Datastream and author's analysis.

where $R_{i,t}$ = Return on index i at time t
$\quad\quad i$ = B (banking index) and M (market index)
$\quad\quad \ln$ = Natural logarithm
$\quad\quad S_{i,t}$ = Index value at time t
$\quad\quad t\text{--}1$ = Prior observation point of i, here: one trading day earlier

We then determined the overall risk of the index as the standard deviation of the rate of return over the prior ninety trading days:[145]

$$\sigma_i = \sqrt{\frac{1}{90-1}\left[\sum_{t-90}^{t}\ln\left(\frac{S_{i,t}}{S_{i,t-1}}\right)^2 - \frac{1}{90}\left[\sum_{t-90}^{t}\ln\left(\frac{S_{i,t}}{S_{i,t-1}}\right)\right]^2\right]} \qquad (2.3)$$

where σ_i = Estimated volatility (standard deviation) of the rate of return of index i

Since[146]

$$\sigma_B^2 = \underbrace{\beta^2 \cdot \sigma_M^2}_{systematic} + \sigma_{specific}^2 \qquad (2.4)$$

where $\sigma^2_{\ i}$ = Total risk for index i (as defined above)
$\quad\quad \beta$ = Beta = $\sigma_{B,M}/\sigma_M^2$, where $\sigma_{B,M}$ is the covariance between B and M
$\quad\quad \sigma^2_{\ specific}$ = *Specific* risk (unexplained by the broad market)

we can determine the component *systematic* and *specific* risk over the same ninety days by determining the beta value (and hence *systematic* risk) and the difference between the two (*specific* risk).

We then rolled the ninety-day window forward over time so that we have 1,996 observation points (number of trading days between May 5, 1992 and December 31, 1999) with the determined split between systematic and

---

[145]As a critique of the chosen approach one could argue that daily returns usually lead to more erratic estimates, due to higher fluctuations, than weekly or monthly returns. However, the ninety-day windows represent averages of these observations, normalizing some of these effects. Besides, choosing weekly or monthly returns did not significantly change the results.
[146]Note that we return to discrete space notation here.

specific risk.[147] We subsequently run a linear regression on these observation points to display the long-term trend.[148]

Figure 2.5 shows that, despite our hypothesized reduction of specific risk due to risk-management actions at the individual transaction level, systematic risk decreased for the overall banking industry. These industry level results for the banking industry can be replicated at the individual bank level.[149] Note that in the beginning of the sample period the systematic risk constitutes roughly 80% of the overall risk—which is in line with the fact that bank betas are roughly around 1.0, meaning that banks fluctuate basically as the market does. However, this component decreases over time to below 65%.[150] Note also that the betas over time were fairly stable for all banks and hence the banking industry overall. An exception is the aftermath of the financial crisis in the fall of 1998, which led to an increase in the betas.[151]

We compared these results for the banking industry to the development in other industries. Even though we looked at basically all available (DJ EURO STOXX) industry indices and conducted the same analysis as above, we would like to present three representative results here (as a control sample). We selected three industries that had an index performance similar to that of the banking industry (320.90%) over the selected time period (as summarized in Table 2.1).

Additionally, one could argue that all of these three industries tend to be as cyclical as the banking industry.[152] However, the results were very different with regard to the development of the split between systematic and specific risk. Whereas the energy sector (the same results can be observed for

---

[147]An alternate method would have been to run regressions as described in the market model [see, for example, Steiner and Bruns (1995), pp. 32+] for each of the ninety-day windows and determine the adjusted R^2. Running a regression on these results would have resulted in the same graph for systematic risk because the adjusted R^2 explains the systematic risk contribution.

[148]Regression equation and R^2 for systematic risk observations are also displayed in Figure 2.5.

[149]Even though we will not display all results of our analysis, we refer to the Appendix to this chapter and the results for Deutsche Bank.

[150]The split for example, for Deutsche Bank shows that the systematic to specific risk goes down from 85% : 15% to 70% : 30%.

[151]The effects show up in the shift of systematic to specific risk in the beginning of 1999.

[152]Note also that all of these three industries had a similar level of betas over time as the banking industry.

TABLE 2.1 Industry Control Sample

DJ EURO STOXX Index	Index Performance
Energy	314.24%
Consumer Cyclical	311.19%
Utilities	320.71%

Source: Datastream and author's analysis.

autos and chemicals) showed a steeper change[153] in the split between systematic and specific risk, the cyclical consumer goods industry basically experienced no change (both trend lines are essentially flat for this industry). For utilities the reverse holds true, meaning that the component systematic risk increased over time.[154]

Therefore, given that the index performance of these four industries is so similar, there is no clear-cut answer as to which risk component (systematic or specific risk) should be chosen to manage in order to maximize value. This (somewhat contradictory) result motivates a closer examination of the problem, which we will provide for the banking industry in the subsequent chapters.

Choice of the Risk-Management Strategy   The last dimension for the choice of the goal of risk management is the risk-management strategy a bank would like to choose. The spectrum of choices runs from a complete elimination of all risks to a (lethargic) "do nothing at all" risk-management strategy,[155] with the following options in between:

- Eliminate all risks (i.e., complete hedging)
- Eliminate risk selectively (i.e., selective hedging)
- Allow for profits (i.e., selective speculation)
- Actively seek profits (i.e., (outright) speculation)[156]
- Do not manage risks at all

---

[153]Meaning that the component systematic risk decreased more than that in the banking industry.

[154]The results are displayed in the Appendix to this chapter.

[155]The choice of specific risk-management instruments cannot be naïvely delegated to the financial specialist. Senior management needs to understand how the instruments link up to the overall risk-management strategy. See Froot et al. (1994), pp. 98–102.

[156]In this context, derivatives are used to increase the exposure to risk in order to enhance earnings. See Fenn et al. (1997), p. 22.

By anecdotal evidence, typically the goal of risk management in banking is not the complete protection against risk, because this would also remove all opportunities to create value. It is rather to implement as much protection against risk as makes sense, given the marginal benefits and costs of acquiring the protection. We will also closer examine this statement in later chapters in order to find out how much protection makes sense, while still allowing the organization to create value.

We have explained in this section that there are multiple goals for conducting risk management at the corporate level. We have also seen that it is difficult for a bank to identify what its primary goal for managing risks is. We can summarize the discussion as follows: If the objective of a bank is to maximize its value, risk management should be undertaken, as long as it increases the present value of the firm's expected cash flows. Therefore, a proper risk-management strategy does not seek to insulate banks completely from risks of all kinds. The banks' stock price, earnings, return on equity, and so on will fluctuate with the underlying risk factors. If, for example, the economy is doing badly, a bank will be less valuable. But, there is nothing risk management can do to improve the underlying economics of being in a specific business such as banking. The goal of risk management is, therefore, not to insure investors and other stakeholders against the risk that is inherent in economic development per se.[157] Trying to do so could destroy value. However, as soon as concerns outside the neoclassical finance world— such as a concern with lower-tail outcomes—enter the decision-making process, protection against default, and hence the management of specific risk, can make sense.

Ways to Conduct Risk Management in Banks

In this section, we will describe and discuss the various ways to conduct risk management in banks. Figure 2.6 provides an overview and indicates that there are two broad categories that need to be distinguished when discussing the various options: First, the bank needs to determine which approach or set of actions it wants to apply when managing risks, and second, the bank then has to choose a set of instruments to actually manage these risks.

We will discuss the three approaches or sets of actions[158] and within them the various instruments[159] that are available to banks and how they can be applied.

---

[157]See Froot et al. (1994), p. 98.
[158]This distinction is adapted from Allen and Santomero (1996), pp. 19+.
[159]The instruments are distinguished as in Mason (1995), pp. 9+, and Allen and Santomero (1996), pp. 19+.

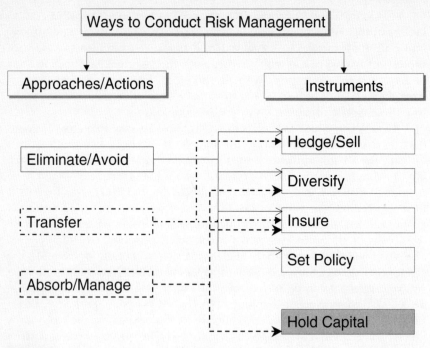

Figure 2.6   Overview of ways to conduct risk management.

Eliminate/Avoid   The bank can decide to eliminate certain risks that are not consistent with its desired financial characteristics or not essential to a financial asset created.[160] Any element of the systematic risk that is not required or desired can be either shed by selling it in the spot market or hedged by using derivative instruments such as futures, forwards, or swaps.[161] Moreover, the bank can use portfolio diversification[162] in order to eliminate specific risk.[163] Additionally, it can decide to buy insurance in the form of options[164] or actuarial insurance, for example, for event risks. Furthermore,

---

[160]Recall from above that banks do bundle and unbundle risks to create new assets. See Merton (1989).

[161]This could also include securitizations.

[162]Note that diversification is something shareholders and other stakeholders can do on their own—but potentially only at a higher cost than the bank can.

[163]Usually, risk elimination is incomplete because some portion of the systematic risk and that portion of the specific risk, which is an integral part of the product's unique business purpose, remain. See Allen and Santomero (1996), p. 19.

[164]Note that Mason (1995), p. 9, classifies options as insurance.

the bank can choose to avoid certain risk types up front by setting certain business practices/policies (e.g., underwriting standards, due diligence procedures, process control) to reduce the chances of certain losses and/or to eliminate certain risks *ex ante*.

Transfer   Contrary to the bank's decision to (simply) avoid some risks, the transfer of risks to other market participants is decided on the basis of whether or not the bank has a competitive advantage in a specific (risk) segment and whether or not it can achieve the fair market value for it. The alternative to transferring risks is to keep (absorb) them, which will be discussed in the next point.

The transfer of risk eliminates or (substantially) reduces risk by selling (or buying) financial claims (this includes both selling in the spot market and hedging via derivative instruments, as well as buying insurance, as described above[165]). As long as the financial risks of the asset (created) are well understood in the market, they can be sold easily to the open market at the fair market value. If the bank has no comparative advantage in managing a specific kind of risk, there is no reason to absorb and/or manage such a risk, because—by definition—for these risks no added value is possible. Therefore, the bank should transfer these risks.[166]

Absorb/Manage   Some risks must or should be absorbed and managed at the bank level, because they have one or more of the following characteristics:[167]

- They cannot be traded or hedged easily.[168]
- They have a complex, illiquid, or proprietary structure that is difficult, expensive, or impossible to reveal to others.[169]
- They are subject to moral hazard.[170]

---

[165]Note that diversification is no means of transferring risks to other market participants for obvious reasons.

[166]As we will see later, Froot and Stein (1998a) come to the same conclusion; however, their model uses a different approach.

[167]See Allen and Santomero (1996), pp. 20–21.

[168]Therefore, hedging or selling is not an option in this context, because the costs of doing so would exceed the benefits.

[169]This is due to disclosure or competitive advantages. For a discussion of the optimal information release to the public in order to maximize value see Schröck (1997), p. 88.

[170]For instance, even though insurance is provided for a certain risk type, other stakeholders may require risk management as a part of standard operating procedures to make sure that management does not misbehave.

■ They are a business necessity. Some risks play a central role in the bank's business purpose[171] and should therefore not be eliminated or transferred.[172]

In all four of these circumstances, the bank needs to actively manage these risks by using one of the following three instruments:

■ **Diversification:** The bank is supposed to have superior skills (competitive advantages), because it can provide diversification more efficiently/at a lower cost than individual investors could do on their own.[173] This might be the case in illiquid areas where shareholders cannot hedge on their own.[174] We know that banks care about the internal diversification of their portfolios and especially the management of their credit portfolio, because the performance of a credit portfolio is determined not only by exogenous factors but also by endogenous factors such as superior *ex ante* screening capabilities and *ex post* monitoring skills.[175] Diversification, typically, reduces the frequency of both worst-case and best-case outcomes, which generally reduces the bank's probability of failure.[176]

■ **Internal insurance:** The bank is supposed to have superior risk-pooling skills[177] for some risks, that is, it is cheaper for the bank to hold a pool of risks internally than to buy external insurance.

■ **Holding capital:** For all other risks that cannot be diversified away or insured internally and which the bank decides to absorb, it has to make sure that it holds a sufficient amount of capital[178] in order to

---

[171]For instance, if the bank offers an index fund, it should—by definition of the product—keep exactly the risks that are contained in the index and should not try to manage, for example, the systematic part of the constituent stocks. See Allen and Santomero (1996), p. 21.
[172]If the bank has superior skills in transferring some assets, this is considered to be a competitive advantage in this situation, but not as described in the previous point.
[173]Individual investors lack specific knowledge relative to banks.
[174]Some level of diversification of specific risk of credits must be valuable to shareholders. Otherwise, they would hold, for example, (corporate) loans directly.
[175]See Winton (2000).
[176]Winton (2000), p. 2, shows that "pure" diversification in credit portfolios into areas where the bank does not have these superior screening and monitoring skills can result in an increase in the bank's probability of failure.
[177]See Mason (1995), p. 9.
[178]A conservative financial policy is considered to be an alternative to the other instruments of risk management. See Tufano (1996), p. 1112.

ensure that its probability of default is kept at a sufficiently low level.[179]

However, the decision to absorb risks internally should be based on competitive advantages that reimburse the bank more than the associated costs, that is, when value is created. A bank should have appropriate instruments to identify uneconomic risk taking, which allows it to decide when risk absorption is not the right choice and to decide when it is better to transfer risk to the market, or to avoid it altogether.[180] Again, we can observe that the complete hedging of all risks should almost never be an option, or as Culp and Miller put it, "most value-maximizing firms do not hedge."[181]

We have seen in this section that there are many other ways to conducting risk management than just hedging.[182] Again, the decision as to which approach is most appropriate and which instrument should be chosen should be based on the trade-off between costs and value created. The key, however, is to have a competitive advantage vis-à-vis the market in order to be able to create value.[183] In order to find this out, the bank needs to monitor both risks and returns.

Empirical Evidence

We have seen in the previous two sections that—from a theoretical point of view—there is no clear and detailed answer as to how banks should structure and conduct their risk management in order to increase value. In this section we will discuss whether and what empirical evidence there is on the link between risk management and value creation.[184]

Despite everything that has been written about corporate risk management, researchers and academics know very little about how risk manage-

---

[179]Note that equity finance is costly. We will discuss this point in more detail in Chapter 3.

[180]See Allen and Santomero (1996), p. 21. We will address this issue in Chapter 6.

[181]See Culp and Miller (1995), p. 122.

[182]Note that some risks can be hedged at low costs, others are expensive or impossible to hedge.

[183]Hedging/selling in liquid markets is a zero NPV transaction and does not create value in itself; it just shifts the bank along the Capital Market Line (CML). It seems problematic to systematically earn a positive return in highly liquid and transparent markets that exceed the costs of doing so.

[184]For an overview and summary of the theoretical and empirical evidence, see Smithson (1998).

ment is applied in practice.[185] A major difficulty facing researchers is that the data needed to measure a firm's risk exposure and its derivative positions is generally not available.[186] Since hedging operations are typically off-balance sheet transactions, they are not included in databases such as COMPUSTAT. This lack of well-developed databases has made empirical work very difficult (especially for banks) and has led researchers to collect survey data on firm risk-management policies.[187] However, these surveys may have major drawbacks:

- Many of the surveys do not seem to be conducted according to correct academic practices and are therefore not particularly useful. For instance, surveys are typically sent to a very limited number of firms and different surveys draw typically different samples.[188] Nonetheless, many surveys try to claim generality and draw conclusions that are presented as universally valid. Another difficulty, in our context, is that some surveys use risk management and hedging—or what is even worse, risk measurement and risk management—as synonyms, making it difficult to reveal the level of differentiation we are looking for.

- Survey questions are sometimes ambiguous, rendering it difficult to interpret responses. Additionally, surveys only convey what respondents say their firms do and not what they actually do in the real world, because the wrong people, who have the wrong perception of what their firms do, answer the questions. If surveys do not ask the right control questions, the reliability of the survey results could be

---

[185]Tufano (1996), p. 1097, summarizes the situation as follows: "Academics know remarkably little about corporate risk-management practices, even though almost three-fourths of corporations have adopted at least some financial engineering techniques to control their exposures. While theorists continue to advance new rationales for corporate risk management, empiricists seeking to test if practice is consistent with these theories have been obstructed by a lack of meaningful data. Corporations disclose only minimal details of their risk-management programs, and, as a result, most empirical analyses have to rely on surveys and relatively coarse data that at best discriminate between firms that do and do not use specific types of derivative instruments. Case studies of individual firms, while providing greater detail on firm practices, typically lack cross-sectional variation to test whether existing theories explain behavior."

[186]See Fenn et al. (1997), p. 20.

[187]See Froot et al. (1993), p. 1652.

[188]Surveys may not even be necessarily from the same industry(ies).

questionable.[189] For instance, firms that use risk management to speculate might be reluctant to admit doing so in a survey.[190]

- Surveys are often based on year-end financial statements and annual reports.[191] However, our current ability to judge whether one firm hedges more than another has important limitations:[192]
    - There are potentially huge differences in the disclosure of corporate hedging activities. Some firms with essentially equivalent hedging policies might appear different, because they voluntarily disclose more than required or the industry average does.
    - Even with complete access to hedging data, if two firms use different risk-management instruments, judging which firm conducts more risk management can be difficult.[193]

Therefore, we can conclude that survey-based data on risk management is associated with (fundamental) difficulties and can lead to inconsistent results that are not of much use for our purposes. Additionally, there are hardly any surveys and studies that are tailored specifically to banks, which is also due to the fact that banks are perceived to be opaque institutions. The empirical studies that are available so far can only give an indication as to what other players are doing in very specific areas.[194] But, as we have seen previously, drawing conclusions from surveys might not only be difficult, but also dangerous because, for example, the supposedly evolving industry standard could be completely off from what organizations should really consider from a theoretical perspective. The message should be rather

---

[189]Glaum and Förschle (2000), pp. 47+, reveal, for example, that hedging strategies often differ substantially from the actual hedging, meaning that internal guidelines are not strictly followed. This could indicate that there is a severe agency problem: The ranks and files are not maximizing value, because they potentially have the wrong incentives.

[190]See Smith (1995), p. 28.

[191]A major drawback of using such data is that the information they contain is often limited in scope and varies greatly from firm to firm. See Fenn et al. (1997), pp. 20–21.

[192]See Smith (1995), p. 28.

[193]For instance, one of the questions is how notional amounts should be compared to derivatives contracts with different times to maturity and exercise prices. One alternative would be to use the delta of the options. But this depends on the price of the underlying at which it is evaluated—and it is, therefore, unlikely that the results are comparable across firms.

[194]It is also difficult to see firms using risk-management instruments along the dimensions as we have described them above (i.e., hedge, diversify, insure, etc.).

that companies (even) in the same industry should not necessarily adopt the same risk-management strategy.[195]

Despite these difficulties, we can observe the following general trends in the empirical findings of the surveys and studies available:[196] Risk-management instruments are typically used to hedge.[197] Despite the reluctance of firms to admit in surveys that they speculate,[198] data limitations that preclude a comprehensive analysis, and the anecdotal evidence that derivatives are used to speculate, there seems to be systematic evidence that firms do not use risk management to speculate. However, when asked for details of their hedging strategy, these firms have open/unhedged positions, when they have a market opinion, of up to 70%. Firms almost never hedge 100% of their risk exposure[199] for the following reasons:

- **Transaction costs:** Hedging should only occur up to the point at which the marginal benefit of risk reduction equals the marginal costs of using derivatives.[200]
- **Errors in risk measurement:** If a firm is uncertain of its true risk exposure, it underhedges, using the best estimate, to minimize the possibility that it is adding rather than subtracting risk.
- **Opportunistic speculation:** Firms seem willing to let their view influence their hedge if it leads to underhedging, but not if it leads to overhedging.[201] This behavior, firms underhedging on average, is often

---

[195]See Froot et al. (1994), pp. 98–102.

[196]We base these statements on studies provided by Glaum and Förschle (2000), p. 24, Raposo (1999), pp. 47+, Mian (1996), Tufano (1996), p. 1097, Dolde (1993), Nance, Smith, and Smithson (1993), Mayers and Smith (1990), Wall and Pringle (1989), Block and Gallagher (1986), Booth, Smith, and Stolz (1984), and the studies additionally mentioned in the overview tables provided by Pritsch and Hommel (1997), pp. 687–689.

[197]See Smith (1995), p. 20.

[198]Typically 99% of the survey respondents answer that they do not speculate.

[199]Indirect evidence against full hedging is provided by a study that uses stock market data to investigate the sensitivity of firm equity values to financial price risk. It finds that the stock price sensitivity of derivatives users and nonusers is roughly the same, implying that users do not fully eliminate their exposure to risk. See Fenn et al. (1997), pp. 23–24, who refer to Hentschle and Kothari (1995).

[200]One model finds that transaction costs of 14 bps reduce the optimal hedge ratio from 100% to 80%.

[201]The explanation for this behavioral asymmetry is that firms confuse reversing their exposure with increasing risk. Overhedging actually reverses the exposure—only negative hedging amplifies the exposure.

described as selective hedging.[202] Even though selective hedging is not explained by theory,[203] it is an observable phenomenon. Like individuals who shed unwanted risks and acquire preferred risks, firms also buy or increase risks (via selective hedging), even if they know that, when things go wrong, these actions will affect firm value adversely.[204]

However, for one of the most fundamental questions—whether risk management can create value—there is almost no (direct) empirical evidence,[205] because the major challenge facing researchers is to design strategies for obtaining such evidence. One possibility for providing such evidence would be, for example, to use event studies. However, they are difficult to implement because the use of certain risk-management tools is rarely publicly announced.[206] Additionally, it is difficult to determine the effects of, for example, derivative usage on other financial characteristics of a firm (an increase in the leverage) that could have counterbalancing effects on the firm's value. Another possibility would be to try to measure the reduction in cash flow volatility through risk management. When trying to do so,[207] the reduction is so low that the benefits of using, for example, derivatives are unlikely to outweigh their costs.

Therefore, we can conclude that the positive link between firm value and risk management is still more of an object of theory than a hard empirical fact[208] because the empirical evidence for such a link is inconclusive. That is why I decided neither to use or derive survey results for this book, nor to try to provide empirical evidence on the value effects of risk management.

---

[202]If a firm has no view or if its view agrees with the market's view, then it tends to hedge almost fully. Conversely, if a firm believes that the price will decrease relative to the market's expectation, it hedges less than 100%.

[203]Market players do not seem to believe in efficient markets and try to outperform the market by using selective hedging and forecasting, which is impossible in most liquid markets. Nonetheless, firms are trying to face risks in which they perceive themselves as having a comparative advantage while managing others. See Raposo (1999), p. 47.

[204]See Mason (1995), p. 33.

[205]See Fenn et al. (1997), pp. 14 and 28.

[206]Dolde (1993) reports that derivative users outperform nonusers over a two-year period. But the difference is very small and could be simply due to the fact that better managers are the first to adopt state-of-the-art risk management techniques.

[207]See Copeland, Joshi, and Queen (1996).

[208]Nonetheless, a seminal paper by Froot et al. (1993) shows that—given the anecdotal and survey evidence on risk management—risk management as it is currently applied can enhance value, but does not optimize it.

SUMMARY

We have seen in this chapter that value maximization is, for banks (as for all corporations), the ultimate objective—even if there is evidence that bank stocks underperform on average and that there are other deviating and strong stakeholder interests. We then went on to define how the terms risk and risk management will be used in this book and identified the central role of risk management in banks as well as indicating that it is a likely source for value creation in banks.

We subsequently presented possible goals of and ways to conduct risk management in the light of how they can be linked to the ultimate objective, which is to maximize value. We finally evaluated whether there is empirical evidence for this link, but recognized that the results are inconclusive and do not provide detailed answers as to which exact risk-management strategy a bank should apply in order to increase value.

We will, therefore, explore in the next chapter whether financial theory offers more detailed answers as to whether banks should conduct risk management in order to maximize value. So far, we can only observe that banks are—by their very nature—in the risk business and that they do conduct risk management as an empirical fact (positive theory for risk management). We are now trying to find out whether there is also a normative rationale/theory for risk management.

APPENDIX

Part A: Bank Performance

TABLE 2.2   Bank Performance

BANK NAME (INDEX = 100% ON January 1, 1992)	INDEX ON December 31, 1999
Bank Austria	76.29%
EuroHypo	93.33%
Banca di Roma	101.27%
Natexis bq pop	110.72%
Baden–Württembergische Bank	120.58%
Banesto	126.99%
IKB Deutsche Industriebank	133.13%
Vereins- & Westbank	168.83%
Bankgesellschaft Berlin	171.70%
Okobank	190.15%
Bca. Toscana	193.07%
Bnc. Prtg. Atlantico	214.21%
RheinHyp	215.84%

Cdt. Bergamasco	219.44%
Bca. Agricola Mantovana	229.55%
BHF–Bank	237.22%
Deutsche Bank	252.71%
Oldenburger Landesbank	277.07%
Banca Intesa RNC	279.39%
Bca. PPO. Bergamo	281.41%
Commerzbank	298.28%
Merita	303.11%
COMIT	314.14%
Deutsche Hypothekenbank Frankfurt Hamburg	316.11%
Societe Generale	325.86%
Dresdner Bank	329.67%
Bayer. Hypo- und Vereinsbank	342.25%
Banca Lombarda	355.03%
BCP R	362.50%
DePfa–Bank	372.12%
Almanij	398.63%
Bnc. Popul. Español R	414.60%
Bca. PPO. Emilia Romagna	422.80%
Bca. PPO. Coml. Indr.	428.97%
CCF	477.24%
Allied Irish Banks	483.76%
Banca Intesa	513.38%
ABN AMRO Holding	527.66%
KBC Bkvs. Holding	529.18%
Unicredito Italiano	529.28%
HSBC Trinkaus & Burkhard	602.01%
BSCH	677.11%
Bankinter R	695.56%
ING Groep Certs.	729.20%
Fortis B	763.75%
BBV Argentaria	785.56%
Bank of Ireland	797.98%

Source: Datastream and author's analysis.

Part B: Systematic versus Specific Risk

See Figures 2.7 through 2.10 on the following pages.

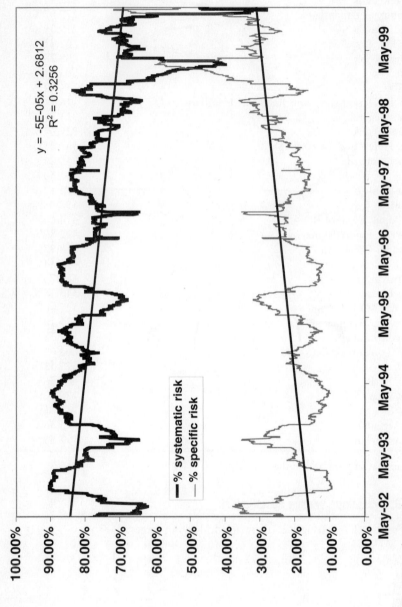

Figure 2.7 Deutsche Bank.
Source: Datastream and author's analysis.

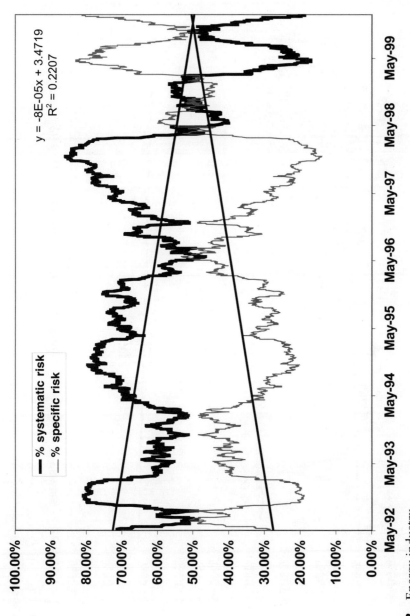

$$y = -8E-05x + 3.4719$$
$$R^2 = 0.2207$$

— % systematic risk
— % specific risk

Figure 2.8 Energy industry.
Source: Datastream and author's analysis.

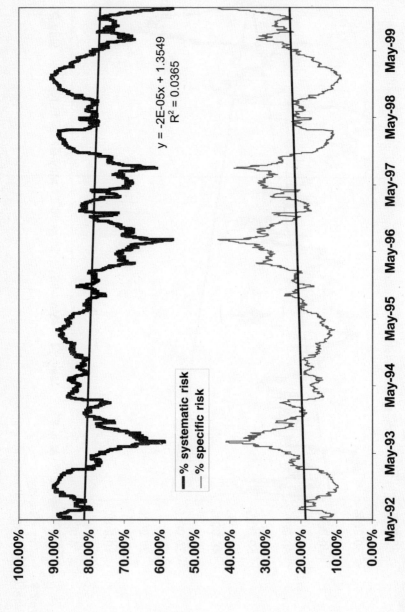

Figure 2.9   Consumer cyclical industry.
Source: Datastream and author's analysis.

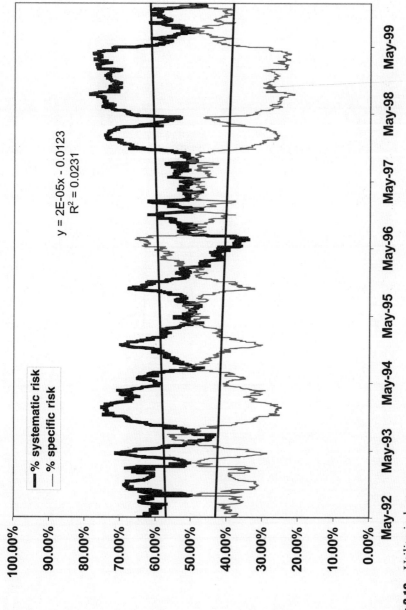

$$y = 2E\text{-}05x - 0.0123$$
$$R^2 = 0.0231$$

— % systematic risk
— % specific risk

Figure 2.10 Utility industry.
Source: Datastream and author's analysis.

CHAPTER 3

Rationales for Risk Management in Banks

As we have seen, we can observe in real life that firms (and banks) do conduct risk management in one way or another[1] and that there is a widespread belief among practitioners that corporate risk management is necessary and useful (positive theory). Both industry experts and analysts often claim risk management to be a strategic weapon in the battle to build (shareholder) value. Since markets penalize firms disproportionately when they perceive the risks of a firm to be higher than they actually are,[2] risk management could help to reduce the sources of this misperception and could bring value to the firm.[3]

Besides the argument used above that risk management should be employed to ensure the survival of the firm, there are numerous other reasons why risk management makes sense in practice[4] and why the interest in and the importance of risk management has grown:[5]

- An increase in international operations: operating abroad offers many opportunities, but also risks (due to, for example, less information,

---

[1]For a discussion of the empirical evidence on risk management see the "Empirical Evidence" section in Chapter 2.

[2]See Damodaran (1997), p. 788.

[3]See Shimko and Humphreys (1998), p. 33. However, it is necessary that this change be communicated and made transparent in adequate ways to the investor community.

[4]All stakeholders (shareholders, debt holders, regulators, managers, employees, customers, etc.) use arguments like their aversion to risk or the protection of their claim on the firm to justify corporate risk management.

[5]See Glaum and Förschle (2000), pp. 9–10.

political risks, foreign exchange risks) that are not compensated for by the benefits of international diversification.

- The increase in the volatility of foreign exchange rates, interest rates, and commodity and securities prices.[6]
- The introduction of regulatory changes and requirements (for many market players, especially banks).
- Technological and methodological advances.

The fact that the (financial) environment has become more volatile, which translates into an increase in the risk to firm value, is only a necessary but not a sufficient condition to manage risks at the corporate level. Given that the overall objective is the maximization of the firm's value—as reflected in Equation (2.1)—the sufficient condition to manage risks is that risk management should increase firm value.[7]

The increase in the volatility of the markets has led to the introduction of risk-management products like forwards, futures, swaps, options, and other derivatives,[8] which are themselves considered to have increased the volatility in financial markets.[9] The improper use of these financial products and the lack of organizational and business process adjustments—as is shown in various vast losses[10] in Figure 3.1—can expose firms themselves to a new set of risks[11] that is beyond their traditional business scope.[12] Therefore, both industry experts and analysts claim that financial risk management is important, but it is also difficult to assess. Since risk management, in practice, is often identified only in terms of not experiencing negative events, a lot of the risk management conducted remains a black box to many constituents. If these negative events (i.e. losses) occur, most people ask immediately for better risk-management systems.[13]

However, to date, there is no or only little consensus on a theory that

---

[6]For an extensive discussion see Rawl and Smithson (1989) and Smithson et al. (1995), pp. 2–21.

[7]See Smithson et al. (1990), p. 355.

[8]See Smithson (1995), pp. 21–28 and 30–44.

[9]See Merton (1995), p. 462, for a different opinion— that derivative products greatly reduced risks in the system instead of increasing them.

[10]Note that any derivatives contract, in order to be useful, has to transfer risk, that is, it can be used equally easily to hedge or to speculate. Many of the losses in the Wheel of Misfortune result from companies using derivatives to speculate. These events are failures of managerial oversight rather than failures of the derivatives markets.

[11]See Fenn et al. (1997), p. 13.

[12]Since financial institutions use derivatives disproportionately more than any other market players, this is even more true for them. See Fenn et al. (1997), p. 28.

[13]See Shimko and Humphreys (1998), p. 33.

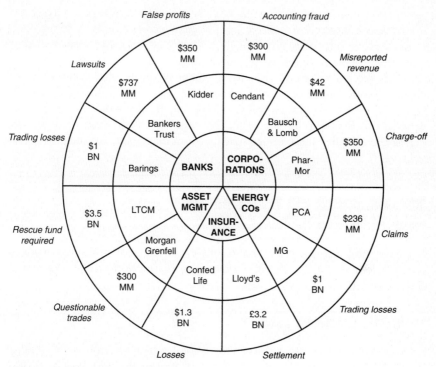

Figure 3.1 The wheel of misfortune.
Source: James Lani (1999): The Wheel of Misfortune, www.erisks.com. Used with permission. The wheel describes (from the inner to the outer circles) the industry of firms experiencing large losses, the company name, the amount of money lost, and the main reason for the losses.

explains why risk management matters for firms, because modern financial theory does not imply that firms should manage their risks at the corporate level (normative theory). Following the arguments of Modigliani and Miller (M&M), it can be shown that—under certain conditions—investors will not reward firms for changing their leverage, paying dividends, or managing and reducing their risks. Because investors can replicate or reverse all of these actions by themselves,[14] they have no impact on the overall value of the firm and are therefore irrelevant.

There are—by relaxing these conditions—a number of theoretical arguments that can explain why risk management can be useful at the firm level. On the other hand, testing these concepts empirically shows—as we have

---

[14]See Fenn et al. (1997), p. 13.

seen previously—only weak or inconclusive evidence.[15] In particular, there is only very limited confirmation that risk management creates (shareholder) value.[16] However, the major challenge for researchers is the fact that data limitations make it very difficult to obtain such evidence.[17]

This section examines risk management in the light of whether it can meet the sufficient condition mentioned above, that is, whether it can be used as a device to increase value (in banks). In discussing the theoretical foundations for the rationale of risk management at the firm level, we will derive the circumstances under which risk management can help to create value.

RISK MANAGEMENT AND VALUE CREATION IN THE NEOCLASSICAL FINANCE THEORY

In this section we investigate if and how risk management at the corporate level can help to create value under the strict assumptions of the neoclassical finance theory.

The Neoclassical Finance Theory

Risk management at the level of individual investors is well established in modern finance theory. However, this neoclassical world is based on rigid assumptions that capital markets are perfect and complete. The details of such markets are defined in the following lists.

Financial markets are *perfect*, if:[18]

- There are no taxes.
- There are no transaction costs (i.e., markets are frictionless, and information is available free of charge).
- There are no costs for writing and enforcing contracts.
- There are no restrictions on investments in securities (no regulation, no limitations on short-selling).
- There are no differences in information across investors (i.e., markets are efficient, and information is simultaneously available to all market players).
- All market players are price takers (i.e., price is a given and is the same for buyers and sellers).

---

[15]For a summary of empirical studies on risk management and value creation see, for example, Fenn et al. (1997) and the "Empirical Evidence" section of Chapter 2.
[16]See Fenn et al. (1997), pp. 14 and 25.
[17]See for example, Fenn et al. (1997), p. 28, and Tufano (1996), pp. 1097–1098.
[18]See for example, Stulz (2000), p. 2-4, Schmidt and Terberger (1997), p. 56.

A market is *complete*, if:

- All streams of cash flows can be traded irrespective of amount, time structure, or risk profile (i.e., all assets are marketable and perfectly divisible).
- A risk-free asset exists whose interest rate is the same for all market participants, irrespective of lending or borrowing.
- Complete information (which is free of charge, as indicated before) leads to homogeneous expectations and to the absence of arbitrage opportunities.

Furthermore, it is useful for our analysis to extend this list of assumptions for the M&M world. Therefore, the following additional neoclassical assumptions apply:[19]

- Firms have a fixed investment program.
- Firms have free access to (frictionless) capital markets.
- There is no (risk of) default (the M&M propositions hold without this assumption as long as default costs are zero[20]).
- Taxes are neutral.

Homogeneous expectations and information-efficient capital markets allow all nonfinancial preferences of the market players to be neglected in the neoclassical world, because they will not affect price-setting and cannot be traded in capital markets.[21] Even though individuals try to maximize the expected utility of their end-of-period wealth,[22] they are assumed to be risk-averse. The characterization of assets can be reduced in the neoclassical world to risk and return, because—additionally and by definition—asset returns are either (jointly) normally distributed or individuals have quadratic utility functions.[23]

While most of these assumptions are not realistic, these simplifications lead to the development of extremely useful models such as the Capital Asset Pricing Model (CAPM).[24] In this model, since individuals are assumed to be risk averse, they prefer a sure thing to a fair gamble—at least, when signifi-

---

[19]See for example, Pritsch and Hommel (1997), p. 675.
[20]See Stiglitz (1969).
[21]See Schmidt and Terberger (1997), p. 57.
[22]See Copeland and Weston (1988), p. 194, making this world implicitly a single-period model.
[23]See Perridon and Steiner (1995), p. 234.
[24]As developed by Sharpe (1964), Lintner (1965), and Mossin (1966).

cant financial stakes are involved[25]—that is, they prefer a certain stream of income to an uncertain stream of income with the same expected value. Therefore risk-averse investors care about the trade-off between risk and return—but, since they are assumed to be well-diversified, only with regard to systematic risks.[26] Hence, they only request a risk premium for taking these systematic risks,[27] meaning that they are only willing to bear additional (systematic financial) risk if they are adequately compensated with higher expected returns.

Risk-averse people, thus, have an incentive to manage (systematic) risk because doing so—as we have just seen—lowers the expected rate of return they require to engage in a risky activity. Individual risk aversion[28] can thus explain the purchase of insurance, but also explains the hedging by small companies in which a substantial fraction of the owner's personal wealth is invested. Risk management at the level of individuals is therefore well established, and investors have two effective instruments for managing their risks: asset allocation and diversification.[29] The usage of these two risk-management tools is sufficient for individual investors to achieve their optimal risk-return trade-off.

However, this logic fails for widely held corporations.[30] Unlike individuals, it is not clear why a corporation would want to manage its risks. The organizational form of the modern corporation was developed precisely to enable entrepreneurs to disperse risk among a large number of small, but well-diversified shareholders, each of whom bears only a small part of the risk. Therefore, it is hard to see why corporations themselves also need to manage the volatility of their income streams. Investors can manage risks on their own, and there is no reason for the corporation to, for example, hedge on behalf of the investor. The above assumptions of the neoclassical world imply that, for firms, investor risk-aversion is a poor reason for risk management.[31] Because companies cannot systematically make

---

[25]See, for example, Bernstein (1996), pp. 113–114, referring to Bernoulli, who provided the basis for this analysis in 1738; see Bamberg and Coenenberg (1992), pp. 73+.

[26]Given these assumptions, investors can diversify specific risks at no extra cost.

[27]See, for example, Bamberg and Coenenberg (1992), pp. 83–84.

[28]Methods for determining risk aversion are discussed, for example, by Krahnen et al. (1997).

[29]See Stulz (2000), pp. 2-2–2-3. Asset allocation defines in which assets investors want to invest their wealth, whereas diversification specifies how their funds are distributed among these assets to achieve this optimum.

[30]See Smith (1995), p. 20.

[31]See Fenn et al. (1997), p. 15.

money by managing risks,[32] they should behave as a risk-neutral agent in the aggregate.[33]

In efficient capital markets,[34] corporate financing decisions only reshuffle cash flows among investors.[35] Since (financial) risk-management decisions are a subset of these financing decisions, corporate risk management does not hurt,[36] but it also cannot create value.[37] Value can—according to M&M—only be created on the left-hand side of the balance sheet when companies make good investments that ultimately increase (expected) operating cash flows. How companies finance those investments on the right-hand side of the balance sheet—whether through debt, equity, or retained earnings—is irrelevant in this world.[38] The financial policy decisions can only affect how the value created by a company's real investments is divided among its investors. But, in efficient and well-functioning capital markets, they cannot affect the overall value of those investments,[39] because the value of (a stream of) cash flows is determined in the market and is the same for all market players.

However, this does not mean that financing and risk management is redundant. It only means that the way in which it is done is irrelevant for value creation under the above assumptions, because investors can always undo or replicate any financing decision by adjusting their own portfolios[40] at the same terms as the firm.

Corollaries from the Neoclassical Finance Theory with Regard to Risk Management

Modern financial theory and its rigid assumptions, as described in the previous section, have also lead to some other interesting corollaries, especially with regard to banks and their risk management.

In frictionless, perfect, and complete markets there would be no intermediation and no role for banks,[41] because everybody would contract directly with the market[42] at the same terms, as described in the traditional

---

[32]Unless they have a competitive advantage, which banks often claim to have.
[33]See Raposo (1999), p. 42.
[34]As described by the above assumptions.
[35]See Fenn et al. (1997), p. 16.
[36]However, if risk management comes at a cost, it destroys value.
[37]See Schmidt and Terberger (1997), p. 61, and Stulz (2000), p. 2-4, and below in more detail.
[38]See *Economist* (1996) and Fenn et al. (1997), p. 15.
[39]See Fenn et al. (1997), p. 16.
[40]See Fenn et al. (1997), p. 16.
[41]See Schmidt and Terberger (1997), p. 63.
[42]See Perridon and Steiner (1995), p. 485.

Arrow-Debreu world. The allocation of resources would be Pareto-efficient, and there would be no room for intermediaries like banks to improve welfare.[43] Likewise, there would be no need for a large number of different financial instruments, since all assets are priced in the market at a fair price and the exchange of various streams of cash flows would be free of charge.

In the CAPM, the world is reduced to the expected return of an asset and its (total) risk (as measured by its return volatility). However, for the individual investor, only the covariance of an asset's return with a broad (market) portfolio (i.e., the systematic risk[44]) matters and is quantified and priced.[45] Modern portfolio theory indicates that because investors can inexpensively manage nonsystematic (specific) risk through diversification,[46] an asset's required rate of return does not depend on its total risk but only on the systematic component of its cash flows.[47] Given the other assumptions of the neoclassical finance theory, the correct and fair (market) price for a banking product or financial instrument would be the same for any bank and for any investor, because it only depends on the return covariance with the market portfolio, which is independent of the bank's or the investor's preexisting portfolio.[48] Again, banks could not add value by offering their services and (risk management) products in this world.

As described above, there are usually multiple owners of a company that all have their own preferences with respect to the time structure and the risk profile of the cash flows generated by the firm they own. In order to make capital-budgeting decisions at the corporate level, they would have to agree on a single cash flow structure that would fit all preferences and which is obviously impossible to achieve. One feasible solution to resolve this conflict is to assume—as defined above—that all cash flows and streams of cash flows can be traded in perfect and complete capital markets.[49] In such a world without transaction costs, each of the owners can sell their claims on the firm and can buy a stream of cash flows that would best fit their (consumption) preferences with regard to time structure and riskiness.[50]

In this world, (corporate) capital-budgeting and capital-structure decisions can be separated without any impact on a firm's value. It does not

---

[43]See Allen and Santomero (1996), p. 22.
[44]The risk that cannot be diversified because it is due to aggregate economic fluctuations. See Stulz (2000), p. 2-24.
[45]See Copeland and Weston (1988), p. 194.
[46]Diversification can only reduce, but cannot eliminate risk altogether, see, for example, Stulz (2000), p. 2-20.
[47]See Smith (1995), p. 20.
[48]See Froot and Stein (1998a), p. 57.
[49]These are similar to the perfect markets for goods as described by Arrow-Debreu.
[50]See Schmidt and Terberger (1997), p. 56.

matter how the "pie"[51] is sliced among the various claimholders of the firm, because the size of the "pie" does not change through these decisions in this neoclassical world. However, that reinforces the ultimate objective of the firm: As soon as the value of the firm is maximized (due to good capital-budgeting decisions), each of the owners will be better off than in the case when the firm tries to choose non-value-maximizing investments by trying to match the individual preferences of the owners.[52] Again, Equation (2.1), and hence the traditional (shareholder) value framework,[53] can be applied: The firm value equals the net cash flows of the firm discounted at the appropriate rates, which only reflect the systematic risk of these cash flows.

Under the above assumptions, risk-management activities are purely financial transactions[54] that do not affect the value of a company's operating assets. Consequently, financial hedging strategies have no impact on firm value, because they affect neither the firm's relevant marginal costs nor its marginal revenues. Analogously to the M&M propositions, there is no reason to worry about risk management—it is as irrelevant as capital-structure or dividend-policy decisions for value creation on the firm level. Therefore, a firm's decision to use financial instruments to manage its risk exposure and its pricing and production decisions are also separable.[55]

This is true because in such a neoclassical world of efficient capital markets and under the M&M assumptions, financing, and hence risk-management decisions by a firm in a specific risk class can always be undone by investors.[56] Even though derivatives can make individual investors better off because they could achieve payoffs they could otherwise not achieve,[57] firms cannot increase value through the use of derivatives.[58] Buying and selling, for example, option contracts, cannot change the company's value, because individual investors in the company's stock can always buy and sell such contracts themselves at the same terms if they care to adjust their exposure to a specific risk factor.[59] Likewise, market players can construct portfolios that offset any position taken by a bank, and hence intermediation cannot create value.[60] Also, there is no need to manage risk at the

---

[51]See Brealey and Myers (1991), p. 401, who use this term for the overall value of the firm.
[52]See Schmidt and Terberger (1997), p. 59.
[53]As, for example, described by Copeland et al. (1994).
[54]This definition excludes changes in operations.
[55]See Smith (1995), p. 23.
[56]See Fenn et al. (1997), p. 16.
[57]For example, a static portfolio investment strategy can achieve only inferior payoffs to a strategy using derivatives.
[58]See Stulz (2000), pp. 2-48 and 2-51.
[59]See Froot et al. (1993), p. 1630.
[60]See Allen and Santomero (1996), p. 2.

corporate level, because all investors are fully participating in the financial markets[61], exploiting all arbitrage opportunities.

The Risk Management Irrelevance Proposition

From all of the above, we can conclude that firms cannot create value by managing risks at the corporate level. This leads us to the postulation of the "risk management irrelevance proposition," which is a natural extension of the M&M capital structure irrelevance proposition:[62] As long as the price of risk taking is determined in perfect and complete capital markets, it is the same within a firm as it is outside the firm. Therefore, corporate risk management is irrelevant, is unnecessary, and can even (as we will show shortly below) destroy value. This is true because firm risk management can always be replicated by "home-made" risk management on the individual investor's level at the same terms.

In the following paragraphs, we will show in detail why the risk management irrelevance proposition holds in the neoclassical world. We are trying to answer the question asked by many firms and banks—once they have identified and measured the various risks in their portfolios—as to whether or not they should try to manage risk.[63]

There are two kinds of risks in modern portfolio theory:

- **Diversifiable or (firm-[64]) specific risks** (for example, the risk that a new production process or marketing approach is unsuccessful): Shareholders are unconcerned with this kind of risk since it can be reduced, if not completely eliminated, by holding a well-diversified portfolio. If we fix the expected value of a company's cash flows, well-diversified shareholders will not pay more for a stock with less firm-specific risk because such risk is offset by (and offsets) the firm-specific risk of other stocks. Holding specific risk is not rewarded in capital markets.[65]
- **Market (-wide) or systematic risks:** These risks cannot be diversified away, because they are caused by economy-wide fluctuations (such as changes in interest rates) and do not vanish even in well-diversified portfolios. Investors are therefore concerned with these systematic risks and hence require a premium for bearing such risk. Systematic risk is the only component that is reflected in expected returns.

---

[61]See Allen and Santomero (1996), p. 22.
[62]See Stulz (2000), pp. 2-45–2-46 and 2-53.
[63]See Damodaran (1997), p. 784.
[64]These can also be risks specific to the industry in which a firm operates.
[65]See Fenn et al. (1997), p. 15.

While keeping in mind that we defined firm value in Equation (2.1) as a function of the present value of the (expected) cash flow and the appropriate discount rate, which reflects both the riskiness and the financing mix of the firm,[66] we need to establish the answer to the question of whether or not to manage risk at the corporate level along three dimensions (see Table 3.1).

- Is the firm trying to manage risks on behalf of well-diversified investors or not well-diversified investors (dimension A. versus B. in Table 3.1)?
- Is the intended risk management done through financial instruments or by changes in operations (dimension I. versus II. in Table 3.1)?
- Is the corporate risk management aimed at specific or systematic risks [dimension (1) versus (2) in Table 3.1]?

Let us first turn to a world where firms try to manage risks on behalf of *well-diversified* investors (A. in Table 3.1). In this world, for risk management through *financial* instruments (I. in Table 3.1) in capital markets to affect firm value, there are the following four potential scenarios (as indicated in the first row of Table 3.1 and as depicted in more detail in Table 3.2).

Let us consider what happens if a firm tries to eliminate *specific risks* on behalf of their investors [dimension (1) in Tables 3.1 and 3.2]. Since we assume in this section that typical investors in the firm are well-diversified, they will not be concerned with (firm-) specific risks. They can always eliminate specific risk by diversification on their own (at no cost) and will therefore not appreciate diversification provided by the firm. Because the discount rate in Equation (2.1) only depends on systematic risk, the overall firm value is also not dependent on specific risk. There are two scenarios in this setting:

TABLE 3.1 Overview of Corporate Risk-Management Scenarios

Investors	Risk Management	(1) Specific Risk	(2) Systematic Risk
A. Well-diversified	I. Financial	❶,❷	❸,❹
	II. Operational	❺	❻
B. Not well-diversified	I. Financial	❼	❽
	II. Operational	❾	❿

---

[66]See Damodaran (1997), p. 784.

TABLE 3.2   Financial Risk Management by the Firm

Corporate Risk Management working on	Scenario	Cash Flows	Discount Rate	Firm Value
(1) Specific risk	❶	o	o	o
	❷	–	o	–
(2) Systematic risk	❸	o	–	+
	❹	–	–	?

o = no change/neutral
– = decrease
+ = increase

Source: Adjusted from Damodaran (1997), p. 784.

Value-neutral scenario (❶ in Tables 3.1 and 3.2): This is the most obvious scenario in the world of perfect and complete markets. Since all risk-management actions are free of charge, the cash flows in the numerator of Equation (2.1) are unaffected. Likewise, all risk-management actions aimed at specific risks will not change the denominator of Equation (2.1). Thus, managing specific risks will not create value—neither on the firm level nor for the individual investor.

Value-destroying scenario (❷ in Tables 3.1 and 3.2): As soon as the firm spends time and money on eliminating firm-specific risks, the cash flows in the numerator of Equation (2.1) are reduced. Because these actions— as in scenario ❶—have no impact on the denominator, managing specific risk may decrease the value of the firm. Since individual investors could have eliminated specific risk themselves at no cost by portfolio diversification, they will not appreciate a firm's effort to do so at a cost.

Scenarios ❶ and ❷ assume that there is no positive feedback from eliminating firm-specific risks, that is, there is no increase in expected cash flows from existing projects, future investment decisions, or the optimal capital structure (and hence a positive effect on the discount rate).[67] Thus, a risk-management instrument that works on specific risk does not provide a lower discount rate for firms whose owners hold well-diversified portfolios, and hence can destroy value, if it comes at a cost.[68]

Let us now consider a firm that eliminates *systematic risk* on behalf of its investors [dimension (2). in Tables 3.1 and 3.2]. There are two possible scenarios:

---

[67]See Damodaran (1997), pp. 784–785.
[68]See Smith (1995), p. 20.

Value-creating scenario (❸ in Tables 3.1 and 3.2): If the firm were able to reduce systematic risk by its risk-management actions without reducing its cash flows, the resulting lower discount rate in Equation (2.1) would induce an increase in firm value. Unfortunately, systematic risk can only be off-loaded at fair market terms, because it is always correctly priced in neoclassical markets. Therefore a reduction in systematic risk will always also have an adverse impact on the (expected) cash flows, making this value-creation scenario unrealistic under the given assumptions (see negative subscenario ❹ below).

Unclear effect scenario (❹ in Tables 3.1 and 3.2): As observed in scenario ❸, risk-management actions in the neoclassical world can only change systematic risk and cash flows at the same time. Depending on the exact change in each of the two components, the net effect on firm value could be neutral, negative, or positive.[69]

- **Neutral:** Changing systematic risk always has a cost or a benefit associated with it. As long as the risk-management instrument or action is priced at fair market terms to reflect its systematic risk, the expected cash flows (from buying or selling the systematic risk) will change in parallel. Therefore, the firm only moves along the Security Market Line (SML[70]) with no effect on firm value[71] and investors would be indifferent vis-à-vis this kind of corporate risk management.
- **Negative:** If the reduction of systematic risk is more costly than the price that can be achieved in the capital markets for it, value will be destroyed.
- **Positive:** The reduction in cash flows is less costly than the price for systematic risk in the market. Therefore, value is created because the effect on the denominator is more profound than on the numerator.

However, the negative and the positive scenarios are unlikely to happen in complete and perfect neoclassical markets. Even if systematic risk is affected, as long as the risk is correctly priced, risk management still will not affect firm value.[72]

Additionally, one should keep in mind that if investors can buy and sell risk at the same terms as corporations, no service is provided to investors by corporate (or intermediated) risk management. Whenever a firm tries to reduce its systematic risk, its shareholders will simply end up with less exposure to systematic risk *and* lower expected cash flows, which in perfect

---

[69]See Damodaran (1997), p. 784.
[70]As described in the CAPM.
[71]See Smith (1995), p. 20.
[72]See Smith (1995), p. 20.

financial markets creates no value for investors. However, investors have chosen their optimal amount of systematic risk during the asset allocation process. Investors will, therefore, reverse corporate actions by changing this allocation and will simply readjust their portfolio without transaction costs, that is, move along the SML until they have reached their optimum risk level again.

Moreover, if a firm without risk management were able to increase its value to investors by providing risk-management services, investors would already have bought this firm's shares and conducted risk management on their own, driving up the stock price in the process and exploiting arbitrage opportunities.[73]

Let us now turn to a world where firms try to manage risks on behalf of well-diversified investors through changes in *operations* (dimension II. as represented in the second row of Table 3.1). In this world, for risk management to affect firm value, there are the following potential scenarios for (1) specific and (2) systematic risk:

Value-neutral or value-destroying scenario (❺ in Table 3.1): Similarly to scenarios ❶ and ❷, operational changes working on specific risk do not induce a lower discount rate for firms whose owners hold well-diversified portfolios. Therefore, these actions have either no effect on firm value or can destroy value, if they are costly.

Value-creating scenario (❻ in Table 3.1): As we have seen, selling systematic risk in financial markets cannot be done at a profit. However, if operations can be changed at little or no cost to decrease systematic risk, cash flows will be basically left unchanged. Since the discount rate will decrease in this scenario, risk management via a change in operations can therefore increase value, as long as the cost effect on the cash flows is smaller in the numerator than the effect of decreasing systematic risk is on the denominator of Equation (2.1). However, this scenario conflicts with the above (M&M) assumption of a fixed investment program with fixed operations.[74]

Scenarios ❺ and ❻ assume that there are no other potential benefits to conducting operational risk management, such as, for example, the avoidance of a costly company default that, in turn, would affect expected cash flows.[75]

---

[73]See Fenn et al. (1997), p. 15.

[74]Even though this flexibility would create value by itself.

[75]Given the above assumptions, there would be either no default costs or no (risk of) default at all.

Let us now turn to a world where firms try to manage risks on behalf of *not well-diversified* investors (B. in Table 3.1). These investors care about specific risks in their portfolios. However, in neoclassical markets, there would be no reason to hold such portfolios because they are inferior to well-diversified portfolios that can be created without any costs.[76] Nonetheless, if those investors and portfolios exist, it is out of the question that risk management conducted on the level of individuals can create value.[77] However, the question here is whether corporate risk management can also create value. Again, we distinguish between *financial* (as represented in the third row labeled I. in Table 3.1) risk management and changes in *operations* (as represented in the fourth row labeled II. in Table 3.1).

Financial risk management scenarios:

Value-creating scenario (❼ in Table 3.1): Corporate risk management working on *specific risks* [dimension (1)] can create value because investors decided not to use the opportunity to diversify their portfolios. Such investors will appreciate diversification provided by the firm. Even though these actions will not increase the overall firm value (which is only dependent on systematic risks), it will increase the consumption stream available to individual investors. However, if costs are associated with such actions at the corporate level, the resulting decrease in firm value has to be outweighed by the overall value increase to individuals in order to be beneficial overall.

Unclear effect scenario (❽ in Table 3.1): Since *systematic risk* [dimension (2)] can always be bought or sold in the market at fair terms, there will be no benefit for individual investors because they can replicate those transactions free of charge on their own. However, the same cases as in scenario ❸ and ❹ need to be considered to decide on whether the net effect on value creation is neutral, positive, or negative.

In the case of not-well-diversified portfolios, asset allocation and diversification can be insufficient risk-management tools, and individual investors can be made better off by using derivatives. However, as mentioned, firms cannot improve value for their investors by using derivatives.[78]

---

[76]According to capital markets theory, investors would only split their assets between the risk-free asset and the market portfolio, which—by definition—is perfectly diversified.

[77]See Stulz (2000), pp. 2--7–2-50.

[78]See Stulz (2000), pp. 2-50–2-51.

Changes in *operations* scenarios:

Value-creating scenario (❾ in Table 3.1): This is a direct analogue to scenario ❼ for *specific risk* (1).

Value-creating scenario (❿ in Table 3.1): This is a direct analogue to scenario ❻ for *systematic risk*(2).

Besides the above-mentioned arguments for corporate risk management, some companies claim to manage risks in order to best fit the wants and needs of certain shareholder clienteles.[79] However, the variation in the goals of such policies is wide—both within and across industries.[80] For instance, one gold-mining company states in its annual report that its "unique gold-hedging program offers investors a predictable, rising earnings profile in the future",[81] trying to guarantee a certain company risk profile. Another gold-mining company states, to the contrary, that its "no-hedging policy permits shareholders to capture the full benefit of increases in the price of gold"[82] by giving them more exposure to gold prices than other companies in the same industry. As long as we assume neoclassical markets and well-diversified investors, these risk-management policies for shareholder clienteles are irrelevant.

Let us first consider *specific risk*. Since investors can diversify those risks easily and because those risks are not compensated by capital markets for holding them, investors will be indifferent vis-à-vis this kind of risk, no matter whether a company provides more or less specific risk. Besides, scenarios ❶, ❷, ❺, ❼, and ❾ need to be considered to evaluate the exact effect on value.

Let us now turn towards *systematic risk*. If a firm tries to eliminate or create systematic risk, shareholders can buy or sell it in the market at the same fair market price on their own. Therefore the clientele argument used, for example, by Homestake is incorrect in perfect financial markets, because it cannot create value for investors. Again, scenarios ❸, ❹, ❻, ❽, and ❿ need to be considered in order to draw exact conclusions as to whether value is created by such actions.

Summary and Implications

We can summarize the economic insights that we derived under the strict assumptions of the neoclassical world in the previous sections as follows:

---

[79]See Stulz (2000), pp. 2-41+.
[80]For an extensive discussion of the risk-management policies in North American gold-mining corporations, see Tufano (1996).
[81]See Stulz (2000), pp. 2-2 and 2-53.
[82]Homestake (1990), p. 12.

First, risk-averse individuals should manage risks, especially if they are not well-diversified.

Second, risk management at the corporate level is irrelevant, unnecessary, and can be harmful:[83]

- Out of the ten scenarios on how risk management at the firm level could potentially create value for its investors, only three (❶,❹ neutral, and ❺[84]) conform exactly to the strict assumptions. However, all of these three scenarios are neutral to value creation. Therefore, the risk management irrelevance proposition holds in the neoclassical world.
- All other scenarios (❷, ❸, ❹ negative and positive, ❼, ❽, ❾) are not consistent with the neoclassical world and can only create or destroy value because they relax one or more of the given assumptions.
- If risk-management decisions are to affect the value of the firm, they must do so by influencing the expected level of cash flows and the discount rate[85] disproportionately, which is impossible given the assumptions.
- The irrelevance proposition even holds for scenarios ❻ and ❿. Albeit changes in operations working on systematic risk are the most promising candidates for value creation in the neoclassical world, they are at stake with the M&M assumption that investment programs, and hence operations, are fixed.
- If there are transaction costs associated with managing risks, no risk management should be conducted at all, because this is a value-destroying proposition.

Third, firm-specific risks do influence the volatility of stock prices and earnings. However, eliminating them is of little value to well-diversified investors, unless there is a concern with bankruptcy.[86] On the other hand, as soon as we remove the assumption that there is no default risk and no transaction costs, it does matter that banks can potentially remove some of the specific risk more efficiently and at a lower cost than diversification by individual investors can.

Fourth, because only systematic risk counts in the neoclassical world, the DCF methodology using the CAPM (or any other standard asset pricing model[87]) is the appropriate measure to determine the value of a transaction and the firm value (see Equation [2.1]).

---

[83]See, for example, Mason (1995), p. 29.

[84]Besides, the clientele argument was also found to be neutral to value creation.

[85]See Fenn et al. (1997), p. 16.

[86]However, this is always the case with investors in banks who often see them as "accidents waiting to happen." We will expand on this point below.

[87]For instance, the Arbitrage Pricing Theory (APT), as first described by Ross (1976).

Fifth, since risk management in this world only redistributes risk across market participants, who charge the same price for bearing it,[88] all banks, for example, would offer similar products at the same price, and their current portfolio constitution would not influence the pricing decision.

Sixth, decisions on capital budgeting, capital structure, and risk management can therefore be determined separately in the neoclassical world,[89] because all market participants face the same price/cost for their actions and are thus able to replicate any of the decisions taken by the firm.

Last but not least, even though risk management is irrelevant for value creation, that is, a NPV = 0 proposition, it could still be useful to ensure and signal a certain company risk profile and hence a certain M&M risk class to the outside world. Therefore, risk management is not per se redundant in the neoclassical theory.

The neoclassical world does not build a sound foundation for an economic rationale for using risk management to create value. However, as soon as we relax one or more of the rigid assumptions, risk management could potentially increase value and there would be an economic rationale for conducting risk management even at the corporate level. As we will see in the following section, many of the assumptions of the neoclassical world appear to be unrealistic because we can observe wide discrepancies between what the neoclassical theory predicts and what we can observe in practice. Therefore, we will analyze the results of relaxing some of the assumptions in the subsequent sections.

Discrepancies Between Neoclassical Theory and Practice

The neoclassical theory predicts that neither banks nor any other (financial) intermediaries would exist,[90] because all market players would contract directly with each other in complete and perfect (financial) markets. And even if banks existed, they would not be able to add value through the provision of their services, since prices are determined in efficient markets and are the same for all participants, irrespective of their preexisting portfolios.

However, what we can observe in reality is that banks do exist and that they offer a variety of different financial products and services that are utilized by investors who are willing to pay a premium for them. One of the reasons that could explain this fact is that there is empirical evidence that investors do not hold diversified portfolios and that there is only limited

---

[88]See Stulz (2000), p. 2-41.
[89]See, for example, Mason (1995), p. 29.
[90]However, the existence of firms is consistent with the neoclassical world. See Mason (1995), p. 27.

market participation.[91] This is due to the fact that there are fixed[92] and marginal[93] costs in order to be able to participate in markets. Uninformed investors can gain access to the markets through the intermediary's services. This adds value to the transaction by reducing the (perceived) participation costs of the uninformed investor. Therefore, participation costs can explain the fact that intermediaries trade risk and undertake risk management. Such costs can also explain why investors prefer to hold debt or debtlike instruments[94] or assets with a relatively stable risk profile that are (synthetically) created by banks by using derivatives, so that investors do not have to monitor the expected distribution of returns.[95]

Likewise, banks do extensively conduct risk management[96] and—as many surveys and annual reports convey—see risk management as one of their most important corporate objectives or core competencies,[97] even if—as we have seen—the neoclassical theory predicts that corporate risk management cannot create any value. However, banks manage their risks with the purpose of increasing value, and there is anecdotal evidence that banks with superior risk-management skills and systems outperform their competitors.[98] Similarly, there must be some benefit to conducting risk management at the firm level, because we can observe a subjective and normative view that risk management is good and necessary, which is also reflected in many regulatory requirements.[99]

We have described previously that the increase in the volatility in financial markets translates into an increased volatility of firm values. Since it is often claimed that risk management can reduce this volatility (and that this

---

[91]For an extensive list of literature on this empirical evidence see Allen and Santomero (1996), pp. 22–23, and for a critique of this reasoning, see Scholtens and van Wensveen (2000).

[92]These are costs of learning about the financial instruments and how the market works. Fixed participation costs are not transaction costs.

[93]For example, the costs of monitoring the markets on a day-to-day basis.

[94]These types of securities typically have low participation costs.

[95]See Allen and Santomero (1996), pp. 22–24.

[96]Even though it is—in the neoclassical world—irrelevant for shareholders, they demand that managers pursue risk management, see Mason (1995), p. 29.

[97]See, for example, Deutsche Bank (1999), p. 123, Raposo (1999), p. 41.

[98]See Shimko and Humphreys (1998), p. 33, who claim that risk management is very important over the long run, because a company's stock will outperform as losses are avoided. Similarly, they claim that good risk-management systems will have the same effect.

[99]For instance the "Mindestanforderungen an das Betreiben von Handelsgeschäften" (1995) for banks and the "Gesetz zur Kontrolle und Transparenz im Unternehmensbereich (KonTraG)" (1998) for industrial companies in Germany reflect this view.

would be useful and is the goal of risk management), the immediate hypothesis would be that all firms would want to manage (all of) their risks. However, there is a wide variation in the use of risk management (instruments) across firms, even within the same industry[100] and even when they have similar exposures.[101] Therefore, there must be other reasons that can help to explain these differences in actual behavior.

Moreover, as is reflected in the recognition of value at risk[102] as an industry standard by choice or by regulation, for banks (and many other market players), the current constitution of their portfolio counts and influences their decisions. Likewise, for many market players not only systematic, but rather total risk (including specific risk, even if they are well-diversified) matters.

Explaining and diminishing these discrepancies between theory and practice was identified as one of the motivations for writing this book. It seems that only market imperfections can help to explain what happens in reality. The neoclassical theory is—at best—only a partial solution, because it is too perfect to describe reality. We, therefore, turn now to the neoinstitutional theory, which is—as we will see below—also only a partial solution.[103]

RISK MANAGEMENT AND VALUE CREATION IN THE NEOINSTITUTIONAL FINANCE THEORY

The risk management irrelevance proposition only holds in the perfect and complete markets of the neoclassical world, because only then is the price for bearing risks the same within and outside the firm. As soon as we introduce market imperfections, this does not necessarily need to be the case. There might be situations where risk management by the firm cannot be replicated by individual investors at the same terms, which in turn can increase the firm's value.

---

[100]See Tufano (1996) for an extensive analysis of the differences in North American gold-mining companies. Likewise, there is anecdotal evidence for differences in the risk-management policies of banks.

[101]See Smith (1995), p. 20.

[102]The value-at-risk measure will be described in detail in Chapter 5. It summarizes risks at an aggregated level, taking into account diversification effects, and can be translated into an amount of equity capital needed to absorb unexpected losses with a prespecified degree of certainty.

[103]See Schmidt and Terberger (1997), p. 53.

Classification of the Relaxation of the Assumptions of the Neoclassical World

The neoinstitutional theory[104] relaxes the rigid assumptions of the neoclassical world, without (completely) ignoring the results derived under the neoclassical paradigm. There are various neoinstitutional approaches that basically try to describe the trade relationships between two or more constituents of a firm, and which can be differentiated as follows:[105]

■ **Incentive-based approaches:** The nucleus of these approaches is the separation of ownership and decision/control power in modern corporations. They can be further differentiated into the following two branches:

– **Property rights theory:** The allocation of resources can only be efficient and optimal when all positive and negative externalities are internalized. This will only be the case when all property rights (authority rights, property rights, and disposition rights) are specified and are tradable in appropriate markets. Even though this approach provides valuable insights by trying to explain the effects of legal and institutional rules on the behavior of the various constituents, it is not helpful in deriving a rationale for how risk management can create value. We will, therefore, not pursue this approach in more detail, but will use its results in our discussion below.

– **Agency theory:** The delegation of disposition rights from principals to agents necessitates the alignment of the diverging interests[106] that are caused by asymmetric information (and the fact that obtaining information is costly), uncertainty, and external effects, and that can also be the consequence of nonfinancial preferences. The resulting so-called agency costs can be minimized via *ex ante* contractual arrangements. They can be split,[107] on the one hand, into *agency costs of equity*,[108] which can be mitigated by financial leverage, which forces the agents (i.e., man-

---

[104]Also often termed as neoinstitutional economics and finance theory, see Jensen and Meckling (1976).

[105]See for example, Perridon and Steiner (1995), p. 486, who refer to Williamson (1985), pp. 23+.

[106]Agents usually maximize their utility, which is not necessarily in the interest of the principal.

[107]See Jensen and Meckling (1976), pp. 305+.

[108]These are, for example, overinvestment and conflicts between shareholders and will be described in more detail below.

agement) to generate enough cash flows to meet the debt's obligations. This is especially important when no single influential shareholder controls the management actions closely or plays an active role in the firm's management. On the other hand, there are *agency costs of debt* that increase with leverage.[109] A higher leverage increases the probability of default and, with it, increases the (indirect) cost of default, that is, it lowers the market value of the firm. Additionally, the higher interest rates charged by the debt holders to reimburse them for the costs of writing and monitoring collateral, covenants, and so on, especially when the firm's risk-profile changes or its leverage is further increased, are also nontrivial. Jensen and Meckling[110] argue that there is an optimal degree of leverage that minimizes the total agency costs from the two sources. Moreover, the market for corporate control[111] and other mechanisms can lower both kinds of agency costs.

■ **Transaction-cost-based approach:** Transaction costs are the costs that are associated with the initiation, determination, transfer, enforcement, and adaptation of contractual arrangements on property rights. They are the result of asymmetric information (that leads to moral hazard and adverse selection) and the limited rationality of the market participants. These problems are resolved via *ex post* monitoring structures, which are costly, because they try to remove these information and incentive problems. The analysis of these costs can determine—based on the difference in transaction costs—where trade relationships should be exchanged. Depending on the specificity and the frequency of a transaction, it can be more cost-efficient to do the transaction in the open market or within a firm.[112]

As can be seen from the above description of the various neoinstitutional approaches, they all require, in one way or another, the relaxation of the assumptions of the idealized neoclassical world to include the concerns of the various stakeholders of a firm (such as, for example, transaction costs, taxes, default costs, conflicts of interest that result from the fact that each party cares only about the financial and nonfinancial advantages and disad-

---

[109]These are, for example, asset substitution and underinvestment and will be described in more detail below.
[110]See Jensen and Meckling (1976), p. 344. However, they analyze each branch of the problem set in isolation to derive their equilibrium. Modern theory would require deriving an integrated solution, which could be very different.
[111]As described above and, for example, by Jensen (1993).
[112]See for example, Jensen and Meckling (1991).

vantages of their part of the firm's cash flows because they are utility maximizers,[113] and so on).

If capital markets are less than perfect, the risk management irrelevance proposition does not hold anymore. Therefore, under these more realistic assumptions, the value of the firm can be increased when risk taking within a firm is rewarded more highly than what can be achieved by selling the risk to the capital markets, that is, than what someone else would be willing to pay for bearing the same risk.[114] From this, one can directly deduce that, in this world, it is not the purpose of risk management to protect the firm's value against changes in market values at any price. These changes can occur, but shareholders are still able to adjust their exposure, just as in the neoclassical world, to the various risk factors according to their preferences. The purpose of risk management is rather to reduce the frictional costs that are associated with these changes in market values and to create value by doing so.

These frictional costs can stem from the following market imperfections,[115] which are a relaxation of the assumptions of the M&M world:

- Asymmetric information
- Agency problems and management incentive structures
- Limited availability of external funds (i.e., external funds are costly)
- Transaction costs
- (Direct and indirect) default costs
- (Convex schedule of) taxes

Additionally, one should also assume that investment opportunities are stochastic, that is, the investment program is not fixed and dependent on the prevailing economic conditions and, hence, a function of the cash flows generated by the firm's assets in place.[116]

Irrespective of these relaxed assumptions, the basic workings of the neoclassical world are still valid, and investors are still able to adjust their portfolios and can undo corporate decisions by home-made risk management. It is therefore obvious, as long as investors are well-diversified,[117] that it is unlikely that risk-management decisions by the firm can influence the denominator of Equation (2.1) by changing the systematic risk. If risk management does not reduce the firm's required rate of return, then it must

---

[113]See Jensen and Meckling (1976), p. 308.
[114]See Stulz (2000), p. 3-3.
[115]See Pritsch and Hommel (1997), p. 675.
[116]See Froot et al. (1993), p. 1638.
[117]See for example, Fenn et al. (1997), pp. 13+, and Smith (1993), pp. 17+.

increase the firm's (expected) cash flows[118] by decreasing the frictional costs (as mentioned previously) to increase the value of a widely held firm.[119]

This can only happen under circumstances[120] that basically turn M&M's Proposition I[121] "upside down",[122] that is, when financial decisions (including risk management) have an impact on taxes, transaction costs, or the investment decisions of a firm.[123] Besides these three reasons (as shown in the gray shaded areas in Figure 3.2 below) stemming immediately from the relaxation of the M&M assumptions,[124] there are other circumstances under which it can make economic sense to manage risks at the firm level. They are the result of the relaxation of other neoclassical assumptions and are, for example, due to managerial risk aversion[125] or other effects of having not-well-diversified investors.[126] Similarly, other market inefficiencies (as discussed in detail below) show that it is not sufficient to just turn the M&M proposition upside down in order to get a comprehensive picture of the economic rationales for risk management in the neoinstitutional world; a more differentiated view is necessary.

Clearly, because we now permit agency and transaction costs, there are not only benefits but also costs associated with risk-management actions.[127] Only as long as the benefits outweigh the costs can risk management be sensible from an economic point of view. In the subsequent sections we will

---

[118]Smithson (1998), pp. 6–13, labels this view the "Real Cash Flow" rationale for risk management.

[119]See Smith (1995), p. 20.

[120]As first identified and discussed by Smith and Stulz (1985).

[121]M&M Proposition I postulates that, in a world without taxes and transaction costs, and given a fixed investment program, financial decisions cannot affect the value of a firm.

[122]See Smithson et al. (1990), pp. 357 and 363, Smithson (1998), p. 7.

[123]See Smith and Stulz (1985), p. 392, and Smith (1993), p. 17.

[124]These three points of turning the M&M Proposition I upside down are labeled by Tufano (1996), p. 1106, as the Shareholder Value Maximization Hypothesis of risk management.

[125]This is labeled the Managerial Utility Maximization Hypothesis by Tufano (1996), p. 1109. Fenn et al. (1997), pp. 13+, also identify this fourth rationale in addition to the three stemming from the relaxation of the M&M assumptions. Likewise, see Froot et al. (1993), pp. 1631+. Smithson (1998), pp. 13–14, calls this view the "Agency Relations with the Firm's Managers" rationale for risk management.

[126]Damodaran (1997), pp. 785+, also distinguishes between risk-management rationales that apply to companies with well-diversified investors and undiversified investors.

[127]Both benefits and costs are difficult to quantify in this context.

first describe and discuss (where appropriate in the context of banks) the circumstances under which corporate risk management can be beneficial in the three broad categories: (1) agency costs, (2) transaction costs, and (3) taxes and other market imperfections. Figure 3.2 provides an overview of the risk-management rationales in the neoinstitutional world. We return to the cost-benefit trade-off later, in Chapters 4 and 6.

However, before doing so, it is worthwhile to mention that the relaxation of the rigid neoclassical assumptions allows now for the existence of banks. It is, therefore, not surprising that the traditional theories of intermediation are based on transaction costs and asymmetric information and are designed to model institutions that take deposits and channel funds to firms in the form of loans. However, this traditional role of intermediation has shifted from reducing the frictions of these transaction costs and asymmetric

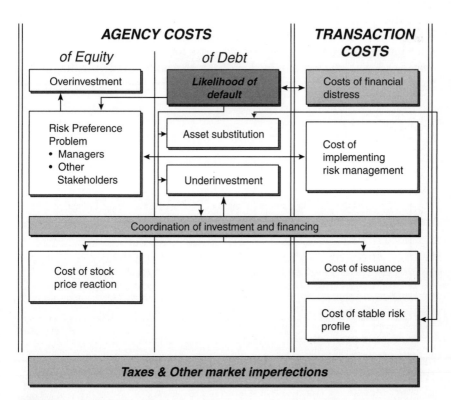

Figure 3.2 Overview of risk-management rationales in the neoinstitutional world.
Note: The gray shaded areas show the areas where turning M&M Proposition I upside-down can be the foundation for conducting risk management in the neoinstitutional world.

information to risk trading and the reduction of participation costs.[128] As we have already mentioned, in facilitating this risk transfer, risk management has become a key area of banking.

The Central Role of the Likelihood of Default

As indicated by the arrows in Figure 3.2 above, the likelihood of default plays a central role in deriving rationales for risk management in the neoinstitutional world and, therefore, forms the starting point of our discussion.

As a firm starts to finance itself through debt, every increase in its financial leverage also increases the probability of default.[129] Risk management can reduce the probability of a firm encountering financial distress, by reducing the variance in the distribution of the firm's value. As shown in Figure 3.3, the asset distribution of a firm without risk management is broader (solid line), and the area below the default point *DP*, that is, probability p_1, is relatively large. By conducting risk management, the firm can narrow the distribution (dotted line). However, since risk management (most likely) only comes at a cost, the expected value of the distribution is lower than in the

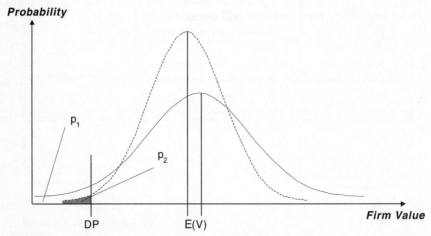

Figure 3.3   Variations in firm value and default point.
Source: Adapted from Smithson et al. (1990), p. 368.

---

[128]See Allen and Santomero (1996), p. 1.
[129]See Stulz (2000), p. 3-39. Without debt of some sort, there are no bankruptcy costs and no tax benefits of debt.

case without risk management. Nonetheless, the (gray shaded) area left of the default point p_2 is considerably smaller than p_1.

Reducing the likelihood of default from p_1 to p_2 does not increase firm value by itself.[130] However, it can lower the agency and transaction costs stemming from the probability of default (and the costs of the various other areas discussed in more detail below). These direct and/or indirect effects indicate the benefit of risk management and hence the ability to create value through it.

Agency Costs as Rationale for Risk Management

Agency conflicts are based on information asymmetries between information insiders and outsiders (e.g., conflicts between shareholders and bond holders, old and new shareholders, and management and shareholders). Agents have incentives to undertake a real investment policy that deviates from that of the principals because of financing and risk.[131] For instance, since shareholders have a residual claim on the firm's cash flows, they tend to favor actions that increase the value of their holdings, even if that means increasing the risk that bond holders (who have a fixed claim on these cash flows) will not receive their promised payments. On the contrary, bond holders want to preserve and increase the security of their claims.[132] However, because the equity investors generally control the firm's management and decision making, their interests will dominate the bond holders' interests, unless bond holders take some protective action.

As mentioned previously, agency conflicts can be the result of adverse selection and moral hazard. All of the agency problems related to risk management result from moral hazard problems[133] and, therefore, occur after contracting. Since the resulting agency costs[134] cause a reduction of the market value of equity and/or debt, they can be split (as already indicated) into agency costs of equity and those of debt. The (potential) benefit of risk management lies in the reduction of these agency costs,[135] which, in turn, can increase firm value and hence can build the basis for a rationale for risk management.[136]

---

[130]As is shown in Figure 3.3, the cost of risk management can even decrease the expected firm value E(V).

[131]See Pritsch and Hommel (1997), p. 675.

[132]This view is also the perspective of bank regulators for other reasons.

[133]See Pritsch and Hommel (1997), p. 676.

[134]Agency costs are the sum of monitoring and bonding costs as well as a residual loss; see Jensen and Meckling (1976), p. 308.

[135]See Pritsch and Hommel (1997), p. 675.

[136]Note that both kinds of agency costs can be reduced via the market for corporate control, as described by Jensen (1993).

Agency Costs of Equity as a Rationale for Risk Management   The agency costs of equity that are relevant for risk management can be split into three groups and are represented by the three (nonshaded) boxes in the left-hand part of Figure 3.2.

The Overinvestment Problem   Managerial discretion[137] may result in a conflict of interest between shareholders and their managers and becomes especially relevant when organizations generate substantial free cash flow.[138] Managers can decide to accept negative NPV projects, that is, projects with which they pursue their own interests (so-called consumption on the job) and/or increase firm size (so-called empire building[139]).

The benefit of risk management in this context is the potential reduction of these "agency costs of free cash flow".[140] Risk management can reduce the volatility of free cash flows both upwards and downwards and can, hence, limit the availability of the cash flows that are at managerial discretion.[141] Additionally, risk management can allow for an increase in the debt ratio,[142] which can lower these agency costs of equity without increasing the default probability of the firm.[143] Note that the past avoidance of overinvestment can be especially important in financial distress situations. If capital markets know of previous incidents where agency costs of free cash flow were incurred, it is especially difficult to raise additional funds.

The Risk Preference Problem   A firm can be viewed as a network of contracts among its various stakeholders,[144] who can have common and conflicting interests. Managers, employees, customers, suppliers, and other stakeholders are frequently less able to diversify their claims on the firm,[145] because it is often important for the firm that these stakeholders make long-term firm-specific investments.[146] Like the owners of a closely held firm,[147] they therefore end up being poorly diversified investors who are affected by

---

[137]As first described by Stulz (1984).

[138]See Jensen (1986), p. 323.

[139]Promotions are still largely based on power, which is an incentive for managers to grow their organizations beyond their optimal size. See Jensen (1986), p. 323.

[140]See Jensen (1986).

[141]See Tufano (1998), p. 69.

[142]As described by Jensen (1986), p. 324, debt reduces the agency costs by reducing the free cash flow available for spending at the discretion of managers.

[143]See Tufano (1996), p. 1106.

[144]Jensen and Meckling (1976), p. 310, label this as a "nexus" for contracting.

[145]See Smith (1993), p. 16.

[146]See Stulz (2000), p. 3-34.

[147]This is the case when ownership is concentrated.

and do care about the specific risks of that firm and who have a preference for the management of these risks (the risk preference problem).

Under these circumstances, risk management by the firm's stakeholders is not an adequate substitute for risk management by the firm. When firms try to hedge these firm-specific risks, stakeholders will not require a higher compensation for bearing these risks, which they otherwise would. Since these higher (risk) premiums would lower the value of the firm's equity (agency costs of equity), avoiding their payment would increase the firm's value. Therefore, the stakeholders' risk aversion can provide an important incentive[148] for the firm to engage in risk-management activities,[149] even if there is no default risk for the firm through debt.

The Risk Preference Problem of Managers   Managers can have a risk preference problem for two reasons. On the one hand, they would like the firm to conduct risk management on their behalf because they are risk averse and not well diversified (as described previously). On the other hand, they would like (the firm) to hedge to be able to signal their true management capabilities to the labor market. We will discuss both arguments in more detail in this section.

> **Managerial risk aversion:** The managerial risk preference problem is due to a shareholder-manager (principal-agent) conflict[150] and determined by the agency relations of a firm with its managers.[151] Risk management may be used by poorly diversified managers who might have private interests in managing risk to maximize their own utility. The proposition here is that corporate risk-management choices might be the product of:
>
> - The managers' risk aversion
> - Their exposure to the success of the firm, as offered by their compensation contracts and their investments in the firm[152]
>
> Let us first address *managerial risk aversion*.[153] Stulz[154] first suggested the economic reasons for why firm managers are concerned with

---

[148]See Mayers and Smith (1987).
[149]See Smith (1993), p. 16.
[150]And, as mentioned, a moral-hazard-type problem.
[151]Managers are often more risk averse than their shareholders when it comes to taking projects, because (the probability of) bankruptcy might have more serious consequences for them.
[152]See Tufano (1998).
[153]See Stulz (1984), Smith and Stulz (1985), and, for example, Mason (1995), p. 30.
[154]See Stulz (1984).

risk management. Like the owners of a closely held firm, managers may have invested a large fraction of their personal wealth in the company in the form of stocks and human capital (i.e., the NPV of their expected future income stream from that firm). This makes them poorly diversified and limits their ability to diversify.[155] Managers are, therefore, not indifferent with regard to firm-specific (unsystematic) risks and care about the total risk of the firm. This sets the preference for them to reduce those risks to which they are exposed.[156]

For risk-averse managers, an increase in the volatility of the underlying cash flows of the firm means a higher probability of default,[157] which results in a decreasing expected utility of their human capital and their stock holdings. Hence, managers have an incentive to adjust the firm's investment, capital structure, and risk-management policy to change the risk profile that is preferred by shareholders (the risk preference problem). They favor a reduction in the variance of total firm value (that is, due to the volatility in the firm's cash flows), because convincing the firm to manage risks makes the managers strictly better off by improving their own utility at little or no expense to other stakeholders.[158] Otherwise, they could sell their stake (which might be impossible in the short run) and invest the proceeds in a diversified portfolio and risk-free assets or keep their stake but conduct risk management on their own (and at a potentially much higher cost).[159]

Therefore, managers can have an incentive to manage risks at the corporate level not to increase the value of the firm, but rather to protect their own wealth position[160] out of self-interest.[161] Managerial risk-aversion can be consequently an important rationale for risk man-

---

[155]See Stulz (1984), Allen and Santomero (1996), p. 14, and the list of references to the literature provided there.

[156]See Tufano (1996), p. 1109.

[157]And hence the (potential) loss of the reputation of their managerial capabilities.

[158]As long as the firm has committed itself to conducting risk management to ensure a stable risk profile and there are little or no transaction costs. See Froot et al. (1993), p. 1631.

[159]See Stulz (2000), p. 3-27.

[160]See Smithson (1998), p. 13.

[161]The economic decision makers face a nonlinear optimization problem, which in turn leads them to be concerned about both the expected firm returns and their distribution (variability is a choice variable usually assumed to be selected by management subject to the usual constraints of optimization) around the expected value. See Allen and Santomero, pp. 13–17.

agement[162] and can make the firm's objective function itself concave,[163] that is, managers behave in a risk-averse way.[164]

Froot, Stein, and Scharfstein[165] contend that this line of reasoning is a transaction cost rather than an agency cost argument. Their assumption is that managers face significant transaction costs for conducting risk management on their own and therefore exploit the opportunity to have the firm manage risk because this is cheaper for the firm (due to the large setup costs) than for them (as is indicated by the arrow to the transaction cost box in Figure 3.2).[166] Besides, the firm might have a competitive advantage in providing that risk-management service.

Let us now turn to the *management's exposure to the success of the firm* as it is offered by their compensation contracts. The extent to which managers have an incentive to adopt risk-management policies is directly related to the terms of their compensation package and the specification of the payoff structure of these claims (e.g., fixed salary, performance-related bonus, compensation in stocks or options on these stocks, which could be at the money, out of the money, etc.).[167]

Managers decide to manage risks in order to reduce the volatility of their own compensation, which is consistent with their individual risk aversion. However, managerial risk-management decisions are not as removed from the interests of the shareholders as it may seem at first sight. Shareholders gain by having management compensation tied to the firm's or its stock price performance, because this provides incentives that lower the agency costs of their principal-agent relationship by aligning their interests. The use of such arrangements is limited, however, by the risk aversion of the managers. Managers and shareholders will be better off to the extent that risk management can reduce the variation in performance-based compensation without destroying the implicit performance incentives.[168]

Depending on the link of managerial compensation to either equity performance or compensation in the form of stocks or options on these stocks, it can produce different incentive structures. In general, managers with greater stock ownership will prefer more risk management, while managers with more option holdings will prefer less.[169] This is true because stocks provide a linear payoff as a function of stock prices,

[162]See Smith (1993), p. 19.
[163]See Allen and Santomero (1996), p. 14.
[164]Note that there is no risk aversion by the firm per se as for individuals.
[165]See Froot et al. (1993), pp. 1631–1632.
[166]Also see Tufano (1996), p. 1109.
[167]See Smith (1993), p. 19.
[168]See Fenn et al. (1997), p. 20.
[169]See Tufano (1996), p. 1109.

whereas options provide a nonlinear payoff. Hence, managers who hold substantial option positions in their company will have an incentive to increase the riskiness of the firm by not managing risks (or even by outright speculation),[170] because higher risk increases the volatility and consequently the value of the expected utility of an option contract for a risk-averse manager.[171] Equity options for less capable managers, hence, increase the incentive to speculate, whereas for capable managers, equity options can even create an incentive to manage risk.[172]

Therefore, due to the risk preference problem, we should find firms with a high investment of human capital and substantial stock holdings (but not equity option holdings) of their managers to have more risk management than vice versa and that is necessary from the shareholders' point of view. This creates agency costs because:

- The firm might diversify beyond its core capabilities, that is, engage in unnecessary diversification (especially when at a cost)
- Managers overinvest
- The leverage of the firm is too low with regard to what would be optimal from a tax shield point of view
- The firm might have to spend additional money to ensure that managers perform appropriately if they have risk management at their discretion, that is, they do not speculate (especially if they hold equity options)[173]

These agency costs reduce the value of the firm's equity. On the one hand, increasing the firm's leverage can reduce them, which can be achieved with the help of risk management even without increasing the probability of default. On the other hand, they can be reduced by using risk management as a device to change the distribution of payoffs from managerial compensation,[174] which will allow the firm to save money because it will then be able to enforce cheaper incentive compensation contracts.[175]

Signaling higher management quality: The delegation of decision/con-

---

[170]See Smithson (1998), p. 13.

[171]See Tufano (1996), p. 1110.

[172]As we will see below, capable managers can signal their quality. See Raposo (1999), p. 47.

[173]Allen and Santomero (1996), p. 17, refer to Metallgesellschaft and Barings as recent and extreme examples of these agency costs.

[174]See Raposo (1999), p. 45.

[175]If manager's compensation depends on the distribution of the firm's payoffs, so does the manager's utility.

trol power from a principal to an agent is sensible as long as the agent has better information or better qualifications than the principal. However, due to uncertainty and asymmetric information the principal is not able to perfectly observe whether the outcome of the agent's decisions is due to his ability and effort or due to circumstances that are outside the agent's control. Therefore, agents have an incentive to use risk management to reduce asymmetric information and thereby increase the transparency of their management capabilities,[176] so that it is easier for the principal to differentiate good management skills and talent from luck (e.g., favorable developments in the financial markets).[177] This attempt of the agents to use risk management as a tool is, therefore, called the "signaling of higher management quality."[178]

There are three lines of reasoning behind this idea:

- The first argument is based on the agency theory explaining the relationship between firm performance and managerial compensation. While the argument might not be immediately convincing, observed outcomes of firm performance may—because of asymmetric information—influence the perception of managerial talent by the labor markets.[179] Since that will be eventually reflected in management compensation, the assumption that managers will behave in a way consistent with a concave objective function, that is, that they are risk-averse, seems to be justified. Therefore, managers may engage in risk management to better communicate their skills to the labor market[180] in an attempt to influence the labor market's perspective.[181]

- The second argument reflects the managers' interest in reducing the volatility of corporate earnings so that financial markets and, hence, the shareholders can better evaluate their true ability and performance.[182] Smoothing the company's performance by risk management can convince shareholders that managers are capable, which improves their prospects, evaluation,[183] and remu-

---

[176]See Pritsch and Hommel (1997), pp. 675–676.
[177]See Brealey and Myers (1991), p. 629.
[178]However, signaling is used in this context not in the sense of the adverse selection theory, that is, before contracting, but rather in the sense of "positive" moral hazard, that is, agents are much better than they are perceived and not dangerous for the organization.
[179]See Froot et al. (1993), p. 1632.
[180]See Breeden and Viswanathan (1996) and Tufano (1996), p. 1111.
[181]See Froot et al. (1993), p. 1632.
[182]See Fenn et al. (1997), p. 20.
[183]See Mason (1995), p. 30, and DeMarzo/Duffie (1991).

neration. This again increases the managers' efforts, which can in turn create additional firm value.

■ Third, if management compensation is linked to firm performance, it is also linked to various types of risks, some of which cannot be influenced by the management's own efforts. Capable managers, that is, managers who have a comparative advantage in managing some of these risks, have an incentive to manage those risks which they cannot influence[184] and for which they do not have a superior ability.[185] Hedging these risks (completely) will reduce "noise" and make their management capability more transparent, which in turn will increase their reputation and their (expected) income.[186] Less capable managers have an incentive to speculate or not to reduce risk at all to hide their disability.[187] However, as mentioned previously, in some incentive system regimes, risk management will reduce the value of the managerial option positions, incurring opportunity costs for the managers. Capable managers will, under these circumstances, only conduct risk management if the gains from an increase in their reputation will be higher than these opportunity costs.

Therefore, the risk-management strategy chosen by the managers might diverge from that which is optimal for the shareholders (the risk preference problem). However, by using risk management to make the managerial efforts more transparent and to remove those risk components that cannot be influenced by the management, managers will show more effort and, therefore, will increase firm value. Yet, all of this will only occur if the managers' compensation scheme is designed accordingly (see above).

---

[184]See for example, Brealey and Myers (1991), p. 629. Risk management can relieve managers of risks outside their control. However, there are no explicit contracts on whether and how to manage the firm's risk exposure. This might lead to additional agency problems and costs.

[185]Or abilities that do not influence shareholder value.

[186]See, for example, Tufano (1996), p. 1127 and Table VI, who finds that less tenured board members are more inclined to manage risk, because they are less capable (or confident) and have a smaller fraction of their total wealth invested in the firm (and its stocks).

[187]See Raposo (1999), pp. 46–47, who also provides a more extensive list of references to the literature. One example of this behavior is the degree of detail on corporate risk-management activities in annual reports: When managers are less capable, they have an incentive to only broadly report on risk management to allow for a wide range of risk-management activities to hide their lack of competence.

The Risk Preference Problem of Other Stakeholders Besides shareholders and management, other stakeholders of the firm are also exposed to firm-specific risks.[188] If these other stakeholders are unable to diversify these risks[189] or manage them otherwise directly, firm-specific risk can affect the future payoffs of these constituents' contracts. Because these stakeholders are risk averse, at a company where the probability of layoff, insolvency, or financial difficulties is significant, they will find it unattractive to invest into the relationship with the firm, that is, to contribute firm-specific capital—unless they receive an extra compensation in the form of an additional risk premium to bear any of these risks.

The following scenarios are possible:

- Investors with block holdings in the firm have only limited opportunities to diversify away firm-specific risks. Even though these investors can improve the efficient monitoring of the firm,[190] they will have a higher risk aversion that they will try to impose on the firm.
- The same argument is true for employees who are not shareholders, but have invested a considerable amount of their human capital in the firm (e.g., knowledge specialized to the firm). If the firm performance is so volatile that the likelihood of default is relevant, these employees will require a higher compensation to work for such a firm[191] or will reduce their loyalty or work effort. On the contrary, incentive considerations command that firms link their employees' compensation to performance measures (share price, earnings, etc.). However, these performance proxies contain significant variation that is often completely unrelated to the employees' actions. This has implications for the design of compensation contracts. Effective compensation plans achieve an appropriate balance between two potentially conflicting goals: strengthening employees' performance incentives and insulating them from risks beyond their control. Firms can achieve this by using risk management to more effectively exclude "noise" from performance measures that serve as the basis for employee evaluations and bonuses and by making the bonus a more constructive motivating force.[192]

---

[188]An important question is to define for the company what is specific risk and what is systematic risk, because this could be differentiated by the holdings in the firm. As we will see later on, this would also define what risk-management tools to use. See Damodaran (1997), pp. 776–777.

[189]Similar to the owners of private or closely held companies.

[190]Especially of its management, which will lower the agency costs of equity.

[191]See Damodaran (1997), p. 788.

[192]See Smith (1995), p. 26.

- Also, if the likelihood of default is significant, managers with alternative opportunities will demand higher salaries (or a higher equity stake in the firm).
- Likewise, suppliers that deliver products with a high degree of firm-specific use will be more reluctant to enter into long-term contracts with the firm or will do so only at a higher price.
- Similarly, other trade creditors will charge more and will be less flexible when contracting with the firm.
- Customers concerned with the firm's ability to fulfill after-sales warranty or service obligations will only buy the firm's products at a lower price,[193] because they anticipate that the likelihood of cheating on product quality is greater the closer the firm is to financial distress.

Therefore, an increase in the likelihood of default will have an impact on the cost of contracting with (undiversified) stakeholders. This will be eventually reflected in a reduction of the firm's cash flows because firms close to financial distress will have to pay more for services and will have to offer lower prices to customers.[194] Additionally, one has to include the effect of the deterioration of valuable relationships with stakeholders who value long-term interactions with the firm.[195]

All of this results in agency costs that lower the value of the firm's equity, because the firm has to set economic incentives that are costly. However, the firm can benefit from conducting risk management since it can be used as a tool to lower the costs of these extra payments by being able to reduce the likelihood of default and improve the design of the contractual arrangements with the other stakeholder groups.[196] Yet, this will only create value when the costs associated with risk management will be smaller than the benefits[197] and the firm has committed to a stable risk profile, that is, when its risk-management program is binding.

Although risk management at the corporate level can reduce the agency costs from the risk preference problem, it can also create other agency problems. On the one hand, for example, stock holdings and performance-related compensation could resolve some of the principal-agent problems. On the other hand, various (undiversified) stakeholders can try to impose

---

[193]Bank customers would charge a higher interest rate, for example, on their savings accounts in such a situation.

[194]See Stulz (1999), p. 6.

[195]See Tufano (1996), p. 1106.

[196]See Damodaran (1997), p. 788.

[197]For example, it is only useful to keep (large) stakeholders with superior monitoring skills when they are more valuable for the firm than the cost of the risk management they try to impose on the firm.

their concave objective function onto the firm, which may imply a subop-timal risk-management strategy for the firm and could destroy value. It is, therefore, very difficult to tell which effect is dominant.

However, from an empirical point of view, concentrated ownership does not seem to be an issue in European banks. For the sample of ninety European banks identified and described in Chapter 2, we were able to obtain ownership data for forty-eight banks.[198] Eliminating group ownership/cross-holdings, we calculated the concentration ratio[199] (CR_r) for the r (with $r =$ 3, 5, 10) largest shareholders in the following way:[200]

$$CR_r = \sum_{i=1}^{r} \frac{x_i}{x} \tag{3.1}$$

where x_i = Share of overall firm (market) value held by shareholder group i

x = Total firm (market) value.

We obtained the following results by binning the outcomes in 5% increments and plotting them in a cumulative way. The deviation from the straight line[201] (the line of equally distributed ownership), as depicted in Figure 3.4, is not too large for any of the three calculated measures, indicating that the risk preference problem is not the driving factor for why banks conduct risk management in practice.

The Cost of Stock Price Reaction   We will describe the costs of stock price reaction in detail in the "Cost of Stock Price Reaction" section.

Agency Costs of Debt as a Rationale for Risk Management   The agency costs of debt are costs associated with the conflicts of interests between shareholders and bond holders. They can be divided into two broad groups: asset substitution and underinvestment (as represented by the middle part in Figure 3.2) and will be discussed in this section in turn. Both problems stem from the likelihood of default by having a firm (partially) financed with debt, which clearly has a tax benefit. However, these agency costs decrease the value of debt, and their avoidance through risk management will increase firm value.

---

[198]The sample of forty-eight banks is summarized in a table in the Appendix to this chapter.
[199]Even though other concentration indices would be more appropriate to identify ownership concentration, the required input data cannot be identified. For a discussion see Clarke (1985), pp. 13–17.
[200]See Clarke (1985), pp. 13+.
[201]Note that the overall number of shareholders (n) cannot be obtained from the chosen data source. It was therefore not our intention to calculate the Gini-coefficient as, for example, described in Bamberg and Baur (1991), pp. 26–28.

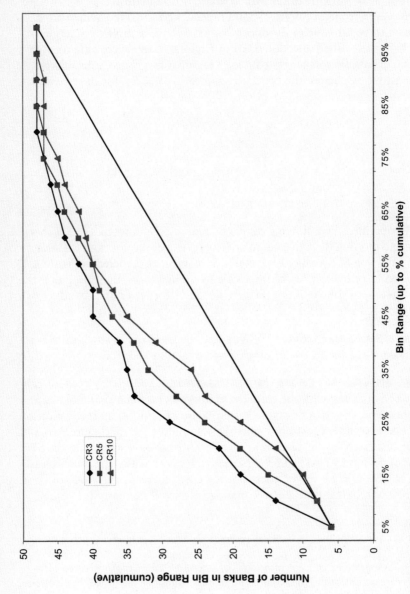

Figure 3.4   Ownership concentration in European banks.
Source: thomson*direct*.com and author's analysis.

The Asset Substitution Problem Debt holders (i.e., all creditors to the firm) hold fixed claims on the firm because they lend money with the expectation that the projects undertaken by the firm will have a certain risk level[202] and (*ex ante*) set the interest rate on the bonds accordingly. On the contrary, shareholders are residual claimants. They hold claims whose value is equivalent to a call option on the value of the firm, since they have the right to take over the firm by buying back all debt at any point in time.[203]

As with any other option, the value of the shareholders' equity rises as the variance in the returns of the underlying asset increases, that is, an increase in the volatility of the firm's cash flows will increase the value of the equity. Therefore, shareholders (and their managers) have an incentive to switch from low-variance investment projects (as promised on the issuance of the debt) to high-variance projects. This behavior is called asset substitution[204] or risk-shifting within the corporation,[205] and increases the value of the shareholders' claims while reducing the value of the fixed claims.[206] This will basically not only transfer wealth from debt holders to shareholders,[207] but will also be—typically—not beneficial to the firm as a whole.

The incentive for asset substitution rises the closer the firm is to distress, because shareholders have a chance to restore the value of their equity by taking large risks. If the risk taking does not work out, then shareholders are not worse off, since their equity had little or no value anyway. This could go as far as accepting negative NPV projects with large upside potential (i.e., very risky projects), because any gains flow to the shareholders, but any losses are borne by the debt holders.[208]

Rational debt holders will anticipate this behavior and will, therefore, require a higher risk premium (i.e., higher yields) on their bonds[209] or try to prohibit this "risk shifting." This can be achieved by writing restrictive covenants into their debt contracts or issuing convertible debt or other options to participate in the value increase of the equity.[210] However, these restrictions can lead to a suboptimal investment policy and can eliminate the flex-

---

[202]As mentioned previously, risk management can be used to ensure a stable risk profile to lower the participation costs of the investors.

[203]The value of debt can be viewed as a portfolio of a risk-free bond and a short-put option. See Merton (1974).

[204]See Jensen and Meckling (1976), pp. 334–337.

[205]See Smith (1993), p. 19.

[206]Due to the increase in default risk, bond holders would require a higher yield on their bonds, meaning that the value of debt would decrease.

[207]See Mason (1995), p. 32.

[208]See Damodaran (1997), pp. 453+.

[209]Or they would be only willing to pay a lower price for the bonds.

[210]To align the interest of the bond holders with those of the shareholders.

ibility needed to take advantage of new investment opportunities,[211] increasing the agency costs of debt. Additionally, because the shareholder incentive increases as the firm is closer to distress, firms may find it difficult in general to raise external funds to finance valuable investment projects.

Risk management can help to reduce these agency costs from risk shifting by balancing conflicting interests. It can:

- Decrease the agency costs from the asset substitution problem by lowering the cash flow volatility of the firm.
- Increase the debt capacity of the firm without increasing default probability. Risk shifting will therefore be less of an issue.[212]
- Reduce the probability of default. Potential debt holders are therefore willing to pay more for the bond or to require lower coupon payments, which will increase the firm value.
- Be more beneficial, the more likely is the breaching of covenants and other restrictive measures. Firms that are more likely to be exposed to this risk will conduct more risk management to avoid additional agency costs.
- Decrease agency costs from risk shifting, which are likely to be greater in firms whose cash flows cannot be easily observed and monitored.[213]
- Be beneficial when credible commitments to manage observable risks can reduce the incentive to substitute assets and the associated agency costs of debt.[214]

The Underinvestment Problem   As defined in Equation (2.1), (operating) cash flows are the sum of debt holders' and stockholders' claims on the company. Having to split these cash flows between the two groups can create problems (so-called shareholder-bondholder conflicts) that might result in a reduction of the value of the firm due to the agency costs associated with them. This problem is especially relevant in the underinvestment problem, which has two facets:

- The firm does not generate enough internal cash flows that are then available for valuable investment projects. This leads to less investment than what would otherwise be possible (underinvestment). We

---

[211]See Stulz (1999), p. 5.
[212]See Smithson (1998), p. 8. Also, a higher debt ratio increases the benefits from the tax shield of debt.
[213]See Damodaran (1997), pp. 453+.
[214]See Raposo (1999), p. 47.

will discuss this phenomenon in more detail in the subsequent section on the coordination of investment and financing.

■ Underinvestment due to excessive leverage (which is the focus of this section): In companies with significant fixed claims and volatile assets,[215] the underinvestment problem arises from the conflict of interest between shareholders and bond holders that stems from the fact that shareholders are only residual claimants. As first described by Myers,[216] firms can decide under these circumstances to forego positive NPV projects, because shareholders choose not to pursue the project if a disproportionate portion of the total available cash flows of a project would accrue to bond holders (as more senior claimants).[217] Likewise, a shareholder value-maximizing management would also have the incentive to pass up positive NPV projects. Even though this behavior decreases overall firm value[218] (thus harming debt holders), it would improve the shareholders' position,[219] because—while shareholders bear all the deadweight costs, that is, agency costs, of this decision—the value created by the new project that flows to the debt holders would be larger. However, it is worthwhile to note, that underinvestment can also occur when, due to the debt overhang and the high probability of default associated with it, shareholders will not provide new funds necessary to finance valuable projects in the first place. This occurs because such activity would benefit mostly the (existing) debt holders by making their debt safer.[220]

As the debt level in the capital structure rises, the underinvestment problem becomes more significant and with it the agency costs resulting from it. For instance, since debt holders will anticipate the potential conflict of interest, they will require a higher yield on their bonds[221] when they sign the agreement, incurring (additional) agency costs.

By reducing the debt/equity ratio, the underinvestment problem gradually disappears, because it becomes then more likely that the shareholders will receive all of their part of the cash flows generated by positive NPV projects. Alternately, risk management can help to decrease the likelihood of default and hence to mitigate the underinvestment problem. This is shown in Figure 3.5.

---

[215]These are firms whose probability of financial distress is not trivial.
[216]See Myers (1977).
[217]See Mian (1996), p. 421.
[218]Maximizing firm value should be—as described previously—the objective instead.
[219]See, for example, Smith (1995), p. 20.
[220]See Stulz (1999), p. 5.
[221]Or they will include this in the pricing of the bond. See Mian (1996), p. 421.

The figure illustrates that an unexpected change in the price of a risk factor (ΔP) causes a reduction in the firm value, as depicted by the dotted line.[222] Adverse changes in P will, therefore, effectively increase the leverage and intensify the underinvestment problem, because it raises the likelihood that the firm will forgo a positive NPV project (as shown by the dark gray shaded area that represents the costs from underinvestment).

By conducting risk management (here: hedging as represented by the light solid line), an unexpected change in the price of the risk factor causes a smaller reduction in the firm value. The bold solid line—which is less steep than the original dotted line—represents this. In this setting, both the induced increase in leverage and the exacerbation of the underinvestment problem are smaller (as depicted by the light gray shaded area that indicates smaller costs from underinvestment). Thus, the real benefit of risk management is not the flattening of the curve from the core business exposure to the net exposure (i.e., after hedging), but the reduction in the underinvestment costs (as represented by the reduction in the size of the shaded wedges).[223]

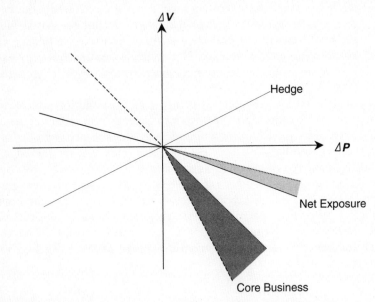

Figure 3.5   The underinvestment problem and risk management.
Source: Adapted from Smith (1993), p. 19, and Smith (1995), p. 25.

---

[222]This assumes that the relationship between the risk factor and the firm value is known and that it is negative.
[223]See Smith (1995), p. 25.

Reducing the probability of firm default—either via reducing debt or by conducting risk management as a substitute (which additionally conserves the tax shield for debt, because this allows the firm to keep the leverage constant or even to increase it)[224]—will also reduce the debt holder-shareholder conflict of underinvestment. Risk management can, thus, reduce the associated agency costs in the form of higher promised payments to debt holders and the turning down of positive NPV projects, and will, therefore, increase firm value.

The underinvestment problem is more pronounced in firms with more shareholder and managerial discretion in the choice of investment projects.[225] This is the case when firms derive a relatively higher proportion of their market value from growth options relative to the assets in place.[226] Therefore, the more growth options and the higher the leverage of a firm are, the more likely it is that the firm conducts risk management to decrease the underinvestment problem.

Coordination of Investment and Financing   In a world of perfect and complete capital markets, a firm's losses accompanied by a reduction in cash flows (and hence the need to turn to external sources) would not affect a firm's investment spending: A project that is worth funding internally would be worth funding externally, and external funds would be always available at fair terms.[227] However, as we have seen above, capital markets are not perfect. And the imperfections can lead to inefficient investment,[228] because (inefficient) capital markets may not be able to evaluate investment projects fairly—due to agency problems and asymmetric information[229]—and hence may not provide external funding for positive NPV projects at all or may do so only at a higher price.[230] Nonetheless, even in the neoinstitutional world the (implicit) key M&M insight is still valid: increasing the firm value can only be achieved by making good investment decisions that will, in turn, increase the firm's (operating) cash flows.[231]

---

[224]Alternately, as we have seen, the debt holders can use restrictive covenants, which have their own agency problems.

[225]However, in general, this has little relevance for banks.

[226]See Mian (1996), p. 421.

[227]See Fenn et al. (1997), p. 19.

[228]See Froot et al. (1993), pp. 1632–1633.

[229]See Fenn et al. (1997), p. 19. For example, agency costs of managerial discretion and other costs resulting from conflicts of interest between managers and outside investors can blur the information about the company prospects.

[230]See Pritsch/Hommel (1997), pp. 675 and 681.

[231]See Froot et al. (1994), pp. 92–93. The authors label the availability of positive NPV projects as the first step in how risk management can help to create firm value.

The observation that external sources of finance are likely to be unavailable or more costly to corporations than internally generated funds provides another rationale for managing risks, because this knowledge can be used to protect a company's (optimal) investment plans.[232] Risk management can increase the firm's value in less than perfect markets when it coordinates the demand for funds with the supply so that a corporation (always) has sufficient internal funds available to take advantage of attractive, that is, positive NPV, investment opportunities[233] that would otherwise be turned down.[234]

In the following sections, we will first examine in more detail why external funds are more expensive than internally generated cash flows and what the consequences of this are. We will then turn to the relaxation of the M&M proposition that there is no interdependency between investment and the financing policy. Third, we will examine variations in the investment program that was assumed to be fixed so far. Finally, we will discuss how risk management can be helpful in this context.

The Pecking Order Theory[235] lays the foundation for why external funds are more expensive than internally generated funds.[236] Due to capital market imperfections, there is an increasing marginal cost to external finance for both debt and equity because of agency and default costs, which make the cost function convex. There are three types of costs that are also represented below the shaded box in the center of Figure 3.2.

The Cost of Stock Price Reaction   The most compelling argument for why external equity is more expensive is the adverse signal sent to investors in capital markets when new equity is issued.[237] Since firms are reluctant to raise new equity when they think it is undervalued, and because it is very

---

[232]See Fenn et al. (1997), p. 19.

[233]See Froot et al. (1993), p. 1633.

[234]These investment decisions can also be postponed or reduced, see Fenn et al. (1997), p. 19. This is the second step of how risk management can create value in this context, see Froot et al. (1994), p. 92.

[235]See Myers (1977), Myers and Majluf (1984), and Myers (1984). Market imperfections lead to increasing marginal costs of external finance, making firms first use their internally generated cash flows, then debt financing, and last new equity to finance positive NPV projects.

[236]However, we need to keep in mind that, if there is asymmetrical information, external financing can be not only much more expensive but also simply unavailable. This is especially true for banks.

[237]See Brealey and Myers (1991), p. 447.

difficult for investors to determine the true value of a company's assets in general and to evaluate the riskiness of the new investment opportunities[238] in specific, firms are inclined to issue equity when it is overvalued to exploit their information advantage vis-à-vis (new) shareholders. Because investors anticipate this behavior, the stock price tends to fall on the announcement by 3% on average.[239] Due to these indirect costs, firms think that equity is (very) costly and prefer to avoid financing via the external equity market.[240] Additional agency costs of equity are incurred if equity is issued when a firm's outstanding debt is sufficiently risky. As discussed previously, this redistributes wealth from shareholders to bond holders.[241]

The Underinvestment Problem Even though these signaling costs are (almost) not observable for the issuance of debt,[242] there are the previously mentioned (indirect) agency costs of potential future bankruptcy[243] associated with the issuance of debt.[244] However, in this context, there is another dimension to the already discussed underinvestment problem: Due to the shortage of available (internal) funds (and not due to agency problems), investment is foregone and its associated positive NPV is lost, making it a direct cost. As we will discuss in more detail, this kind of underinvestment can occur even without excessive leverage (i.e., represented by the bottom-up arrow in Figure 3.2).

The Costs of Issuance Additionally, there are direct and discrete transaction costs associated with obtaining external funds[245] that can be, for example, on the order of 5% of the value of the new equity.[246]

Froot and Stein[247] show that the more difficult (and hence the more

---

[238]See Allen and Santomero (1996), p. 16.

[239]See, for example, Asquith and Mullins (1986). Stulz (2000), p. 4-40, estimates the value of the existing equity falls by about 2.5%. Since the value of the existing equity is decreased, this is an agency cost of equity.

[240]See Froot et al. (1994), p. 94. Also see Miller (1995), p. 484, who states that equity is expensive for banks to raise.

[241]Also see, for example, Miller (1995), p. 484, who describes this problem in the context of banks.

[242]See, for example, Eckbo (1986).

[243]See Allen and Santomero (1996), p. 16.

[244]For highly levered firms, additional debt financing requires a significant premium to compensate lenders for the costs of financial distress.

[245]See, for example, Allen and Santomero (1996), p. 16, and Mason (1995), p. 32. The size of these transaction costs is described, for example, in Brealey and Myers (1991), Chapter 15.

[246]See Stulz (2000), p. 4-40.

[247]See Froot and Stein (1998a).

costly) it is for a bank[248] to raise external funds (on short notice), the more risk averse it will be with respect to fluctuations in its internal wealth. They assume that a bank can enter into new lucrative transactions with an initial cash investment I and a return $f(I)$ that is a concave function.[249] I can be funded by internal sources w stemming from the bank's existing assets or by raising external funds e that have convex costs c (Froot et al. [1993] specify that function in the light of agency and information problems[250]).

The bank's problem is then:

$$g(w) = \max[f(I) - I - c], \text{ subject to } I = w + e \qquad (3.2)$$

It can be shown that g is a concave function[251] and that this shape creates the rationale for risk management. Since c is convex, that is, the more costly it is for the bank to raise external funds, the more the bank will want to make sure that the fluctuations in its internal wealth w are limited in order to have the funds available it needs for investment. The bank therefore cares about the distribution of its end of investment horizon wealth and is not risk neutral anymore.

The increasing costs to raising new external funds (both for debt and equity) make the firm's concern with risk management endogenous,[252] that is, an integral part of the internal decision-making process. In order to avoid these costs, a firm will behave in a risk-averse fashion[253] at the company level (independent of the risk preferences of its stakeholders), even though the firm's objective function itself is not concave.[254]

The necessity to generate sufficient internal funds from the existing assets to finance planned investments is complicated by the fact that (financial) risks cause volatility in the firm's cash flows, which in turn causes difficul-

---

[248]Froot et al. (1993) show the same line of reasoning for industrial corporation.

[249]Here, Froot and Stein assume that the production technology of banks is concave as it typically is for industrial companies.

[250]They assume that cash flows are costlessly observable to company insiders, but are observable to external creditors only at some cost. Cash flows from the existing assets can be observed at a cost, but it is infinitely costly to observe the cash flows from the new investment project. The difference between internal and external funding costs will be greater for firms that are more leveraged and whose types of investment are difficult for outsiders to evaluate and that offer relatively little tangible collateral. See Froot et al. (1993), p. 1636.

[251]See Froot and Stein (1998a), p. 61.

[252]See Froot et al. (1993), p. 1632.

[253]See Froot and Stein (1998a), p. 58. As Miller (1995), p. 484, points out correctly, these costs (especially the underwriting costs) are relatively higher for smaller banks, which should make them even more risk-averse than larger banks.

[254]See Allen and Santomero (1996), p. 14.

ties in coordinating the supply and demand for internal funds.[255] Given the (fixed) set of investment opportunities of the firm, the existence of these difficulties results in underinvestment (even without debt) in some states. Internally generated funds may fall short of the amount of new investment opportunities that would be profitable in the absence of capital market imperfections.

Because it is costly or impossible to raise external financing,[256] the firm is forced to forgo investment unless it can reduce the variability in cash flows via risk management to obtain the highest expected firm value. Risk management at the company level can, therefore, facilitate investment[257] by minimizing the set of circumstances under which external financing is both costly and needed[258] and thus reduces the deadweight losses resulting from incomplete (inefficient) capital markets.

However, Froot et al.[259] show that risk management can only be beneficial when two conditions are met:

- The marginal returns on investment must be decreasing.
- The level of internal wealth must have a positive impact on the optimal level of investment.[260]

They base their analysis on a well-known optimizing model of costly external financing (the costly-state-verification = CSV model)[261] and come to the conclusion that if external financing is costly and the value of the new investment is uncorrelated with the existing assets, then the firm should always fully hedge its cash flows.

---

[255]This is labeled the third step in why risk management can be useful in this context. See Froot et al. (1994), p. 92. Also see Brealey and Myers (1991), p. 629, with regard to financial planning.

[256]See Froot et al. (1993), p. 1633. This is especially true when profits are low and the firm may face (financial) difficulties under any circumstances. Similarly, see Stulz (2000), p. 4-38.

[257]See Pritsch and Hommel (1997), p. 675.

[258]See Fenn et al. (1997), p. 19, stabilizing the firm's cash flow and thus minimizing the reliance on external funds.

[259]See Froot et al. (1993), pp. 1636–1638.

[260]There is anecdotal evidence that corporate investment is sensitive to the levels of internal cash flows.

[261]As referenced in their article, the CSV was developed by Townsend (1979) and Gale and Hellwig (1985). However, as Raposo (1998), pp. 44–45, outlines, the Froot et al. model is only a special case of the CSV and peculiar in that there is no limited liability to an outside investor.

However, this contradicts empirical evidence,[262] because it can be beneficial to have low cash flows at a time when investment opportunities are not lucrative. Therefore, the investment strategy may not be independent of the variability of the cash flows generated by the existing assets.[263] This variability may disturb both investment and financing plans in a way that is costly to the firm. Hence one needs to make two extensions:[264]

Changing investment opportunities: So far we assumed that the firm's investment opportunities are nonstochastic and hence independent (i.e., uncorrelated with) of the cash flows generated by the assets in place. When we relax the M&M assumption of a fixed investment program,[265] risk management can be less valuable because the supply of internal funds can (automatically) match the demand for funds when the two are highly correlated.[266] The derivation of the optimal hedge ratio then needs to consider the direct effect of a change in the risk factor on the firm's output and insulates the marginal value of internal wealth from fluctuations in the variable to be managed.[267] If there is no correlation between investment opportunities and the availability of internal funds, it is still optimal to hedge fully.

However, if the correlation between the two factors is greater than zero, then the firm will not want to fully hedge. The more sensitive investment opportunities are to the risk factor, the smaller is the optimal hedge ratio. Note that—as depicted in Figure 3.6 below—the optimal hedge ratio can be smaller than zero (the firm increases its exposure to the risk) or greater than one (the firm overhedges because investment opportunities are negatively correlated with its current cash flows). This is the reason why firms with different investment opportunities might implement different hedging strategies (even when they are exposed to the same risks or risks that have the same distribution). For instance, higher per-unit development costs can make one company's investment opportunities more exposed to a source of risk. Hence, the company

---

[262]See, for example, Lessard (1990). Additionally, Raposo (1998), pp. 44–45, refers to the criticism provided by Mello and Parsons (1995) that full hedging is not optimal.
[263]See Mason (1995), p. 32.
[264]See Froot et al. (1993), pp. 1638–1642.
[265]Note that the range of investment projects available to the firm also affects the severity of the agency conflicts described above. See Smithson (1998), p. 8.
[266]This is equivalent to having a built-in hedge.
[267]Note that this is not necessarily the same as insulating the total value of the firm from such fluctuations.

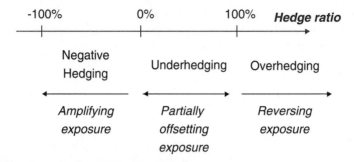

Figure 3.6 Over- and underhedging.
Source: Adapted from Fenn et al. (1997), p. 24.

that is less exposed should hedge more than a firm whose investment opportunities are more exposed to the price of a specific risk factor.

Changing financing opportunities: Negative shocks to a firm's current cash flow might also make it more costly for the firm to raise money from outside investors.[268] Hence the supply schedule for external finance is not exogenously fixed and insensitive to the risks affecting the firm's cash flows from its existing assets. If that is the case, then it may make sense for the firm to hedge more than it otherwise would. This will allow the firm to fund its investments while making less use of external financing in bad times than in good times.[269] The effect of changing financing opportunities on the hedge ratio is as follows: The optimal hedge ratio is greater than one, being greater the more sensitive assets are in place to the risk variable. Hedging must now allow the firm to fund its investments and yet avoid borrowing at those times when external finance is most expensive.

If both investment opportunities and financing opportunities are fluctuating, obviously there are wide-ranging implications for the design of risk-management strategies. Linear hedging—as described previously by asset allocation and diversification[270]—may no longer be optimal. If nonlinear instruments such as options are available, the firm will indeed wish to con-

---

[268]This is especially true for banks.
[269]See Froot et al. (1993), p. 1641.
[270]Stulz (2000) and the line of reasoning above assume that the investment program is fixed.

struct a hedging strategy that leads to nonstochastic investment. Linear hedges can add value, but they will not generally maximize value if nonlinear instruments are available.[271]

Risk management can be beneficial for firms through the coordination of investment and financing.[272] By being able to reduce the variability of internally generated cash flows, risk management can ensure that a company has enough internal funds available to pursue attractive investment opportunities. This avoids the cost of underinvestment and hence increases net cash flows and, therefore, firm value. Risk management can thus make external financing redundant and can lower the direct and indirect costs associated with visiting capital markets.

It can further increase the value of the firm by avoiding unnecessary fluctuations in either investment spending or funds raised from outside investors. If the firm's cash flows are low, obtaining additional funding is even more costly and the probability increases that the firm will postpone positive NPV projects. Risk-management programs that break this dependency of investment on internally generated cash flows can increase the firm's value by doing so[273] and can give firms access to a wider range of lucrative investment projects.[274]

However, the coordination of investment and financing insulates the company from the scrutiny of external markets[275] and can increase agency conflicts between managers and shareholders and, hence, the associated costs.[276]

All of these theoretical arguments derived above for industrial companies generally also apply to banks. However, the protection of the optimal investment program takes on another aspect for banks: The avoidance of a change in the default probability is the main rationale for conducting risk management in banks and not securing the availability of internal funds.

The funds necessary for a bank's investments are almost exclusively obtained from the outside (mostly in the form of deposits). However, only as long as there is no concern with financial distress are banks actually able to (easily) obtain these external funds (both debt and equity) in the capital markets for positive NPV projects.[277] As soon as there is a change in the

---

[271]See Froot et al. (1993), pp. 1645–1648. Note that hedging cannot change the expected level of wealth.

[272]The probability of risk management increases with the demand for funds (which is typically determined by the firm's growth opportunities as indicated by the firm's market-to-book ratio or its Tobin's q) and the unavailability of internal funds.

[273]See Tufano (1996), pp. 1107–1108.

[274]See Smithson et al. (1990), p. 375.

[275]As described by Jensen (1986) and (1993).

[276]See Tufano (1998).

[277]See Smith (1993), p. 21.

bank's creditworthiness, debt and equity not only get much more expensive at the same time but are also simply unavailable,[278] indicating that the pecking order theory might not perfectly apply to banks.

To ensure its creditworthiness, a bank needs to hold a certain amount of equity[279] (as is also required by regulation), which depends on the riskiness of both its existing business portfolio and the new investment opportunities. The availability of equity therefore protects the planned investment program in two ways:

- External funds are available.
- The required pro rata equity investment can be made.

It is thus extremely important for a bank to either invest in positive NPV projects to generate and enhance the value of its equity or to protect its value via risk management.[280]

Transaction Costs as a Rationale for Risk Management

As shown in the right-hand part of Figure 3.2, there are the following four types of transaction costs that can create a rationale for risk management, because the reduction of these transaction costs can increase the firm's value (these are discussed in the sections of the same name later in this chapter):

- Costs of financial distress
- Costs of implementing risk management
- Costs of issuing external financing
- Costs of ensuring a stable risk profile

The Costs of Financial Distress   Most companies, and also banks,[281] perceive equity to be a costly source of financing and tend to avoid it. However, debt financing is not without cost: taking on too much debt limits a company's ability to raise funds later and can lead to situations in which the firm can encounter cash shortfalls that could trigger financial distress or even bankruptcy.[282]

In general, the costs of financial distress are defined as the costs result-

---

[278]As we have seen, bank stakeholders are extremely concerned about whether the bank can meet its obligations.

[279]Since equity is also costly for banks, this can create a rationale for risk management on its own.

[280]As soon as equity is destroyed through losses, no further investment might be possible and at the same time, typically, no external funds are available for banks.

[281]See Miller (1995), p. 484.

[282]See Brealey and Myers (1991), pp. 628–630.

ing from difficulties a firm may have in coping with its debt service.[283] Since the M&M world assumes that there are either no financial distress situations at all or no costs associated with them, a change in the probability of encountering financial distress does not affect firm value in this world. As depicted in Figure 3.7, in such a world a change in the firm value after financial distress costs (especially as shown in the dotted line beyond the default point (*DP*), which is irrelevant in this world) is a linear function of the changes in the firm value before financial distress costs.

However, if financial distress is costly, firms have an incentive to reduce its probability of occurrence,[284] that is, to narrow the distribution (or the variance) of firm values, because it leads to a nonlinear relationship between the firm value before and after financial distress costs. This can increase firm value because one can define:

$$\text{Firm Value} = \text{Firm Value without Transaction Costs} - PV(\text{Expected Financial Distress Costs})^{285} \quad (3.3)$$

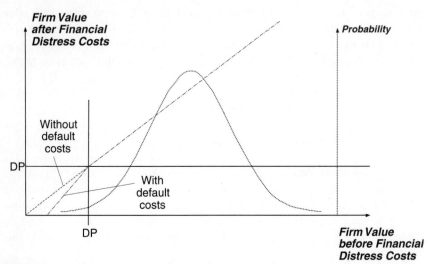

Figure 3.7   Influence of bankruptcy costs on firm value.
Source: Adapted from Stulz (1996), p. 16.

---

[283]See Stulz (2000), p. 3-39.
[284]See Mian (1996), p. 420.
[285]This approach (as suggested by Stulz (2000), p. 3-7) is similar to the Adjusted Present Value concept suggested by Brealey and Myers (1991), p. 458. However it assumes—for the time being—that financial distress costs are the only market imperfections.

and

$$E(\text{Financial Distress Costs}) = p(\text{default}) \times E(\text{default costs})^{286} \quad (3.4)$$

Hence risk management can reduce the expected costs of financial distress by reducing the probability of incurring losses that are large enough to have a firm encountering financial distress, that is, points below the default point (DP) in Figure 3.7.[287]

Equation (3.4) defines the expected value of financial distress costs of healthy as well as troubled but not yet defaulted institutions. It has two components: the probability p of encountering financial distress situations and the expected costs $E(\text{default costs})$ associated with such a situation. We will discuss both components in turn below.

A. **The probability of default:** The probability of default is a function of two factors:[288]
   1. **Ratio of debt (and other fixed costs) to cash flows:** Default is the result of a firm being unable to service its fixed claims.[289] The larger is the size of cash flows on debt obligations and other fixed claims relative to the size of operating cash flows, the higher is the probability of default.
   2. **Volatility of cash flows:** Default is triggered when the firm's cash flow is too low to pay its fixed claims. The more volatile the firm's (operating) cash flow, the more likely it is that the firm will face default.

B. **The absolute amount of default costs:** The absolute amount of financial distress costs can be differentiated into two components:
   1. **Direct costs:** The direct transaction costs related to default are relatively independent of the size of the firm.[290] They are any legal, administrative, accounting, and advisory payments associated with bankruptcy or Chapter 11 filing, reorganization, and liquidation and sale of assets, as well as the present value effects of delays in paying out cash flows.[291] They are estimated to be relatively small for industrial corporations (1–7% of a large firm's

---

[286]See Stulz (1996), p. 13.
[287]See Fenn et al. (1997), pp. 18–19.
[288]See Smithson et al. (1990), pp. 368–369, and Damodaran (1997), p. 451.
[289]Note that there is also a fixed cost for running a risk-management program.
[290]There are, therefore, significant economies of scale with respect to direct costs of financial distress. Also see James (1991), p. 1225.
[291] See Damodaran (1997), p. 451, and Mason (1995), p. 31.

assets),[292] and somewhat larger for financial institutions (approximately 10% of the failed bank's assets)[293]

2. **Indirect costs:** However, the real driving factor for the costs of financial distress is indirect costs, that is, the opportunity costs associated with financial distress situations. They are much more likely to occur than an actual default and can be differentiated into two groups:

   a. Indirect costs due to agency problems associated with financial distress:

      ■ The underinvestment problem (as described previously for "normal" levels of debt) can be exaggerated in financial distress situations in the following ways:

         – Financial distress may trigger debt covenants that place additional (that is, above normal) restrictions on management decision making and hence might induce the systematical passing up of positive NPV projects.

         – Due to the interference of the bankruptcy court in investment and operating decisions, nonroutine expenditures might not be approved, leading to underinvestment.[294]

         – The impossibility of raising external funds in financial distress situations may lead to capital rationing and, hence, underinvestment.[295]

         – The fact of living on the edge of bankruptcy means that, consequently, the benefits of taking on positive NPV projects accrue to debt holders most prominently. Shareholders (and their managers), who then will not expect a normally expected return, will tend to underinvest.

      ■ Financial distress may provide the incentive for management to behave more opportunistically (i.e., to increase the firm's level of risk) than usual in the presence of debt finance (asset substitution).[296]

---

[292]See, for example, Weiss (1990).
[293]See James (1991), pp. 1228 and 1241. The mean of his sample is 9.96% and the median 9.51%.
[294]See Smith (1995), p. 20.
[295] See Damodaran (1997), p. 452.
[296]Stulz (1996), p. 17, provides the supposed behavior of managers of nearly insolvent savings and loans institutions in the United States in the 1980s and 1990s as an example.

b. Financial distress situations fundamentally change the incentives of the firm's various stakeholders, and the higher the default probability, the higher the costs of maintaining contractual relationships with them:[297]

- These indirect costs are likely to be higher for firms that sell products with warranties and long-term service contracts or that provide services for which quality is an important attribute, but that is difficult to determine in advance. Customers who are unsure whether they can take advantage of these services in the future (because of the threat of bankruptcy) are willing to pay only a lower price for the products, decreasing the firm's (operating) cash flows and hence its value. The quality of service might also become another facet of the underinvestment problem: for example, troubled airlines tend to avoid investing in further maintenance, because the benefits of doing so disproportionately accrue to the bond holders. Rational customers expect this behavior and will avoid doing business with such a firm.

- Financial distress can also lead to the loss of valuable (key) employees with specialized knowledge and labor skills needed by the firm. They would only be willing to stay with the company for a higher compensation.

- Likewise, financial distress will trigger unfavorable credit terms, delivery schedules, and service by suppliers, whose production facilities are customized to the troubled firm. For example, when suppliers provide specialized input and there are long periods of time between incurring production costs and the ultimate receipt of the revenues, they will demand either cash in advance or collateral, increasing the troubled firm's liquidity problems.

For banks, additional aspects of indirect costs need to be considered. On the one hand, the business of troubled banks might immediately vanish (as described above) since credit-sensitive customers and suppliers of funds stop doing business with a bank that approaches bankruptcy. Also, the same argument is true for bank customers as it is for the airline customers: Reputation plays a significant role in whether a customer will put money into a bank in the first place. Therefore, there is either a significant reduction in the bank's cash flows the closer it is to bankruptcy

---

[297]See Mason (1995), p. 31.

or it will face unfavorable terms, that is, it has to pay above-market rates for deposits or has to offer below-market rates on credit to attract customers/business.

On the other hand, banks are subject to systemic risk and (therefore) threatened by bank runs, both events being associated with banks in financial distress situations. Because of extensively lending to and borrowing from each other, banks tend to be more interconnected than firms in any other industry and, hence, especially subject to this systemic risk, that is, that adverse events at one bank will be quickly transmitted to the other banks in the system. Disregarding deposit insurance and the "too-big-to-fail" doctrine,[298] depositors are aware of this fragility of the banking system and will withdraw their deposits more than they otherwise would[299] when they anticipate a bank is approaching financial distress.[300] There are presumably considerable[301] (indirect) costs associated with such bank runs that are—to the best of my knowledge—unfortunately not quantified by any study.

Additionally, there is significant lost going concern value[302] in bank failures[303] and the costs associated with the withdrawal of the bank charter and hence the loss of its value.[304] James (1991) calculates the indirect costs of a bank failure in his study on FDIC[305] data[306] and measures losses on assets as the difference between the book value of a failed bank's assets and the market value of the asset at the time of the failure (net of direct costs associated with the failure).[307] He comes to the conclusion that

[298]The reasoning behind this doctrine is that regulatory bodies will bail out or otherwise arrange an orderly termination for failed banks, when the bail-out costs are considered lower than those of a systemic crisis of the financial system.

[299]The Federal Reserve Bank of Cleveland defines a bank run as a withdrawal of more than 1% of total deposits per working day that cannot be explained by seasonal or other factors unrelated to depositors' confidence. See Gup (1998), p. 13.

[300]See Gup (1998), p. 132.

[301]The social costs of bank failure may be higher than those borne by investors. See Winton (2000), p. 30.

[302]That is, loss of reputation or franchise value and goodwill. This was, for example, the reason why the market values of banks exposed to the "Russian Crisis" declined by a multiple of the actual credit exposure of these banks in 1998.

[303]See James (1991), pp. 1241–1242.

[304]See James (1991), p. 1225.

[305]Federal Deposit Insurance Corporation.

[306]James (1991) analyzes 412 bank failures during 1985 and mid-year 1988.

[307]See James (1991), p. 1226.

the indirect costs average ca. 30% of the failed bank's assets.[308] Even though his approach might be the only feasible one—given the difficulty of estimating the exact amount of indirect costs, some of which are simply unobservable—it appears to be unrealistic that book values (as of initiation of the assets) represent the true value of assets just before the financial distress situation and are, therefore, a good predictor. Similar studies of Oliver, Wyman & Company come to the conclusion that the sum of both direct and indirect costs average 27%,[309] indicating that the asset value just before default may be much lower than the book value.

So far, we have only discussed the components of Equation (3.4). However, what we are really interested in is the second component in Equation (3.3): the present value of the expected financial distress costs. This brings us to the question:[310] What is the correct time horizon for estimating the default probability and what is the appropriate discount rate to derive the present value (PV) of the payments/cash flows associated with default? We will return to this question in a valuation context in Chapter 5.

Although the distribution of unhedged firm values as depicted in Figure 3.7 does not matter per se to well-diversified shareholders or bond holders, both investor groups will become concerned if negative deviations incur losses that materially raise the probability of financial insolvency. This is mainly due to the fact that the costs of financial distress can cause a significant reduction in a firm's value.[311]

No matter whether the risks causing these (negative) deviations are specific or systematic, in the presence of default costs the capital markets have a comparative advantage over the firm to bear risks: if the risk is specific, it can be diversified in the capital markets, and hence the cost of having the markets bear this risk is zero (i.e., no risk premium will be paid). However, the costs of bearing this specific risk within the firm are equal to the present value of the bankruptcy costs associated with them. If the risk is

---

[308]See James (1991), pp. 1225 and 1228. The mean of his sample is 30.51% and the median 27.68%. Starr et al. (1999), p. 7, estimate for a different sample of failed U.S. banks, an average loss of 13.8% of assets.

[309]Even though the Oliver, Wyman & Company sample is much smaller than James', it spreads over longer periods of time (than just 1985–1988) and across continents (as opposed to just reflecting the U.S. experience). Note that the Oliver, Wyman & Company method has a different background and is used to quantify the *loss given default,* the fraction of the exposure amount that a bank is likely to recover in the event of default, see Ong (1999), p. 56.

[310]This question is also not addressed in the James (1991) approach.

[311]See Smith (1995), p. 20.

systematic, the market will charge a risk premium for bearing it, which will be the same as a shareholder would require in the absence of bankruptcy costs. The market still has a competitive advantage over the firm because it does not have to bear the present value of the financial distress costs.[312]

Therefore, both specific and systematic risks do influence the firm value, and stakeholders do worry about specific risk because it is one source of the costs of financial distress. However, there is nothing investors can do about these risks on their own to avoid incurring financial distress costs at the firm level. Home-made risk management by the investors is no substitute for risk management by the firm in this case.[313] This observation builds one of the main rationales for corporate risk management: when financial distress is costly,[314] the firm will try to avoid lower-tail outcomes and will behave in a risk-averse manner,[315] meaning it will behave as if it had a concave objective function.[316] Since the (in)direct costs for financial distress situations appear to be higher and more important in regulated industries, banks will behave more risk-averse than their industrial counterparts because it is more valuable for them to avoid such situations.[317]

The possible contribution of corporate risk management to value creation is quantified in Equations (3.3) and (3.4). Risk management can increase the firm value by reducing cash flow volatility and hence decreasing the variability in future firm values. This reduces the probability of facing default[318] and thus the present value of the direct and indirect transaction costs[319] associated with financial distress. This, in turn, will increase the firm value net of financial distress costs[320] and will benefit shareholders and

---

[312]See Stulz (2000), p. 3-8.

[313]See Stulz (2000), p. 3-8.

[314]The cost of financial distress must be nonlinear because linear cost functions do not lead to the required behavior. See Allen and Santomero (1996), p. 16.

[315]See Allen and Santomero (1996), p. 14.

[316]Note that the objective function itself is not concave.

[317]Charter withdrawal and the loss of a monopoly position offer some insight into why banks themselves may choose low-risk strategies; see Allen and Santomero (1996), p. 16. Therefore, risk management to reduce financial distress costs may be far more valuable than is implied by the calculations given above, but difficult to quantify.

[318]In that respect, firm risk management can be a substitute to additional equity. See Stulz (1995), p. 8.

[319]As we have discussed previously, risk management can not only decrease the probability, but also the expected value of indirect (agency) costs associated with financial distress itself.

[320]See Tufano (1996), p. 1106, Raposo (1999), p. 44, and Smithson et al. (1990), p. 368.

bond holders as well as any other stakeholders in the firm.[321] Since the volatility in firm values is caused by total risk, avoiding specific risk—that is, a part of it—at the corporate level can increase the firm value. Note that Equation (3.3) quantifies the contribution of risk management when the firm is healthy. In the event that cash flows and value decline sharply from current levels, the value added by risk management increases in absolute terms and even more on a percentage basis.[322]

The Costs of Implementing Risk Management   As mentioned previously, the relative ability of firms and individuals to efficiently implement risk management[323] is influenced by the existence of transaction costs.[324] Poorly diversified stakeholders, in particular, might prefer the firm to conduct risk management on their behalf, because the transaction costs are lower for the firm than for the individual. This seems plausible given the high costs for acquiring the necessary knowledge (e.g., qualified personnel), the required technological infrastructure[325] to identify the optimal hedge position, and the existence of economies of scale in transaction costs to be able to trade, for example, in derivatives markets (that can additionally require a minimum deal size and/or turnover).[326] However, besides saving on the costs of trading, one should keep in mind that risk management by the firm can also incur agency costs to ensure that the agents (managers and/or traders) transact appropriately.[327]

For financial institutions, the fixed costs of asset evaluation, especially, mean that intermediaries have an advantage over individuals, because they allow such costs to be shared across a large number of deals.[328] Similarly,

---

[321]Banks that maximize firm value will, therefore, incorporate the expected costs of financial distress in their objective function. See Winton (2000), p. 30.

[322]See Stulz (1996), p. 13.

[323]See Mason (1995), p. 31.

[324]For instance, transaction costs can prevent individuals from diversifying their portfolio perfectly. See, for example, Perridon and Steiner (1995), p. 247, who refer to Garman and Ohlson (1981).

[325]However, it is debatable which part of the investment in information systems is sunk costs. Computer systems are necessary for firms to know who their customers are, for reporting, for controlling, and also for regulatory purposes, with risk management being just one of the many reasons for building the technological infrastructure.

[326]See Mian (1996), pp. 422+.

[327]See Allen and Santomero (1996), p. 17. Recent scandals, as represented in the Wheel of Misfortune on page 57, are extreme examples of such agency costs.

[328]For instance, banks can—given their specialized knowledge—evaluate loans more efficiently than individual investors.

the effects of trading costs mean that intermediaries can more easily be diversified than individuals.[329]

The Costs of Issuance The direct transaction costs associated with the issuance of external funds have already been described in detail in the previous section on "Coordination of Investment and Financing."

The Costs of a Stable Risk Profile We have already seen previously in the discussion of the asset substitution problem that the (pre-)commitment of a firm to a stable risk profile (by using risk-management tools) can increase shareholder value. And many firms already use this opportunity with respect to some firm-specific risks when they cover some specifics of supplier, work, and customer contracts by insurance. However, only rarely do we see an employment contract that, for example, specifies that interest rate risk should be managed by the firm on an ongoing basis.[330]

In this section, we view the importance of a stable risk profile from a different point of view. The information asymmetry between managers and (outside) investors can have the following two facets with respect to transaction costs and a stable risk profile:

- If managers and/or the firm have access to information about risks that shareholders do not have, then shareholders cannot optimally diversify or hedge their portfolios. Risk management by the firm can only reduce the transaction costs (as argued in the last section on costs associated with the implementation of risk management), if its goal is to keep the risk exposure constant. Otherwise, it will incur additional transaction costs for the shareholders for monitoring the firm's risk profile and its risk-management policy in order to be able to rebalance their portfolios accordingly.[331]

---

[329]See Allen and Santomero (1996), p. 3. Even though Allen and Santomero base their line of reasoning for the existence of intermediaries on increasing participation costs (because transaction costs, as one of the market imperfections, diminished over time), Scholtens and van Wensveen (2000), p. 1248, prove them wrong.
[330]See Smith (1995), p. 26.
[331]See Smith (1995), p. 26. Shareholders have heterogeneous risk preferences. Since they have very different views and incentives in regard to risk-management actions, they do not favor one risk-management policy over another. Risk management that is intended to minimize transaction costs can lead to costly compensating portfolio adjustments by shareholders. In some circumstances where other stakeholders would value risk management highly, shareholders may have big incentives to unwind a hedge. One well-known example of this phenomenon is the Metallgesellschaft debacle, as described by Stulz (1996), pp. 10-11, and Culp and Miller (1995), p. 63.

Therefore, risk management at the firm level can create shareholder value, when it guarantees a certain (observable) risk profile to which shareholders need to adjust their portfolios only once,[332] which will, in turn, save transaction costs. Likewise, the firm (and especially banks) can set their long-run "target" capital structure when they commit to a certain risk profile (and hence rating). By only taking risks that are in line with this risk profile,[333] the firm can avoid the costly adjustment of the current capital structure to achieve this target in the short run.[334]

■ Managers/firms are often not willing to disclose inside information to investors (and hence the public in general) because this proprietary information could be exploited by competitors. This is also true with regard to the detailed disclosure of risk exposures, risk-management policies, and which risk-management tools are used within firms and to what degree. This is especially true for banks, for whom the management of risk is the most important source of competitive advantage. Given the current reporting of firms and banks, risk transparency (inside and outside the firm) is only rarely found, and so investors have to try and reveal this private information, which is—due to transaction costs—costly. However, risk management can be used as a substitute for the publication of internal information.[335] As long as it guarantees a stable risk profile of the firm and the costs for conducting the necessary risk management are lower than the costs associated with the information disclosure, it can increase the value of the firm.[336] The same argument is valid for another facet of the same problem on a different (not the firm) level: Banks, in particular, use risk management to create assets or products with stable distributions so that customers can save on both transaction and participation[337] costs.

---

[332]See Mason (1995), pp. 31–32.
[333]See Shimko and Humphreys (1998), p. 33.
[334]See Froot and Stein (1998a), p. 60.
[335]Albeit there are many advantages of increasing the transparency (especially of banks) via better disclosure and educating the analysts' community—as suggested by Shimko and Humphreys (1998), p. 33—it can be counterproductive and even dangerous to do so for strategic and competitive reasons.
[336]See DeMarzo and Duffie (1992) and Smithson (1998), pp. 9–10.
[337]As defined in Allen and Santomero (1996), p. 1.

Taxes and Other Market Imperfections as Rationales for Risk Management

In the first part of this section, we will discuss the effects of taxes and how risk management can help to reduce them in order to increase firm value. In the second part of this section, we will turn to other market imperfections neglected so far and discuss how risk management can be used for value creation within their context.

Taxes   So far, we have neglected the fact that firms have to pay taxes. Since taxes are an important component of doing business and tax savings can substantially influence the firm value, optimally all valuations should be conducted on an after-tax basis. Equation (2.1) for determining the firm value, therefore, needs to be adjusted in one of the following two ways:

- Both the cash flows in the numerator and the discount rate(s) in the denominator are now to be estimated on an after-tax basis.
- Alternately, we can—while ignoring for the moment financial distress costs as derived in the last section—use an adjusted present value (APV) approach to derive the after-tax firm value:[338]

$$\text{Firm Value} = \text{Firm Value without Taxes}^{339} - PV(\text{Tax Effects}) \quad (3.5)$$

As is immediately obvious from Equation (3.5), decreasing the present value of the tax payments can increase the firm value. However, that is an overall firm objective. The question in this section is how risk management can help to achieve this goal.

There are two conditions necessary—as we will describe in more detail below—for a risk-management strategy to generate tax benefits:[340]

- The tax schedule must be convex.
- Some portion of the range for pretax income needs to lie within the convex section of the tax schedule.

A convex tax schedule is defined as one in which the firm's average effective tax rate rises as pretax income[341] rises,[342] that is, when the marginal tax rate exceeds the average tax rate, as depicted in Figure 3.8.

---

[338]See Brealey and Myers (1991), pp. 458+.
[339]As derived in Equation (2.1).
[340]See Smithson et al. (1990), pp. 366–367.
[341]As taken from the financial reporting.
[342]See Smithson et al. (1995), p. 102, and Smithson (1998), p. 7.

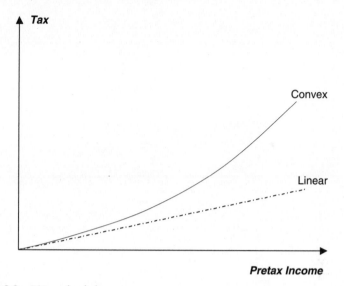

Figure 3.8 Tax schedules.
Source: Adapted from Smithson et al. (1995), p. 103.

In a tax system with a linear tax schedule risk management cannot have any impact on firm value, since—as we know from statistics:

$$E(g(X)) = g(E(X)) \qquad (3.6)$$

where g = Linear tax function
       X = Random variable = pretax income
       $E(\cdot)$ = Expected value of $(\cdot)$.

So when, for instance, a firm can have pretax income of +300 or –100 with equal probability and the tax rate is fixed at 50%, $g(X) = 0.5X$[343] and hence $E(g(X)) = g(E(X)) = 50$.

If the effective tax schedule is convex (as indicated by function $f(X)$ in Figure 3.9), risk management will reduce the firm's expected taxes, because Jensen's inequality[344] indicates that a reduction in the volatility of pretax income X (hedged position) induced by (financial price) risk will decrease the tax liability (the expected value of the unhedged position), because:

$$E(f(X)) \geq f(E(X)) \qquad (3.7)$$

---

[343]This is equivalent to allowing for unrestricted tax-loss carry forwards.
[344]See Smith (1995), p. 26, and Bamberg and Baur (1991), p. 121.

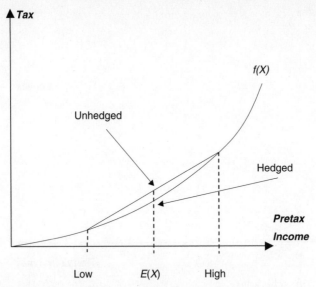

Figure 3.9   Effects of convex tax schedules on tax liabilities.
Source: Adapted from Smithson et al. (1995), p. 104.

Therefore, the firm saves the difference in taxes between the expected tax payment without risk management and the lower taxes due to hedging.

The same line of reasoning can be used when we apply this knowledge about the convexity of the tax function and plot after-tax income as a function $e(X)$ of pretax income X, as shown in Figure 3.10. Here, the expected value of the concave function e of a random variable X is less than the concave function evaluated at the expected value of X or:

$$E(e(X)) \leq e(E(X)) \tag{3.8}$$

Equation (3.8) again indicates that reducing the volatility of pretax income can reduce the expected value of the tax payments.

Tax codes are both historically and internationally highly nonlinear,[345] and their convexity arises from the following three sources:[346]

- Statutory progressivity of the tax rate
- Limitations on the use of tax preference items (e.g., tax-loss carry forwards, foreign tax credits, investment tax credits)

[345]See Allen and Santomero (1996), p. 15.
[346]See Smith (1995), p. 26.

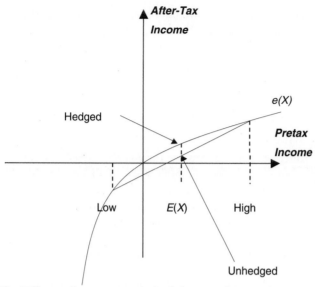

Figure 3.10 Effects of convex tax schedules on after-tax income.
Source: Adapted from Smithson et al. (1995), p. 104.

- Alternative minimum tax (e.g., difference between reported and taxable income)

The increases in the progressivity of the tax code have only limited applicability to corporations,[347] because there is only a narrow range of marginal corporate tax rates,[348] which make this argument only a weak motive for conducting risk management.[349] However, the other arguments—such as, for example, the presence of tax preference items—are much more likely to apply and can make the effective tax rates convex[350] despite the limited progressivity of corporate tax rates. The convexity of the tax function is, therefore, plausible, especially when firms face a significant prob-

---

[347]This is especially true for large publicly quoted banks.
[348]See Mason (1995), p. 30.
[349]See Fenn et al. (1997), p. 18.
[350]Graham and Smith (1996) examine the degree of convexity of the tax function in the United States. For most corporations the tax function is convex due to tax-loss carry forwards. However, for some corporations, Graham and Smith observe a concave tax function.

ability of negative earnings and are unable to carry 100% of their tax losses forward to subsequent periods.[351]

So, if taxes are a convex function of earnings, it will generally be optimal for firms to hedge.[352] However, the economic incentives to conduct risk management in order to increase firm value should be greater for firms whose:[353]

- Income is close to the level at which there is a large shift in the marginal tax rate
- Tax function is more convex than other firms' tax functions (i.e., firms that have more tax preference items or that have a greater potential to have a tax liability under the alternative minimum tax)
- Pretax income is more volatile, and especially for those whose income often switches between profits and losses

However, since reported (pretax) earnings can be very different from economic earnings, the question is how accounting reasons can justify economic decisions.[354] Given the above discussion of tax issues, the goal of risk management is, then, to reduce the volatility of earnings and hence the firm's average tax liability. However, hedging earnings is not the same as hedging firm value,[355] and reducing the volatility of earnings may require a very different risk-management strategy than reducing the volatility of the firm value. This is especially true for banks, whose hedge positions are marked to market, but underlying exposures (assets and liabilities) are kept at historical book values on the balance sheet. Reducing the volatility of the firm value in this setup might increase the volatility of pretax income,[356] and hence might not achieve the intended goal.

Again, even though the firms' objective function itself is not concave, firms behave in a risk-averse manner due to the nonlinearity of taxes.[357] They will conduct risk management at the corporate level, because it can increase the firm value under a convex tax schedule. By reducing the expected tax liability of the firm (either by reducing expected taxes directly or

---

[351]See Froot et al. (1993), p. 1632. Even if they could carry forward tax losses without restrictions, the present value effect of taxes saved in later periods would make the schedule convex.

[352]See Froot et al. (1993), p. 1632.

[353]See Smith (1995), pp. 26–27.

[354]See Allen and Santomero (1996), p. 15.

[355]This is the appropriate goal when the costs associated with the probability of default are more relevant for the firm.

[356]See Smith (1995), p. 27.

[357]See Allen and Santomero (1996), p. 14.

by increasing the present value of the various tax shields via the smoothing of corporate earnings)[358], risk management can increase the (after-tax) cash flows[359] and hence firm value. Note that home-made risk management on the part of the investors cannot replicate these benefits of risk management by the firm, and it is therefore more valuable to conduct risk management at this level.

Other Market Imperfections   The following market imperfections can be additional reasons for conducting risk management at the firm level:

- **Dividend policy:** Because of the signaling effect of dividends,[360] firms often have the desire to maintain stable dividends and hold back cash that could or should be paid out to shareholders because of the concern that income is volatile over time. If this cash is invested in negative NPV projects, firm value is destroyed. If risk management can reduce cash retention and hence result in the taking on of fewer poor projects, firm value can be increased.[361]
- **Perceived risk:** Markets may perceive firms to be riskier than they actually are. If a certain risk factor is the source of this misperception and if risk management can eliminate or reduce that misperception,[362] then risk management can reduce the perceived probability of financial distress (and the associated costs), and it will increase the current market value of the firm.[363]
- **Other market inefficiencies:** Because of limited liability, the amount of risk that can be allocated to the shareholders is limited by the capital stock of the firm. This can obviously limit the firm's overall risk capacity. In companies that are thinly capitalized and where the claims of managers and employees are likely to be large relative to the claims of the shareholders, there may be substantial benefits from managing, or at least coordinating (not necessarily reducing), risks. Risk management can then allow for a concentration on those risks where the firm has comparative advantages[364] and hence those risks where the firm is most likely to increase its value.

---

[358]See Mian (1996).
[359]See Pritsch and Hommel (1997), p. 675.
[360]See Copeland and Weston (1988), pp. 584+, for an extensive discussion and a list of references to the literature for the Signaling Hypothesis of dividend announcements.
[361]See Damodaran (1997), p. 788.
[362]See Damodaran (1997), p. 788.
[363]See Stulz (1996), p. 13.
[364]See Pritsch and Hommel (1997), p. 675.

Additional Rationales for Risk Management in Banks

As we have described above, theory would predict, in general, that the higher the debt ratio, the more risk management a firm should conduct. Since banks have a very high leverage (see "The Role of Capital in Banks" section of Chapter 5), this statement should be especially relevant for banks. Accordingly, Diamond (1984) argues that risk management (actually diversification) mitigates incentive problems associated with debt finance in financial institutions.[365]

Besides this argument, there is a fundamental interest of all stakeholders in a "no default" situation. The provision of financial services[366] is crucially dependent on the creditworthiness of financial firms. According to Merton and Bodie,[367] it is important to distinguish between investors in and customers of a bank to emphasize the significance of creditworthiness in banking. Investors (stockholder, bond holders, etc.) expect to earn a return on their investment commensurate with their risk taking, and the creditworthiness of a bank represents the risks inherent in the investment.[368]

Bank customers are usually also significant bank liability holders, who almost always hold much larger financial claims than the investors. However, they have a different view of creditworthiness: depositors want to know that their money will be repaid with certainty and not just that their claim is due *and* the bank is still solvent. In theory, customers could manage the bank default risk by diversification or by buying third-party insurance or banks could offer actuarially fair price reductions of the default risk in their contracts. But customers prefer a default-free contract with the bank. Their concern with the bank's creditworthiness is best addressed by the bank's use of risk management to guarantee a stable risk profile. However, this is difficult to communicate and difficult for customers (and all other stakeholders) to monitor since banks are opaque, flexible in their portfolio composition,[369] and complex with regard to the instruments they hold (e.g., exotic derivatives).[370]

---

[365]See Diamond (1984).

[366]In particular, the provision of risk-management services and the facilitation of risk allocation are critical.

[367]See Merton and Bodie (1992), p. 89.

[368]Since bank failure is costly, investors require a compensation for such costs. Therefore, the bank has an incentive to minimize the probability of failure, all else being equal. See Winton (2000), p. 1.

[369]Because of the nature of participating in capital markets, banks can basically change their risk profiles completely within minutes.

[370]See Mason (1995), pp. 34–37.

This is why regulation often tries to ensure a certain creditworthiness of the bank and governments insure deposits or intervene on the basis of the "too-big-to-fail" doctrine. Even though firms in regulated industries typically face lower contracting costs and, therefore, have less incentive to hedge,[371] the preceding arguments are much stronger and show that there is a predominant concern with risk management in banks for good reason.

However, note that risk management by the bank cannot be a substitute for risk management conducted by the bank's customers. This kind of risk management makes the customers more profitable[372] and, since customers are then less subject to financial distress situations themselves, reduces the bank's loss exposure.[373] Obviously, bank risk management cannot achieve this result.

SUMMARY AND CONCLUSIONS

In this section we removed (some of) the strict assumptions of the neoclassical world, because we were not able to explain why corporations would conduct risk management in such a world to increase value. By doing so, we essentially followed the development of financial theory starting from the mid-1980s, when Smith and Stulz first introduced the existence of market inefficiencies[374] in their analysis to derive the conditions under which risk management at the corporate level can be useful and value enhancing.

As we have seen above, the rationale for conducting risk management in the neoinstitutional world lies in the benefits that are entailed with it: risk management allows firms to decrease the present value of:

- The agency costs of equity, by allowing firms to increase their leverage (without increasing the probability of default)
- The agency costs of debt, by using risk management as an equity substitute
- Transaction costs, especially the cost of financial distress
- Tax payments

---

[371]See Mian (1996), p. 422.
[372]They will buy risk-management products from the bank and hence will increase fee income.
[373]See Smith (1993), p. 20.
[374]See Stulz (1984) and Smith and Stulz (1985), who included, for example, the cost of financial distress, the problems of coordinating capital-budgeting decisions with financing decisions, agency problems between managers and stockholders, and taxes.

By doing so, risk management can reduce the expected payments to the various stakeholders of the firm and can additionally ensure that enough (internal) cash flows are generated to fund positive NPV projects,[375] all of which will increase the firm value. We have also seen that, because of these benefits (that can be achieved by conducting risk management at the corporate level), firms behave as if they were risk averse, even though they are not in and of themselves. Therefore, these benefits form the basis for the design of a comprehensive risk-management approach for banks, to which we will return in Chapter 6.

However, as we have also indicated in the beginning of this section on the neoinstitutional rationales, there are also costs associated with implementing risk management, which could outweigh the benefits.[376] These costs can be thought of as the transaction costs directly associated with risk-management actions, such as the sum of any out-of-pocket fees,[377] the implicit cost of the bid-ask spread when trading, the opportunity cost of management's time in the administration of the risk-management program,[378] significant investments in the systems environment,[379] and so on. Following the line of reasoning from the neoclassical section, one should keep in mind that as the transaction costs of reducing risk increase, risk management becomes less attractive, because one does not have to pay these transaction costs for risks borne within the firm.[380]

Since we explicitly allowed for such costs (including also the costs for writing, enforcing, and monitoring contracts), they should be considered when making the decision whether risk management is useful and value enhancing on the basis of a cost-benefit analysis. However, it is very difficult to estimate exact dollar amounts on both the cost and the benefit side. Therefore, we evaluate and rank the various benefits discussed in this section and depicted in Figure 3.2 on a subjective and relative basis from worst to best with regard to their potential for value creation (for firms and, where appropriate, for banks).

The tax argument seems to provide the weakest rationale for conducting risk management at the firm level. Even though taxes are otherwise a very important source for value creation, conducting risk management for achieving additional tax savings seems less than convincing. This approach

---

[375]See Stulz (2000), p. 4-3.

[376]See Shimko and Humphreys (1998), p. 33.

[377]Option premiums paid are not costs of conducting risk management because they represent a fair market price for the respective product.

[378]See Smith (1995), p. 27.

[379]See Allen and Santomero (1996), p. 17. Footnote 325 of this chapter discusses whether these costs should be viewed as sunk costs.

[380]See Stulz (2000), p. 3-2.

only makes sense as long as the costs for doing so are lower than the present value of the expected tax savings.[381] In reality, this appears to be unlikely, because the costs of risk management seem to be much higher than the small gains from tax savings. Since the actual convexity of the tax schedule is much lower than depicted in Figures 3.9 and 3.10, the difference between the straight line (i.e., the unhedged position) and the curved line (i.e., the hedged position) is even smaller. Also, except for Graham and Smith (1996),[382] there is very little or only contradictory[383] empirical evidence that strongly supports the concept that taxes should represent a significant rationale for conducting risk management. Therefore, and because it is also very difficult to allocate tax obligations to a single transaction level, taxes are ignored in the further analysis of risk management below.

Other market inefficiencies and transaction-cost-based benefits (cost of implementing risk management and guaranteeing a stable risk profile) also appear to be of less significance. The benefits stemming from the reduction of the agency costs of equity and debt (overinvestment, the risk preference problem, asset substitution, underinvestment) are important from an incentive-setting point of view and for the alignment of the interests of the various stakeholders in a firm. But, when viewing the contribution of risk-management actions to the benefits of avoiding the consequences of management self-interest and capital market imperfections from a pure value creation perspective (counterbalancing it with the tremendous costs[384]), it seems unlikely that the benefits are significant enough.[385]

Likewise, the coordination of investment and financing[386] (and its associated agency and transaction costs) seems less relevant in a banking context. Here, the estimates of the large costs of financial distress, which originate from the likelihood of default, and the value increases stemming from their avoidance seem to significantly outweigh the costs. Even when weighted with the (relatively small) probability of default (for banks[387]),

---

[381]See Damodaran (1997), p. 785.

[382]Graham and Smith (1996) employ an accounting data-driven simulation-based analysis to find that roughly 12% of the firms in their sample could achieve tax savings from risk management, if the firms were able to adequately control the volatility of their income through derivative instruments.

[383]Some studies (e.g., Nance et al. [1993] or Geczy et al. [1995]) find that the expected tax liability is negatively correlated with the availability of internal funds, and hence firms with a convex tax function conduct less risk management.

[384]See the "Role and Importance of Risk and Its Management in Banks" section in Chapter 2.

[385]See Allen and Santomero (1996), p. 18.

[386]As discussed by Froot et al. (1993) and (1994).

[387]As we have observed above, banks typically have high credit ratings.

bankruptcy costs are substantial and can, therefore, explain a large part of the risk-management activities, which makes them the most plausible rationale.[388]

The direct and indirect costs from financial distress situations are the most compelling argument for using risk management to reduce the expected value of these (transaction) costs and to increase firm value. Since risk management can achieve this by reducing the firm's default probability, it can increase the firm's debt capacity.[389] By allowing for an increase in the leverage, risk management can, additionally, reduce a firm's tax obligations[390] and, moreover, can implicitly mitigate almost all of the agency problems (e.g., reduce the agency cost of free cash flows) that have been discussed. Also, this use of risk management can allow a firm to move closer to its optimal capital structure,[391] which, in turn, minimizes its cost of capital and can increase its firm value. However, the lower costs of capital need to be balanced with a potential increase in the expected costs of financial distress and the costs for risk management.[392] A possible optimum state where firm value is maximized could be where the marginal costs of debt (i.e., costs of financial distress) equal the marginal benefits of debt (i.e., reduction in agency costs). However, it is not clear why alternate strategies such as increasing the amount of equity[393] are not superior, given the costs associated with risk management.[394]

---

[388]See Allen and Santomero (1996), p. 18.

[389]See, for example, Damodaran (1997), pp. 786–787, Froot et al. (1993), p. 1632, Pritsch and Hommel (1997), p. 675.

[390]See Mason (1995), p. 31. Note that here risk management is no substitute for capital.

[391]Although it has been long discussed in finance theory, there seems to still be no conclusion on what such an optimal capital structure would look like.

[392]The gains in value from moving to the optimal debt ratio can be, according to Damodaran (1997), p. 786, substantial and justify even expensive risk management.

[393]Note that equity is a substitute for risk management.

[394]See Allen and Santomero (1996), p. 18.

APPENDIX

TABLE 3.3 Sample of European Banks Selected for Testing Ownership Concentration

Number	Bank Name
1	Banca Agricola Mantovana SpA
2	Banco Bilbao Vizcaya Argentaria SA
3	Banco Popular Español
4	Banco Pinto & Sotto Mayor
5	Banco Espirito Santo SA
6	Banca Popolare di Verona
7	Banca Popolare Sondrio
8	Banca Monte dei Paschi di Siena SpA
9	Banca Carige SpA Cassa di Risparmio di Genova e Imperia
10	Bankinter SA
11	Barclays PLC
12	Banca di Roma SpA
13	Banca Intesa SpA
14	Bank Austria AG
15	Bipop Carire SpA
16	BHW Holding AG
17	BHF Bank AG
18	Bayerische Hypo- und Vereinsbank AG
19	Bank of Scotland
20	BNP Banque Nationale de Paris
21	DePfa Deutsche Pfandbriefbank AG
22	Deutsche Bank AG
23	Credit Suisse Group
24	Commerzbank AG
25	Comit Banca Commerciale Italiana
26	Christiania Bank og Kreditkasse
27	CCF Credit Commercial de France
28	Dexia
29	Dresdner Bank AG
30	KBC Bankverzekeringsholding
31	ING Groep NV
32	IKB Deutsche Industriebank AG
33	HSBC Trinkaus & Burkhardt KGaA
34	HSBC Holdings PLC
35	Halifax Group PLC
36	Fortis Inc
37	Erste Bank der Österreichischen Sparkassen AG
38	Lloyds TSB Group PLC
39	Northern Rock PLC
40	Vontobel Holding AG
41	Unidanmark

(continued)

42	UniCredito Italiano
43	Standard Chartered PLC
44	Sparebanken Nord-Norge
45	Societe Generale
46	San Paolo IMI SpA
47	Royal Bank of Scotland Group PLC
48	Woolwich PLC

Source: thomson*direct*.com and author's own analysis.

CHAPTER 4

Implications of the Previous Theoretical Discussion for This Book

In the previous chapter(s), we have closely investigated the circumstances under which risk management at the corporate level can increase the value of a firm. We can draw the following conclusions from this theoretical discussion.

First, even though the neoclassical theory with its strict assumptions has laid the foundation for the development of extremely useful theories like the CAPM and the M&M propositions, we saw that in such a world risk management at the bank level is irrelevant, unnecessary, and can even be harmful with respect to the corporate objective of value creation.

Second, we also saw—by relaxing these strict assumptions—that in the neoinstitutional world various market imperfections can build the rationale for conducting risk management. Here, managing risk at the corporate level can create value, because it can reduce the present value of, for example, agency and transaction costs.

Third, neither of the two theories offers a general framework that can be used to guide risk-management strategies and that gives detailed instructions on how to apply these conditions in practice (a normative theory of risk management). This is due to the fact that the previous analysis has focused on why risk management at the corporate level is necessary and desirable from a value creation perspective, rather than on how much or what sort of risk management is optimal for a particular firm. Therefore, much of the previous academic work comes to the extreme conclusion that firms should always fully hedge (when they decide to hedge), completely insulating their market values from risk.[1] Although there are only very narrow empirical studies that offer some valuable information on what the prevailing (best) practice is in firms, full hedging is not what we observe in reality.[2]

As an example of how unspecific some academic recommendations can be with regard to risk management, we refer to the following two propositions:[3]

- If risk can be managed at no or at a very low cost[4] it should be. At worst, risk management will have no effect on value, and at best it will provide positive feedback effects that will increase value.
- If risk can be managed at a cost, it makes sense to hedge the risk only if the benefits[5] that arise from hedging exceed the costs.

One could also extend these propositions and infer the following (also from our previous discussion):[6]

- Closely held or private firms typically gain more from risk management than widely held firms with well-diversified investors.
- Firms that experience significant agency problems between managers and shareholders, and between shareholders and bond holders, are likely to gain more from risk management than firms that do not.
- Firms that are exposed to large indirect bankruptcy costs will gain the most from risk management. This would imply that banks should conduct more risk management than industrial corporations, because they have higher costs associated with financial distress situations.[7]
- Risk management can help to increase the leverage of corporations to their optimal debt ratio to minimize the costs of capital.[8]

---

[1]See Froot et al. (1993), p. 1630.
[2]See also the "Empirical Evidence" section of Chapter 2 for a discussion of this behavior, which is called selective hedging.
[3]See Damodaran (1997), p. 788.
[4]Possible instruments are, for example, changes in operations, financial decisions, or the usage of derivatives.
[5]Examples are reduced taxes, increased debt capacity, or better investment decisions.
[6]See Damodaran (1997), pp. 788–789.
[7]This is implied by both the results of various studies mentioned in "The Costs of Financial Distress" section of Chapter 3 (see e.g., James (1991)) and the reductions in market values during the Russian crisis in 1998 that exceeded the credit exposure of various banks by a multiple.
[8]There are two open questions with respect to banks: (1) Why do banks all have capital ratios around 8%? and (2) Would banks be able to use risk-management techniques to adjust to the "optimal" capital structure because of regulatory constraints?

In contrast, finance theory based on the neoclassical paradigm offers sophisticated answers as to what "risk-management mechanics"[9] can be used (e.g., calculating the hedge ratio by using Black-Scholes-type models). However, it has less specific answers to the questions that must logically be asked first in order to design a coherent risk-management strategy:[10]

- Which risks should be hedged and which risks should be left unhedged?
- To what degree (partially or fully)?[11]
- What kind of instruments and trading strategies are appropriate?

Rather than simply demonstrating that there is a role for risk management, a well-designed strategy—both in terms of the amount of risk management and the instruments used[12]—can enable a firm to maximize its value.[13] We will return to this issue in Chapter 6 when we analyze a metric that is used in banks (Risk-Adjusted Performance Measures = RAPM) to answer the question of whether a risk-management activity creates value.

Such a metric is important because managers should be able to identify what is worth hedging. Worrying about stock-price volatility in itself is not worthwhile, because individual investors can better manage this volatility through their portfolio strategies.[14] Also, there is an intertemporal trade-off as to whether the firm should manage the risks of the present value of all cash flows or whether it should insulate the level of cash at each point in time.[15] It is especially interesting how sensitive these cash flows, and hence firm value, are to various risk variables and the changes in the economic environment.

Understanding this connection between a company's investment/growth opportunities and the key economic variables is critical in developing a coherent risk-management strategy because it defines how much hedging is necessary: If there is no correlation between the two, a firm should fully

---

[9]See Froot et al. (1993), p. 1629.
[10]See Froot et al. (1993), p. 1629, and Chapter 2.
[11]However, even if the above framework comes to the conclusion that it is best to fully hedge, the framework does not address the fact that not all of the risks affecting a firm's cash flows are marketable and thus can be hedged.
[12]Even the best risk-management programs will incur losses in some trades. However, more severe is the opportunity cost for using the wrong instrument and taking positions in derivatives that do not fit well with the corporate strategy, meaning that a (coherent) risk-management strategy needs to be integrated with the overall corporate strategy.
[13]See Froot et al. (1993), p. 1631.
[14]See Froot et al. (1994), pp. 98–102.
[15]See Froot et al. (1993), p. 1655.

hedge. However, if they are correlated, it might not be necessary for the firm to hedge at all, because the company has a natural hedge already built into its business.[16] Likewise, it is important to understand the impact of fundamental economic/risk factors on the firm value rather than only on the cash flows of specific projects to ensure the long-term survival of the company, to retain its competitiveness, and to meet its strategic objectives.[17]

Fourth, the likelihood of default is the central component and forms the foundation for practically all of the potential rationales for conducting risk management in the neoinstitutional world. Its most obvious manifestations are the (expected) costs of financial distress that are the key argument for managing risks at the corporate level, particularly when viewed from a cost-benefit perspective, but also because this factor influences almost all of the other components. Therefore, value gains seem to be most profound when a firm tries to avoid the costs of financial distress via risk management. This is especially true for banks for which unexpected external financing needs and financial distress are associated with higher costs (because of the central role of creditworthiness in the provision of financial services[18] and the potential loss of their franchise value) than for industrial corporations.

Fifth, therefore, firms, and especially banks, are trying to avoid lower-tail outcomes or are trying to decrease the likelihood of their occurrence by using risk management, which results in a (quasi[19]) risk-averse behavior. Increases in total risk (and not only in the systematic part of it) make it more likely that a firm will end up in a situation where it cannot take advantage of valuable projects. In the neoclassical world with costless and perfect contracting, a firm can always recapitalize at fair market prices. However,

---

[16]Banks can have extremely large "hidden hedge funds" in their portfolios that they might be completely unaware of, because it is an unavoidable consequence of a wider business strategy. Due to the multidimensionality and the complexity of the counterbalancing effects in such large portfolios of risky assets, firm behavior is not always value enhancing, and the practical solutions to risk management do not always increase firm value. See, for example, Drzik et al. (1997), p. 1, and Pritsch and Hommel (1997), p. 685.

[17]See Froot et al. (1994), pp. 98–102. Also, risk-management strategies should depend on both (1) the nature of the product market competition and (2) the competitors' risk-management strategies. For instance, when investment is a "strategic substitute" a firm will want to hedge more when its rival hedges less (as in the product market). However, the overall industry equilibrium will involve some risk management by both firms. When investment is a "strategic complement" (as in the case of research and development, where firms want to invest more when their rivals invest more), firms will want to hedge more when their rivals hedge more. See Froot et al. (1993), pp. 1650–1652.

[18]See Mason (1995), p. 28.

[19]Firms/banks are not risk-averse themselves.

in the neoinstitutional world, firms with a nontrivial probability of financial distress may not be able to invest in projects they would in the neoclassical world, because they may not be able to raise funds to invest in such projects or may be able to do so only at a price so high that it is not worthwhile.

Sixth, in the neoinstitutional world, with costly external finance and where total risk (including specific risk) matters (and is costly due to financial distress costs), not only systematic risks, but also unmarketable (i.e., nonhedgable) idiosyncratic risks will impose real costs on the firm. Therefore, firms can increase their value through risk management by decreasing these total risk costs. Capital-budgeting procedures should, therefore, take the cost of a project's impact on the total risk of the firm into account.[20]

Seventh, this makes risk management inseparable from capital-budgeting decisions and the current capital structure choice (see Figure 4.1).[21] Because both risk-management and capital-structure decisions can influence

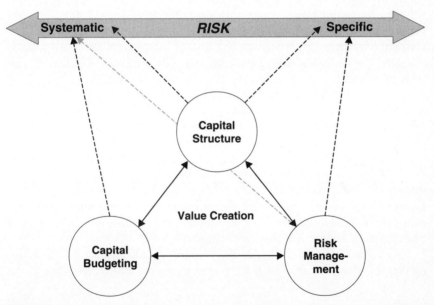

Figure 4.1 The interdependency of capital budgeting, capital structure, and risk management when risk management can create value.

---

[20]See Froot et al. (1993), p. 1650, and Stulz (1999), p. 7.
[21]For instance, negative NPV projects under this paradigm could be turned into positive NPV projects by reducing their contribution to total risk. See Stulz (1999), pp. 8–9.

total risk costs, capital budgeting can also no longer only be concerned with the systematic components of a firm's cash flow (as depicted by the arrow in the left-hand part of Figure 4.1), as it is in the neoclassical theory.

Therefore, the CAPM and the traditional DCF methodology might no longer be universally valid as a capital-budgeting tool,[22] and using the traditional NPV rule might not always be the correct way to decide whether or not to undertake a project and whether value is created. Removing any of the perfect market assumptions, typically, but not always, destroys the intellectual foundations for the capital-budgeting rules used in the neoclassical world.[23] Therefore, one needs to evaluate the magnitude of the deviations from traditional capital-budgeting principles and establish where and when they apply.

On the one hand, there are certainly (capital) markets where the assumptions of the neoclassical world are not completely unrealistic and liquid assets are traded. Here, only the systematic component counts and Equation (2.1) can still be applied. Similarly, if there were no costs for holding equity capital, firms would tend to hold a capital buffer that is large enough so that there would be no issue with default risk. In such a situation, risk management can be separated from the investment decisions, and the neoclassical paradigm still applies.[24] The firm's (quasi) aversion to risk should not enter the decision-making process, and only the risks' correlation with systematic factors should matter when risks are marketable.

On the other hand, if holding equity is costly for tax or agency reasons, risk management typically cannot be separated from capital budgeting.[25] Also, there are other (capital) market segments where comparative advantages[26] lead to the fact that specific risk counts and the costs of financial distress have to come into play. Therefore, it can be more expensive for the firm to bear risk within its own portfolio than it is for the market, because the firm has to consider the costs of financial distress when holding risk. Corporate risk-management considerations and the constitution of the existing portfolio should then enter into the pricing of those risks (that cannot be hedged and for which total risk counts).

Therefore, one can conclude that a bank should always sell or hedge marketable (liquid) risk or only keep it when the price also compensates the

[22]See Froot et al. (1993), p. 1650.
[23]See Stulz (1999), p. 2. As we have mentioned, in the neoclassical world we assume that capital-budgeting, risk-management, and capital-structure decisions can be determined independently.
[24]See Froot and Stein (1998a), p. 58.
[25]See Froot and Stein (1998a), p. 58.
[26]Note that competitive advantages can only persist in illiquid markets, where there are information asymmetries.

bank for the risk's contribution to its total risk costs.[27] This logic should even hold when the risk is uncorrelated with factors that are priced in the capital markets, that is, for diversifiable or specific risk.

Returning to Figure 4.1, it is worthwhile to emphasize that a bank's capital structure should be determined by the bank's exposure to total risk (i.e., to both systematic and specific risk) and driven by its concern with creditworthiness. Even though some of the post-modern models realize how critical financial policy/structure can be in enabling companies to make valuable investments,[28] none of these models includes the role of risk management in accepting value-enhancing projects. Additionally, while the current practice in risk management seems to aim mostly at specific risk, it became clear in the above discussion that risk management should also aim at systematic risk and hence the totality of risk.[29]

Eighth, the market imperfections introduced in the neoinstitutional section seem to indicate that firm (stakeholder) value maximization might be a better corporate objective for banks than shareholder value maximization, since the costs entailed in shareholder value maximization might have adverse effects on all (bank) stakeholders.[30]

The differences between the two theories can be summarized as shown in Table 4.1.

We can, therefore, deduce the following implications for the further structure of this book:

- First, we need to define and derive an adequate total risk measure for banks, because (especially in a non-normal world) neither systematic nor specific risk capture the concern with lower-tail outcomes well. We also need to discuss the interrelation of such a risk measure with the capital structure of banks, both of which we will do in Chapter 5.
- Second, we need to define an adequate capital-budgeting tool that reflects the interrelation of capital budgeting, capital structure, and risk management, and that provides a consistent merger of the two theories, that is, encompasses market as well as bank internal portfolio considerations. We will, therefore, investigate in Chapter 6

---

[27]The only way to control the firm's risk exposure to nonmarketable risks is by investing less aggressively in illiquid risk.

[28]According to Myers (1977) and Myers and Majluf (1984), firms face real trade-offs in how they finance their investments.

[29]See Chapter 2 for a more detailed discussion of this issue in a banking context.

[30]This is especially true for banks, since they care about total risks for good reasons. As shown previously, "bank runs" induce a state in which all of the business is lost immediately (which is relevant for all stakeholders) and, in general, bank stakeholders are extremely credit sensitive and cannot diversify that risk.

TABLE 4.1 Summary Table for Comparison

Neoclassical Finance Theory	Criterion	Neoinstitutional Finance Theory
Irrelevant for value creation	Risk management at the bank level	Can increase value
Broad market portfolio	Relevant risk universe	(Existing) bank portfolio
Systematic risk	Relevant risk dimension	Total risk
Separated	Capital budgeting, capital structure, and risk management	Integrated
DCF/traditional (shareholder) value framework	Valuation approach	Stakeholder value framework?/RAROC?

whether a measure that is currently used in banks in practice and that uses the risk measure derived in Chapter 5 (RAROC), can help to decide if risk borne within a bank is more valuable than risk borne outside.

However, this can only be the case when a bank has a competitive advantage[31] in holding some risks within its own portfolio.[32] The key prerequisite to a value-enhancing risk-management strategy is, therefore, to understand this comparative advantage and to know how to identify it.[33] "Good" risks are hence those risks that banks understand[34] and thus where they can have a comparative advantage, whereas "bad" risks are the risks that they do not understand.[35]

---

[31]As we have discussed, firms/banks only have a limited overall risk capacity and should, therefore, concentrate on those risks where they have a comparative advantage and where they can hence create value.

[32]Banks require a special measure because they are so different from industrial companies with respect to risk management for two reasons: banks may be able to (1) create portfolios of assets that gain from diversification more than what can be achieved by other companies and (2) acquire the expertise to evaluate risks more efficiently (due to repeated exposure to that risk). However, an open question is what is the core value added of these activities and how can banks develop a key competency, that is, what determines where they trade (risk) and how they add value by doing so.

[33]See Stulz (1996), pp. 14–15.

[34]Leland and Pyle (1977) argue that intermediaries can signal their informed status by investing wealth in assets about which they have special knowledge.

[35]See Shimko and Humphreys (1998), p. 33. However, it seems that many market players do not even know what risks they have.

CHAPTER 5

Capital Structure in Banks

We saw in Chapter 3 that the costs of financial distress are especially relevant market imperfections, creating the rationale for conducting risk management at the bank level in order to maximize value. Therefore, total risk matters to banks.

Banks can manage risk and thus the cost of total risk through transactions in financial markets (selling or hedging risks) or (up front) through the choice of projects they accept (i.e., capital-budgeting decisions). However, since taking risks on their books is one of the fundamental parts of the business of banking, managing all risks in such a way cannot be the business objective for banks.[1] Given that banks hold risks, increasing their (financial) leverage increases the probability of incurring the costs of financial distress. Therefore, holding (equity) capital commensurate with the risks on the bank's books is sensible from both an economic and a regulatory point of view and can be considered as an alternative form of risk management.[2]

This view is consistent with the role of capital in banks as discussed from a theoretical point of view. However, in practice, the various bank stakeholders have diverging opinions on how much equity capital the bank needs to hold. Since a bank can hold only one amount of capital for its risks, we are going to try and derive this amount in this chapter. We will find that "risk capital" is the relevant and correct measure for both quantifying total risk and determining the required amount of capital in banks. We will also find that for practical purposes "economic capital" is a feasible proxy for risk capital. We will subsequently present and discuss various ways in which economic capital can be estimated.

---

[1]See Berger et al. (1995b), p. 398.
[2]See Stulz (2000), p. 4-4, and as also shown in Chapter 2.

THE ROLE OF CAPITAL IN BANKS

In this section we will discuss the role of (equity) capital in banks, which can be seen—at least for the purposes of this book—first and foremost as a substitute for risk management.

Capital as a Means for Achieving the Optimal Capital Structure

As we saw in Chapter 3, the neoclassical setting is not particularly relevant to explaining the existence of banks and their risk-management functions. This setting (and especially the M&M propositions) would suggest that a bank's capital structure is irrelevant for value creation and that there is no interconnection between the risk-management actions of a bank and the amount of equity capital it needs to hold.

Additionally, the M&M propositions would predict that capital structures should be distributed randomly across firms and industries. However, as can be observed in reality, banks have the highest leverage of firms in any industry.[3] As exemplified in Table 5.1, not only is the capital ratio of banks extremely low, but also fairly consistently so across the sampled 474 U.S. banks in the six selected asset-size buckets. Given this observation alone, one might be tempted to conclude that banks basically violate one or more of the M&M assumptions and that, therefore, the capital structure is relevant for banks and can be used to create value.[4] Under such conditions, the value of a bank is a function of its financial leverage.

This line of thought is not the focus of this chapter. It is not the intention here to develop a model for determining the optimal capital structure for banks that are trying to maximize value by trading off various leverage-related costs[5] against leverage-related benefits[6] when determining the opti-

---

[3]See Berger et al. (1995b), p. 394. Of course, there are always exceptions to the rule: some banks report BIS capital ratios of up to 76%. See Blanden (1999), p. 131.

[4]This means that banks will destroy value when they hold too much or too little capital. (If leverage is too low, hostile [leveraged] takeover bids [or financial restructuring from within] are likely and will bring the leverage closer to the optimal level. If the leverage is too high, this implies a high risk of bankruptcy and high associated financial distress costs). Adjusting the leverage can therefore create value.

[5]The costs of debt financing are, for example, the increased risk of bankruptcy that leads to higher financial distress costs and increased constraints and restrictions (i.e., incentives for suboptimal investment).

[6]The advantages of debt financing are, for example, that interest is tax deductible and that debt imposes discipline on the management.

TABLE 5.1 Bank Book Capital Ratios

Asset Size Bucket 1996 (in $bn)	0.5–1	1–2	2–5	5–10	10–30	> 30
Number of Banks	203	112	65	33	32	29
Tier-1 Capital/Average Assets (in %)	8.58	8.57	7.80	8.46	7.50	7.14
Total Capital (Tier-1 + Tier-2) / Risk-Weighted Assets (in %)	14.47	14.23	13.46	13.75	13.25	12.80

Source: Adapted from Davis and Lee (1997), p. 37. Tier-1 and Tier-2 capital are defined in the "Available Capital" section later in this chapter. Used with permission.

mum where the marginal effects equal out.[7] Typically, the reduced form of such models tries to find the optimal capital structure where the marginal tax benefits equal the marginal increase in bankruptcy costs.[8] As we saw in Chapter 3, in such models, it can be easily shown that risk management can contribute to value creation, because it allows the firm to increase its leverage while keeping the probability of bankruptcy low.

These simple models do not cover banking reality, because manifold other departures from the frictionless M&M world could explain the economically driven leverage of banks. For instance, the capital requirement is:

- Reduced by tax benefits
- Increased in response to a rise in the expected costs of financial distress[9]
- Ambiguous with regard to other transaction and agency costs[10]
- Reduced by regulation[11]

---

[7]See, for example, Johnson (1998), pp. 47–48, who refers to an extensive list of references to the literature.

[8]See, for example, Opler et al. (1997).

[9]See Berger et al. (1995b), pp. 396 and 399.

[10]Some of the agency problems between shareholders and debt holders are reduced by an increase in leverage, whereas some other conflicts between shareholders and managers are reduced when leverage is increased. Given that the corporate finance literature has made little progress in quantifying this trade-off, the net impact of economically induced capital requirements can be best described as ambiguous. See Berger et al. (1995b), p. 399.

[11]The introduction of the safety net and the subsequent effects on the capital ratios (as discussed in regard to Figure 5.1) basically insulates banks from market discipline. See Berger et al. (1995b), p. 400.

These factors make it difficult to determine the net value effect[12] of changes in bank leverage.

Although theory suggests that a firm should pick the mix of debt and equity that maximizes its firm value, the most common approach is to set the leverage close to that of the peer group to which the firm belongs.[13] If (and only if) firms in the peer group are similar in their fundamental characteristics (e.g., tax rates and cash-flow variability) and tend to be right in their capital structure choice, at least on average, it can be argued that this approach provides a shortcut to arriving at the optimum. It is likely to fail, however, when banks differ on any of these following characteristics:[14]

- Similarity of asset mix
- Relative risk in the loan portfolio
- Degree of concentration in the loan portfolio
- Level of loan loss reserves
- Ability to generate noninterest income consistently
- Similarity in characteristics of the local/regional economy

Nevertheless, this behavior could explain why banks have consistently low capital ratios (see Table 5.1).

Capital as Substitute for Risk Management to Ensure Bank Safety

However, when we view holding capital as a substitute for selling or hedging risks (as shown in Chapter 2[15])—which is the focus of this chapter—we can also see that Table 5.1 contains valuable information to prove some of the predictions made in Chapter 3: Smaller banks tend to have concentrated ownership and owner-managers,[16] suggesting that they prefer more risk management to less. Since they have only limited access to sophisticated risk

---

[12]Whereas bank debt and the associated monitoring by banks can increase firm value (see, for example, James [1987]), and hence also the leverage in firms (see, for example, Johnson [1998]), little is known on the (net) value effects of the capital structure in banks.

[13]See Damodaran (1997), pp. 465+, and Kimball (1998), p. 44.

[14]See Davis and Lee (1997), p. 38.

[15]See also Allen and Santomero (1996), p. 18, who state that it is not clear why alternate strategies like increasing the amount of equity are not superior given the high costs associated with risk management. For an opposite opinion, see Stulz (2000), pp. 4-41–4-42, who claims that financial instruments are the cheapest way to conduct risk management, but ignores the costs associated with establishing a risk-management function in that context.

[16]This is true at least in the U.S. market.

management,[17] they need to hold (relatively) more capital (which is confirmed in the data in Table 5.1). Additionally, other reasons may account for the relatively lower leverage of smaller banks.[18] Smaller banks tend to have:

- More operating risk[19] due to the lack of management depth
- A lack of fee-based income that has a stabilizing effect on the earnings volatility, thus making risk management less necessary[20]
- A lack of diversification of their credit portfolios (with geographical and/or industry concentrations).

Therefore, we can infer that the capital structure choice in banks is closely related to the underlying risks held on the books of a bank. The role of equity capital in banks is that of a substitute for transferring risk and, hence, that of a buffer that protects the bank against costly unexpected shocks to its capital base.[21] Equity capital, therefore, ensures a bank's safety.[22]

The Various Stakeholders' Interests in Bank Safety   As we have also seen in Chapter 2, all of a bank's stakeholders have an interest in the safety of the bank, but all have different views with regard to how much equity capital a bank should hold. We will discuss these different views and which role equity capital plays for all of the various stakeholder groups briefly below.

- **Depositors/customers:** Bank customers are those bank liability holders who are most interested in the bank's high credit quality, that is, they would like no risk[23] associated with the repayment of their

---

[17]It may not be worthwhile hiring an expensive risk professional for a part-time job.

[18]See Davis and Lee (1997), p. 38.

[19]Including business risk; for a definition see the "Operational Risk" section later in this chapter.

[20]Whereas an average of 38% of the earnings in the ">30 bn" bucket stem from fee-based income, only 18% do so in the "0.5–1 bn" bucket in Table 5.1.

[21]These shocks are costly—as we saw in Chapter 3—when the financial distress costs from high leverage are substantial and the transaction costs of raising new capital quickly are high for the bank, that is, when total risk matters. See Berger et al. (1995b), p. 398, also see Diamond and Rajan (1999), p. 4.

[22]See Diamond and Rajan (1999), p. 4. Additionally, bank capital has an effect on the bank's ability to refinance at low cost and on the bank's ability to extract repayment from, or its willingness to liquidate, borrowers. See Diamond and Rajan (1999), p. 42.

[23]This is because customers usually do not want to be compensated for increases in the bank's credit risk. They prefer a safe repayment of their deposits. Moreover, for many forms of deposits (e.g., checking accounts) no compensation for risk is possible because no interest is paid.

deposits and savings.[24] These credit-sensitive customers increase the importance of risk management and hence the amount of equity capital to be held by the bank.[25]

- **Bond holders:** Bond holders are also concerned about the likelihood of the repayment of their interest and principal. However, they are less credit sensitive because they are (and want to be) compensated for the risk they bear—often depending on the seniority[26] of their claim. External bond ratings are a useful, but only an imperfect, estimate of a bank's ability to repay its bond obligations. A bank with a higher default risk will need to pay its bond holders a higher rate of interest or will need to hold more equity capital instead. Therefore, a bank needs to understand how the uncertainty of outcomes (risk) of its activities affects its overall default risk and the degree of risk management required by that stakeholder group.

- **Shareholders:** Shareholders, as residual claimholders of a bank, are aware that their return[27] will fluctuate with the profits and losses of the bank, that is, they choose points further out on the risk-expected return frontier[28] than either of the other two stakeholder groups discussed so far, knowing that they are the first to be hit by adverse events. Shareholders are thus the stakeholder group that is least credit quality sensitive as long as they are compensated appropriately for their risk taking in the market.[29]

- **Regulators:** Banks differ from most other firms because they are protected by a regulatory safety net. By that we mean all government actions[30] that are intended to ensure the safety and soundness of the banking system, such as explicit[31] as well as implicit[32] deposit insurance, payment guarantees, access to the discount window, and so on, all of which protect banks from bankruptcy and the costs of

---

[24]See Merton (1995b).

[25]See Merton and Perold (1993), p. 16.

[26]For the sake of the argument, we distinguish between senior and junior bond holders, even though these groups might be further differentiated by the kind and quality of collateral backing their repayment.

[27]Shareholders care about dividend payments and share price appreciation. Share prices are determined by the bank's (expected future free) cash flows and the (expected) volatility of these free cash flows.

[28]See Berger et al. (1995a), p. 27.

[29]See Merton and Perold (1993), p. 16.

[30]Other than regulatory capital requirements.

[31]Which is only available in that form in the United States.

[32]Implicit deposit insurance induces government intervention if a bank is considered too big to fail. See Diamond and Rajan (1999), p. 39.

financial distress. This kind of regulation obviously affects the economically driven capital requirements of the other three stakeholder groups—and reduces them because regulation insulates banks from market discipline.[33]

Regulators[34] require banks to hold capital for very similar reasons as other uninsured creditors: To protect themselves against the costs of financial distress,[35] which they would have to bear, and the reduction in market discipline caused by the safety net. As can be seen in Figure 5.1, the capital ratios (defined as book equity as percent of assets) of U.S. commercial banks steadily declined between the 1840s and 1950s, from which point on they were fairly stable. Only following the implementation of the Basle (I) Accord,[36] when regulators around the world became worried about the erosion in capital ratios, can we observe an increase in the capital ratios, in the beginning of the 1990s, to the intended 8% (as depicted in the enlargement in Figure 5.1 below).

Even though the recent increase in capital ratios might also have been driven by market or economic concerns about the likelihood of financial

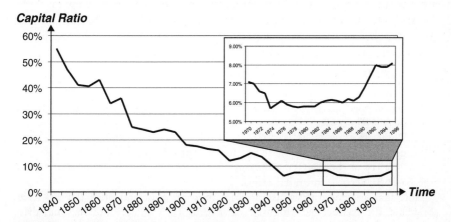

Figure 5.1 Capital ratios in U.S. banks over time.
Source: Adjusted from Berger et al. (1995b), p. 402. Enlargement taken from Davis/Lee (1997), p. 36, who focus on a broader sample of FDIC registered U.S. banks.

---

[33]See Berger et al. (1995b), p. 400.
[34]As representatives of the government, taxpayers, and so on.
[35]Note that regulators are vulnerable to the same costs of financial distress and expropriations of value as other creditors. See Berger et al. (1995b), pp. 403–404.
[36]See Basle Committee on Banking Supervision (1988).

distress in the banking system,[37] "it seems [nonetheless] plausible that regulatory changes accounted for much of the [changes] in capital ratios"[38] over time.[39]

The high social costs associated with threats to the soundness and stability of the international banking system[40] led regulators to try to achieve a higher degree of safety by requiring banks to hold a minimum amount of capital with the intention to lower the risk of bank failures. These capital ratios are, therefore, higher than what uninsured creditors[41] would require and are meant to protect the economy from negative externalities caused by bank failures—especially by systemic risk.[42] These external effects are also often neglected when determining economically driven capital requirements.[43]

In spite of the fact that this regulatory view is convincing from the standpoint of ensuring the safety of banks in specific and the banking system in general, it is unclear how it is interrelated with the economically driven views of the other three stakeholder groups (as described previously). On the one hand, the discussion above indicates that regulatory capital would exceed economically driven capital requirements because (1) it does include some of the externalities and (2) in order to be binding.[44] This binding, regulatory-required, minimum capital level can, therefore, in turn impose a significant cost on banks.[45] On the other hand, since the regulatory view takes the perspective of an uninsured bank creditor, regulators expect to bear some of the losses before the insured depositors, who would therefore have a higher (economically driven) capital requirement than regulators.

---

[37]Which is especially true for the early 1990s in the United States, caused by the Savings & Loan crisis.

[38]See Berger et al. (1995b), p. 403.

[39]Leading to both the decrease (e.g., after the introduction of the Federal Reserve Bank in 1914 or the FDIC in 1933) and increase (e.g., after the implementation of the Basle [I] Accord) in capital ratios.

[40]Note that systemic risk is also a major motivation behind the safety net itself. Systemic risk is associated with high social costs: The chain reaction that may damage the stability of the financial system can either lead to bank runs (on other solvent, but then illiquid banks; see *Economist* [1992], pp. 9+) or is transmitted quickly through the interbank markets to other banks (exacerbation of regional and macroeconomic difficulties, threatening of the payment system, and undermining of the effectiveness of the monetary policy; see Berger et al. [1995b], p. 425).

[41]See Berger et al. (1995b), pp. 404–405, and the extensive list of references to the literature mentioned there.

[42]See Berger et al. (1995b), p. 424.

[43]Note that we assume an imperfect world here.

[44]See Berger et al. (1995b), pp. 418–419. Regulatory capital requirements are also set higher for simple safety reasons, which in turn destroy value.

[45]See Davis and Lee (1997), p. 33.

Additionally, given the opaqueness of banks, it is impossible for outsiders—and even for regulators with some insight[46]—to determine the exact capital requirement. Therefore, regulators have to rely on higher capital requirements (than the private sector with the same perspective would) because they do not have the option to ration credit or their guarantees, or other means the private sector has for this. Regulatory requirements also have to differ from economically driven capital requirements because they have to be general, crude guidelines that cannot be tailored exactly to the riskiness of an individual bank.[47] The optimal regulatory capital ratio is, hence, likely to differ from the economically optimal capital ratio, and any deviation from that will reduce the value of the bank and will incur social costs.[48]

Therefore—given the focus of this book on value creation in banks—we adopt the purely economic perspective that encompasses the views and interests of *all* stakeholder groups to determine the (economically driven) capital requirement.

Available Capital Before we turn to how the differing views of the various stakeholders can be combined into a single (equity) capital amount, it is worthwhile to briefly discuss what regulators accept as capital when they compare their (relatively undifferentiated capital) requirements with the actual capital available at a bank. We will take the regulatory view as a starting point for our discussion of the purely economically driven view, because it is unclear in the first place what should be accepted as a buffer against unexpected losses and how the required capital amount should be compared to observable and actual capital amounts.[49] Table 5.2 provides an overview of the terms for this discussion.[50]

---

[46]This is true despite the fact that regulators (may) have an informational advantage because they have access to information during the examination process that the private sector does not have. See Berger and Davies (1994).

[47]Note that the unavoidable inaccuracies in setting the regulatory capital requirements will destroy value. For instance, the current risk-weighted (credit) assets approach (Basle [I] Accord) does not reflect the obvious determinants of credit risk such as the differences in credit quality across loans; concentrations of risk in a specific asset class or to a specific borrower, industry, or geography; or the covariances between these components.

[48]The optimal regulatory capital ratio would trade off between the marginal benefits from reducing the risk of bank failure and the marginal (social) costs of diminishing intermediation (i.e., banks would increase the prices to their customers to pass through the regulatory costs, and the customers would then do less business through banks). Inaccuracies in setting the regulatory capital requirement will worsen this trade-off. See Berger et al. (1995b), p. 425.

[49]Note that equity capital is a residual amount.

[50]Note that these four measures of capital may not be equal.

TABLE 5.2   Overview of Capital Concepts in Banks

	Regulatory[1]	Economic
Required	Simple, relatively undifferentiated capital requirement[2] based on a bank's assets = *Regulatory Capital*[3]	More granular, differentiated, and risk-related capital requirement = *Risk Capital*
Actual	Balance sheet-based capital measurement (Tier-1 and Tier-2 capital) = *Book Capital*[4]	Market-oriented capital measurement (?) = ?

Notes: [1]Neither regulatory nor book capital provides an ideal measure of the capital level required to support risky activities.
[2]The newly released Basle Accord takes a much more risk-related view.
[3]Regulatory Capital is the level of capital required for the institution by outside regulators.
[4]Book Capital is an accounting measure of the capital that the bank is actually holding, and can be observed on the balance sheet (assets minus liabilities).

From a theoretical point of view, capital that is available to be compared to the regulatory requirements should have the following three characteristics:[51]

- It should be a claim that is junior to the deposit insurers' one. This will create a buffer against losses before the government/regulators have to step in.[52]
- It should be "patient money," that is, a stable source of funds even during bank runs. It should, therefore, reduce the risk of bank runs and should allow the regulators time to evaluate the situation.
- It should reduce the banks' moral hazard incentives to exploit the benefits of the safety net by having excessive leverage or risk in their portfolios.

We can identify the following candidates[53] for regulatory capital, which we will briefly evaluate in turn:

---

[51]See Berger et al. (1995b), pp. 408–409.
[52]This characteristic is mostly relevant for a U.S.-type of government deposit insurance.
[53]Insured deposits are the most senior claims that should be protected (the most) against any losses (which is also the regulatory intention). They are, therefore, not even a candidate for regulatory capital.

■ **Equity (book) capital:** This is the most junior claim there is and cannot be withdrawn in times of crisis (making it "patient money"). However, equity capital may not always limit risk taking. Whereas equity limits risk taking in the form of (financial) leverage, it does not always limit portfolio risk taking—at least as long as it is not closely enough tied to portfolio risk, which is the case for book equity. Therefore, higher equity ratios do not always predict a lower probability of default and often explain little of the variation in bank performance.[54]

■ **Subordinated debt:** This is the second most junior claim after equity. It can be considered "patient money," since it usually has a long-term maturity and is difficult to redeem even in a crisis. Whereas it may increase the (financial) leverage risk of a bank, it can reduce portfolio risk taking: if subordinated creditors are not protected by deposit insurance (which they are usually not[55]), they have an incentive to closely monitor the bank's risk taking and restrict it if necessary.[56]

■ **Uninsured debt (senior debt and other uninsured deposits):** It immediately appears that these claims are not junior (enough). Since they are additionally not considered to be "patient money," because they are likely to be the first to be withdrawn during a "run,"[57] uninsured debt is not considered to be regulatory capital—even though it creates the incentive to more closely monitor the bank's risk taking.

Therefore, from a regulatory point of view, so-called Tier-1 and Tier-2 capital is accepted[58] as such a buffer. Both are actual (book) capital amounts

---

[54]As Berger et al. (1995b), p. 409, state after an extensive discussion of the literature: "The theoretical issue of how higher required equity ratios affect bank risk-taking is unresolved." Also, empirical evidence proves that higher equity ratios are associated with a lower default probability—although the relationship is often relatively weak.

[55]Differing views often assume that "too-big-to-fail" intervention applies even to subordinated debt and will, therefore, reduce the willingness to monitor.

[56]This view of the subordinated debt holders is similar to the view of many stakeholder groups: being exposed to downside risk that exceeds shareholder equity.

[57]For instance, according to Gup (1998), p. 53, Continental Illinois (which defaulted in 1984) relied heavily on uninsured (senior) deposits provided by institutional investors (because they were not allowed to run branch banks under the then-valid regulation). After the first rumors of trouble at Continental Illinois, these uninsured deposits were the first hit by the "run" leading to withdrawals of US$ 8 billion per day.

[58]For instance, the EU Capital Adequacy Directive based on the recommendations of the Basle Committee defines these capital amounts in detail.

and can be easily observed from the bank's balance sheet. They are defined—in broad terms—as follows:

- Tier-1 capital ("basic" equity)[59]
  - Equity capital[60]
  - Disclosed reserves
- Tier-2 capital ("supplementary" capital)[61]
  - Undisclosed reserves[62]
  - Revaluation reserves[63]
  - General provisions/general loan-loss reserves[64]
  - Hybrid debt capital instruments[65]
  - Subordinated term debt[66]

Note that, since these two capital amounts are determined on the basis of accounting/balance sheet information, they have the additional[67] advantage that they are relatively stable over time and can be objectively determined—which is sensible from a regulatory point of view.

However, one of the problems with regard to this balance-sheet-based

---

[59]Without discussing the specifics, one can deduce, in general, from the regulatory guidelines that Tier-1 capital—net of goodwill—must at least amount to 50% of Tier-1 + Tier-2 capital.

[60]Issued and fully paid common shares and (perpetual noncumulative) preference shares are considered equity capital under this definition.

[61]Consequently, Tier-2 capital must amount to less than Tier-1 capital.

[62]As an exception to the rule, these cannot be identified in the published balance sheet.

[63]In order to reflect their current value, assets valued at historic costs are allowed to be revalued to their market values under certain circumstances.

[64]Reserves held against presently unidentified losses that are freely available to meet losses that subsequently materialize and that are limited to not exceeding 1.25% of the bank's risk-weighted assets.

[65]For instance, the following instruments may qualify for inclusion: titres participatifs and titres subordonnés à durée indéterminée in France, Genussscheine in Germany, perpetual debt instruments in the United Kingdom, and mandatory convertible debt instruments in the United States. The qualifying criteria for such instruments are in line with the above defined characteristics: (1) they are unsecured, subordinated, and fully paid-up; (2) they are not redeemable at the initiative of the holder or without the prior consent of the supervisory authority; (3) they are available to participate in losses without the bank being obliged to close down its operations.

[66]Unlike instruments included in the previous category, "hybrid debt capital instruments," these instruments are not normally available to participate in the losses of a bank. For this reason, these instruments are limited to a maximum of 50% of Tier-1 capital.

[67]Meaning, besides meeting the previously defined characteristics.

approach is that it is difficult to measure equity, because it is a residual claim on the bank and depends on how the bank's assets and liabilities are valued. Therefore, the book value of equity might not be suitable because it measures most on-balance-sheet assets and liabilities on an historical cost basis (that may deviate substantially from fair actual [market] values—and can lead to gains trading[68]) and does not include most off-balance sheet items. Accounting-based measures of capital may, therefore, overstate the actual value of capital that is available to absorb losses.[69]

A possible alternative to using the book value of equity is the usage of the market value of equity. However, this amount is not suitable for regulatory purposes because:

- It is also difficult to compute the economic value of equity as the difference of the market value of assets minus the market value of liabilities. Most of the bank's assets are not traded or not tradable in the open market because the bank has specific knowledge or informational advantages, and outside investors are not willing to buy those assets because of this asymmetric information. Therefore, no market value can be determined for many bank assets.[70]
- The observable market capitalization of the bank's traded shares is too volatile a measure[71] and, therefore, prone to not satisfying the previously mentioned characteristics.[72]

---

[68]Gains trading is defined as the (fire) sale of assets whose market value is above book value, to cash in the profit and to increase the reported equity. However, only assets whose value is below book value then remain, exacerbating the lack of equity.

[69]See Cordell and King (1995).

[70]Note that the introduction of fair value accounting does not really help to resolve this problem. Marking tradable financial instruments to market is not the problem. The question is how the market value of an essentially unmarketable asset (e.g., a loan to an information-intensive small customer) can be derived. Also, establishing the effect of fair value accounting on hedge positions can be difficult: If the hedge position is marked to market but not the underlying exposure, this can create artificial volatility in the reported earnings and equity, even if the bank as a whole has a matched book.

[71]Markets are very sensitive to changing conditions. For instance, even though Barclays Bank only had an overall credit exposure of GBP 300 million to Russia, it experienced a GBP 2 bill. decline in market capitalization during the "Russian" crisis/default in the fall of 1998.

[72]Additionally, using the market value of equity is not suitable for regulatory purposes because it contains the value of the bank's limited liabilities, that is, the value of its option to put the bank's assets on the creditors. As Berger et al. (1995b) explain, regulators should exclude the value of this put option from their considerations because they bear all the costs when the option is exercised. One must also consider that the market value of equity could trade at a discount on its book value.

Note that many banks hold capital in excess[73] of the regulatory minimum as an extra buffer[74] to avoid regulatory intervention[75] in the form of "prompt corrective action" and the subsequent costs associated with increased oversight and restricted business activities.[76]

Required Capital from an Economic Perspective   After discussing the regulatory views on (equity) capital in some detail, we now turn to the economic view on capital (requirements) in banks that focuses on its buffer function against future, unidentified losses.[77] We depart here from the traditional form of risk management of holding equity capital as an "all-purpose" cushion for absorbing risk without the need to know the exact source for the unexpected losses.[78] We have already identified hedging as an alternative form of risk management—which is a very targeted means of limiting risk, because the bank needs to specify exactly what kind and which quantity of risk it is exposed to in order to determine the most suitable (financial) risk-management instrument. However, once the firm has acquired the necessary capability of measuring and quantifying its risks and decided to keep some risks on its books, it can use this knowledge to tailor the capital requirement to it—from a purely risk-based and insider's perspective.

Before we turn to the detailed determination of the economically driven capital requirement in the "Ways to Determine Economic Capital for Various Risk Types in Banks (Bottom-Up)" section, we will discuss how the various bank stakeholders' interests can be aligned so that they can agree on a single capital amount. We will then briefly discuss how the bank determines whether it has sufficient capital funds to support the riskiness of its portfolio of assets.

As we have already described above, the various stakeholders of a bank have very different views on how much capital a bank should hold. These different opinions can be best summarized in Figure 5.2.

Figure 5.2 depicts (in stylized form) the overall value distribution of a bank, whose shape is determined by the riskiness of the bank's assets. As can

---

[73]Additionally, excess capital can be held as extra cushion for unexpected negative shocks (see Berger et al. [1995b], p. 418), for lucrative new business (i.e., unexpected profitable) opportunities, or for acquisitions.

[74]Failure to meet these capital requirements will not necessarily result in default, but will probably trigger regulatory intervention against the management of the group.

[75]See Berger et al. (1995b), p. 403.

[76]See Davis and Lee (1997), pp. 36–37.

[77]However, Schmittmann et al. (1996), pp. 651 and 653, argue that equity is not a cushion because all of the troubled banks in Germany over the past 50 years only tapped into their equity resources to default at the same time.

[78]See Merton (1995a), p. 464.

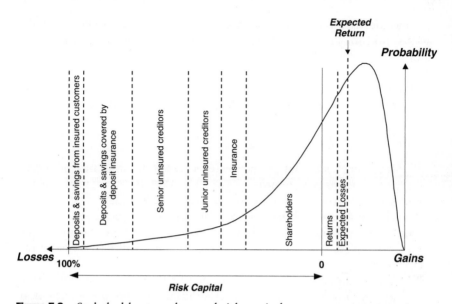

Figure 5.2 Stakeholder tranches and risk capital.
Note: The distribution is only schematically correct. In particular, the Expected Return of the distribution should be much farther to the left than actually depicted.

be easily seen, the bank has a positive expected return on its assets.[79] However, since the bank holds a risky portfolio, the outcomes fluctuate around this expected value. Because a large part of a typical bank's portfolio consists of credit assets, which can experience rare, but very severe downside events, the distribution is skewed to the left and is non-normal. The bank will, therefore, suffer large losses with a positive probability and will default[80] at some threshold level. At that critical point, the bank will incur distress costs, which are the main driver and rationale behind conducting risk management and why total risk matters to banks. However, the more capital a bank holds (in this case the critical threshold level is moved to the left), the less likely it becomes that losses will exceed the default point and trigger default. Holding more capital, therefore, makes the bank safer, which is consistent with the regulatory view.

---

[79]Otherwise, the bank would/should exit/restructure its current business.
[80]Unlike regulatory default—which occurs when a bank's net assets (i.e., book assets minus book liabilities) fall below the required minimum (regulatory) capital amount set by the regulators—a bank enters economic default when the market value of its assets falls below the market value of its liabilities.

Since decreases in asset values are associated with economic losses, the various stakeholders have to bear these losses in the sequence of the seniority of their claims:

1. As we will shortly see, the bank should set aside an insurance pool that covers all expected (actuarial) losses (especially from credits). This pool is the first tranche that is hit by losses and is fed by deducting "insurance premiums" from (expected) returns on the portfolio of assets.
2. Incurring losses that exceed the resources of this insurance pool then eat up (expected) returns.
3. Once there are no revenues left, shareholders—as residual claimholders—will have to bear all subsequent losses.[81]
4. Since the bank has bought insurance[82] to cover the declines in the value of some assets,[83] insurance companies will bear some of the subsequent losses.
5. Then junior debt holders—knowing that they bear the highest probability of being hit by losses exceeding equity (and insurance)—bear the next tranche of losses.
6. Senior debt holders are next hit by even higher losses. Note that 5. and 6. are both uninsured creditors of the bank.
7. Since at some level of losses between 5. and 6. the likelihood of a "bank run" will increase dramatically, the government/regulatory bodies will step in and try to rescue the bank (see the previous description). Nonetheless, if depositors are hit by losses, deposit insurance in almost all banking systems will cover all losses up to a certain amount (either provided by the government, as in the U.S. for US$ 100,000 per customer,[84] or by private organizations formed by the banking industry[85]).
8. Only deposits and savings exceeding this amount are then nonrecoverable for the insured customers, who then have to bear losses exceeding this amount.

---

[81]Once the shareholder funds are eaten up, (economic) default occurs.

[82]A good example is credit (re-) insurance for a decline in the value of credit assets (for instance, provided for export financing by government (backed) agencies like EXIM (Export-Import Bank) in the United States or Hermes in Germany). Some other insurance policies will cover losses before the equity tranche is hit (e.g., fire insurance for the bank's buildings).

[83]In most cases the shareholders also have to bear the deductible before the claim on the insurance can be exercised.

[84]See Stulz (2000), p. 4-5.

[85]For instance the "Einlagensicherungsfonds" in Germany, see, for example, Obst and Hintner (1991), p. 689.

Figure 5.2, therefore, summarizes economic reality, although the size of the various tranches is not intended to be drawn to scale and is not meant to indicate the actual size and split of the losses borne by the respective stakeholder groups at any bank. However, it clearly indicates that—at one end of the spectrum—for example, insured customers only have to bear the most extreme of losses and are only hit in the rare event when their deposits with the bank exceed the insured maximum amount. Both the low probability of such an event happening and the small amount of losses borne by insured depositors are represented in the smallest of tranches in the far left of Figure 5.2.[86] At the other end of the spectrum, shareholders always bear all residual losses and basically provide so-called "credit enhancement",[87] which they also do in reality.[88]

In reality, however, the different stakeholder groups might not be aware of this sequential loss taking and do require the bank to hold capital up to the level where they would be hit by losses. This explains, on the one hand, why—looking at the problem from an individual point of view—all different stakeholder groups have different capital requirements to make their investment basically risk-free, as has already been indicated. On the other hand, from a collective point of view, all stakeholders are interested in ensuring that the bank holds enough capital so that they will not be hit by a bank run. This is true because they all have an interest to ensure—that the bank, by holding enough capital, will be able to operate at the same level of capacity, that is, to maintain the same level of business and associated profitability.[89] Since credit-sensitive customers will only enter into a transaction when they believe that the bank itself will survive until the contract is due, most of the value of a bank is dependent on the bank being able to continue operations. The entire bank and its capital—as measured by the credit standing of the overall bank—back this belief.[90] We will address both views in turn below.

Risk Capital If all stakeholders wanted their investment free of default risk, the bank would need to hold capital for 100% of the potential losses. However, since there are considerable costs associated with holding capital for banks, this would be too expensive.[91]

---

[86]Note that this is exactly what customers require before they enter into doing business with a bank.

[87]See for example, Merton and Perold (1993), p. 19.

[88]Note that the picture drawn in Figure 5.2 is very similar to the various tranches of a credit default swap/credit securitization, which basically works according to similar principles.

[89]See Matten (1996), pp. 8–9.

[90]See Merton and Perold (1993), p. 17.

[91]See for example, Schröck (1997), p. 112, for a discussion of this point.

Alternately, the bank could decide to split up the losses so that each stakeholder group would reach its required level of confidence, but would, however, have to bear some of the losses, while being compensated for doing so on fair economic terms. We will describe below how the bank could achieve this.[92]

We can define *Risk Capital* as the minimum capital amount that has to be invested to buy insurance that fully protects the value of a bank's net assets against a decline in value,[93] so that completely default-free financing of these net assets can be obtained.[94] Risk capital therefore differs from regulatory capital (which attempts to measure risk capital according to a particular accounting standard[95]) and from cash capital (i.e., up-front cash that is required to execute the transaction and that is a component of the working capital of a bank).[96, 97]

Risk capital is, thus, completely determined by the shape of the distribution of the changes in the value (i.e., the riskiness) of net assets. Note that, as long as the liabilities of a bank are fixed and not contingent on the payoff of the bank's (gross) assets (which is usually the case), the gross assets show the same fluctuations as the net assets. It is, therefore, sufficient to know the distribution of the value changes in the gross assets to determine the required amount of risk capital of a bank.

However, when the liabilities are completely contingent (e.g., mutual funds usually make all of their payoffs completely contingent on the value development of their gross assets, that is, customer returns exactly match the fund's portfolio returns[98]), the riskiness of the net assets is reduced to zero (even though the gross assets are risky). Therefore, under such circumstances, the bank would not have to hold any risk capital.[99]

Despite the fact that in reality a bank's liabilities are partly fixed and partly contingent (i.e., the riskiness of the net assets will, in general, differ from the riskiness of the gross assets), we are assuming for our further discussion that all bank liabilities are fixed. Note that, since the underlying

---

[92]For definitions of risk capital that ignore this global approach, including all stakeholder groups, see, for example, Lister (1997), p. 19, and Johanning (1998), p. 46.
[93]As indicated in Figure 5.2.
[94]See Merton and Perold (1993), p. 17. Note that net assets are defined as gross assets minus (default-free) customer liabilities in this context.
[95]However, the regulatory approach has, as stated previously, a different focus and, therefore, measures up to a different level, because the regulators' view is very similar to that of uninsured creditors.
[96]Therefore, the amount of initially provided cash capital (both debt and equity) is irrelevant in that context from a purely economic point of view.
[97]See Merton and Perold (1993), p. 17.
[98]The returns are (usually) net of an administration fee for managing the portfolio.
[99]See Merton and Perold (1993), pp. 23–24.

asset (and its riskiness) that is the basis to determine the required amount of risk capital is always the same, risk capital does not at all depend on the form of the financing of the (net) assets.

We also assume that all of the required risk capital is initially provided by the shareholders as residual claimholders of the bank. However, as we have already indicated above, since holding equity capital for all possible circumstances is too expensive, the shareholders decide to buy asset insurance[100] either (explicitly) from external third-party insurers or (implicitly) from the bank's other stakeholders. By doing so, shareholders redistribute the risk of the loss of the risk capital to the other stakeholders of the bank.

The other stakeholders initially required a completely risk-free investment. Therefore, they could only ask for the risk-free rate to compensate them for their investment. By taking some of the default risk, they now require compensation above the risk-free rate, which should be commensurate with their respective risk taking. Note that this difference above the risk-free rate is an insurance premium paid by the shareholders (from the risk capital resources they provided in the first place). It is not equivalent to the liability held by a specific stakeholder group (which is an accounting view of the problem), but rather represents the economically measured decline in asset value that hits the respective tranche in the order of seniority.

The same result can be achieved when we view this redistribution of taking tranches of the bank's overall default risk as a sequence of reinsurance contracts.[101] Here, the shareholders will sell all default risk they do not want to bear to the next most junior tranche, which in turn will also sell the remainder of the default risk they do not want to hold to the next most junior tranche, and so forth.

What is important here is that all stakeholders agree on the overall amount of risk capital that is necessary to back the amount of losses that can be accumulated by the bank's assets. How this overall amount is split between the various stakeholders is the result of a negotiation process until an (economic) equilibrium is reached. This negotiation process can be very complex[102] and is not the focus of this book. However, as an indication of how that process for reaching equilibrium might work, one can think of the following: Even though the creditors decide to bear the risk of being hit by losses for a fair economic compensation, they might not be willing to also bear the expected value of financial distress costs. Therefore, they will de-

---

[100]As shown—under simplifying assumptions—by Merton and Perold (1993), p. 19, the provision of asset and liability insurance is economically equivalent and therefore has the same price.

[101]See Merton and Perold (1993), p. 23, footnote 15, and their list of references to the literature.

[102]Therefore, we present a "reduced" version for determining risk capital below.

mand a higher compensation in the form of higher interest rates on their debt and will, in doing this, shift the entire costs of financial distress to the shareholders, who may choose to reduce these expected costs by decreasing the leverage. Therefore, banks may decrease their leverage to assure creditors that the bank is safe and to align the interests of shareholders and debt holders.[103]

The beauty of this eventual synthesis of interests of the various individual views of the stakeholder groups is that, in the end, everybody holds exactly that part of the overall risk of losses that they want to bear. For instance, shareholders are economically only interested in the "normal" fluctuations in the bank's asset value (i.e., the "normal" volatility of returns), for which they are compensated in the capital markets. Since they are residual claimholders, they are willing to bear all losses—however, only up to a certain amount. If that amount is exceeded, other stakeholders have to step in and bear all subsequent losses.

Economic Capital   Even if all stakeholder groups individually bear the part of the losses they want to bear, they all have an interest that the bank is not being hit by a "bank run" because that would immediately result in the discontinuation of the bank's operations. Therefore, all stakeholders are collectively interested in the point when this critical threshold[104] is reached and how much capital (at minimum) they need to hold in order to avoid this occurrence.

Economic default is triggered when the market value of the equity falls below the market value of the liabilities. However, this event might not coincide with a bank run, even though it results—at least—in a default on the bank's junior liabilities. Since these junior liabilities are, even from a regulatory perspective, accepted as a buffer to protect the other stakeholders from experiencing losses (Tier-2 capital), one could argue that banks have (implicitly) received a "guarantee"[105] that specifies that they can continue to operate even after defaulting on their subordinated liabilities.[106]

The bank's credit standard is typically expressed by the (external agency) rating of its senior (uninsured) debt. This benchmark is the basis for most market participants' and bank customers' business decisions.[107] It is, there-

---

[103]See Berger et al. (1995b), pp. 396 and 399.

[104]Meaning the threshold that triggers a bank run.

[105]In the absence of such a guarantee, defaulting on subordinated debt would automatically result in insolvency.

[106]One could further argue that such a guarantee would result in costly legal actions from the junior debt holders to recover their losses, which would increase the likelihood of a bank run.

[107]Even though external agency ratings might be also available for junior bonds.

fore, plausible that the critical threshold that triggers a bank run is reached as soon as losses exceed junior liabilities and hit the senior debt tranche.[108] Therefore, many market players argue that a bank should hold, from an economic perspective, (risk) capital (at least) up to this senior debt level. This indicates that the amount of capital that a bank would need to hold is dependent on its desired safety level (or target credit rating) of its senior debt.

However, it is worthwhile to mention that the rating agencies' evaluation of how secure a bank's senior debt is considers more factors than just equity requirements. For instance, S&P consider size, asset strength and credit quality, geographic and funding diversity, and earnings as more important.[109] Capital ratios are only a secondary factor.[110] Similarly, Fitch IBCA ranks risk as being the most important component of their rating analysis (credit, market, legal, operational risk), followed by funding, capital, performance/ earnings, market environment and planning, prospects, ownership, auditing, and contingent liabilities.[111] In contrast, Moody's does not rank their seven "pillars" of their bank analysis; these are operating environment (competitive, regulatory, institutional support), ownership and governance, franchise value, recurring earning power, risk profile (credit, market, liquidity and asset-liability management, agency reputation, operational) and risk management, economic capital analysis, and management priorities and strategies.[112]

In order to focus on the critical threshold when a bank run occurs, we will simplify the complex picture and negotiation process that defines the split of the loss-taking between the various tranches and will abstract certain aspects of some of them.

First, we will neglect externally bought insurance, for two reasons:

- This tranche is explicitly paid for and therefore appears as an asset on the bank's (economic) balance sheet.
- There is no need for a bank to hold capital for that tranche because the insurance will cover the losses.

---

[108]Also see the example of Continental Illinois described previously as potential further proof of this argument.

[109]DeStefano and Manzer (1999), pp. 28–31, point out that S&P's rating factors are (in order of importance): economic risk, industry risk, customer base, regulation and deregulation, ownership structure, market position, diversification, management and strategy, credit risk, market risk, trading risk, funding and liquidity, capitalization, earnings, risk management, and financial flexibility.

[110]See Davis and Lee (1997), p. 39.

[111]See Fitch IBCA (1998), pp. 4 and 11–17.

[112]See Theodore et al. (1999), pp. 11–43.

Second, we will ignore the deposit insurance and the deposits and savings tranche, for the following reasons:

- The insured amount will be paid from external sources (mostly backed by a government guarantee). Therefore, there is no need for the bank to hold capital internally.
- The part of deposits and savings exceeding the insured amount is very small. Trying to estimate the extreme tail of the assumed value distribution is associated with very high uncertainty and can, therefore, hardly be done with meaningful accuracy.
- All of this only becomes relevant when the bank is in default and the bank run has already occurred. Regulators will intervene in order to minimize the probability of this happening as early as possible.

Therefore, we can simplify the illustration in Figure 5.2 to the one depicted in Figure 5.3. Note that the asset distribution is drawn without the three tranches that we have ignored. It, therefore, has a slightly different shape and does not cover all possible losses. Even though the tranches "left" of the senior debt tranche are ignored, the critical threshold level is still driven by the concern to secure the repayment of all of these tranches by avoiding a bank run. To differentiate the estimated capital requirement up to this critical threshold level from the amount of risk capital derived previously, we use the industry-standard label for this and call it *Economic Capital*.

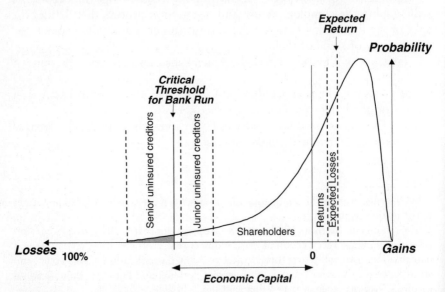

Figure 5.3 Economic capital.
Note: Again, the Expected Return should be farther to the left than actually depicted.

Economic capital is an estimate of the overall level of capital necessary to guarantee the solvency[113] of the bank at some predetermined confidence level[114] that is consistent with the target credit rating of its senior debt.[115] It is, therefore, risk capital that is estimated up to a critical threshold level and provided by shareholders and junior debt holders.[116] Even though economic capital is (like risk capital) a fictional amount of capital[117]—and therefore different from (book) equity capital—it takes a very similar view to that of the regulatory standpoint.

However, there are some problems associated with the economic capital approach. First and foremost, it is only a shortcut to the full-blown economic analysis of determining (the various tranches of) risk capital. It does, therefore, not look at the overall value distribution, and determines the required capital amount only at a—(at least at first sight) more or less arbitrarily chosen—level of confidence. However, the economic reality is, as we have shown previously, not as simple as this, and one should keep in mind that the various stakeholders would eventually have to bear their tranche of the losses. Additionally, and as stated previously, using the asset value distribution to determine economic capital is only valid when the bank's liabilities are fixed and not contingent.

Nonetheless, economic capital might be the only practicable way to estimate how much capital is necessary, because it tries to avoid specifying the complex negotiation process as required to determine the amount of risk capital while still adopting a risk-related perspective that is much more accurate than the regulatory approach. It has, therefore, developed into the best practice standard for doing this in the banking industry. Moreover, economic capital is an amount that is comparable to actual capital levels, as we will see shortly when we discuss capital adequacy in the economic world.

Additionally, economic capital has the advantage that it uses an observable benchmark to determine the critical (bank run) threshold and, hence, the required capital. External agency ratings are a calibrated indicator of

---

[113]That is, avoiding a bank run.

[114]The objective of the regulatory approach is also to require an adequate cushion for depositors and senior lenders against a loss in asset value. Even though no confidence level is specified, the intention is similar to that of economic capital: to define a level of capital that will ensure solvency. However, the "one-size-fits-all approach" is just a simplification of the economic reality, and the risk weights that are used do not adjust for the degree of concentration/diversification in the bank's asset portfolio. However, this view is about to change for credit risk (see Basle II) and has already changed for market risk (VaR is allowed to be used for regulatory purposes).

[115]See Davis and Lee (1997), p. 34.

[116]As explained previously, we ignore the insurance tranche in this world.

[117]As Davis and Lee (1997), p. 34, put it, economic capital is a theoretical construct.

how likely it is that a bank's senior debt will be hit by losses. Rating agencies regularly publish[118] the default probabilities of their ratings. For instance, the AA-rated senior debt of a bank typically has a default probability of between 1 and 3 basis points (bps).[119] Therefore, it is easy to determine the critical threshold as the point of the distribution where the confidence level that the senior debt experiences no losses is 99.97%.[120] This point, slightly exceeding the junior debt tranche, is indicated in Figure 5.3.[121]

In practice, banks actually seem to try and hold enough (risk) capital so that the credit rating for their senior debt matches the required safety level (and default probability).[122] This guarantees that these banks have access to both low costs of funds and credit-sensitive customers (especially for off-balance sheet activities).[123] Since the bank's shareholders have a special interest in that being the case,[124] they might be willing to provide more capital than they otherwise would. However, it seems unlikely—given the above discussion—that they provide all of the economic capital,[125] as it is often falsely claimed.

Determining Capital Adequacy in the Economic Perspective   Deriving the capital requirement from a purely economic perspective (i.e., from a more granular, differentiated, and risk-related view than regulatory capital) by itself is not meaningful. A bank would like to determine this requirement in order to find out whether it holds enough capital to satisfy its various stakeholders' interests.

However, for both risk capital and economic capital, the alignment with observable capital is unclear, because they are both fictional[126] amounts of capital that have no real-life counterpart and both have nothing to do with the cash capital invested in a bank.[127]

The comparison with a reference amount of (actual) capital is most

---

[118]See, for example, Standard & Poor's (1997).

[119]See, for example, Brand and Bahar (1999), p. 10.

[120]The confidence level is (1 − default probability on the senior debt). Obviously, we assume here a 3 bps default probability when determining the confidence level.

[121]Note that this is not the 99.97% confidence level of the distribution plotted.

[122]See, for example, Zaik et al. (1996).

[123]See Davis and Lee (1997), pp. 36–37.

[124]Banks are, therefore, different from other companies. For a discussion on why banks are different in their assets and functions, see, for example, Diamond and Rajan (1999), p. 2.

[125]Including the junior debt holders' tranche.

[126]Therefore, both risk capital and economic capital seem to be binding constraints and hence need to be linked to actual capital.

[127]They are determined by a decline in the (net) asset value (and not in the book value) that hits the tranches sequentially.

difficult for risk capital. On the one hand, the value of (book) equity (determined as residual) is usually not equal to the bank's risk capital (which is determined by the riskiness of the net assets of the bank). The true economic values of debt and equity are determined by netting the asset insurance against the provision of risk-free cash capital and risk capital. However, since most of the insurance is provided implicitly, it does not appear on the balance sheet. On the other hand, one is tempted to assume that risk capital borne by the shareholders is closely aligned with some market-based metric.[128] However, as Merton and Perold show,[129] when they determine the (market) value of the equity by treating it as a put option on the firm, the value of the equity can be larger than what is required as insurance contribution (risk capital from shareholders). This is due to the fact that the other stakeholders also bear some of the total risk.

Ideally, the economic capital requirement should also be compared to an economic measure of capital that corresponds to the intrinsic value of the bank.[130] As discussed previously in the regulatory context, there is no good approximation for such an actual capital amount because of the lack of data needed to arrive at such a figure. However, since the use of economic capital represents a very similar view to the regulatory one—while being more accurate—we could use an approximation of intrinsic value based on book capital as the reference for determining capital adequacy.[131] If we take the regulatory definition of Tier-1 and Tier-2 capital and replace general loan-loss reserves with the insurance pool held for expected losses[132] and subtract subordinated debt, we can derive such a proxy for actually available equity.[133] But, despite the difficulties with that benchmark already discussed in the regulatory view, we would still have to add the more difficult to observe junior debt holders tranche to this amount in order to arrive at a completely comparable number.[134] For simplicity, it seems sensible to add (back) subordinated liabilities instead to arrive at the final benchmark. As discussed in the regulatory view, the market value of equity is too volatile a measure and

---

[128]For the difficulties arising from using market-value-based actual capital numbers, please refer to the discussion of such numbers in the section on capital adequacy in the regulatory context above.

[129]See Merton and Perold (1993), pp. 22–23.

[130]See, for example, Drzik et al. (1998a), p. 27.

[131]This seems also to be reasonable because economic capital is a simplified version of the full-blown risk capital approach.

[132]This insurance pool is also based on the riskiness of the loan portfolio.

[133]Unlike book equity, this number contains (hidden) reserves and allows for reasonable, market-driven adjustments to the book value of assets.

[134]Of course, the expected revenues are ignored in the regulatory view because they are too uncertain to count as reliable buffer for losses.

would always exceed economic capital because it considers all components of the (net) asset value distribution.[135]

The comparison of (actual) available capital with that economically required[136] is often extended by matching both up against regulatory capital,[137] which is the most binding capital requirement.[138] Often, when regulatory capital exceeds the economic capital requirement, banks decide to sell, securitize, or syndicate assets,[139] because all of these actions have the effect of reducing regulatory capital more than economic capital.[140] These actions—often labeled as regulatory arbitrage[141]—obviously have the (at least from the regulatory standpoint) unintended effect that they increase the bank's portfolio risk, which will eventually result in both higher regulatory and economic capital requirements.

Summary and Consequences

We can infer from the above discussion that a bank's capital providers accomplish three basic functions:[142]

- All bank stakeholders provide cash capital so that the bank can conduct its underlying business.

---

[135]We will address this problem in more detail in the "Suggestion of an Approach to Determine Economic Capital from the Top Down" section later in this chapter.
[136]For a discussion of what to do about the surplus or deficit between the two capital measures from a value-oriented perspective, see e.g., Drzik et al. (1998a), p. 27.
[137]Also, for an extensive discussion of a practical approach for resolving the capital structure problem in banks, on aligning the various capital types, and what to do with excess capital, see Davis and Lee (1997), pp. 33+. They suggest the following procedure: (1) Determine economic capital as a lower bound for the bank's target level of capital. (2) Compare (1) against the regulatory minimum requirement (as indicated above, most banks want to exceed (2) in order to avoid the risk of regulatory intervention; alternately, they could decide how much regulatory intervention and hence business disruption they are willing to accept—observing the volatility of (1) over time can indicate how large the margin should be). (3) Balance (1) and (2) against other factors such as peer group capital ratios (which could be dangerous, see above), the bank's (future) risk appetite, its target credit rating on senior debt, and so on.
[138]Since risk/economic capital is only a fictional amount of money and it is difficult to match it with actual capital, it is obvious that it is less binding than the regulatory requirement.
[139]See Davis and Lee (1997), p. 41.
[140]However, as Jagtiani et al. (1995) and Calstrom and Samolyk (1995) claim, securitizations are driven more by economic than by regulatory factors (e.g., to exploit comparative advantages while still maintaining sufficient [economic] capital).
[141]See, for example, Pfingsten and Schröck (2000), p. 9.
[142]See Merton and Perold (1993), p. 23.

■ All stakeholders are sellers of (asset) insurance to the bank. Whereas depositors sell only very little or no insurance,[143] the bulk of the insurance is borne by debt holders and shareholders (unless it is purchased from external third-party providers).
■ The cash required to purchase the (asset) insurance, that is, the risk capital, is (initially) provided by the bank's shareholders.

The suggested approach to determine the required amount of risk capital is much more accurate than the regulatory "one-size-fits-all approach," since it uses the overall shape of the distribution of the changes in (net) asset values, which is determined by the riskiness of the portfolio of assets. And it is also more flexible: banks have relatively liquid "balance sheets,"[144] that is, they can fundamentally change the size and the risk profile of their overall portfolio in very little time. An adequate measure should, therefore, be able to take that into account. Regulatory capital does not appear to be able to reflect that necessity as short-term, as it should do, whereas risk capital does.

All stakeholders agree on this overall amount of risk capital from their individual perspective, because they want their investment to be initially risk-free, meaning the bank to be safe. They also all agree on the split of this amount in a complex negotiation process (which is not specified in this book), and this results in each stakeholder group's holding the most appropriate tranche of the overall risk of loss by selling insurance to the shareholders. However, from a collective point of view, the required capital amount can also be determined at a critical threshold level where a bank run becomes likely. This is most likely the level where senior debt is hit by losses, but it is basically independent of the tranches as determined above. Even though this approach is a shortcut to the full-blown risk capital approach (i.e., why we called it economic capital), it takes a calibrated default benchmark (the external agency rating) as the reference level and is very similar to the regulatory view (although more accurate). It is, therefore, accepted as the best practice approach in the banking industry and even about to be accepted by regulatory bodies.[145]

The challenge with the economically determined capital requirements is, however, to translate them into specific instruments and/or balance sheet numbers. A comparison to objective, balance-sheet-based capital measures

---

[143]Because they want their deposits and savings repaid with certainty and do not want to worry about whether or not the bank will still be solvent when their contracts are due.
[144]See Merton and Perold (1993), p. 16.
[145]See Basle Committee on Banking Supervision (2001), p. 22.

can be useful, but is less meaningful since they are theoretical constructs that fit with neither the accounting nor the regulatory world.

Given the focus of this book on value creation, we will not use regulatory capital requirements as a constraint to our framework—neither at the single transaction level nor at the bank/business unit level where it would be a binding restriction. This is the case because a value perspective is completely market driven (and therefore binding by itself), and the regulatory requirements are about to change and have been adopting this economic perspective more and more.[146]

However, since risk capital is a theoretical construct, the traditional performance and value creation measures (which are mostly accounting based) will not work any longer. We will develop an appropriate new metric in the next chapter.

To put it in a nutshell, risk capital links the bank's riskiness to its concern about financial distress situations—which are caused by the totality of the risks it faces—and is economically driven rather than being a general (regulatory) rule. Not only, therefore, does it determine best the (economically) required amount of capital, but we can also identify it as a candidate for an adequate risk measure for banks. We will discuss its practical workings in more detail in the next section.

DERIVATION OF ECONOMIC CAPITAL

Before we turn to the detailed derivation of economic capital in banks in the "Ways to Determine Economic Capital for Various Risk Types in Banks (Bottom-Up)" and "Suggestion of an Approach to Determine Economic Capital from the Top Down" sections later in this chapter, it is worthwhile to classify the types of risk a bank is typically exposed to, each of which contributes to the total (economic) risk of the bank (see the "Types of Risk" section, which follows), and to introduce value-at-risk-based risk measures in the "Economic Capital as an Adequate Risk Measure for Banks" section later in this chapter.

Types of Risk

As already defined in Chapter 2, risk arises from any transaction or business decision whose result may deviate from the expected outcome, that is, due to unexpected (negative) changes in its value. For banks, we can draw a

---

[146]See Basle Committee on Banking Supervision (1999) and (2001) as well as *Economist* (2001), p. 71.

simplified picture of their business activities (see Figure 5.4) and can infer three broad categories of risk:[147]

- **Credit risk:** Risk of loss due to unexpected deterioration in the credit quality of borrowers (including transfer or country risk)
- **Market risk:** Risk of loss due to unexpected changes in market prices or liquidity (including all balance sheet risks)
- **Operational risk:** Risk of loss due to:
  - **Business (or banking) risk:** Unexpected changes in business volume, margins, and costs (including legal and regulatory risks)
  - **Event risk:** One-time events that are not related to business risk/operations (including political risks and natural disasters)

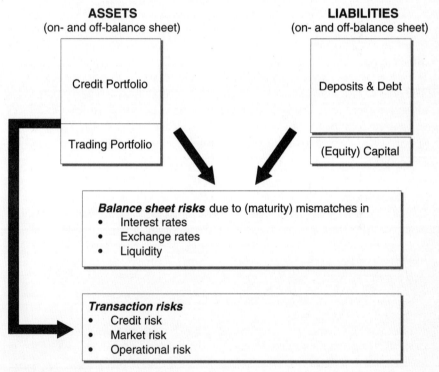

Figure 5.4 Types of risk in banks.
Source: Adapted from Reyniers (1991), pp. 10+, *Economist* (1993), pp. 4 and 35, Grübel et al. (1995), pp. 624–625, and Schröck (1997), pp. 34–36.

---

[147]A detailed definition will be given below when discussing the determination of the capital requirement for them.

Since most of these (credit and market) risks are (continuous) financial risks, we can find (standardized) models for quantifying them and also adequate hedging instruments in the capital markets. This is, however, less the case for operational (discontinuous) risks.[148]

Economic Capital as an Adequate Risk Measure for Banks

The driving force behind determining a bank's capital requirement is its risk exposure.[149] However, for risk management to be useful in order to maximize bank value, we need to define how risk is measured.[150] As we have seen above, an adequate risk measure for banks needs to correspond to the probability that a bank will lose business[151] because of its own credit risk,[152] which is in turn driven by the total risk of the portfolio of its transactions. Understanding and being able to determine this relationship is the key to a bank's benefiting from conducting risk management.

For assets that are marked to market we can directly observe a change in value.[153] This change corresponds to a gain or loss, that is, it directly affects a bank's return. Note that the probability that a negative change in value (i.e., a loss) can create problems for a bank cannot be reduced to zero.[154] The goal of risk management is to keep this probability of experiencing such a serious event (i.e., financial distress) as low as possible—at least at a level so that customers are not concerned.[155] In order to do so, the bank has to specify for itself a critical loss size[156] and a probability that it will (not) be exceeded.

---

[148]Glaum and Förschle (2000) rank various risk types for German industrial companies by degree of importance. They find the following order: (1) business risk, (2) financial risk, (3) firm-specific (event) risk, and (4) macroeconomic risk. However, there seems to be a gap between this perceived importance of risks and the degree of risk management, which is mostly due to the lack of models and (standardized) hedging instruments for (1) and (3).

[149]See also Merton (1995a), p. 470, for a discussion of this point.

[150]See Stulz (2000), p. 4-3.

[151]For banks, it is important that all stakeholders be extremely sensitive with regard to small changes in the creditworthiness of the financial institution, making shareholder value very fragile and the management of risks crucial.

[152]See Stulz (2000), p. 4-7.

[153]By that we are able to derive the distribution of the gains and losses of the portfolio.

[154]See Stulz (2000), p. 4-7.

[155]Note that customers already accepted a certain probability when they decided to put money into the bank.

[156]As we will see below, for determining VaR, this does not have to be the confidence level where the critical threshold for a bank run would be experienced.

The risk measure, which calculates that a certain dollar loss[157] will only be exceeded with a given probability (α%) over some measurement period, is commonly called (in the banking industry) value at risk (VaR).[158] Therefore, we can generally define:

$$p(\Delta V \le - \text{VaR}) \le \alpha\%^{159} \qquad (5.1)$$

where p = probability
ΔV = change in value V; in this case a loss

The VaR at the probability level of α% is equivalent to the α-quantile of the cumulative probability distribution F of the changes in the portfolio value[160] (see Figure 5.5) between now and date H,[161] the end of the predetermined measurement period. Therefore, without making any assumptions about the shape of the distribution function, we can reformulate:

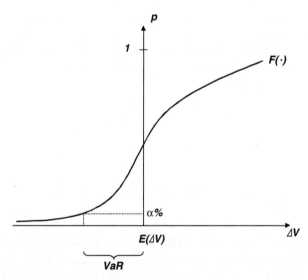

Figure 5.5 Value at risk.

---

[157]This loss is usually stated as a positive number.
[158]See Stulz (2000), p. 4-9.
[159]See for example, Schröck (1997), p. 43, and Hirschbeck (1998), p. 143, with a list of references to the literature.
[160]See Stulz (2000), p. 4-9.
[161]See Artzner et al. (1997), p. 68. In a later version of their paper, Artzner et al. emphasize that the definition relates to future values, that is, expectations; see Artzner et al. (1999), p. 205.

$$F(-\text{VaR}) = \alpha\% \text{ or } -\text{VaR} = F^{-1}(\alpha) \tag{5.2}$$

So, the bank can be $(1 - \alpha\%)$ confident that losses will not exceed VaR, that is, at the (one-sided) confidence level $(1 - \alpha\%)$ the maximum loss will be VaR.

This kind of risk measure is exactly what we are looking for. VaR reflects the bank's concern with the risk of bad outcomes that would create problems for the bank. Neither volatility, systematic risk, nor unsystematic risk provides this information. And except for the normal distribution (as we will see below for market risk), there is no direct relationship between VaR and volatility or systematic and unsystematic risk. Hence, it is possible that the volatility of a complex financial instrument increases, while the VaR falls at the same time.

Despite the theoretical concerns with VaR, which we will discuss shortly, it has many advantages that are especially relevant for practical purposes. These can best be explained by the following example: A bank has access to a lottery ticket for free (with a small probability of a large payoff). Adding the lottery ticket to the bank's portfolio of assets will increase the volatility of the potential gains and losses in the value of the bank's portfolio. If the bank focuses on volatility as a risk measure,[162] it would conclude that taking the lottery ticket would make it worse off.[163] However, taking the lottery ticket will not increase the VaR of the bank's portfolio. This is exactly what we would have concluded from an economic point of view. It makes sense to take the lottery ticket because it is associated only with upside potential. Therefore, we can conclude that volatility is not useful in evaluating the risk of lower-tail events. This downside risk is even less well captured by systematic or unsystematic risk than by volatility.[164]

The reason for computing VaR is that the bank wants to measure, monitor, and manage the size of lower-tail outcomes so that the probability of financial distress is low. It is, therefore, crucially important for banks to understand the distribution of value changes in their portfolio.

As is depicted in Figure 5.5, VaR measures risk as a negative deviation from the expected outcome[165] and is, hence, a measure for total risk. Therefore, we can use VaR as the basis for a "common currency" to quantify each of the three types of risk as defined in the last section in a similar way by:

---

[162]We assume here that the bank is averse to increases in risk.

[163]See Artzner et al. (1997), p. 68. This is only true when we ignore the expected return as the second decision component.

[164]For constructing the distribution of value changes of the portfolio, the beta to a broad market portfolio is not useful.

[165]VaR, therefore, matches exactly our definition from Chapter 2.

■ Estimating the distribution of value changes for the specific risk type at the end of the measurement horizon H

■ Estimating the confidence level to the target solvency probability for the institution

■ Measuring the difference between the expected outcome and the chosen confidence level

Note that whereas VaR is typically calculated at a somewhat arbitrarily chosen confidence level of the distribution (mostly 95% or 99%), we are now adopting the above-derived industry standard for doing so. As mentioned, this industry standard is called *economic capital* and scales the VaR confidence level to the critical threshold level for avoiding a bank run by determining what amount of capital is necessary to protect the bank against adverse events. Economic capital is therefore a function of the riskiness of the bank's activities and the bank's desired likelihood of solvency.[166]

Therefore, we determine

$$p[(X_H - E(X_H)) \geq \text{economic capital}] \leq \alpha\% \qquad (5.3)$$

the probability that the distance between the expected (positive) outcome X and the unexpected (negative) deviations $E(X)$ will not exceed economic capital, which guarantees a certain solvency, with $\alpha\%$ at/until time H.[167] Note that we assume that we do not need to hold economic capital for the positive expected return X_H that accumulates until the end of the measurement period,[168] because it will eventually also be available as a buffer against losses (see above), but that we need to hold economic capital for all risks, including bank-specific risks.

By doing so, we accept that economic capital is—as has been shown— a shortcut to adopting the full-blown economic perspective to determine risk capital. However, economic capital seems to be the only realistic practical way to determine the required amount of capital. Note that—unlike VaR that takes some confidence level of the overall distribution—economic capital quantifies risk at a confidence level of what matters most to banks: securing the senior debt tranche with a certain probability.

So far, we have only provided a very general idea of how economic capital is determined. We now turn to the specifics of quantifying economic capital for each of the three broad types of risk for banks. Even though the "devil" is in the details and the actual implementation of these approaches (which

---

[166]This is indicated (objectively) by the credit rating of the bank's senior debt.
[167]Deviations may be due to losses, credit defaults, and so on.
[168]As defined above, net of expected (credit) losses.

we will not address), we are trying to provide a detailed and consistent approach that:

- First, estimates economic capital "bottom-up," that is, we:
  - Determine economic capital for each of the three types of risk separately, transaction by transaction, at a consistent time horizon (H) and confidence level, and then aggregate the capital requirements within that risk type.[169] Note that, therefore—unlike what is often done for limiting and management purposes—only the marginal risk contribution of a single transaction to the (total) portfolio risk (of that risk type) counts.
  - Then aggregate economic capital across the three types of risk in a second step by using the correlations between these three categories, because this seems to be the only realistic way to accomplish aggregation up to the bank level.
- Second, uses a newly suggested "top-down" approach to provide a meaningful check for the bottom-up results.

Ways to Determine Economic Capital for Various Risk Types in Banks (Bottom-Up)

In this section, we will discuss how economic capital can be calculated from the bottom up for the various types of risk introduced previously. We will start with credit risk, followed by market risk, and then operational risk. We will close this section by discussing potential ways of aggregating economic capital across these three types of risk and concerns with using such a bottom-up approach.

Credit Risk   In this section we will first define what credit risk is. We will then discuss the steps to derive economic capital for credit risk and the problems related to this approach.

Definition of Credit Risk   Credit risk is the risk that arises from any nonpayment or rescheduling of any promised payments (i.e., default-related events) or from (unexpected) credit migrations (i.e., events that are related to changes in the credit quality of a borrower) of a loan[170] and that gives rise to an economic loss to the bank.[171] This includes events resulting from changes in

---

[169]This, of course, assumes that our total risk measure can be broken down to the single transaction level.

[170]This includes all credit exposures of the bank, such as bonds, customer credits, credit cards, derivatives, and so on.

[171]See Ong (1999), p. 56. Rolfes (1999), p. 332, also distinguishes between default risk and migration risk.

the counterparty as well as the country[172] characteristics. Since credit losses are a predictable element of the lending business, it is useful to distinguish between so-called expected losses and unexpected losses[173] when attempting to quantify the risk of a credit portfolio and, eventually, the required amount of economic capital.

Steps to Derive Economic Capital for Credit Risk In this section, we will discuss the steps for deriving economic capital for credit risk. These are the quantification of Expected Losses (*EL*), Unexpected Losses (*UL* – Standalone), Unexpected Loss Contribution (*ULC*), and Economic Capital for Credit Risk.

Expected Losses (EL) A bank can expect to lose, on average, a certain amount of money over a predetermined period of time[174] when extending credits to its customers. These losses should, therefore, not come as a surprise to the bank, and a prudent bank should set aside a certain amount of money (often called loan loss reserves or [standard] risk costs[175]) to cover these losses that occur during the normal course of their credit business.[176]

Even though these credit loss levels will fluctuate from year to year, there is an anticipated average (annual) level of losses over time that can be statistically determined. This actuarial-type average credit loss is called expected loss (*EL*), can therefore be viewed as payments to an insurance pool,[177] and is typically calculated from the bottom up, that is, transaction by transaction. *EL* must be treated as the foreseeable cost of doing business in lending markets. It, therefore, needs to be reflected in differentiated risk costs and reimbursed through adequate loan pricing. It is important to recognize that *EL* is not the level of losses predicted for the following year based on the

---

[172]Country risk is also often labeled transfer risk and is defined as the risk to the bank that solvent foreign borrowers will be unable to meet their obligations due to the fact that they are unable to obtain the convertible currency needed because of transfer restrictions. Note that the economic health of the customer is not by definition affected in this case. However, any changes in the macroeconomic environment that lead to changes in the credit quality of the counterparty should be captured in the counterparty rating.

[173]See, for example, Ong (1999), pp. 56, 94+, and 109+, Kealhofer (1995), pp. 52+, Asarnow and Edwards (1995), pp. 11+.

[174]Following the annual (balance sheet) review cycle in banks, this period of time is most often set to be one year.

[175]See for example, Rolfes (1999), p. 14, and the list of references to the literature presented there.

[176]See Ong (1999), p. 56.

[177]See, for example, the ACRA (Actuarial Credit Risk Accounting) approach used by Union Bank of Switzerland as described in Garside et al. (1999), p. 206.

economic cycle, but rather the long-run average loss level across a range of typical economic conditions.[178]

There are three components that determine EL:

■ The probability of default (PD),[179] which is the probability that a borrower will default before the end of a predetermined period of time (the estimation horizon typically chosen is one year) or at any time before the maturity of the loan
■ The exposure amount (EA) of the loan at the time of default
■ The loss rate (LR), that is, the fraction of the exposure amount that is lost in the event of default,[180] meaning the amount that is not recovered after the sale of the collateral

Since the default event D is a Bernoulli variable,[181] that is, D equals 1 in the event of default and 0 otherwise, we can define the expected amount lost (EL) in the event of a default as follows (see Figure 5.6):

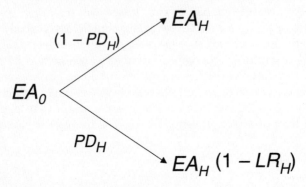

Figure 5.6   Deriving expected losses.
Source: Adapted from Ong (1999), p. 101.

---

[178]Note that Expected Losses are the unconditional estimate of losses for a given (customer) credit rating. However, for a portfolio, the grade distribution is conditional on the recent economic cycle. Thus, losses from a portfolio as predicted by a rating model will have some cyclical elements.

[179]Often also labeled expected default frequency (EDF); see, for example, Kealhofer (1995), p. 53, Ong (1999), pp. 101–102.

[180]Therefore also called severity, loss given default (LGD), or loss in the event of default (LIED); see, for example, Asarnow and Edwards (1995), p. 12. The loss rate equals (1 – recovery rate), see, for example, Mark (1995), pp. 113+.

[181]See Bamberg and Baur (1991), pp. 100–101, that is, a binomial $B(1; p)$ random variable, where $p = PD$.

Hence,

$$EL_H = EA_H - E(EA_H)$$

$$= EA_H - [(1 - PD_H) \cdot EA_H + PD_H \cdot (EA_H \cdot (1 - LR_H))]$$

$$= PD_H \cdot EA_H \cdot LR_H \qquad (5.4)$$

where PD_H = Probability of default up to time H (horizon)
EA_H = Exposure amount at time H
LR_H = Loss rate experienced at time H
$E(\cdot)$ = Expected Value of $(\cdot)$

The expected loss experienced at time H (EL_H), that is, at the end of the predetermined estimation period, is the difference between the promised exposure amount (EA_H) at that time (including all promised interest payments) and the amount that the bank can expect to receive at that time—given that, with a certain probability of default (PD_H) between time 0 and H, a loss ($EA_H \cdot LR_H$) will be experienced.[182]

Therefore, *EL* is the product of its three determining components, which we will briefly describe in turn below:

1. **Probability of default** (*PD*): This probability determines whether a counterparty or client goes into default[183] over a predetermined period of time. *PD* is a borrower-specific estimate[184] that is typically linked to the borrower's risk rating, that is, estimated independently[185] of

---

[182]This assumes—for the sake of both simplicity and practicability—that all default events occurring between time 0 and the predetermined period of time ending at H will be considered in this framework. However, the exposure amount and the loss experienced after recoveries will be considered/calculated only at time H and not exactly at the time when the actual default occurs.

[183]Default is typically defined as a failure to make a payment of either principal or interest, or a restructuring of obligations to avoid a payment failure. This is the definition also used by most external rating agencies, such as Standard & Poor's and Moody's. Independently of what default definition has been chosen, a bank should ensure an application of this definition of default as consistent as possible across the credit portfolio.

[184]This assumes that either all credit obligations of one borrower are in default or none of them.

[185]This is not true for some facility types such as project finance or commercial real estate lending where the probability of default (*PD*) is not necessarily linked to a specific borrower but rather to the underlying business. Additionally, *PD* is not independent from the loss rate (*LR* – as discussed later), that is, the recovery rates change with the credit quality of the underlying business. This requires obviously a different modeling approach (usually a Monte Carlo simulation), whose specifics will not be discussed in this book.

the specifics of the credit facility such as collateral and/or exposure structure.[186] Although the probability of default can be calculated for any period of time, probabilities are generally estimated at an annual horizon. However, *PD* can and does change over time. A counter-party's *PD* in the second year of a loan is typically higher than its *PD* in the first year.[187] This behavior can be modeled by using so-called migration or transition matrices.[188] Since these matrices are based on the Markov property,[189] they can be used to derive multiperiod *PD*s—both cumulative[190] and marginal[191] default probabilities.[192]

The remaining two components reflect and model the product specifics of a borrower's liability.

2. **Exposure amount** (*EA*): The exposure amount *EA*, for the purposes of the *EL* calculation, is the expected amount of the bank's credit exposure to a customer or counterparty at the time of default. As described above, this amount includes all outstanding payments (including interest) at that time.[193] These overall outstandings can often be very different from the outstandings at the initiation of the credit. This is especially true for the credit risk of derivative transactions (such as swaps), where the quantification of *EA* can be difficult and subject to Monte Carlo simulation.[194]

3. **Loss rate** (*LR*): When a borrower defaults, the bank does not necessarily lose the full amount of the loan. *LR* represents the ratio of actual losses incurred at the time of default (including all costs associated with the collection and sale of collateral) to *EA*. *LR* is, therefore, largely a function of collateral. Uncollateralized, unsecured

---

[186]Amortization schedules and credit lines (i.e., limit vs. utilization) can have a significant impact on the exposure amount outstanding at the time of default. The same is true for the credit exposure of derivatives.

[187]This statement is only true (on average) for credits with initially low *PD*s.

[188]See, for example, Standard & Poor's (1997) and Moody's Investor Services (1997).

[189]See, for example, Bhat (1984), pp. 38+.

[190]That is the overall probability to default between time 0 and the estimation horizon *n*.

[191]That is the probability of not defaulting until period *i*, but defaulting between period *i* and *i*+1. These are also often derived as forward *PD*s (similar to forward interest rates).

[192]However, this can—by definition—only reflect the average behavior of a cohort of similarly rated counterparties and not the customer-specific development path.

[193]Obviously, there are differing opinions as to when the measurement actually should take place. See Ong (1999), pp. 94+.

[194]See, for example, Dowd (1998), p. 174.

loans typically have much higher ultimate losses than do collateralized or secured loans.

EL due to transfer or country risk can be modeled similarly to this approach and has basically the same three components (*PD* of the country,[195] *EA*, and *LR* due to country risk[196]). However, there are some more specific aspects to consider, which we will not deal with in this book. For instance, since a borrower can default due to counterparty and country risk at the same time, one would need to adjust for the "overlap" because the bank can only lose its money once.

Likewise, we will not deal with the parameterization[197] of this model in this book, but there are many pitfalls when correctly determining the components in practice.

By definition, *EL* does not itself constitute risk. If losses always equaled their expected levels, there would be no uncertainty, and there would be no economic rationale to hold capital against credit risk. Risk arises from the variation in loss levels—which for credit risk is due to unexpected losses (*UL*). As we will see shortly, unexpected loss is the standard deviation of credit losses, and can be calculated at the transaction and portfolio level. Unexpected loss is the primary driver of the amount of economic capital required for credit risk.

Unexpected loss is translated into economic capital for credit risk in three steps, which are—as already indicated—discussed in turn: first, the standalone unexpected loss is calculated (see the "Unexpected Losses" section which follows). Then, the contribution of the standalone *UL* to the *UL* of the bank portfolio is determined (see the "Unexpected Loss Contribution" section later in this chapter). Finally, this unexpected loss contribution (*ULC*) is translated into economic capital by determining the distance between *EL* and the confidence level to which the portfolio is intended to be backed by economic capital (see the "Economic Capital for Credit Risk" section later in this chapter).

---

[195]Typically estimated using the input from the Economics/Research Department of the bank and/or using the information from the spreads of sovereign Eurobonds, see Meybom and Reinhart (1999).

[196]The calculation of *LR* due to country risk is broken into (the product of) two parts: (1) loss rate given a country risk event, which is a function of the characteristics of the country of risk (i.e., where *EA* is located) and (2) the country risk type, which is a function of the facility type (e.g., recognizing the differences between short-term export finance and long-term project finance that can be subject to nationalization, and so on).

[197]We will not deal with the estimation and determination of the various input factors for specific customer and product segments. See, for a discussion, Ong (1999), pp. 104–108.

Unexpected Losses (UL–Standalone) As we have defined previously, risk arises from (unexpected) variations in credit loss levels. These unexpected losses (UL)[198] are—like EL—an integral part of the business of lending and stem from the (unexpected) occurrence of defaults and (unexpected) credit migration.[199] However, these ULs cannot be anticipated and hence cannot be adequately priced for in a loan's interest rate. They require a cushion of economic capital, which needs to be differentiated by the risk characteristics of a specific loan.[200]

UL, in statistical terms, is the standard deviation of credit losses, that is, the standard deviation of actual credit losses around the expected loss average (EL). The UL of a specific loan on a standalone basis (i.e., ignoring diversification effects) can be derived from the components of EL. Just as EL is calculated as the mean of a distribution, UL is calculated as the standard deviation of the same distribution.

Recall that EL is the product of three factors: PD, EA, and LR. For an individual loan, PD is (by definition) independent of the EA and the LR, because default is a binary event. Moreover, in most situations, EA and the LR can be viewed as being independent.[201] Thus, we can apply standard statistics to derive the standard deviation of the product of three independent factors and arrive at:[202]

$$UL = EA \cdot \sqrt{PD \cdot \sigma_{LR}^2 + LR^2 \cdot \sigma_{PD}^2} \qquad (5.5)$$

where σ_{LR} = Standard deviation of the loss rate LR
σ_{PD} = Standard deviation of the default probability PD

Since the expected exposure amount EA can vary, but is (typically) not subject to changes in the credit characteristics itself, UL is dependent on the default probability PD, the loss rate LR, and their corresponding variances, σ^2_{LR} and σ^2_{PD}. If there were no uncertainty in the default event and no uncertainty about the recovery rate, both variances would be equal to zero,

---

[198]For a detailed discussion of UL see, for example, Ong (1999), Chapter 5, pp. 109–118.

[199]See Ong (1999), p. 111.

[200]To be more precise and as we will see shortly below, the amount of economic capital depends on the risk contribution of a specific loan to the overall riskiness of a loan portfolio.

[201]However, in practice it is not clear as to whether the assumption of statistical independence is well justified. See Ong (1999), p. 114. If they were not independent, a covariance cross-term needs to be introduced, but would have only a small overall impact on the absolute amount of UL in practice.

[202]See Ong (1999), pp. 116–118, for a detailed derivation.

and hence *UL* would also be equal to zero, indicating that there would be no credit risk. For simplicity, we have ignored the time index in this derivation. But all parameters are estimated, as was done previously, at time *H*.

Note that, since default is a Bernoulli variable with a binomial $B(1;PD)$-distribution:[203]

$$\sigma^2_{PD} = PD \cdot (1 - PD) \tag{5.6}$$

Since it is typically difficult in practice to measure the variance of the loss rate σ^2_{LR} due to the lack of sufficient historical data, we will have to assume in most cases a reasonable distribution for the variations in the loss rate. Unfortunately, unlike the distribution for *PD*, the loss rate distribution can take a number of shapes, which result in different equations for the variance of *LR*. Possible candidates are the binomial, the uniform, or the normal distribution. Whereas the binomial distribution overstates the variance of *LR* (when a customer defaults, either all of the exposure amount is lost or nothing), the uniform distribution assumes that all defaulted borrowers would have the same probability of losing anywhere between 0% and 100%. Therefore, the most reasonable assumption is the normal distribution, because of the lack of better knowledge in most cases.[204] The shape of this assumed normal distribution should take into account the empirical fact that some customers lose almost nothing, that is, almost fully recover, and it is very unlikely that all of the money is lost during the work-out process.[205]

Like *EL*, *UL* can also be calculated for various time periods and for rolling time windows across time. By convention, almost always one-year intervals are used.[206] Hence, all measures of volatility need to be annualized to allow comparisons among different products and business units.[207] Again, the same methodology can be applied to derive the *UL* resulting from country risk using the three components of country *EL*.

---

[203]See Bamberg and Baur (1991), p. 123.

[204]Also see Ong (1999), p. 132.

[205]As mentioned above, even unsecured loans almost always recover some amount in the bankruptcy court, see, for example, Eales and Bosworth (1998), p. 62, or Carty and Lieberman (1996), p. 5.

[206]Sec Ong (199), p. 121.

[207]For convenience and again due to lack of data, the volatility of *LR* is assumed to be constant over time (intervals).

Unexpected Loss Contribution (ULC)   Credit risk cannot be completely eliminated by hedging it through the securities markets like market risk.[208] Even credit derivatives and asset securitizations can only shift credit risk to other market players. These actions will not eliminate the downside risk associated with lending. However, they can transfer credit risk to the market participant best suited to bear it, because the only way to reduce credit risk is by holding it in a well-diversified portfolio (of other credit risks).[209] Therefore, we need to change our perspective of looking at credit risk from the single, standalone credit to credit risk in a portfolio context.

The expected loss of a portfolio of credits is straightforward to calculate because *EL* is linear and additive.[210] Therefore:

$$EL_P = \sum_{i=1}^{n} EL_i = \sum_{i=1}^{n} EA_i \cdot PD_i \cdot LR_i \qquad (5.7)$$

where EL_P = Expected loss of a portfolio of *n* credits.

However, when measuring unexpected loss at the portfolio level, we need to consider the effects of diversification because—as always in portfolio theory—only the contribution of an asset to the overall portfolio risk matters in a portfolio context. In its most general form, we can define the unexpected loss of a portfolio UL_P as:

$$UL_P = \sqrt{\sum_{i=1}^{n} \sum_{j=1}^{n} \omega_i \omega_j \rho_{ij} UL_i UL_j} \qquad (5.8)$$

where

$$\sum_{i=1}^{n} \omega_i = 1 \text{ and } \omega_i = \frac{EA_i}{\sum_{i=1}^{n} EA_i} \qquad (5.9)$$

ω_i = Portfolio weight of the *i*-th credit asset
ρ_{ij} = Correlation that default or a credit migration (in the same direction) of asset *i* and asset *j* will occur over the same

---

[208]Credit risk only has a downside potential (i.e., to lose money), but no upside potential (the maximum return on a credit is limited because the best possible outcome is that all promised payments will be made according to schedule).
[209]See Mason (1995), pp. 14–24, and Ong (1999), p. 119. As Mason shows, the same argument can be applied to the management of insurance risk.
[210]See Ong (1999), p. 123.

predetermined period of time (usually, again, between time 0 and H [one] year)

UL_i = Unexpected Loss of the i-th credit asset as defined above in Equation (5.5).

Therefore, considering a loan at the portfolio level, the contribution of a single UL_i to the overall portfolio risk is a function of:

- The loan's expected loss (EL), because default probability (PD), loss rate (LR), and exposure amount (EA) all enter the UL-equation
- The loan's exposure amount (i.e., the weight of the loan in the portfolio)
- The correlation of the exposure to the rest of the portfolio

To calculate the unexpected loss contribution[211] ULC_i of a single loan i analytically, we first need to determine the marginal impact of the inclusion of this loan on the overall credit portfolio risk. This is done by taking the first partial derivative of the portfolio UL with respect to UL_i (for loan i):

$$ULMC_i \equiv \frac{\partial UL_P}{\partial UL_i} = \frac{\partial \left(UL_P^{\,2}\right)^{1/2}}{\partial UL_i} = \left(\frac{1}{2}\right) \cdot \left(UL_P^{\,2}\right)^{-1/2} \cdot \frac{\partial \left(UL_P^{\,2}\right)}{\partial UL_i}$$

$$= \left(\frac{1}{2UL_P}\right) \cdot \frac{\partial \left(\sum_{j=1}^{n}\sum_{k=1}^{n} UL_j \cdot UL_k \rho_{jk}\right)}{\partial UL_i} = \frac{\sum_{j=1}^{n} UL_j \rho_{ij}}{UL_P} \qquad (5.10)$$

where $ULMC_i$ is the marginal contribution of loan i to the overall portfolio unexpected loss.

Note that in the above formula, the marginal contribution only depends on the (UL-) weights of the different loans in the portfolio, not on the size of the portfolio itself. In order to calculate the portfolio volatility attributable to loan i, we use the following property for a marginal change in portfolio volatility:

$$dUL_{Port} \equiv \sum_{i=1}^{n} \frac{\partial UL_P}{\partial UL_i} \cdot dUL_i = \sum_{i=1}^{n} ULMC_i \cdot dUL_i \qquad (5.11)$$

---

[211]Note that we follow the argument made by Ong (1999), p. 133, in this discussion and ignore the weights w_i in the derivation of ULC. We can do so if we assume that UL_i is measured in dollar terms rather than as a percentage of the overall portfolio.

The marginal contribution of each loan is constant if the weights of each loan in the portfolio are held constant. Hence, integrating the above equation, holding the weight of each loan constant (i.e., UL_i/UL_P is constant, which is true for practical purposes on average), we obtain:

$$UL_{Port} \equiv \sum_{i=1}^{n} ULMC_i \cdot UL_i \qquad (5.12)$$

Therefore, the portfolio UL can be viewed to split into n components, each of which corresponds to the marginal loss volatility contribution of each loan multiplied by its standalone loss volatility. Hence, we define the total contribution to the portfolio's UL as:[212]

$$ULC_i \equiv ULMC_i \cdot UL_i = \frac{\sum_{i=1}^{n} UL_j \rho_{ij}}{UL_P} \cdot UL_i \qquad (5.13)$$

It is easy to see from the above formula that ULC has the important property that the sum of the ULCs of all loans will equal the portfolio-level UL (i.e., the sum of the parts equals the whole, which is exactly the intended result):[213]

$$\sum_{i=1}^{n} ULC_i = \sum_{i=1}^{n} UL_i \frac{\sum_{j=1}^{n} UL_j \rho_{ij}}{UL_P} = \frac{\sum_{i=1}^{n} \sum_{j=1}^{n} UL_i \cdot UL_j \cdot \rho_{ij}}{UL_P} = \frac{UL_P^2}{UL_P} = UL_P \qquad (5.14)$$

Assuming now that the portfolio consists of n loans that have approximately the same characteristics and size ($1/n$), we can set $\rho_{ij} \equiv \rho =$ constant (for all $i \neq j$). Rewriting Equation (5.8) according to standard portfolio theory:

$$UL_P = \sqrt{\sum_{i=1}^{n} \sum_{j=1}^{n} cov_{i,j}} = \sqrt{\sum_{i=1}^{n} var_i + \sum_{j,i \neq j}^{n} cov_{i,j}} \qquad (5.15)$$

where $cov_{i,j}$ is defined as the covariance and var_i as the variance of losses; one could further derive:

---

[212]See Ong (1999), p. 126, for more details on his derivation of this equation pp. 132–134.
[213]See Ong (1999), p. 127.

$$UL_P = \sqrt{\sum_{i}^{n} UL_i^2 + 2\sum_{j,\, i<j}^{n} \mathrm{cov}_{i,j}} = \sqrt{\sum_{i}^{n} UL_i^2 + 2\sum_{j,\, i<j}^{n} \rho UL_i UL_j}$$

$$\approx \sqrt{n \cdot UL_i^2 + 2\frac{n(n-1)}{2} \cdot \rho \cdot UL_i^2} = \sqrt{[n + \rho n(n-1)] \cdot UL_i^2} \qquad (5.16)$$

and hence:

$$UL_P = UL_i \sqrt{n + \rho(n^2 - n)} \qquad (5.17)$$

Using the assumption of similar credits within the portfolio previously described, we can now rewrite:

$$ULC_i = \frac{UL_P}{n} = \frac{1}{n} UL_i \sqrt{n + \rho(n^2 - n)} = UL_i \sqrt{\frac{1}{n} + \rho\left(1 - \frac{1}{n}\right)} \qquad (5.18)$$

which reduces for large n to:

$$ULC_i = UL_i \sqrt{\rho} \qquad (5.19)$$

Combining Equation (5.13) with (5.19) and rearranging the terms, we can arrive at:

$$\sqrt{\rho} = \frac{\sum_{j=1}^{n} UL_j \rho_{ij}}{UL_P} \qquad (5.20)$$

which clearly shows that ρ is the (weighted) average correlation between loans in the portfolio (as was assumed above).

This derivation provides some important insights:

■ If one tried to estimate the portfolio UL by using Equation (5.8), one would need to estimate $[n(n-1)]/2$ pairwise default correlations.[214] Given that typical loan portfolios contain many thousand credits, this is impossible to do. Additionally, one needs to consider the fact that default correlations are very difficult, if not impossible, to observe.[215]

---

[214] As indicated above, one would also need to estimate the correlation of a joint movement in credit quality.

[215] However, they can be estimated from observable asset correlations. See e.g., Gupton et al. (1997), Ong (1999), pp. 143–145, Pfingsten and Schröck (2000), pp. 14–15.

- Equation (5.19) is a practicable way to calculate ULC. However, it basically ignores the fact that loans are of different sizes and show different correlations (e.g., by industry, geography, etc.). Therefore, using Equation (5.19) does not reveal potential concentrations in the credit portfolio. But banks try to avoid exactly these concentrations. It is easy to show[216] that Equation (5.19) can be decomposed for various segments of the portfolio so that, for example, default correlations between various industries or even of a single credit can be included. Using this approach (instead of the impractical "full-blown" approach, as indicated by Equation (5.8), allows banks to quantify exactly what they have done by intuition, prudent lending policies, and guidelines for a very long time.[217]
- Default correlations are small, but positive. Therefore, and as indicated previously, there are considerable benefits to diversification in credit portfolios.
- Overall, the analytical approach is very cumbersome and prone to estimation errors and problems. To avoid these difficulties, banks now use numerical procedures[218] to derive more exact and reliable results.

Viewing the UL of a single credit in the context of a credit portfolio[219] reduces the standalone risk considerably in terms of its risk contribution (ULC).[220]

Economic Capital for Credit Risk As defined previously, the amount of economic capital needed is the distance between the expected outcome and the unexpected (negative) outcome at a certain confidence level. As we saw in the last section, the unexpected outcomes at the portfolio level are driven by UL_P, the estimated volatility around the expected loss. Knowing the shape of the loss distribution, EL_P, and UL_P, one can estimate the distance between the expected outcome and the chosen confidence level as a multiple (often labeled as capital multiplier, or CM[221]) of UL_P, as shown in Figure 5.7.

---

[216]See Ong (1999), pp. 133–134.

[217]These guidelines often state that a bank should not lend too much money to a single counterparty (i.e., the size effect ignored in Equation [5.19]), the same industry or geography (i.e., the correlation effect ignored in Equation [5.19]).

[218]Such as Monte Carlo simulations; see, for example, Wilson (1997a) and (1997b).

[219]An alternative for determining this marginal risk contribution would be to calculate the UL of the portfolio once without and once with the transaction and to build the difference between the two results.

[220]The same approach is applicable to country risk. However, instead of borrower default correlations, country default correlations are applied.

[221]See Ong (1999), p. 163.

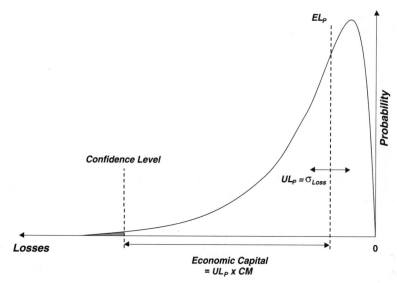

Figure 5.7 Economic capital for credit risk.
Source: Adapted from Ong (1999), p. 169.

Since the sum of ULC_is equals UL_p, we can attribute the necessary economic capital at the single transaction level as follows:

$$Economic\ Capital_p = UL_p \cdot CM \qquad (5.21)$$

Therefore:

$$Economic\ Capital_i = ULC_i \cdot CM \qquad (5.22)$$

that is, the required economic capital at the single credit transaction level is directly proportional to its contribution to the overall portfolio credit risk.

The crucial task in estimating economic capital is, therefore, the choice of the probability distribution, because we are only interested in the tail of this distribution. Credit risks are not normally distributed but highly skewed because, as mentioned previously, the upward potential is limited to receiving at maximum the promised payments and only in very rare events to losing a lot of money.

One distribution often recommended[222] and suitable for this practical

---

[222]See Ong (1999), p. 164. Other recommended distributions for finding an analytic solution to economic capital are the inverse normal distribution (see Ong (1999), p. 184) or distributions that are also used in extreme value theory (*EVT*) such as Cauchy, Gumbel, or Pareto distributions. For a detailed discussion of *EVT*, see Reiss and Thomas (1997), Embrechts et al. (1997 and 1998), McNeil and Saladin (1997), and McNeil (1998).

purpose is the beta distribution. This kind of distribution is especially useful in modeling a random variable that varies between 0 and c (> 0). And, in modeling credit events,[223] losses can vary between 0 and 100%, so that $c = 1$.[224] The beta distribution is extremely flexible in the shapes of the distribution it can accommodate. When defined between 0 and 1, the beta distribution has the following probability density function:[225]

$$f(x;\alpha,\beta) = \begin{cases} \dfrac{\Gamma(\alpha)\Gamma(\beta)}{\Gamma(\alpha+\beta)}\, x^{\alpha-1}\,(1-x)^{\beta-1}, & 0 < x < 1 \\ 0, & \text{otherwise} \end{cases} \tag{5.23}$$

where
$$\Gamma(z) \equiv \int_0^\infty t^z e^{-t} dt$$

By specifying the parameters α and β, we completely determine the shape of the beta distribution. It can be shown[226] that if $\alpha = \beta$, the beta distribution is symmetric and that in our case (0 < c < 1) the mean of the beta distribution equals:

$$\mu = EL_p = \int_0^1 x\, f(x;\alpha,\beta)\, dx = \frac{\alpha}{\alpha+\beta} \tag{5.24}$$

and that the variance equals:

$$\sigma^2 = UL_p^2 = \int_0^1 x^2\, f(x;\alpha,\beta)\, dx - \mu^2 = \left[\frac{\alpha\beta}{(\alpha+\beta)^2 \cdot (\alpha+\beta+1)}\right] \tag{5.25}$$

Therefore, the form of the beta distribution is fully characterized by two parameters: EL_p and UL_p. However, the difficulty is fitting the beta distribution exactly to the tail of the risk profile of the credit portfolio.[227] This tail-fitting exercise is best accomplished by combining the analytical (beta

---

[223]It can be shown that the beta distribution is a continuous approximation of a binomial distribution (the sum of independent two-point distributions).

[224]In Figure 5.7, a credit loss is depicted as a negative deviation, so that $c = -1$ in that case.

[225]See Greene (1993), p. 61.

[226]See Greene (1993), p. 61, and Ong (1999), pp. 165–166.

[227]The tail of a fitted beta distribution depends on the ratio of EL_p/UL_p. For high-quality portfolios ($EL_p > UL_p$) the beta distribution has too fat a tail. Here, the beta distribution usually overestimates economic capital. In contrast, for lower-quality portfolios ($EL_p < UL_p$) it has too thin a tail. See Ong (1999), pp. 184–185.

distribution) solution with a numerical procedure such as a Monte Carlo simulation.[228]

Since we try to determine the distance between EL_P and the confidence level, we try to estimate:

$$p\left(\frac{X_H - EL_P}{UL_P} \leq CM\right) \leq \alpha \qquad (5.26)$$

the probability p that the negative deviation of the random variable X exceeds the confidence level only in $\alpha\%$ of the cases[229] (as indicated by the gray shaded area in Figure 5.7) in the end of the predetermined measurement period, that is, at time horizon H. Taking the inverse of the beta function at the chosen confidence level, we can determine CM, the capital multiplier, to determine the required amount of economic capital. Obviously, CM is dependent on the overall credit quality of the portfolio and the confidence level. At the typically chosen 99.97% confidence level, CM is between 7.0 and 7.5,[230] which is—given the skewness of the loss distribution—far higher than the capital multiples for the normally distributed events in market risk.

Note that the derivation of the economic capital cushion for country risk is identical to the previously described derivation. However, country risk is more "lumpy," that is, the correlations between single transfer events are higher and there are fewer benefits to diversification because there are only a limited number of countries in the world. Additionally, one needs to consider the correlation between country and counterparty events in deriving the overall economic capital amount.

Problems with the Quantification of Credit Risk Despite the beauty[231] and simplicity of the bottom-up (total) risk measurement approach just described, there are a number of caveats that need to be addressed:

- This approach assumes that credits are illiquid assets. Therefore, it measures only the risk contribution (i.e., the internal "betas") to the losses of the existing credit portfolio and not the correlation with

---

[228]See Ong (1999), pp. 164 and 170–177, as well as, for a detailed description of the workings of such a model, pp. 179–196.

[229]Mathematically, this implies that the bank needs to hold an economic capital cushion ($CM \times UL_P$) sufficient to make the area under its loss probability distribution equal to 99.97%, if it targets a AA target solvency.

[230]See Ong (1999), pp. 173–177.

[231]Contrary to the regulatory approach that assigns roughly 8% equity capital to credits on a standalone basis, this approach reflects the economic perspective with respect to both a differentiated capital attribution by borrower quality as well as in a portfolio context reflecting the benefits to diversification.

risk factors as priced in liquid markets. Since the credit risk of bank loans becomes more and more liquid and is traded in the capital markets, a value approach would be more suitable. Such an approach would estimate the expected return and value of the promised payments and would try to model the probability distribution of changes in the value of the loan portfolio to derive the necessary economic capital.

■ This, however, would require modeling the multiperiod nature of credits and, hence, the expected and unexpected changes in the credit quality of the borrowers (and their correlations). Even though this can be easily included in the analytical approach, the more precise numerical solutions get very complex and cumbersome. Therefore, almost all of the internal credit risk models used in practice[232] use only a one-year estimation horizon.[233]

■ Although this approach considers correlations at a practicable level, that is, within the same risk type, it assumes, when measuring, that all other risk components (such as market and operational risk) are separated and are measured and managed in different departments within the bank.

Market Risk   In this section we will first define what market risk is. We will then discuss the steps to derive economic capital for market risk and the problems related to this approach.

Definition of Market Risk   Market risk is the risk of experiencing losses due to unexpected and adverse changes in the market price factors (such as interest rates, exchange rates, equity prices, and commodity prices[234]) that cause the mark-to-market value of a bank's single (trading) position[235] or its overall (trading) portfolio to decrease. It, therefore, includes the effects on all on- and off-balance sheet assets of the bank's trading book as well as those on all positions taken by the treasury[236] function[237] that can lead to a bank's

---

[232]For instance CreditMetrics™/CreditManager™ as described by Gupton et al. (1997), CreditPortfolioView as described by Wilson (1997a and 1997b), and CreditRisk+ as described by CSFP (1997).

[233]See Ong (1999), p. 122.

[234]This includes also changes in the volatility and the liquidity of these market price factors, which are important input factors to determine the value of, for example, derivative instruments.

[235]Therefore, market risk is also often called "position" risk.

[236]Typically also labeled asset-liability management (ALM) function.

[237]Which also includes, for example, the market risk components (such as interest rate or foreign exchange rate risk) of credit instruments and that can, therefore, have an impact on the overall bank value.

default at any time between now ($t = 0$) and a predetermined period of time ending at time horizon H.[238]

Steps to Derive Economic Capital for Market Risk For market risk, just as for credit and operating risk, we try to estimate the amount of economic capital that is required to ensure a target solvency standard of the bank over a one-year horizon.[239] Again, we will view a single transaction in a portfolio context, that is, only the incremental contribution to the overall portfolio risk counts.

The derivation of the necessary economic capital amount for a business unit exposed to market risk requires a metric that models the level of (market) risk taken by that unit. By now, the industry standard that has evolved for market risk measurement is *Value at Risk (VaR)*,[240] which will be defined in detail in the discussion that follows. VaR is a useful foundation for determining the required capital amount, but differs fundamentally from economic capital in that:

- VaR for market risk typically is a daily measure,[241] whereas economic capital is usually determined on an annual basis.
- VaR and economic capital are defined at different confidence levels (α_1 versus α_2 as depicted in Figure 5.8 on page 193).
- VaR for market risk is usually based on relatively strict assumptions about the distribution of outcomes (normality of trading results), while the economic capital calculation can relax some of these assumptions.

Each of these points will be discussed in detail in the sections that follow, and we will show how VaR can be used to derive economic capital, that is, how we can transpose and use daily VaR for market risk in a value creation framework that reflects total risk over a one-year horizon.

Daily Value at Risk (VaR) For managing and limiting market risk, banks internally use VaR, which is probably the best single metric for measuring market risk, because it unites both the magnitude of losses and the probabil-

---

[238]Which is typically chosen to be one year (see the discussion below).

[239]For instance, the bank's target could be to default only with a probability of (less than) 3 bps on its senior debt within the next year, which is equivalent to saying that the bank's economic capital will ensure solvency for the coming year at a 99.97% confidence level. As pointed out previously, this ensures that we measure total risk consistent across all types of risk.

[240]See Hirschbeck (1998), p. 143.

[241]VaR is used for limiting and managing market risk on a daily basis.

ity of their occurrence. Therefore, VaR has evolved as the standard methodology for measuring market risk. It is defined as the loss to the portfolio due to an adverse and unexpected move in one or more market risk factors that is only exceeded with a given probability $\alpha\%$ over a predetermined period of time. In the case of trading units, the time interval typically chosen is a one-day (holding) period. VaR is therefore the α-quantile of the cumulative probability distribution of the value changes in the portfolio over the measurement period H, and α is typically 2.5% or 1%. Hence, there is a $(1 - \alpha)\%$ probability that the critical threshold loss will not be exceeded.[242]

Mathematically, we can express the probability that a loss will exceed VaR over a predetermined period of time and that this will occur less than $\alpha\%$ of the time as:

$$p\left(\left[\Delta V_H - E(R_H)\right] > VaR_H\right) \le \alpha\% \Leftrightarrow \int_{-\infty}^{VaR} f(R_H)dR_H \le \alpha\% \qquad (5.27)$$

where p = Probability
ΔV_H = Change in the portfolio value V over period H, which equals R_H, the return of the portfolio over the same time horizon
$E(R_H)$ = Expected (or mean) return of the portfolio over time horizon H
VaR_H = Value at risk for period H, which is a negative number
α = Confidence level for not exceeding threshold VaR_H
$f(R_H)$ = Assumed distribution of the portfolio returns over time horizon H

Note that this definition so far does not make any assumptions about the distribution function of the value changes. We assume now that the (daily) returns are (as mostly assumed in modern finance theory and especially for tradable market instruments) normally distributed[243] with mean return μ and standard deviation of the return σ_R, that is $f(R) \sim N(\mu; \sigma_R)$. We can then rearrange terms[244] and eventually derive the dollar amount for VaR as:[245]

$$VaR = \left(\left[\Phi^{-1}(1 - \alpha)\cdot\sigma_R\right] - \mu\right) \cdot V = (c\cdot\sigma_R - \mu) \cdot V \qquad (5.28)$$

where Φ^{-1} = Inverse standard normal cumulative density function

---

[242]See Stulz (2000), pp. 4-9–4-10, Hirschbeck (1998), p. 143, Dowd (1998), p. 41, Jorion (1997), Guldimann et al. (1995).
[243]See Dowd (1998), p. 42.
[244]By using the property that we can transform R to a standard normal variable by the following transformation $[(R-\mu)/\sigma]$.
[245]See Hirschbeck (1998), p. 154.

c = $(1 - \alpha)$-quantile of the standard normal distribution[246]
V = Value of the portfolio

and which is also depicted for confidence level α_1 in Figure 5.8.

Since we are looking at a one-day period in this section, we have ignored time index H in Equation (5.28). For the same reason, the expected return μ will be very small[247] and is, therefore, almost always ignored when calculating the daily VaR (hence *VaR* reduces to $c \cdot \sigma_R \cdot V$).[248]

Assuming that the returns of the positions constituting the portfolio are distributed normally greatly reduces the bottom-up calculation of the overall portfolio VaR_P:

$$VaR_P = \sqrt{\sum_i \sum_j VaR_i VaR_j \rho_{ij}} = \sqrt{\mathbf{VaR}^T \cdot \Sigma \cdot \mathbf{VaR}} \qquad (5.29)$$

where ρ_{ij} = Correlation between value changes in assets i and j
Σ = Correlation matrix of value changes in the portfolio positions
$\mathbf{VaR}$ = Vector of single transaction *VaR* (**T** indicates the transposed vector thereof)

This approach is called the parametric approach[249] and clearly shows that only the marginal contribution (expressed by the correlation with the remainder of the portfolio[250]) of a single position to the overall portfolio risk counts.[251]

However, the normality assumption is just an approximation of the true

---

[246]c is, for example, for $\alpha = 2.5\%$ roughly 1.96, for $\alpha = 1\%$ roughly 2.33, and for $\alpha = 0.03\%$ roughly 3.43, as can be read off any statistics table of the standard normal distribution; see, for example, Bamberg and Baur (1991), p. 313.
[247]Compared to the volatility; see Stulz (2000), p. 4-13.
[248]See, for example, Hirschbeck (1998), p. 154, and Dowd (1998), pp. 41 and 43.
[249]See, for example, Dowd (1998), pp. 42 and 63–98. For a discussion of the various variants such as the delta-normal or the delta-gamma approach to include nonlinear positions see Wilson (1996), pp. 193–232.
[250]Another way to calculate the marginal contribution of a single position to the overall portfolio risk is to calculate VaR for the portfolio without the position, next for the portfolio including the position, and then build the difference between the two. However, this can be cumbersome and difficult to do; see Dowd (1998), pp. 48–50, for a discussion and the derivation of a shortcut formula in which the change in VaR = marginal VaR = $w_A \beta_{A,P} VaR^{without}$, where w_A = value weight of new asset A with respect to the portfolio value, $\beta_{A,P} = \sigma_{A,P}/\sigma^2_P$, and $VaR^{without}$ = portfolio VaR without new asset A.
[251]Hirschbeck (1998), p. 156, also defines this equation for a combination of long and short positions.

(empirical) distribution, which usually has fatter tails than assumed by normality, that is, losses exceeding *VaR* happen more often than predicted by the normal distribution. Similarly, nonlinear positions, such as options, cannot be easily included in the parametric approach. Therefore, banks also apply so-called Historical[252] and Monte Carlo simulations[253] to include both the nonlinearity of the positions and deviations from normality.[254]

It is not the purpose of this section to discuss and evaluate these various approaches[255] to calculating portfolio VaR for market risk in detail. However, all three approaches use historical time series[256] and a number of assumptions (e.g., that correlations are stable over time) to estimate the input parameters. They are, therefore, subject to misspecification and estimation errors. Potential remedies are to conduct either all three "alternative" VaR approaches,[257] or both backtesting[258] and stress-testing[259] to validate that the model works appropriately.[260]

Typically, the confidence interval $(1 - \alpha)$ chosen for the internal management and limit purposes of market risk is the 97.5% or 99% level. Even though this choice seems somewhat arbitrary, it is not the level that is important, but rather that it is applied consistently across time and products. At these levels, we can expect that VaR can and will be exceeded on an average of 5 to 6 days per year for the 97.5% confidence level and 2 to 3 days per annum for the 99% confidence level. Even though the estimates at these confidence levels are much more reliable than at higher confidence

---

[252]See Hirschbeck (1998), pp. 182–187, Dowd (1998), pp. 99–107.

[253]See Dowd (1998), pp. 108–120, Hirschbeck (1998), pp. 177–182.

[254]Even though the Monte Carlo simulation can include non-normal positions, it generates random draws on the basis of a correlation matrix that assumes normality and does therefore not model deviations from normality.

[255]For such an evaluation See for example, Hirschbeck (1998), pp. 188–196.

[256]Even the Monte Carlo Simulation uses correlation and distribution assumptions that are typically based on historical time series.

[257]The three results should be compared to find out what the "real" VaR is. Some banks take the most conservative estimate out of the three results.

[258]This procedure evaluates whether the number of losses greater than VaR are in line with the prediction by the assumed probability distribution. It can therefore identify whether the underlying model is correct. For a detailed discussion of these methods see Stahl and Traber (2000), pp. 85–106.

[259]For a stress test, a standard change in the risk factors is set (e.g., ± 5%, ±10%) and the change in portfolio value is calculated. There are two drawbacks: (1) this procedure does not relate the movements to a probability of occurrence and (2) it only assumes a simple (0; 1) correlation with other moves. For a discussion see for example, Dowd (1998), pp. 121–138, or Hirschbeck (1998), pp. 198–200.

[260]If the models do not work appropriately, they need to be adjusted accordingly.

levels,[261] a capital allocation on basis of these estimates would not be sufficient, because the bank would be forced into bankruptcy due to losses in market risk too often compared to its set target solvency.

Moreover, VaR is calculated at a one-day horizon, which assumes that—in case of emergency—all positions in the portfolio can be closed/sold in the market within a day. However, because of the size of a single position and/or changes in the liquidity of the markets, this might be impossible or might be possible only at a price not modeled in the derivation of daily VaR.[262]

Both problems (confidence level and modeling horizon/liquidity) are also a concern to regulators and are addressed in the regulatory approach to VaR discussed in the following paragraph. Nonetheless, note that daily VaR is a natural starting point for the calculation of market risk (economic) capital.

Regulatory Approach to Market Risk Because of the two concerns mentioned above, regulators—despite allowing banks to use their own internal models[263]—require banks to extend daily VaR in the following ways:

- α is set to be 1% (α_R) irrespective of the bank's internally used confidence level.
- A holding period is defined as ten trading days and is based on the assumption that an orderly liquidation of the market risk positions can take up to ten working days, which is a very conservative estimate for positions traded in liquid markets. The transformation from a one-day horizon to a ten-day horizon is done by multiplying daily VaR by $\sqrt{10}$, assuming that the changes in portfolio value are serially uncorrelated and are identically and independently distributed (iid).[264] Therefore, the sum of the variance over t days is $t \cdot \sigma_R^2$, and the standard deviation for t days $\sqrt{10} \cdot \sigma_R$.[265]
- Additionally, regulators require banks[266] to multiply the resulting ten-day VaR with a "conservatism" factor CF that is between 3 and

---

[261]See, for example, Dowd (1998), pp. 52–53. A proper validation of these models is only possible at lower confidence levels, because observable events become very rare at higher levels.

[262]Bangia et al. (1999) develop a VaR model that includes the liquidity component and estimate that ignoring the liquidity effects can underestimate the market risk (in emerging markets) by as much as 25%–30%.

[263]Following the 1996 market risk amendment to the Basle Accord (I); see Stulz (2000), p. 4-56, and Hirschbeck (1998), pp. 15–32.

[264]For a discussion see Stulz (2000), pp. 6-4–6-6.

[265]Regulators require banks to use the past 250 trading days for estimating this daily standard deviation of returns.

[266]Banks are also required to compare the most recent ten-day VaR with the average ten-day VaR across the past 60 trading days and to take the maximum of the two.

4, according to the quality of the model used, which is determined during the backtesting.

Therefore, the daily *VaR* (= $([\Phi^{-1}(1-\alpha_1)\cdot\sigma_R])\cdot V$) is transformed into the regulatory VaR_R by the following formula:

$$VaR_R = VaR \cdot \sqrt{10} \cdot CF \cdot \frac{\Phi^{-1}(1-\alpha_R)}{\Phi^{-1}(1-\alpha_1)} \tag{5.30}$$

which results in multiplying σ_R by a factor between 22.07 and 29.43, instead of just 2.33.[267]

Note that this approach—even though calculated for a longer period of time—still ignores the fact that there is an expected return on the portfolio that eventually flows to the real capital resources. This expected return would, therefore, reduce the capital requirement. However, as discussed previously, expected earnings are not relevant as a capital resource from a regulatory point of view. It is, therefore, reasonable to assume that $E(R) = 0$ when calculating VaR_R.

Economic Capital for Market Risk   Economic capital for market risk is the amount of (virtual) capital required to ensure a certain solvency standard of a bank over a one-year horizon at a certain confidence level. This higher confidence level usually differs from the one chosen by the bank for internal purposes and is depicted in Figure 5.8 as α_2.

Taking (daily) VaR as a starting point for the calculation of economic capital for market risk, we will have to make three adjustments to translate VaR into economic capital:[268]

- As already indicated, VaR is typically calculated at a 97.5% (or 99%) confidence level, whereas economic capital is calculated at, for example, a 99.97% level.
- VaR is a daily measure of total risk, while economic capital is typically measured on an annual basis. As already discussed, we can scale daily VaR to an annual VaR by multiplying it by $\sqrt{t}$ (i.e., applying the "square-root-of-time rule"), with the caveat that this only holds under

---

[267]This would be correct when we assume that changes in the portfolio value are normally distributed.
[268]These three adjustments ensure that VaR is transformed into economic capital in a way that is consistent with the calculation of economic capital for the other types of risk.

certain assumptions.[269] This scaling has nothing to do with holding and/or liquidation periods.[270] This is a simple way to reflect what the cumulative volatility effect on the portfolio is over a one-year horizon. However, this procedure basically extrapolates past history and also assumes that the portfolio is left constant (i.e., there are no changes to the positions composing the portfolio currently and no active management of the overall market risk position).[271]

■ As can be easily seen in Figure 5.8, the expected return (μ) over a one-year horizon can be quite substantial and should therefore be considered in the amount of (economic) capital required from an economic point of view (i.e., reducing it). Average daily earnings[272] can build up an additional capital cushion against potential (future) losses and can, therefore, mitigate the required amount of economic

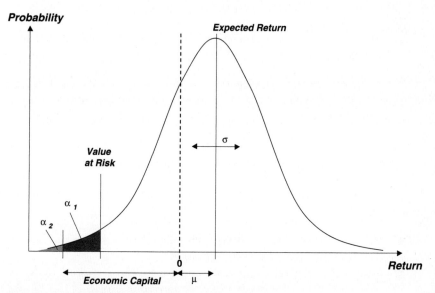

Figure 5.8 Typical distribution for market risk.

---

[269]As already mentioned, this assumes that daily VaR is *iid* (identically and independently distributed). However, VaR often exhibits strong serial correlation (since positions are usually held for more than one day), see Stulz (2000), p. 6-6. Likewise, this scaling assumes constant volatility throughout the trading year. However, actual VaR time series tend to exhibit considerable heteroscedasticity.

[270]These periods are shorter for obvious reasons.

[271]This assumes that the management never lowers limits or closes positions in adverse market conditions.

[272]A business unit should have positive expected earnings in the long run, since otherwise it would be shut down from an economic perspective.

capital. However, economic capital does not exist in the form of tangible funds, and there is no economic capital "account." Gains or losses generated by a unit do not actually increase or decrease the unit's economic capital. Instead, the gains or losses pass directly to the bank's book capital account and can, therefore, be available as an additional cushion only after their recognition.[273] Hence, we need to make an appropriate adjustment in the transformation process.

Therefore the economic capital for market risk (VaR_{EC}) can be derived as a transformation of daily or regulatory VaR:

$$VaR_{EC} = VaR \cdot \frac{\Phi^{-1}(1-\alpha_2)}{\Phi^{-1}(1-\alpha_1)} \cdot \sqrt{250} - \mu_{year} \quad = VaR_R \cdot \frac{\Phi^{-1}(1-\alpha_2)}{\Phi^{-1}(1-\alpha_R)} \cdot \frac{\sqrt{250}}{\sqrt{10}} - \mu_{year}$$

(5.31)

where μ_{year} = The sum of the geometric daily returns over 250 trading days[274]

Note that at a 99.97% confidence level $\Phi^{-1}(1 - \alpha_2) = 3.43$.[275] Multiplying it further with $\sqrt{250}$ (i.e., assuming 250 trading days per annum) results in an overall factor of 54.26 (which is more than double the regulatory requirement).

Problems with the Quantification of Market Risk   Despite the fact that VaR is a practicable way to measure total risk and that it has been adopted by the BIS to set regulatory capital requirements for banks, it has some important limitations:

- We have already discussed the theoretical deficiencies in the general section on deriving economic capital.
- Despite the relatively large scaling factor for the daily VaR to derive economic capital for market risk (as derived in Equation [5.31]), we are assuming normality and do not yet capture the risks associated with extreme market crashes or other extreme "events".[276] The

---

[273]Note that booked losses can increase the required capital amount.

[274]Since the daily returns are fairly small, we can approximate the arithmetic returns by geometric returns, which are much easier to sum. See Dowd (1998), p. 41.

[275]Again, assuming that the changes in the portfolio value are normally distributed.

[276]For a discussion of the problems converting short-term volatility estimates to longer terms, see Christoffersen et al. (1998). For a discussion of the pitfalls and opportunities of applying "extreme value theory" (EVT) for risk-management purposes, see Diebold et al. (1998).

empirical distributions for changes in the portfolio value are not normal and show leptokurtosis, or fat tails. VaR is, therefore, a poor predictor of what can happen in crises[277] and should be supplemented by other measures such as scenario tests or stress tests.

- VaR relies on stable correlations between the market risk factors and the assumption that the portfolio remains unchanged until the end of time horizon H, that is, there is no management intervention and the associated closing of positions will occur.

- One might expect that any of the strict assumptions on which the derivation of VaR is based may be violated to one degree or another. In combination, these violations can have a significant impact on the overall market risk capitalization.

- Economic capital for a single transaction is attributed to its contribution to the annualized risk of the existing portfolio. The correlation with a broad market portfolio, which is typically used to derive the value of such a position, is ignored in that context.

- As we have seen in our previous discussion, if the bank simply scales the daily VaR (which assumes that the expected return equals zero) to a yearly horizon, it will overallocate economic capital to its market risks. However, due largely to data availability and computational power, daily VaR is measured and calculated at the end of each trading day. This obviously ignores the fact that intraday losses, that could lead to default, can occur.[278] Scaling such a daily VaR to a yearly horizon would then basically ignore intrayear defaults and, therefore, the particular path of economic capital consumption *during* the year.[279] The bank, however, wants to hold enough economic capital to ensure that it will remain solvent at a certain confidence level at any point in time and would monitor its default status continuously. Taking such intrayear losses into account leads to the allocation of a greater amount of economic capital, since one must now ensure not only that capital is not depleted at the end of the year, but also that it is never depleted at any point during the year.

---

[277]Some practitioners, therefore, evaluate VaR in the following way: "when you really need it, it doesn't work." Also see Culp and Miller (1998), p. 26, who conclude that VaR has been of limited value in avoiding "disasters."

[278]This would only matter at the overall bank level and not for a single business unit. Unlike losses due to credit risk (which is an absorbing barrier in a Markov sense), one could always recapitalize a trading unit that could then run profitably again.

[279]This assumes that default could only occur at the end of the year.

Therefore, the simple scaling (ignoring expected returns) of daily VaR may not overallocate capital and might just compensate for the extra amount of economic capital needed.[280]

Operational Risk   In this section we will first define what operational risk is. As we will see, operational risk can be split into event risk and business risk. We will, therefore, discuss the steps to derive economic capital for each of these types of risk and the problems related to the two approaches.

Definition of Operational Risk   Even though there is no universally agreed definition,[281] we define operational risk[282] in this book as the risk of experiencing unexpected (financial) losses due to failures[283] in people, processes or systems[284] and their (internal) controls[285] or from external (nonmarket or non-credit-risk) events[286] and a bank's business strategy[287]/business environment.[288] These risks are common to all companies,[289] not just banks, and can lead to a bank's default at any time between now ($t = 0$) and a predetermined period of time ending at time horizon H.[290]

This definition goes beyond the reflection of only financial risks[291] in

---

[280]This obviously depends on the way VaR is measured and calculated.

[281]Operational risk is often described as "residual" risk, that is, any risk that is not due to credit (including transfer risk) or market risk; see Lam and Cameron (1999), p. 94. Even though this negative definition may have the advantage that it tries to capture all remaining sources of risk, it does not necessarily create an incentive to explore the specifics and (avoidable) reasons for operational risk.

[282]Often other labels are used for operational risk: organizational, business, or residual risk.

[283]This includes (human or technical) error, omissions, fraud, or failure to perform in a timely manner or damage to a bank's franchise value in some other way by employees exceeding their authority or through their unethical or risky behavior. See Basle Committee on Banking Supervision (1998), p. 1.

[284]See Cooper (1999), p. 6

[285]See Buhr (2000), p. 202. The Basle Committee on Banking Supervision (1998), p. 1, expands this to the breakdown of the corporate governance system of a bank in general.

[286]The Basle Committee on Banking Supervision (1998), p. 1, includes the failure of IT systems, fires, and other disasters under this label. Additionally, often changes in the legal and political environment as well as (natural) catastrophes and terror are included, see Buhr (2000), p. 202.

[287]See Buhr (2000), p. 202.

[288]See Wills et al. (1999), pp. 29–31.

[289]See Lam and Cameron (1999), p. 81.

[290]The time horizon, again, is typically chosen to be one year. For a discussion see below.

[291]These risks are, according to Damodaran (1997), p. 777, mostly continuous risks.

credit and market risk[292] used so far and tries to measure the generally much larger impact of event (or discontinuous) risks on a bank's cash flows and value.[293] However, it (mostly) does not include the (indirect) impact on the entire organization (and its employees) and the bank's overall liquidity.[294]

In order to clarify the broad definition given previously, we split operational risk into two subcategories of risk, which will be discussed in the light of its measurement and management in turn below:

- Event risk is the risk that losses to the bank are caused by rare events[295] such as a major systems failure,[296] process and control failures (e.g., errors and omissions),[297] fraud,[298] legal risk,[299] and external disruption (e.g., fire or other catastrophes).[300, 301]
- Business risk is the risk that the bank will experience losses through unexpected changes in either (future) revenues (affected by volume and price) or (fixed) costs that are not due to credit or market risk,[302] but rather driven by fundamental (and unexpected) changes in the bank's competitive environment[303] (e.g., price wars, new competitors,[304] changes in regulation, etc.).

---

[292]This book will not, however, cover the measurement and management of insurance risk.

[293]See Damodaran (1997), p. 777. All recent big losses to banks basically stem from event risks and were already summarized in the Wheel of Misfortune (see Chapter 3).

[294]Due to or leading to bank runs, see Cooper (1999), p. 7.

[295]For a list of descriptions/definitions of such events see Lam and Cameron (1999), p. 85, Table 2.

[296]Losses due to failed management information systems, communication, or computer systems.

[297]Unintentional losses due to human error or noncompliance with established business guidelines.

[298]Losses due to employee or third-party theft, mismanagement, or deceit.

[299]Cost of legal fees, fines, and lost settlements resulting from legal actions and lawsuits or fines, and opportunity costs resulting from regulatory actions.

[300]Losses due to, for example, natural disasters, failure of public infrastructure, labor disputes, terrorism, or kidnapping.

[301]This includes the risks from back-office operations such as processing or settlement and their systems; see Lam and Cameron (1999), p. 82.

[302]This is especially important since the fee-based income of banks increased proportionally.

[303]This part of operational risk is not restricted to back-office operations. It, rather, addresses front-office applications such as strategy, client management, product development, pricing, and distribution. See Lam and Cameron (1999), p. 82.

[304]Despite the high entry barriers in the banking market, those competitors from the new economy, in particular, challenge traditional, old-economy banks.

Steps to Derive Economic Capital for Operational Risk   In this section, we discuss the effort to measure operational risk with the same analytical objectivity as market and credit risk (as described previously) using a similar, VaR-like approach. However, one should keep in mind that operational risk indicators, such as the number of failed deals or the number and loss rate of errors and omissions,[305] have no easily identifiable set of risk factors that drive unexpected losses as in market or credit risk. These factors are mostly only qualitative and, for example, used in the (internal) auditing assessments.[306]

Given the broad definition for operational risk, it is not surprising that there is neither a singly accepted framework or methodology[307] nor that no single approach will be sufficient[308] to cover the diversity of operational risks. Operational risk is mostly managed by traditional approaches (e.g., internal auditing or guidelines)[309] and only leading banking organizations calculate and allocate economic capital for operational risks.[310]

Between these two extremes, there are many other means to counter operational risk (e.g., buying insurance against losses from various sources). In fact, holding economic capital for all operational risks can be sub-opti-mal, and a bank should opt for the least expensive form to manage those risks. Of course, not every option is available for every event. Some events, such as natural disasters, cannot be controlled by tighter risk controls. Other events cannot be insured against. The key is to identify the sources of operational risk, estimate the exposure to each source of risk, and determine the most appropriate course of action, that is, the one that creates the most value. In practice, most institutions apply a combination of the available options to find an acceptable answer to managing operational risks and how much capital they need to hold against them.[311]

---

[305]See Wills et al. (1999), p. 61; for a more comprehensive list of such indicators, see ibid, p. 62.

[306]See Basle Committee on Banking Supervision (1998), p. 4.

[307]Since most banks are in the early stages of developing a framework, there are no binding regulatory guidelines to specify a consistent measurement methodology at the moment; see Basle Committee on Banking Supervision (1998), pp. 1, 2, and 7.

[308]See Wills et al. (1999), p. 11.

[309]These are, according to the Basle Committee on Banking Supervision (1998), p. 6, the major tools for managing operational risk. Note that this form of risk management is also costly to the bank.

[310]See Buhr (2000), p. 202.

[311]See Wills et al. (1999), p. 98.

The spectrum runs from simple, top-down estimations[312] to sophisticated, bottom-up[313] approaches.[314]

In the following sections some best-practice approaches for both event and business risk are presented and discussed.

Economic Capital for Event Risk   In this section we will first define which alternatives are available to manage event risks. We will find that some of the exposure to event risk is best "outsourced" to third parties and that a bank only needs to hold event risk capital for the remaining part; the derivation of the amount of this type of economic capital will be discussed subsequently.

The Choice of Risk-Management Options for Event Risk   In general, we can distinguish between two broad categories of losses due to event risk, both of which can be seen as risks that only have a downside (similar to credit risk):[315]

- Relatively small, but fairly frequent event losses resulting from occasional human or technical errors in typical banking processes
- Infrequently occurring major event losses that endanger the existence of the bank due to their substantial impact on the capital resources of the institution

Trying to quantify these risks increases the awareness of their existence.[316] By not ignoring or covering up these types of risks (and hence the fact that mistakes can and do happen), a bank can learn valuable lessons[317] and can devote adequate resources to trying to avoid experiencing such event losses.

As we have seen, there are other options for managing operational/event risk beyond holding economic capital. These options can be divided into three categories:

---

[312]For instance, some banks calculate the capital they would like to hold against operational risks as the difference between their book or regulatory capital and the amount of (economic) capital that they calculated was necessary to hold against market and credit risk.

[313]For instance, some banks take data from so-called event risk databases and (Monte Carlo) simulate the implied distributions to determine the probability of extreme losses via a statistical/actuarial approach.

[314]For a full description of currently used methods for estimating economic capital see Wills et al. (1999), pp. 93–97.

[315]See Basle Committee on Banking Supervision (1998), p. 4.

[316]See Basle Committee on Banking Supervision (1998), p. 2.

[317]See Lam and Cameron (1999), p. 84.

1. **Third-party insurance of risks ("outsourcing" of risks):** By paying a premium (i.e., at a cost), banks can (fully) insure event risks externally. Banks are then no longer subject to the event risks insured and, hence, are not required to hold event risk capital for that part of their event risks. Because insurance companies can build a portfolio of assets that benefits more from diversification effects than can be achieved within a bank and because insurance companies might have accumulated more expertise in evaluating these risks, they can offer the insurance contracts at a lower price.[318]
2. **Self-insurance of risks:** For a number of reasons, including cost considerations, a bank may choose not to buy external insurance for some risks. This can make sense especially if the bank can achieve the benefits of risk pooling on its own—and more economically than provided by a third party.[319]
3. **Controlling risk internally:** Some risks, such as internal fraud, are best managed internally through tight guidelines and controls. However, establishing and running these instruments also comes at a cost.

Since 2. and 3. can considerably reduce the bank's exposure to certain event risks (by limiting the adverse effects through either internal insurance or better/more effective controls), the bank only needs to hold economic capital for the remaining part of its event risks.[320] Therefore, before calculating the required amount of capital, we need to consider the effects of these other options. And the bank needs to determine which option or combination of options it prefers to choose—especially in terms of what is most economically appropriate from a value-creation point of view.

With regard to the two types of event risks defined previously, banks should choose the following options:

■ Banks should manage the small and more frequent event risks by using their internal experience of what can go wrong. Banks should align their processes within a total quality management (TQM)[321] framework and should always try to stay within a predetermined "three sigma" range, where only acceptable losses occur.[322] For these

---

[318]See Damodaran (1997), p. 789.
[319]See Damodaran (1997), p. 789.
[320]This is in line with the previous theoretical discussion, where we concluded that this tranche can be excluded from our considerations.
[321]See, for example, Mitra (1993) for a book-long discussion.
[322]In order to do so, you need to identify the driving variables and determine the causes of variation in performance (i.e., to collect data internally).

expected losses,[323] the bank should either calculate an internal insurance premium (similar to expected losses for credit risk) or should buy insurance at a premium. For the remaining (small) probability that event risks outside the three sigma range lead to larger losses, the bank should hold economic capital (see below).[324]

■ Banks should insure as much of the risk of experiencing major event losses as they can. Even though buying insurance externally is frequently perceived as expensive because of the direct and observable costs that are associated with it, buying catastrophe insurance might be the most appropriate way to hedge against event risk.[325] Despite the fact that such catastrophe insurance for banks is more or less in the early stage of development,[326] insurance companies now offer mitigation options at competitive prices.[327] Therefore, the other available option, to try and exploit the internal potential for self-insurance, seems to be less attractive but should be used where appropriate, that is, where the market price is higher.

■ Assuming that a bank has insured itself up to its intended level and has executed controls to the extent desired, the bank should hold economic capital for the remaining part of its event risks; the derivation of the amount of this economic capital will be discussed in detail below.

The Derivation of Economic Capital for Remaining Event Risks As already mentioned, event risk has no upside potential. Therefore, the methodology to determine economic capital for event risk should be similar to the one for determining economic capital for credit risk, especially with respect to the fact that an event can occur with probability PE_H or not with probability $(1 - PE_H)$ at any time over the predetermined time horizon up to H.[328] In a manner similar to that used in the credit risk framework, we can also estimate the expected size of the loss at any time up to H and can, hence, determine an expected loss (in dollar terms) for event risks (EL_{ER}). As for

---

[323]One could also rate/score the underlying processes and calibrate them to probabilities of occurrence (despite the fact that there is very little historical data to do so), see Buhr (2000), pp. 203–205, and then determine expected losses and in a VaR-like approach the required economic capital amount.

[324]See Lam and Cameron (1999), p. 83.

[325]See Damodaran (1997), p. 777, and Lam and Cameron (1999), p. 88.

[326]Banks have only just realized the potential for large losses since they have been trying to measure event risks.

[327]See Wills et al. (1999), pp. 79–81 and 111.

[328]Since we will use a consistent time horizon of one year, again we will drop time index H from our discussion.

EL for credit risk, a bank should build (loss) reserves for what it can expect to lose on average due to event risks[329] and should also include that in its pricing.

However, as we have also seen previously in the credit risk framework, if losses are "lumpy" or are experienced only rarely,[330] then the expected losses amount will not be sufficient to cover the (unexpected) losses up to a certain level of confidence. Therefore, we also need to hold economic capital for event risks.[331] In general, this amount of economic capital can be derived in the same way as for credit risk. The problem, however, is that the number of observable event risk losses for estimating the event risk loss distribution is even scarcer than the data points for credit risk. Because of the lack of sufficient data for a historical analysis, a variety of assumptions need to be made for the calculation of event risk capital, making the approach subject to challenge and criticism.

In almost all of the cases, banks will have no or insufficient (historical) internal experience with major event risk losses, because—by definition—those events are very infrequent. To increase the number of observations, data points (mostly in the form of case studies) from as many banks and events as possible are being collected in so-called event loss databases, which are currently being built around the world.[332] Since there are many different types of event risk to which a bank can be exposed, it is useful to create different categories[333] of such events and adjust them for the bank's risk profile before conducting the quantitative analysis.[334]

These adjustments need to be made in two dimensions:

■ **Adjustment of the potential size of the loss due to event risk:** The event database is a good starting point for the estimation of the potential size of the loss due to an event in a certain category. However, a bank should use the input from its risk experts to allow for a customization of the potential size of the loss for the bank, adjusting for both the size and the risk characteristics of the bank.[335]

---

[329]See Lam and Cameron (1999), pp. 87–88.

[330]Indicating that the normal assumption might not be appropriate and the distribution is skewed.

[331]Recall that the total amount of capital available to "burn" before a bank goes into default is EL_{ER} plus the economic capital held for event risks.

[332]See Wills et al. (1999), pp. 11 and 66–70.

[333]For a possible list of categories, see the event risk definition above.

[334]This data collection and interpretation can be very costly. The expected costs for conducting the analysis should, therefore, be evaluated against the expected value of losses from event risks in a cost-benefit analysis.

[335]Obviously, this is very subjective, but also the only way to derive meaningful results.

■ **Estimation of the probability of an event occurring at a bank:** Having assessed the potential magnitude of an event in each category, we must next assess the probability of each event occurring at a bank. However, not all banks are equally likely to experience losses due to an event.

Therefore, we need to adjust the observable (average) probability in the event database as follows:

$$PE_j = \frac{E_j}{n_j \cdot a_j} \qquad (5.32)^{336}$$

where PE_j = Probability of an event occurring in category j
E_j = Total number of observed events in category j
n_j = Overall number of banks in the event database in category j, which is the sum of banks weighted for size and riskiness (ranked, for example, on a risk index)
a_j = Number of years of data history in the event database in category j

Since we now have an estimate for both the size and the probability of events occurring at a bank, we can now estimate the expected losses due to event risk in category j ($EL_{ER,j}$) as the product of the two. Again (similar to the credit risk framework discussed above), we can sum these expected losses and derive $EL_{ER,P}$, the expected losses due to event risk at the (bank) portfolio level across all j categories:

$$EL_{ER,P} = \sum_j EL_{ER,j} \qquad (5.33)$$

The unexpected loss due to event risk ($UL_{ER,P}$) at the portfolio level can then be derived as an analogue to the UL in credit risk:

$$UL_{ER,P} = \sqrt{\sum_i \sum_j w_i w_j \rho_{ij} UL_i UL_j} \qquad (5.34)$$

where,

w = Weight of events in a category in the portfolio (weighted according to their $EL_{ER,i}$)
$\rho_{i,j}$ = Correlation between event risk events i and j
UL = Unexpected loss, defined as above as the standard deviation of events around the expected value (EL_{ER})

---

[336]This formula assumes that the number of banks and years exceed the number of actually observed events in order to lead to meaningful probabilities.

All events can be assumed to be independent of each other and of events in other event risk categories. The probabilities of a fire, systems failure, or fraud are, in the vast majority of cases, not related to each other. Therefore, ρ_{ij} is assumed to be zero, and hence Equation (5.34) reduces to

$$UL_{ER,P} = \sqrt{\sum_i w_i^2 UL_i^2} \qquad (5.35)$$

Again, similar to credit risk, we can derive the required amount of economic capital for event risk by assuming a shape of the portfolio distribution of events.[337] We can determine the capital multiplier (*CM*) by estimating the distance between the expected level of losses and the cut-off point of the distribution, which is determined by the chosen confidence level, expressed as a multiple of the standard deviation of losses, as shown in Figure 5.9.

Of course, and again similar to credit risk, these results can also be achieved by more sophisticated Monte Carlo simulations.

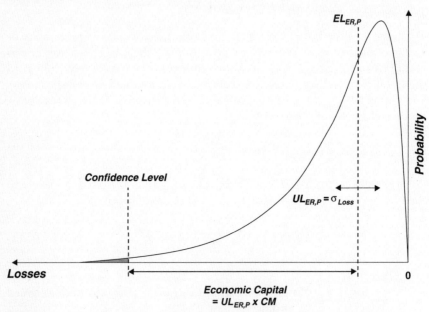

Figure 5.9 Distribution for deriving economic capital for event risk.

---

[337]Given that event risk is more similar to insurance risk than to credit risk, that is, the distribution is even more skewed than for credit risk, assuming a beta distribution here is less appropriate. Some authors, therefore, suggest using a Weibull distribution, see, for example, Ong (1999), p. 201.

The difficulty, however, is to break these results down to a single transaction level. Since the input parameters are determined at the level of an event risk category (which does not need to coincide with the event risk of a single business unit), some sort of capital allocation key has to be determined, which will always be subjective and imprecise.

Economic Capital for Business Risk   Conceptually, business risk can be thought of as the possibility that a bank's (expected) revenues may become insufficient to cover its (expected) fixed cost base and the (rigid) variable expenses not related to market or credit risk, causing the bank's capital to be eroded over the predetermined period of time (ending at time H).[338]

As can be easily seen in Figure 5.10, the problem basically reduces to revenue volatility versus the rigidity of the relevant costs that can—if they cannot be covered—cause losses for which the bank needs to hold economic capital.

Therefore, business risk has three key drivers that need to be modeled when trying to quantify business risk (capital):

1. First, business risk stems from the *volatility of revenues*. Both business volumes and margins can vary as the result of various factors

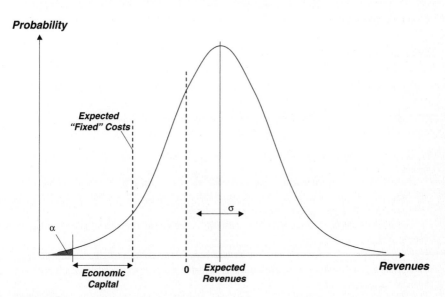

Figure 5.10   Distribution for deriving economic capital for business risk.

---

[338]Business risk has become more important for banks since the percentage of total revenues stemming from fee-based income have increased over time.

that are not (necessarily) under the control of the bank. Such external factors include the intensity of competition in the market and the effect of the economic cycle on the customer base.[339] Additional revenue volatility may also stem from the bank's products moving through their life cycle.

2. Second, business risk tends to grow proportionally to a bank's *fixed cost base*, that is, the larger the fixed cost base, the higher will be the need for business risk capital. While this assumption does not hold for all banks and/or business units, the fixed cost base tends to be the most predictive driver of the amount of business risk capital.

3. The last of the three key drivers is the *volatility (or rigidity) of variable costs*. Here we are concerned with the unexpected fluctuations in variable costs that are not direct responses to the variations in revenues. These unexpected fluctuations are caused by rigid variable costs that do not change in a timely fashion and that cannot be reduced even by strict cost management.

The sum of the fixed cost base (2.) plus the rigid variable costs (3.) form the threshold level (labeled in Figure 5.10 above as "fixed" costs) from which the bank needs to hold economic capital.[340]

There are basically two approaches to derive the required amount of economic capital for business risk.

Historical Accounting-Based Approach   After defining the level at which granular historical revenue and cost time series can be obtained,[341] the (cleaned[342]) historic data series[343] need to be adjusted. We need to remove the gains and losses of trading[344] and credit[345] activities,[346] as well as adjust for any extraordinary items[347] before we can estimate the expected value and the

---

[339]These factors are, therefore, also considered in the agency ratings process.

[340]Consistent to the other approaches, the bank only needs to hold economic capital for business risk up to a certain confidence level.

[341]This assumes that all costs are correctly allocated at the chosen level of reporting.

[342]For outliers, and so on.

[343]To adjust the data for the impact of the economic cycle and the bank's general (expected) growth, we need to obtain as long a time series as possible—at least over the last economic cycle.

[344]Including treasury activities, assuming that they are correctly transfer priced to the business units.

[345]Including transfer risk and any default-related losses.

[346]See Wills et al. (1999), p. 94.

[347]We need to adjust for changes in the internal accounting conventions and any other general structural or reporting inconsistencies.

volatility of a bank's residual business revenues and the (expected) value of the "fixed"[348] costs.[349]

Assuming then that (residual business) revenues are normally distributed (as indicated in Figure 5.10) and that we are able to estimate the expected value of "fixed" costs with reasonable confidence, we can determine the required amount of economic capital for business risk as follows: Similar to the above described approaches, we first determine the α-quantile of the revenue distribution that is consistent with the bank's chosen solvency standard by calculating:

$$\Phi^{-1}(1 - \alpha) \cdot \sigma \cdot E(Revenues) \qquad (5.36)$$

However, as also indicated in Figure 5.10, we do not need to hold econom-ic capital for this full amount. Since the bank is only exposed to (unexpected) losses, when the costs cannot be reduced below the identified threshold level (within a reasonably short period of time), we can subtract the difference between the expected revenues and this threshold level from the capital requirement, so that:

Economic Capital for Business Risk

$$= \Phi^{-1}(1 - \alpha) \cdot \sigma \cdot E(Revenues) - E("Fixed" \ Costs) \qquad (5.37)$$

Despite the simplicity of this approach, it is heavily dependent on a sufficiently long time series of historical accounting data. Directly analyzing this data to estimate the business risk capital can be difficult due to the adjustments that must be made to correct data for market and credit risk. Additionally, the accounting data might be biased by the bank's (current) balance sheet policy, making it difficult to separate true business volatility from purely accounting-driven P&L volatility. Moreover, this approach assumes that historic trends will be continued. This approach, therefore, only reflects the economic cycle and the changes in the competitive environment inappropriately. To adjust for these caveats, the following approach might offer solutions.

Monte Carlo Simulation Approach Even though this approach also relies heavily on historical observations[350] to simulate potential future revenues

---

[348]As already discussed, the amount of economic capital will be sensitive to the level to which costs can be managed in response to revenue changes. Costs that are independent of revenues should be considered as fixed, while costs that are directly linked to the revenue volume should be considered variable.

[349]Since these "fixed" costs will vary over time, we need to determine the expected value for the period ending at time H.

[350]Time series are also obtained over at least one business cycle.

and cost levels,[351] it does not depend as heavily on adjusted P&L data as the previously described approach. Additionally, the Monte Carlo model has the advantage that it can link the input parameters volumes and margins (to model revenues) as well as fixed and variable costs to a proper macroeconomic model. By doing so, the simulation approach is able to consider the correlations between these input parameters as well as their interrelationship to the way that market- and credit-risk-driven gains and losses will develop over the projected time horizon in the context of the projected business environment.[352] Moreover, we are also able to consider (fundamental) changes in the competitive environment and the marketplace in such a model.

Since all of these influencing factors, and especially their common movement, can be modeled much more accurately than can be reflected by just historical observations of accounting data, we can estimate both the distribution of "net" business revenues and the threshold level of "fixed" costs with more confidence.[353] To determine the required economic capital for business risk at the desired solvency standard of the bank, we can follow the previously described procedure exactly and determine first the α-quantile of the revenue distribution and subtract the simulated, most likely level of "fixed" costs from that amount.

Both of the approaches previously described provide a similar route to determine the required capital amount for business risk. However, it can be helpful to use a combination of the two approaches in order to make best use of the available data. Additionally, the results of either of the two approaches could be compared to the capitalization of companies observable in the market.[354] This approach is especially helpful when bank data does not supply sufficient information to determine the requirement for business risk capital. Market data of nonbanks engaged in banking-related activities can fill this gap. Besides addressing the difficulty that we then need to assume that observable book or market capital equals required business risk capital, a number of other assumptions must be met. The analogue company must:

---

[351]If data available are sufficiently granular, this approach can also be applied directly at the business unit level.

[352]For instance, we could model the impact of the economic conditions on (expected) credit performance, and hence losses, or the impact of shifts in the interest rate curves on the treasury result.

[353]Of course, the quality of the model is dependent on the stability of the business and the quality and quantity of the data available. This requires proper adjustments for growth, economic cycles, and other factors such as inflation.

[354]Therefore, often called "market analogues."

- Be exposed to the same fundamental and similar business risks with the same volatility[355] and diversification benefits from the mix of activities
- Have the same certain solvency standard (or one needs to adjust for it)
- Be exposed to a minimum of market and credit risk or must have the same (stable) credit rating history
- Have the same "fixed" cost base
- Be present in same geographical areas

All of these assumptions make it very difficult to find appropriately comparable companies. Nonetheless, the results of this benchmarking exercise can be useful for checking the results of the historical accounting-based approach and the Monte Carlo simulation approach.

If business risk capital is not determined at the aggregate bank level but rather at the business unit level, for aggregating the results, one also needs to consider the benefits of diversification when calculating the overall required capital amount. In order to calculate these diversification benefits, we need to estimate a correlation matrix that produces the overall bank-wide business capital figure, when applied to the business units' capital figures. However, the difficulty lies both with determining the correlations and in how the overall capital amount is then allocated back to the single business units.

In practice, the overall amount of business risk capital is allocated back to the business units as a percentage of their fixed costs base (mostly as a percentage of noninterest expenses) because, as we have seen, fixed costs tend to be the most predictive driver of business risk capital. Even though this approach ignores the fact that some percentage of the variable costs are also considered to be fixed when deriving the capital amount, it has the advantage of giving incentive to the business unit managers to reduce (overall) costs or to move to a more variable cost structure.

Problems with the Quantification of Operational Risk   Even though "pure" statistics is less powerful for measuring operating risk[356] than for measuring credit and market risk, the "Basle II proposal" (beyond focusing on credit risk) for the first time calls for explicit (regulatory) capital requirements for event risks.[357] This means that the new regulatory framework will be com-

---

[355]The analogue company must have the same mix of activities. Only some business lines, such as asset management or data processing, have directly comparable analogues in the market.
[356]For a similar line of reasoning, see Stulz (2000), pp. 4-15–4-16.
[357]Also, for the first time, interest rate risk in the banking book is subject to regulatory requirements.

prehensive across types of risk—which is a major change in philosophy but consistent with the industry's best practice,[358] which has been described previously.

However, the lack of (loss) data, internal experience, and awareness of operational risk leads to having little confidence in the economic capital numbers and, consequently, to only low recognition by the management[359] and almost no usage of the results in the economic decision-making process.[360] Despite this lack of data, measurement,[361] and management[362] acceptance, we have seen that dealing with operational risk is, in many cases, more a management than a measurement issue.[363] The statistical approach must, therefore, be complimented by management and process initiatives. Only a set of integrated processes, tools, and mitigation strategies (e.g., to reduce the exposure, frequency, or severity of events) works well.[364] The best results are achieved when process and culture are in balance.[365] Therefore, collecting "insurance" premiums for expected losses via adequate pricing is only appropriate for some kinds of operational risks, while for some others (also) holding economic capital is required.

In the discussed measurement approaches, again, only the correlation of the operational risks with the existing bank portfolio counts. However, operational risk tends to be highly specific risk, so that it does not make a real difference whether uncorrelated events are measured against the bank's portfolio of such risks or against a broad market portfolio.

Aggregation of Economic Capital across Risk Types   We have seen above that it is difficult to determine the correlations between various transactions even within the same risk type. We nonetheless have tried to do so because we wanted to determine the overall required capital amount for a whole portfolio of transactions. Although this may look fairly straightforward at first sight, since all of the risks were of the same type and we used the same measurement methodology, it is not—for very simple practical estimation reasons.

---

[358]See Oliver Wyman Report (2000), p. 1.

[359]See Wills et al. (1999), p. 87.

[360]See Wills et al. (1999), p. 90.

[361]The effort to try and measure operational risk can substantially improve the data situation and, hence, the accuracy of the estimates.

[362]Linking the results of the measurement process to performance measurement and (pecuniary) compensation also greatly helps to improve the acceptance.

[363]See Cooper (1999), p. 6.

[364]See Wills et al. (1999), p. 11.

[365]See Wills et al. (1999), p. 109.

Therefore, it appears not only appropriate but also a simple practical necessity to determine the correlations between the types of risk in a second step to thus aggregate the capital requirements for the overall bank level. This multistage correlation approach,[366] therefore, applies two correlation matrices: one within the risk type and a second one across the types of risk.

However, it is even more difficult to determine the correlations for the second matrix. Therefore, in practice, these correlations are ignored altogether, and the aggregated capital requirements by risk type are simply summed to determine the overall amount. This obviously overstates the capital requirement as long as the correlations are smaller than one. This approach is often justified by the fact that banks want to create an extra capital buffer (for simple safety reasons) for all risks that are not quantified in any of the three types of risk. This seems to be especially valid, for example, for model risk, the risk that the measurement model itself is ill specified. On the other hand, some other banks try to determine the correlations for the second matrix by employing a macroeconomic simulation model. Despite its usefulness (especially when also modeling operational risks with it), this approach seems difficult to implement and will lead to a mistake[367] by ignoring some of the true correlations between transactions belonging to various types of risk. This is especially relevant when we try to disaggregate the capital requirement to the single transaction level.

The overall, aggregated capital requirement at an average bank is typically split as shown in Table 5.3.[368]

TABLE 5.3 Split of Economic Capital[1]

Type of Risk	Economic Capital Requirement as a Percentage of Overall Economic Capital
Credit Risk	53%
Market Risk	17%
Operational Risk	30%

[1]Note that the split of economic capital depends heavily on the chosen confidence level.

---

[366]See Schröck (1997), pp. 73+, Buhr (2000), pp. 205+.

[367]We are not trying to make a statement on how big that mistake is here.

[368]See Wills et al. (1999), p. 92. These numbers are similar to the average of the observations in Drzik et al. (1998a), p. 25, who give the following (rough) split: credit risk: 53%, market risk: 20%, operational risk: 27%. However, the new Basle proposal (see Basle Committee on Banking Supervision (2001), p. 28, paragraph 161) indicates that banks hold on average only 20% of their economic capital for operational risk.

Concerns with the Suggested Bottom-Up Approach   In this section we will discuss both the practical as well as the theoretical concerns when economic capital is calculated bottom-up according to the suggested approach.

Practical Concerns   As indicated in the introduction to this section, we will first discuss practical concerns such as the aggregation and allocation of economic capital, and the consistent application of the suggested bottom-up approach.

Aggregation and Allocation of Economic Capital   The first and foremost concern with economic capital, calculated as described above, is that the incremental or marginal economic capital amount of a single transaction[369] in a portfolio context differs from the economic capital calculated for that transaction on a standalone basis (as long as the correlations are smaller than 1).[370] Since the latter approach obviously ignores any correlations, that is, any potential for diversification of the transaction to the rest of the portfolio, the sum of the standalone economic capital amounts overestimates the overall required capital amount at the portfolio level.

When deciding on whether a transaction adds value to the overall bank, that is, making a marginal decision, obviously the marginal capital amount is relevant.[371] Therefore, considering the diversification benefits is crucial for determining the correct capital requirement at the bank level. However, this approach creates problems for the full allocation of all economic capital back to the constituting transactions.[372] This is so because the sum of the marginal amount of economic capital—calculated, for example, by the "with and without" approach—will result in too little capital as compared to the overall sum calculated at the portfolio level. Therefore, some of the overall required economic capital remains unallocated. And the amount of unallocated capital increases the smaller the correlations between the transactions are. Only in the extreme case, when the transactions are all perfectly corre-

---

[369]The best way to determine that marginal economic capital is, as described previously, to calculate the economic capital requirement for a portfolio of transactions once with and once without the respective transaction ("with and without" approach). By building the difference of the two capital requirements at the portfolio level, we can determine the marginal or incremental capital requirement of the transaction under consideration.

[370]Note that we have not calculated the standalone VaR in the previous sections.

[371]See Merton and Perold (1993), p. 27. Note that for making other decisions on limiting and managing positions, the standalone economic capital may be more appropriate.

[372]See Merton and Perold (1993), p. 27.

lated, is all of the economic capital allocated by that approach.[373] "Grossing up"[374] the single allocated amounts by the percentage of unallocated economic capital also does not really address the problem, because it provides the wrong incentives. For instance, it would indicate higher benefits from reducing economic capital by shedding business units or transactions than would actually appear to be the case.

The suggested approach for the three types of risk and the consideration of correlations between these types of risk calculates the marginal economic capital, which is sensible for determining whether a transaction creates value or not. However, because we basically use proxies for the "with or without" approach to do so, the aggregation and allocation problem, as indicated, is unresolved.

This problem is fundamental to using VaR-type-based approaches to determine the required capital amount and is also identified by Artzner et al.,[375] for example, who relate the problem that top-down and bottom-up results may not be the same[376] to the problem that VaR is not coherent.[377] They formulate four conditions required for a risk measure to be coherent.[378] VaR violates the so-called subadditivity condition (while meeting the other three), that is:

$$VaR \ (X + Y) \neq VaR \ (X) + VaR \ (Y) \tag{5.38}$$

the condition that the sum of the standalone VaR of two positions X and Y be equal to the VaR of the portfolio consisting of the two positions is violated, making VaR a risk measure that is not coherent.

Practitioners as well as theorists mention another problem of calculating VaR on a standalone basis.[379] VaR can be subject to manipulation, because there are situations in which all traders are within their VaR limit but the overall bank might experience losses larger than VaR in any of the possible economic situations.

---

[373]For a mathematical proof of this proposition, see for example, Merton and Perold (1993), p. 32.

[374]See Merton and Perold (1993), p. 29, footnote 29. For a discussion of the various methods to reallocate the difference (e.g., proportional scaling after diversification, using internal betas), see Kimball (1998), pp. 44–52.

[375]See Artzner et al. (1997) and (1999).

[376]They approach the problem, however, from the perspective of an exchange calculating margin requirement of single transactions. Here it is impossible and also not desired to view a single position in a portfolio context.

[377]A term first introduced by Artzner et al. (1997), p. 68.

[378]These are subadditivity, homogeneity, monotonicity, and a risk-free condition. For a detailed definition of these conditions see Artzner et al. (1997), pp. 68+.

[379]See, for example, Johanning (1998), p. 95, and Artzner et al. (1997), p. 68.

Consistent Application of the Measurement Framework   In order to make the risk measurement across the three types of risk compatible, we must apply the framework for determining economic capital consistently. We will briefly discuss three areas that are especially important in this respect.

Consistent choice of the measurement period: As indicated in the discussion of the derivation of the economic capital for each of the three types of risk, the measurement period over which this forward-looking total risk measure is applied should be consistent across these three types of risks. However, in general, the economically relevant distribution of (gains and) losses is the one that corresponds to (gains and) losses the bank can do nothing about after having itself committed to a portfolio of financial assets, that is, the time horizon throughout which the bank has no control over the distribution.[380]

This differentiated holding period perspective—which is the relevant perspective from a management intervention point of view—has little to do with the gains and losses when we view them from a value-creation perspective. There are various reasons[381] why this is the case and why a consistent one-year horizon for risk quantification makes sense:

- We use the external rating agencies' estimation of the one-year default probability as the anchor point of our calibration of the confidence level (this point is discussed later). Therefore, we need to use a consistent distribution across risk types to make sensible use of this external benchmark.
- Since value creation should be always linked to pecuniary incentives for the employees[382] and the review cycle for employees is typically on an annual basis, we should choose the same (consistent) time horizon to evaluate the performance and riskiness.
- Likewise, the typical review cycle for a credit customer is on an annual basis—upon the presentation of the annual financial statement.
- Because of the lack of data for observing the (economic) value changes of the positions in the portfolio (this is especially the case for illiquid credits and operational risk), we need to use the profit and loss (P&L) statement as a fallback proxy of the economic returns.[383] Even though many companies and banks have switched their reporting cycle to

---

[380]See Stulz (2000), p. 4-14.
[381]Culp and Miller (1998), p. 28, provide a list of other determinants for choosing a consistent time horizon: key decision-making events, major reporting events, regulatory examinations, tax assessments, external quality assessments, and so on.
[382]See, for example, Stewart (1991), p. 225.
[383]For a different opinion see Kimball (1998), p. 44, footnote 13.

quarterly, much of the relevant data is (accurately) only available on an annual basis. Therefore, the shortest, consistent time horizon is annual.[384]

■ As was shown in the market risk section, short holding periods and the possibility of the quick liquidation of a position do not explain the (accumulated annual) volatility of gains and losses in a bank's trading book. Since we can observe that the volatility in the annual P&L is often greater than a daily or monthly VaR, it seems advisable to use an annual (and more conservative[385]) horizon for the quantification of the risk in the accrued overall trading position.

Therefore, using the annualized deviation from the expected outcome consistently across all types of risk, that is, setting H equal to one year, is a fair way to compare the relative contribution of the sources of risk to the bank's overall return volatility.

Consistency of loss versus value-based approach: As was indicated above, the ultimate distribution for determining economic capital is the distribution of changes in the value of the underlying portfolio. However, banks do not always have the information to compute the changes in the riskiness, and hence the value of illiquid loans, on, for example, a daily basis. At best, banks can acquire and evaluate such data on a quarterly or, more commonly, on a yearly basis. Unless the bank has a sophisticated mark-to-model method available to determine the value of illiquid credits assets, no value changes can be calculated. Therefore, the suggested *EL/UL* framework, which is consistent with the VaR idea of estimating the distance between the expected and the unexpected outcome, is the only way to determine an adequate proxy. Moreover, as long as the lending book is not liquid, the loss volatility of the *EL/UL* framework is a good estimate for the value volatility determined by a mark-to-model methodology.[386] Besides, the results can be checked by the suggested top-down approach as presented later in this chapter.

Consistent choice of the confidence level: As already mentioned, external rating agencies use a one-year time horizon for their estimate of the

---

[384]The caveat of this hypothesis is, however, that it assumes that all risks are eventually fed through a bank's P&L and are, therefore, reflected in the earnings distribution. Vis-à-vis the (economic) return distribution, macroeconomic risks may only show up with a large time difference.

[385]Of course, extrapolating a one-day VaR to one year assumes that an institution will not take any intervening steps if it incurs large losses.

[386]For example, Garside (1998), p. 24, shows the difference between the economic capital requirement of the two approaches basically diminishes to below 10% when the confidence level is chosen high enough (i.e., higher than 99.95%).

default probability of a bank's senior debt. We use this data point as the only objectively observable calibration point of our confidence level, which allows us to anchor economic capital requirements on an absolute basis. We apply this confidence level consistently across risk types. The difficulty, however, is to determine the senior debt confidence level of the various distributions. Often, as a shortcut and as a conservative estimate, the 99.97% confidence level (for a AA-rated bank) of the overall distribution[387] under consideration is taken. This might also be the only practical way to determine the economic capital requirement, because breaking down the senior debt confidence level to a single transaction/ subportfolio level might just be impossible.

Other General Concerns   As mentioned, the approach of basing the economic capital estimate on the asset distribution is based on the assumption that the bank's liabilities are fixed and not contingent. Otherwise, we need to consider the distribution of net assets, which can easily lead to the result that no economic capital is necessary.[388]

The approach just presented concentrates on financial risks. Therefore, it mostly ignores the relevance of a fundamental change in the macroeconomic environment that leads to a change in one or more of the relevant risk factors. For instance, a significant change in the dollar exchange rate can indicate a fundamental shift in the business conditions for banking in North America, for example, decreasing the fee income. Another example would be the impact of a serious event risk hitting an organization and leading to a dramatic disruption of its business. Unless the submodeling for each of the three types of risk is not linked to a proper macroeconomic model, these risks will be ignored in the suggested framework. However, as we will present shortly, the top-down approach implicitly includes the market's perception/ information on all of these interdependencies, so it will usually lead to a higher result than the bottom-up procedure and can therefore provide a useful benchmark.[389]

---

[387]This basically ignores the discussion that the critical threshold should be determined at a confidence level of the senior debt tranche thereof.

[388]Even though we do not consider insurance risk in this book, this is exactly what can happen there: Many insurance liability payoffs are contingent on the asset management's performance (except for a minimum guaranteed return). Therefore, the presented asset approach will lead to false results.

[389]Of course, to get to a final evaluation of such a general opinion, banks would have to publish more detailed information on their economic capital numbers. The third pillar of the new Basle Accord (see Basle Committee on Banking Supervision [2001], pp. 33+), which is market discipline, should greatly help in that respect.

Theoretical Concerns Schröder was one of the first[390] to point out that VaR-based risk measures have a serious shortcoming in that they lack a sound theoretical foundation.[391] We can define the so-called lower partial moment (*LPM*) of a distribution as:

$$LPM_n(t) = \int_{-\infty}^{t} (t - X)^n f(X) dX \qquad (5.39)^{392}$$

where t = Target (minimum) return
X = Realized return
n = Moment of the distribution
f = Probability density function of the returns X

The moment n of the distribution determines (theoretically) the type of the utility function used.[393] For instance, for $n = 0$,[394] this approach[395] assumes a risk-neutral investor who is only interested in the probability of falling short of the target minimum return t, ignoring the extent (or severity) of this event when it occurs. For $n = 1$, we consider a risk-averse investor who is interested in both the probability and the extent (severity) of the actual return falling short of the target return t. It therefore calculates the expected value of the shortfall.[396] For $n = 2$, the result is similar to the semivariance and is, therefore, also often called target semivariance.[397]

Replacing the target return t with VaR_α, the value at risk at the $(1 - \alpha)$ confidence level, it is easy to show, because:

$$LPM_0(-VaR_\alpha) = \int_{-\infty}^{-VaR} f(X) dX = F(-VaR_\alpha) = \alpha\%, \text{ that}$$

$$-VaR_\alpha = F^{-1}(LPM_0) \qquad (5.40)$$

where F = Cumulative probability function
F^{-1} = The inverse of the cumulative probability function

---

[390] At least in discussing this in the context of VaR approaches.
[391] See Schröder (1996), pp. 1–2. Obviously, Markowitz (1959) already points into the same direction.
[392] See Fishburn (1977), p. 116.
[393] See Wittrock (1995), p. 43.
[394] Obviously, this is the least restrictive shortfall risk measure possible.
[395] As can be easily seen, LPM_0 reduces to the (cumulative) probability distribution.
[396] In the above methodology, we would call this expected loss.
[397] See Copeland and Weston (1988), p. 152. This measure is also suitable for risk-averse investors.

RISK MANAGEMENT AND VALUE CREATION IN FINANCIAL INSTITUTIONS

Therefore, VaR is the same kind of risk measure as the LPM_0.[398] $LPM_0(-VaR_\alpha)$ and $(-)VaR_\alpha$ look at the same point of the cumulative probability distribution—but from opposite angles.[399] However, since LPM_1 is a necessary condition for second-order stochastic dominance,[400] VaR is not a risk measure that is compatible with maximizing the expected utility. Because VaR only measures the probability, but not the extent (severity), of the losses when they occur,[401] it shows merely first-order stochastic dominance.[402] VaR is, therefore, a suitable risk measure for risk-neutral investors.[403] Thus, Schröder comes to the conclusion that only LPM_n measures with $n > 0$ provide the basis for the development of a generalized VaR measure that takes into account risk aversion.[404]

Similarly, approaches from extreme value theory[405] are being used to try to answer the question "how bad is bad?" by considering not only the probability but also the extent to which losses occur beyond a critical threshold. These approaches can be defined as:

$$E[-X \mid X \leq VaR_\alpha] = LPM_1(-VaR_\alpha) = \int_{-\infty}^{-VaR_\alpha} (-VaR_\alpha - X)f(X)dX \quad (5.41)$$

They measure the average of the future values of the return X of a position or portfolio, conditional on the fact that the value is below a certain threshold value or VaR at a certain quantile α (VaR_α) of the value or return distribution. Therefore, they are also called "tail conditional expectations."[406] These measures can best be explained in a simulation context. If, for example, VaR is calculated at the $\alpha = 1\%$ level and we have 10,000 simulation runs, then $VaR_{1\%}$ is the largest of the 100 smallest realizations in the simulation, whereas the tail conditional expectation calculates the average of the 100 smallest realizations,[407] thus being more conservative than VaR.[408] Given that the tail conditional expectation can be related back to the lower partial moment one (LPM_1) of the distribution (as was shown in the above equa-

[398]VaR can be, therefore, viewed as a special case of the shortfall risk measures; see Schröder (1996), p. 1.
[399]See Guthoff et al. (1998), pp. 32+.
[400]See Hirschbeck (1998), p. 271, and his references to the literature. For an extensive discussion of this point see Guthoff et al. (1998), pp. 24+.
[401]See Johanning (1998), p. 57.
[402]See Guthoff et al. (1998), p. 33.
[403]See Schröder (1996), pp. 1–2.
[404]See Schröder (1996), pp. 12+.
[405]See, for example, Embrechts et al. (1997).
[406]See Artzner et al. (1999), p. 204.
[407]See Artzner et al. (1997), p. 68.
[408]See Artzner et al. (1999), p. 204.

tion), this measure is compatible with maximizing the expected utility and with the assumption of risk-averse investors.

Therefore, some authors[409] suggest that this measure is more suitable both for risk management and from a regulatory perspective. Even though tail conditional expectations are more complicated to calculate, they do not require more input data than the calculation of VaR-based economic capital measures. However, the difficulty is that they cannot be as easily calibrated to an external benchmark as VaR-based economic capital measures. Additionally, as we have shown previously, banks themselves are risk-neutral in the first place and only behave as if they were risk-averse because of financial distress costs.[410]

On the contrary, (risk-averse) investors are indeed not only interested in the probability but also in the severity of such a lower-tail event. However, again, banks are different in this respect. Almost all of the customers' deposits are insured and almost all of the negative events following the threat of a bank run are avoided by regulatory intervention. Therefore, one could argue that most of the stakeholders[411] do not really have to care about the severity element and are only interested in the probability (i.e., the threat of this lower-tail event happening). Nonetheless, (junior) debt holders in particular really care about severity as much as they do about the probability of a lower-tail event hitting their tranche.

Despite the practical and theoretical concerns discussed previously, economic capital is a useful and practical measure for total risk in banks. The danger that any of these concerns will lead to problems can be avoided by checking the results calculated from the bottom up by another method, such as the Merton, or top-down approach, which we will discuss in the next section.

Suggestion of an Approach to Determine Economic Capital from the Top Down

While the other capital measures (Tier-1 capital, book capital, and market capitalization of the bank's outstanding stocks) are directly observable, we need to estimate the fictional capital measure economic capital. As we have seen, since the bank cares about total risk and tries to avoid financial distress situations, we need to use a downside risk measure in order to derive economic capital at the corporate level. There are two ways to do this:

---

[409]See, for example, Guthoff et al. (1998) and Artzner (1999).

[410]This is not the same risk aversion assumed in a traditional CAPM world.

[411]Deposits are usually the largest source of funds in a bank, see, for example, Davies and Lee (1997), p. 33.

■ As described in detail, we can use the sophisticated, value-at-risk-based risk measurement models for market, credit, and operational risk to derive the total required economic capital for the bank in a bottom-up procedure. In order to do so, we would need data on a transaction-by-transaction level.[412] Since the aggregation of thus-derived economic capital numbers is associated with difficulties in estimating the correct correlations between the various types of risk as well as substantial modeling risk (especially for operational risk capital), the results tend to be ambiguous.[413]

■ Economic capital can be estimated from a top-down perspective using an approach based on option pricing theory.[414] We will present in this section a new version of this approach that uses the (future) development of the (market) value of a firm's assets to model default risk. Since default occurs when the value of a firm's assets falls so low that they are worth less than the firm's liabilities, one can use this fact to estimate the probability of default.[415] However, in this section we will turn this approach upside-down. We will infer the probability of default from publicly available agency ratings[416] (for senior debt issues of the bank). We then use this estimate in combination with an assumed asset distribution to find the distance between the default point (i.e., is the critical threshold point of the asset distribution at the implied default probability) and the expected value of the assets. As we have seen, the distance (expressed in dollar terms) between these two points of the distribution is similar to a VaR-based estimate of economic capital. We will use this newly suggested top-down approach to check the results from the bottom-up procedure.

---

[412]Unfortunately, the complete set of such information is unavailable to bank outsiders for disclosure and competitive reasons and, hence, such an analysis cannot be provided in this book.

[413]Additionally, often—according to anecdotal evidence—operational risk capital is estimated to match the difference between economic capital from other sources and the total of either book or market value of equity and is, hence, associated with relatively large uncertainty.

[414]See Gupton et al. (1997), p. 59. Consulting companies such as Oliver, Wyman & Company can use their broad experience in the financial services industry and can use benchmarks for comparable financial institutions to derive reasonable top-down estimates of economic capital.

[415]The leading commercial version of this approach is a model provided by KMV; see Gupton et al. (1997), p. 59.

[416]From Standard & Poor's (S&P) or Moody's.

In this section, we will first set the theoretical foundations for applying this approach and subsequently describe the suggested top-down approach based on option theory in more detail, before we apply it in a real-life example. We will then briefly evaluate the suggested approach.

Theoretical Foundations   As indicated, we will first discuss the theoretical foundations—both general and specific—for applying the suggested top-down approach.

General Theoretical Foundations   Merton first applied the basic option-pricing approach developed by Black and Scholes[417] to value corporate securities[418] by assuming that (limited liability) shareholders have the right, but not the obligation, to take over the firm by paying off the debt holders.

Assuming that we can calculate or observe the current (market) value of the firm[419] at time $t = 0$ ($V_{A, 0}$), we can use the underlying assumptions of a geometric Brownian motion (which state that the returns on the firm's assets are instantaneously normal and have a drift rate of μ and a constant asset volatility σ_A) to model the value of the firm's assets $V_{A, t}$ at time t, which is uncertain and dependent on the general economic conditions. Using the resulting differential equation:

$$\frac{dV_{A,t}}{V_{A,t}} = \mu dt + \sigma_A dz \tag{5.42}$$

where z follows a Wiener process.

We can express the value of the firm's assets $V_{A, t}$ at time t as:

$$V_{A,t} = V_{A,0} \cdot e^{\left[\left(\mu - \frac{\sigma^2}{2}\right)t + \sigma\sqrt{t}Z_t\right]} \tag{5.43}$$

which also indicates that the firm's assets are assumed to be lognormally distributed (Z_t is normally distributed with zero mean and variance t[420]). Hence, the expected value of the firm's assets at time t is:

$$E\left(V_{A,t}\right) = V_{A,0} \cdot e^{\mu t} \tag{5.44}[421]$$

---

[417]See Black and Scholes (1972).
[418]See Merton (1974), p. 449.
[419]This value is ideally derived as the present value of the firm's future (free) cash flows.
[420]See Crouhy et al. (1999), p. 9.
[421]See Hull (1997), pp. 210–216.

We now assume for simplicity that there is only one class of equity and one class of debt in the bank. At least for the debt this assumption does not seem unrealistic, because in the case when the bank approaches default, basically all debt holders will want to reclaim their liabilities at the same time (bank run), making different classes of seniority and maturity less relevant.[422]

We further assume an M&M world with respect to the value additivity[423] of these two classes of debt and equity so that the financing decision has (initially) no impact on the total value of assets. Therefore:

$$V_{A,t} = V_{E,t} + V_{D,t} \tag{5.45}$$

where $V_{E,t}$ = Market value of equity at time t
$V_{D,t}$ = Market value of debt at time t
$V_{D,t} = V_{D,T} \cdot e^{-r'(T-t)}$

assuming that the debt matures at time T and that $V_{D,t}$ is the value of a zero-coupon bond with face value $V_{D,T}$ (which is equal to the book value of debt) discounted at interest rate r' (which is typically not the risk-free rate).

From that we can infer—given that shareholders have to repay the debt holders and can then claim the remainder of the asset value—the payoff for the shareholders at time T is:

$$V_{E,T} = \max[(V_{A,T} - V_{D,T}); 0] \tag{5.46}$$

which is identical to the payoff structure of a call option. Thus, in the simplified case, where we allow for only one class of equity and one class of outstanding debt, equity can be viewed as a call option on the underlying assets of the firm with a strike price equal to the value of the firm's liabilities.

Since we evaluate the value of the shareholders' claim at the time of maturity T of the debt, we can use the Black-Scholes formula for pricing European call options to price V_E at any time t before T:[424]

$$V_{E,t} = V_{A,0} \cdot N(d_1) - V_{D,T} \cdot e^{-r(T-t)} \cdot N(d_2) \tag{5.47}$$

---

[422]See discussion above.
[423]Note that this assumption only relates to value additivity and not the overall top-down approach.
[424]See Hull (1997), p. 241. Of course this assumes that hedging using the underlying is possible and that all assets are fully tradable. Additionally, all other assumptions of the Black-Scholes world need to be met.

where
$$d_1 = \frac{\ln\left(\dfrac{V_{A,0}}{V_{D,T}}\right) + \left(r + \dfrac{\sigma_A^2}{2}\right)\cdot(T-t)}{\sigma_A \cdot \sqrt{T-t}}$$

and
$$d_2 = \frac{\ln\left(\dfrac{V_{A,0}}{V_{D,T}}\right) + \left(r - \dfrac{\sigma_A^2}{2}\right)\cdot(T-t)}{\sigma_A \cdot \sqrt{T-t}} = d_1 - \sigma_A \cdot \sqrt{T-t}$$

where $N(\cdot)$ = Cumulative standard normal probability distribution function

T = Time of maturity

r = Risk-free rate

We use the risk-free rate as the expected rate of return here, because we are in a world of risk-neutral evaluation.[425] As can be easily seen, the Black-Scholes equation does not include any variables that are affected by the risk preferences of the investors.

We can diagrammatically summarize the above as follows (see Figure 5.11).

As we can see in Figure 5.11, r represents the expected return on the bank's assets in such a risk-neutral world[426] and σ_A the volatility of the bank's assets, which drive the probability that $V_{A,T}$ is smaller than (or equal to) $V_{D,T}$ and hence the probability that the bank is in default at time T.

Specific Theoretical Foundations As was already indicated, the purpose of the suggested approach is to apply the previously depicted approach to banks and turn it upside-down by using the default probability implied in publicly available agency ratings. Since these ratings try to estimate the probability of a company's specific debt issue being in default in one year's time, we set our horizon T equal to 1.[427] However, this complicates the analysis: Usually, we do not know for certain how much of the total debt is due in one year's time.[428] The only reasonable proxy we can use is the balance sheet information on debt due in one year.[429] However, companies typically have the possibility of refinancing some of their short-term debt as long-term liabili-

---

[425]See Hull (1997), pp. 239–240.
[426]It will later be replaced by μ, the actual return on assets.
[427]Other reasons are, for example, that the reporting cycle in most European countries is one year and the previously mentioned arguments in the horizon discussion.
[428]Deposits can be withdrawn at any time without prior notice.
[429]This will typically be the book value and not the required market value (that is unobservable in most of the cases).

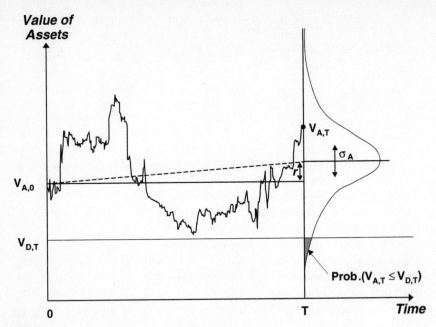

Figure 5.11 Distribution of asset values and default probability.
Source: Adapted from Ong (1999), p. 83.

ties when they approach financial difficulties. Therefore, the critical threshold for companies to go into default lies somewhere between the amount of the long-term liabilities and the short-term debt[430] and will be labeled in our methodology default point (*DP*).[431]

Without further elaborating how we can estimate *DP*, we need to replace $V_{D,T}$ by *DP* in our equations. Therefore, the probability of the bank being in default at time *T* is defined by:

$$p\,[V_{A,T} \le DP] = p\left[\ln(V_{A,0}) + \left(r - \frac{\sigma_A^2}{2}\right)\cdot T + \sigma_A \sqrt{T} \cdot \varepsilon \le \ln(DP)\right] \quad (5.48)$$

where $p(\cdot)$ = Probability

---

[430]See Ong (1999), pp. 83–84, who suggests that the default point *DP* should be defined as the amount of short-term debt plus 50% of the amount of long-term debt.
[431]Even though we do not specify *DP* for the time being, it will typically differ from $V_{D,T}$.

ε = A random change in the bank's return as defined by z, the Wiener process

r = The risk-free rate, as we still assume a risk-neutral evaluation world

It is straightforward to show[432] that:

$$p[\cdot] = N(-d_2) \qquad (5.49)$$

and that $(-d_2)$ is the normalized distance between $V_{A,T}$ and DP.[433] Since we can infer from the public rating how large p is, we could solve Equation (5.49) for DP and can calculate the difference between $V_{A,T}$ and DP, which is a proxy for the required economic capital given the risks a bank holds on its books and that protects it against lower-tail outcomes up to a predetermined level, that is, the probability of default.

Obviously, this approach has various caveats:

■ This procedure implicitly assumes risk-neutral default probabilities. However, default probabilities induced from public ratings are actual probabilities. Therefore, as Crouhy and Mark[434] show, r, the risk-free rate, in Equation (5.48) needs to be replaced by μ, the expected return on the bank's assets, to obtain consistent results.

■ This procedure assumes that the probability distribution of the asset values is known and lognormal. Whereas the transformation used to induce default probabilities from a standard normal distribution is valid, the true distribution of asset values is unknown and might be very different.

■ The empirical distribution to map the normalized distance between $V_{A,T}$ and DP to default probabilities cannot be calibrated for banks, since too few actual bank defaults can be observed.[435]

■ Neither V_A nor σ_A can be observed in reality. Likewise, other input parameters are also either unobservable or are difficult to estimate.

Suggested Top-Down Approach   In this section we will describe the suggested top-down approach based on option theory in more detail, before we apply it in a real-life example.

Theory Underlying the Suggested Top-Down Approach   Given these caveats, I would like to suggest the following methodology to determine a bank's economic

---

[432]See Ong (1999), p. 86.
[433]It is, therefore, often called "distance to default."
[434]See Crouhy and Mark (1998) and Crouhy et al. (1999), p. 10.
[435]This is especially true for banks rated as investment grade.

capital by adjusting the top-down approach based on option theory. In short, we will first estimate realistic values for V_A and σ_A and then employ the results to infer a theoretical default point DP using the normalized distance to default (DTD)[436] in combination with the observed (i.e., actual, not risk-neutral) default probability. Even though all of the eventual input parameters for deriving economic capital are inferred, we will use real, observable data as a starting point for the estimation.

We start with Equation (5.45) and assume that the total value of a bank's assets is the sum of the value of its debt and its equity. If all assets were traded, equity would be the difference between the market value of the bank's assets (on- and off-balance sheet) and the market value of the bank's liabilities (also on- and off-balance sheet).[437] Even though we would like to use market values as best estimates, they are often not observable. For instance, market values of bank liabilities are very difficult to determine, because a bank's liabilities mostly consist of customer deposits and other short-term obligations that are not publicly traded and that have a nominal yield typically below their fair market return. It is, therefore, rather difficult to determine the market value of these obligations.[438] However, since banks have to repay the nominal amount of these obligations, it is fair to take the book value of these obligations into account, rather than their unobservable market value, as a first proxy. Additionally, banks have significant off-balance sheet obligations that we need to consider in estimating the default point and hence the probability of default (PD).

As a starting point for the estimation, we use balance-sheet and off-balance-sheet data from annual financial statements:[439]

$$BV_A \quad = \text{ Book value of total assets}$$
$$BV_{OBS} = \text{ Book value of off-balance sheet liabilities}$$

We must also consider the split of the on-balance sheet liabilities. We assume that if a bank is approaching default, basically all of the short-term and customer liabilities become due immediately (bank run) and 50% of the other liabilities[440] (see the previous discussion of the default point and the

---

[436]An exact definition will be given below.

[437]This equation does implicitly assume that the bank has to repay even the insured deposits in the case of default. See Berger et al. (1995b), p. 411.

[438]See Copeland et al. (1994), p. 479. Also see Berger et al. (1995), p. 412.

[439]Even though balance sheet information is often manipulated (known as "window dressing") around the reporting dates.

[440]These other liabilities can be mostly viewed as subordinated debt (or Tier-2 capital in the definition of the Basle Accord) and are characterized by having a long maturity and being difficult to redeem quickly in times of crisis. See Berger et al. (1995), p. 409.

critical threshold at which a bank goes into default). Hence, we also extract the following two percentages from annual reports:

$ST\%$ = Customer and short-term liabilities as percent of total assets
$Other\%$ = Other (long-term) liabilities as percentage of total assets

Additionally, we assume that all off-balance sheet liabilities will become due immediately if the bank approaches default. Since we use annual financial statement figures and apply the information from publicly available ratings, we set the horizon for our analysis to $T = 1$.
Therefore, as a first proxy, we estimate the default point DP' as:

$$DP' = \left(ST\% + \frac{1}{2} Other\% \right) \times BV_A + BV_{OBS} \qquad (5.50)^{441}$$

where $'$ = indicates a first proxy.

Contrary to the value of bank debt, the market value of equity (V_E) is fairly easy to observe. We can derive V_E either by calculating (share value) $\times$ (number of shares outstanding) or by directly taking sanitized market values from sources such as Datastream.
Therefore, we are able to calculate as a starting point for our estimations the market value of assets V_A' as:

$$V_A' = DP' + V_E \qquad (5.51)^{442}$$

As we saw in the Merton approach, we can view the (market) value of equity as a call option on the underlying assets of the firm. Using the Black-Scholes option-pricing formula for European call options, we can therefore write:[443]

$$V_E = V_A' \cdot N(d_1) - DP' \cdot e^{-r \cdot T} \cdot N(d_2) \qquad (5.52)$$

where:
$$d_1 = \frac{\ln\left(\dfrac{V_A'}{DP'}\right) + \left(r + \dfrac{\sigma_A^2}{2}\right) \cdot T}{\sigma_A \cdot \sqrt{T}}$$

---

[441]Basically following Ong (1999), pp. 83–84.
[442]This approach is also used by other authors. For example, Mian (1996), p. 420, and Tufano (1996), p. 1108, use as a proxy for firm size, book value of assets minus book value of common equity plus market value of common equity = firm value.
[443]See Hull (1997), p. 241.

$$\text{and} \quad d_2 = \frac{\ln\left(\dfrac{V_A'}{DP'}\right) + \left(r - \dfrac{\sigma_A^2}{2}\right) \cdot T}{\sigma_A \cdot \sqrt{T}} = d_1 - \sigma_A \cdot \sqrt{T}$$

where $N(\cdot)$ = Cumulative standard normal probability distribution function

r = Risk-free rate (note that we are still in a risk-neutral evaluation world[444] for deriving the value of V_E)

T = Time to maturity (= 1 [see horizon discussion above])

Whereas in Equation (5.52) V_A' is only a first proxy of what the true value of the assets of a bank is, σ_A is unknown. Yet, both input parameters are unobservable. However, since we know that equity is a call option on the firm's value, equity can be also defined as a portfolio that consists of Δ units[445] of firm value and a short position in the risk-free asset. Therefore, we can infer that the return on equity is perfectly correlated with the return on the value of the firm for small changes in the value of the firm[446] and can show that the volatility of the rate of return (σ_E) of the option V_E is:

$$\sigma_E = \Delta \frac{V_A}{V_E} \cdot \sigma_A \qquad (5.53)$$

This means that the volatility of equity is equal to $\Delta V_A/V_E$ times the volatility of the firm σ_A and the Δ is equal to the option delta $N(d_1)$.[447]

Given that we can observe the volatility of the rate of return σ_E in the stock market, we have now two unknowns and two equations: Equations (5.52) and (5.53). Therefore, we can now determine V_A and σ_A. However, as when trying to determine implied volatilities for quoted option prices, we cannot invert the option-pricing formula and need to apply an iterative search procedure[448] to solve both equations simultaneously.[449]

We use as observable input V_E, DP', r, and T, and estimate σ_E as the annualized volatility of the stock market returns in the year prior to the estimation point in time (i.e., year end). As defined previously, we use as a starting point for the iterative procedure:

$$V_A' = DP' + V_E \text{ (see Equation [5.51] above) and } \sigma_A = \sigma_E/4$$

---

[444]See Hull (1997), pp. 239–240.
[445]As we will see shortly, Δ is the option delta $N(d_1)$.
[446]A small change in the value of the firm d changes the value of the equity by ΔdV_A, see Stulz (2000), p. 18-9.
[447]See Cordell and King (1995), p. 538.
[448]See Hull (1997), p. 246.
[449]See Stulz (2000), p. 18-12.

since asset volatilities are very low for banks compared to the volatility of its traded equity[450] reflecting the high leverage (that magnifies the low σ_A).

We then proceed by iterating on Equations (5.52) and (5.53) until the V_E inferred from the option-pricing formula deviates from the observed input value V_E, and σ_E inferred from the other simultaneous Equation (5.53) deviates from the observed value σ_E less than ε (reasonably small), each by changing V_A and σ_A.

Hence, we have now derived a realistic estimate for V_A and σ_A and have thus been able to use the information implied in the stock market to derive forward-looking measures instead of backward-looking accounting information.

We will now use the publicly available (long-term [senior debt] bank) rating and the results from Brand and Bahar[451] to map ratings to (one-year) default probabilities (PDs).[452]

As we indicated previously, the following relationship between the probability of default (PD) and the distance to default (DTD) exists:

$$PD = N(-DTD) \qquad (5.54)$$

and therefore:

$$DTD = -N^{-1}(PD) \qquad (5.55)$$

where N^{-1} = The inverse of the standard normal cumulative distribution

As we have also mentioned, we are now applying actual instead of risk-neutral default probabilities. Therefore, we need to use μ instead of the risk-free rate to derive the normalized distance to default (DTD):

$$DTD = \frac{\ln\left(\dfrac{V_{A,0}}{DP}\right) + \left(\mu - \dfrac{1}{2}\sigma_A^2\right)T}{\sigma_A \cdot \sqrt{T}} \qquad (5.56)[453]$$

where μ = Expected return on the bank's assets

---

[450]No adjustment is necessary to directly observed equity volatility because it already reflects the higher leverage of banks.
[451]See Brand and Bahar (1999), p. 15.
[452]For more details see example below.
[453]See Crouhy et al. (1999), p. 10.

A reasonable estimate for μ is[454] the market value[455] weighted average costs of capital:

$$\mu = \frac{V_E}{V_A} \cdot \left(r + \beta(R_M - r)\right) + \left(1 - \frac{V_E}{V_A}\right) \cdot (r + s) \qquad (5.57)$$

where r = Risk-free rate
       R_M = Return on the market portfolio M
       $R_M - r$ = Market risk premium
       β = Stock market beta as derived in the market model version of the CAPM
       s = Spread above the risk-free rate commensurate with the bank's rating

Combining and rearranging Equations (5.55) and (5.56), we can solve for DP. By doing so, we improve on the prior estimate DP' for the default point, and again we use the information implied in the stock market. This seems reasonable because banks experience a relatively higher liquidity of their assets when they approach default. However, only the stock market implicitly contains information of how big the effects are.[456]
Hence:

$$DP = e^{\ln(V_A) + \mu - 0.5\,\sigma_A^2 - \sigma_A \cdot DTD} \qquad (5.58)$$

This reflects the fact that the true DP also deviates from its first estimate using book values. We assume here implicitly that the stock market information and the rating contain additional information.
Therefore:

$$Economic\ Capital = V_A - DP \qquad (5.59)$$

We will summarize the suggested approach diagrammatically, both to clarify the required input parameters and to show the dependencies between them (see Figure 5.12).

The suggested derivation of economic capital heavily depends on the fact that the top-down approach is based on a closed system of dependent variables. We are using this property to solve for one of these variables (DP) in order to be able to determine economic capital.

---

[454]Even though asset growth and equity growth are also reasonable candidates for μ, they have relatively little to do with the return on assets.
[455]As derived previously in the iterative procedure.
[456]Additionally, this information also considers the fact that banks are heavily regulated and that the "too-big-to-fail" doctrine might apply to them.

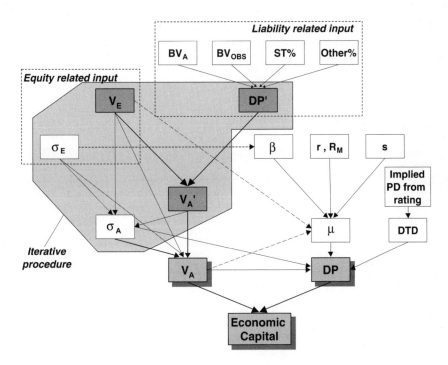

Figure 5.12 Input and output variables for suggested top-down approach.

Applying the Top-down Approach in Practice   Since Deutsche Bank published their bottom-up estimate of economic capital[457] using sophisticated risk measurement models in their annual reports of 1998 and 1999, we can test the suggested approach of whether it leads to reasonable numbers.

For the purposes of this exercise we will set T equal to one and use 5% as a rough estimate for the risk-free rate.[458] We first use balance-sheet and off-balance sheet data from these two annual reports and BankScope to derive BV_A (book value of total assets) and BV_{OBS} (book value of off-balance sheet liabilities) as well as the split of the liabilities ($ST\%$ and $Other\%$ as defined previously) to calculate the first estimate for DP'.

We use sanitized market values from Datastream to determine the market value of equity (V_E) and then calculate as a starting point for our other estimations the market value of assets V_A' as the sum of $DP' + V_E$. This data is summarized in Table 5.4.

---

[457]Except for Deutsche Bank in 1998 and 1999, none of the other European banks published economic capital numbers in their annual reports.
[458]This is not completely unreasonable given the yield overview for government bonds in, for example, Bundesbank (2000), p. 51.

Table 5.4   Input Data from Publicly Available Sources

Deutsche Bank AG (IAS) in bn. EUR	December 31, 1999	December 31, 1998
Total Assets = BV_A	805	604
Off-Balance Sheet Items = BV_{OBS}	224	165
V_E	52.0	35.6
Reported Economic Capital	19.3	15.9
Customer/ST Funds = $ST\%$	67.40%	70.50%
Other Funds = $Other\%$	10.60%	9.50%
$ST\% + 0.5 \times Other\%$	72.70%	75.25%
DP'	809	620
V_A'	861	655

Before we can apply the iterative procedure, we need to determine σ_E as the annualized volatility of the stock market returns in the year prior to the estimation point in time. We start with:

$$R_E = \ln\left(\frac{S_t}{S_{t-1}}\right) \qquad (5.60)$$

where R_E = Return on Deutsche Bank's stock
ln = Natural logarithm
S_t = Stock price at time t
$t-1$ = Earlier observation point of S, here: one week, that is, five trading days earlier[459]

We infer the weekly variance of stock returns by applying the following unbiased formula for sample estimation:

$$\sigma^2_{E,W} = \frac{1}{n-1}\left[\sum_{t=1}^{n}\ln\left(\frac{S_t}{S_{t-1}}\right)^2 - \frac{1}{n}\left[\sum_{t=1}^{n}\ln\left(\frac{S_t}{S_{t-1}}\right)\right]^2\right] \qquad (5.61)$$

where $\sigma^2_{E,W}$ = Variance of weekly stock returns

and transform this into the annualized volatility of the stock market returns by applying:

[459]We use weekly returns calculated on the basis of Wednesdays and applying common replacement rules: If the prior Wednesday was not a trading day, we use the prior Tuesday's stock price. If that was no trading day, we use the prior Monday's, and so forth.

$$\sigma_E = \sqrt{\sigma_{E,\,w}^2 \cdot 52} \qquad\qquad (5.62)^{460}$$

As defined above, we use as a starting point for the iterative procedure:

$$V_A' = DP' + V_E \text{ and } \sigma_A = \sigma_E/4$$

We then proceed by iterating on Equations (5.52) and (5.53) until the inferred values deviate from the observed input values less than $\varepsilon = 0.01\%$. The results for V_A and σ_A are shown in Table 5.5.

In order to calculate the distance to default (*DTD*), we first need to determine the implied default probabilities. For Deutsche Bank, we use the long-term senior debt rating from Standard & Poor's and the results from Brand and Bahar.[461] By using an exponential regression on the S&P default observations, we can infer the following equation from mapping rating [AAA; CCC] to numbers [1; 18]:[462]

$$PD = 0.004\% \cdot e^{(0.4699 \cdot Rating\text{-}Number)} \qquad\qquad (5.63)$$

Smoothing the results, we can derive the results shown in Table 5.6.

By applying the inverse standard normal function, we arrive at the results shown in Table 5.7.

Setting the market risk premium equal to 6% and estimating β (from the same weekly returns as σ_E) and s (the bond spreads above the risk-free rate[463]), we can estimate μ, the market value weighted average costs of capital, as shown in Table 5.8.

And we finally arrive at the results shown in Table 5.9.

Table 5.5 Iterative Procedure

	1999	1998
Input		
V_E	52.0	35.6
DP'	809.0	620.0
σ_E [1]	37.0%	41.5%
Output from iterative module		
V_A	821.530	625.329
σ_A	2.35%	2.38%

[1]*Note:* The actual results were rounded (37.1% and 41.7%).

---

[460]This formula assumes a constant volatility over time.
[461]See Brand and Bahar (1999), p. 15. Since the two authors are with S&P, the results should be consistent.
[462]Obviously, this is only a shortcut for deriving exactly calibrated results.
[463]We used again Bundesbank (2000), p. 51, for a rough estimate that is not exactly trimmed to Deutsche Bank bond issues.

Table 5.6   Approximate S&P Default Probabilities

Rating Number	S&P Rating	Implied Probability of Default (PD)
1	AAA	0.01%
2	AA+	0.02%
3	AA	0.03%
4	AA-	0.04%
5	A+	0.05%
6	A	0.07%
7	A-	0.11%
8	BBB+	0.17%
9	BBB	0.27%
10	BBB-	0.44%
11	BB+	0.70%
12	BB	1.12%
13	BB-	1.80%
14	B+	2.88%
15	B	4.60%
16	B-	7.37%
17	CCC+	11.79%
18	CCC	18.85%

Table 5.7   Distance to Default

	1999	1998
Standard & Poor's, LT-Rating	AA	AA+
Implied Default Probability	0.03%	0.02%
$-N^{-1}(PD) = DTD$	3.431924	3.540190

Table 5.8   Weighted Average Asset Return

	1999	1998
Market-based leverage V_E/V_A	6.33%	5.69%
β	1.15	1.11
s	0.20%	0.40%
μ	5.62%	5.76%

Table 5.9   Final Results

	1999	1998
Implied DP	801.55	608.72
Economic capital = $V_A - DP$	*19.98*	*16.61*
Economic capital as reported	19.30	15.90
Difference from reported (in %)	3.70%	4.20%

Assessment of the Suggested Approach We have introduced this new top-down approach for deriving economic capital because we wanted to check the results from the differentiated bottom-up measurement. We can observe that the difference between the reported and the inferred economic capital amount (via the newly suggested approach) is small (below 5%).[464] One is, therefore, tempted to conclude that the two approaches lead to very similar results and that one would be indifferent as to which one should be used.[465]

However, Deutsche Bank does not report whether it considered correlations between the various types of risk to aggregate their bottom-up results to arrive at the final overall economic capital amount. If this is not the case, one can conclude that—since the top-down approach considers also macroeconomic risks and risks ignored by the three suggested bottom-up risk measurement approaches—the effects of ignoring the correlations and the risks that were unconsidered just canceled out. On the other hand, if correlations are considered in the aggregation process, we can then conclude that the bottom-up approach is fairly comprehensive and accurate. However, given that we have only two data points, neither of these two conclusions has to be the case.

Likewise, we cannot conclude from the results that the capital requirement in the top-down perspective is (always) higher for Deutsche Bank than what is reflected in the bottom-up procedure, because the top-down approach uses market data that includes more comprehensive information than what the bank can estimate internally.[466] If such a difference can be consistently observed, the bottom-up results could then be used as a basis for reallocating the difference back to individual transactions.

However, the above-derived results are heavily dependent on the input parameters. Since there were not enough data points available to calibrate the model to declare it robust, we are not able to conduct a full sensitivity analysis of all the input factors. However, when implementing the suggested approach, we found two effects worthwhile mentioning:

---

[464]This obviously assumes that Deutsche Bank uses a one-year horizon for calculating capital requirements from the bottom up. However, according to anecdotal evidence, this is the current best practice approach in the banking industry.
[465]Taking this line of thought to the extreme, and if one is only interested in the aggregate amount, one would conclude that a bank could save the costs and efforts of detailed bottom-up risk measurement. However, although it would avoid going through this hassle, the bank would not be able to understand the sources of its risks.
[466]When implementing the model, we tested various other assumptions that lead to results being both higher and lower than what is published from the bottom-up procedure.

- The final result is heavily dependent on V_E as an input factor. Even though we can assume that the market assesses the bank's risks fairly and that this is reflected in the current market value of the bank's equity, we could observe that if V_E becomes too low, economic capital can become negative. Or—turning this statement upside-down—the approach basically assumes that economic capital will always be smaller than V_E. Given the discussion in the first section of this chapter, this does not necessarily have to be the case, at least from a theoretical point of view.
- Likewise, the estimated economic capital amount is fairly sensitive to changes in μ. Therefore, the assumption that it is equal to the weighted average return needs closer examination.[467]

However, none of these statements is founded on solid ground, because we would need more than just two data points. Given that we estimated some of the input factors fairly roughly (from an external or regulators' point of view), we can expect that the usage of internal knowledge would lead to further improvement and accuracy.

The current version of the model only considers the capital requirement so that the bank has enough economic capital to avoid a bank run over the course of one (the next) year. Even though the model could be easily extended to horizons beyond one year, it would be difficult to interpret the results. On the one hand, we would not have (easily available) a calibrated benchmark for the probability of default on senior debt issues of the respective bank. On the other hand, the question is whether such a multiple-year estimate generates an accumulated capital requirement where one would need to back out the marginal capital requirement for each of the years via a more or less sophisticated approach.

Evaluation of Using Economic Capital

The advantage of VaR-based economic capital measures is that they are simple, forward-looking[468] summary measures of risk and allow for a consistent quantification[469] of total risk across all types of risk[470] and—in our

---

[467]According to Crouhy et al. (1999), p. 11, this assumption and the numbers used in the example are in line with theory.

[468]Since it is probability-based and calculated at the end of the measurement horizon H.

[469]Note that even though economic capital is a good and adequate risk measure for banks, it is not a substitute for good risk-management decisions. It is rather only a necessary foundation.

[470]See Culp and Miller (1998), p. 26.

context of value creation—at a consistent time horizon.[471] They are, therefore, measures that can be considered a common currency for risk across all types of risk.

However, an implicit assumption in the calculation of economic capital is that the portfolio of transactions under consideration is kept constant over time until H, the end of the measurement period. This assumption was less of an issue when VaR was first developed in the trading arena,[472] where only very short horizons are relevant (often only hours or days). On the contrary, practical experience shows that—at least so far[473]—credit portfolios are kept fairly constant over time[474] and (still) constitute the bulk of a bank's risk exposure. It is also worthwhile to mention here that economic capital calculated on VaR basis seems only appropriate for banks, because only they are concerned about the reduction in the total value of their portfolio of assets. Industrial companies, which are concerned about preserving the level of cash flows to finance valuable projects,[475] should choose other measures of total risk.[476]

Yet another problem with economic capital is that it typically only considers the risk contribution to the overall bank portfolio and not to the broad market. It is, therefore, difficult to use it as the basis for the valuation of assets.[477]

SUMMARY

We have derived an adequate risk measure for the bank's concern with total risk in this chapter. Even though we identified risk capital as the most appropriate measure, we concluded that (the shortcut measure) economic capital is the only practical way to determine the economically based capital re-

---

[471]We only suggested a framework to calculate the capital requirement at a one-year horizon, H. Since value creation occurs multiperiod, we will have to extend this approach beyond H below.

[472]See Culp and Miller (1998), pp. 28–29.

[473]Before the broad usage of credit derivative instruments that significantly increased the liquefaction in the credit markets.

[474]Even though credit portfolios grow over time, their riskiness hardly changes significantly because of the consistent application of credit guidelines.

[475]As described by Froot et al. (1993).

[476]See Culp and Miller (1998), p. 35, or for a more extensive discussion, Stulz (2000), Chapter 4.

[477]Froot and Stein (1998a) suggest a mix of the two approaches, which we will address below.

quirement for banks.[478] We developed and discussed a detailed methodology to determine the required economic capital from a value-creation perspective from the bottom up, differentiated by three types of risks, and discussed how these results can be checked via a newly suggested top-down approach.

Since economic capital can be interpreted as an "insurance premium" paid by the bank's stakeholders, which "insures" them against a bank run, it should be part of the performance and value measurement. However, since this insurance does not appear on a bank's balance sheet (because it is only provided implicitly), it needs to enter a bank's economic "P&L" statement (which determines the value creation) in another way. Otherwise, if the underlying assets perform well, "economic profits" are overstated,[479] because decreasing the cost of total risk is costly for banks[480] and should therefore be reflected in the bank's capital-budgeting framework.[481] Thus, computing a project's NPV using CAPM and accepting all positive NPV projects does not seem to be the right solution for a bank that is concerned with total risk, and hence economic capital.[482] We will discuss possible solutions to this problem in the next chapter.

---

[478]This might also be the reason why it has developed as the standard approach at best practice institutions in the financial industry.

[479]If not, "economic profits" are understated. See Merton and Perold (1993), pp. 24–25.

[480]See Stulz (1999), p. 9.

[481]See Froot and Stein (1998a), p. 58.

[482]See Stulz (2000), p. 4-21.

CHAPTER 6

Capital Budgeting in Banks

EVOLUTION OF CAPITAL-BUDGETING TOOLS IN BANKS

As we have seen, banks are different from industrial corporations in many respects. This statement is also true for the measurement of (economic) profitability, especially when such performance measures are used in order to determine whether a bank's chosen (risk-management) activities are consistent with value maximization, that is, when they are used as a capital-budgeting tool.

Bank performance measures developed over time in the following way:[1] Until the 1970s, many banks took a purely accounting-driven approach and focused on measuring their (net) revenues or earnings. This, obviously, generated the incentive to maximize earnings by increasing the bank's assets. Since this approach obviously lacks the connection to a reference asset (e.g., the underlying risks of the transactions), banks subsequently set these (net) revenues in relation to their assets as determined in their balance sheets (i.e., calculating a return on assets [ROA] ratio). As off-balance sheet activities grew substantially[2] and the riskiness of the underlying assets gradually became more important,[3] banks realized that the scarce resource in their business is equity. Therefore, they decided to focus on ROE (return on equity) ratios and measured net revenues in relation to their book equity in order to find out which businesses were most profitable and where to invest.

The introduction of the BIS regulatory capital requirements (after 1988)

---

[1]For a more extensive discussion of this evolution, see, for example, Schröck (1997), pp. 77–81.

[2]This development obviously made this measure inappropriate.

[3]Banks moved (due to increasing pressure on their margins) into types of lending with higher credit risk and experienced increased credit losses, especially during the first country risk crisis during the 1980s.

reinforced the view throughout the banking industry that assets can have very different risks. Even though regulatory requirements do not offer a sophisticated modeling of these risks,[4] they focused the view on the notion that regulatory required capital can be very different from (current) book equity, that these requirements are binding restrictions on the banks' activities, and that the amount of equity should be linked to the overall riskiness of the bank. These facts subsequently lead to the adjustment of the capital ratios in banks[5] and the calculation of return on regulatory (equity) capital numbers as performance measures.[6]

However, increased shareholder pressure forced banks to focus more and more on value creation. Financial institutions realized that accounting-driven ROE measures based on either book or regulatory capital do not have the economic focus of a valuation framework. They fail to take the actual riskiness of the underlying business, the value of future cash flows,[7] and the opportunity cost of equity capital—which needs to be included in order to calculate economic "profits"—into account. But, as already discussed in Chapters 1 and 2, the appropriate flows-to-equity shareholder value framework—which estimates the bank's (free) cash flows to its shareholders and then discounts these at the cost of equity capital[8] to derive the present value (PV) of the bank's equity[9]—is often cumbersome to apply in a banking context. Additionally, banks realized that this traditional valuation framework[10] does not address their fundamental problems and that it also does not work from a theoretical point of view, because total risk matters to them.

Therefore, we can observe that none of the approaches for calculating a bank's profitability presented so far adjusts for (total) risk in a systematic way.[11] But we have seen in the extensive discussion of how to determine economic capital in the previous chapter that this fictional capital measure is calculated to reflect exactly the riskiness of the bank's transactions and also the bank's concern with total risk. It is, thus, an obvious next step to

---

[4]They are basically determined only by the so-called "risk-weighted assets." The newly proposed Basle Accord takes a much more risk-oriented view, as described in the last chapter.

[5]See the previous chapter.

[6]Possible other alternatives not discussed here are to calculate the return on invested equity capital or the return on a market-driven evaluation of equity, such as market capitalization, and so on.

[7]See Crouhy et al. (1999), p. 5.

[8]As, for example, derived via the Capital Asset Pricing Model (CAPM).

[9]So-called Equity Approach or Flows-to-Equity Approach, as described by Copeland et al. (1994), Strutz (1993), Kümmel (1993), and many others.

[10]Recall that this neoclassical approach only considers systematic risk.

[11]See Crouhy et al. (1999), p. 5, and Grübel et al. (1995), p. 618.

try to determine a bank's economic profitability by calculating the return on economic capital. Doing so is often summarized under the abbreviation RAPM (Risk-Adjusted Performance Measures), or better known as RAROC (Risk-Adjusted Return on Capital), which is their most famous representative. Many of the leading institutions around the globe calculate such a modified return on equity[12] measure and take a purely economic perspective by trying to link it to a market-determined minimum required return[13] (so-called hurdle rate) to find out whether a transaction adds value to the bank or not. Wills et al. (1999)[14] find that out of fifty-five selected leading banks worldwide, 59% have established an "economic capital /RAROC process",[15] 12% plan to do so, and 29% do not use such an approach.

Even though it is crucially important to determine the returns (or net revenues in dollar terms) in all of the mentioned performance measures in an economically correct way,[16] this book will not address the problem of how accounting measures have to be calculated and transformed[17] to arrive at such numbers. However, it is worthwhile to mention that the correct allocation of expenses and costs as well as the transfer pricing method employed are critically important in finding correct approximations.[18] Any inaccurate allocation will lead to the wrong management incentives, because all of the mentioned approaches have in common that the rates of return are much more critical for banks than for industrial companies. For industrial companies, uncertainties associated with the modeling of future cash flows are so large that modeling the appropriate rate of return is, in most of the cases, of second order. However, getting the rates of return right for banks is much more critical because—given the narrow margins in the banking industry—a small error can have a very large impact.[19]

The focus of this chapter will be to rather closely examine RAROC and its currently hypothesized linkage to value creation in banks. After defining this risk-adjusted performance measure, we will investigate its (implicit) assumptions, its advantages and shortcomings, and whether it can be used

---

[12]See Grübel et al. (1995), p. 616.

[13]See, for example, Schröck (1997), pp. 93+.

[14]Wills et al. (1999), p. 88.

[15]In their study, Wills et al. (1999) use the two expressions interchangeably.

[16]Returns are best calculated on a mark-to-market basis rather than on an accrual-based accounting measurement. See Wilson (1992), p. 114.

[17]For instance, accounting measures typically do not consider the time value of money and risk associated with a transaction. Additionally, they are subject to management manipulation in order to "window dress" external reporting.

[18]For the difficulty of allocation and issues with transfer pricing systems in banks, see, for example, Kimball (1998), p. 41.

[19]See Merton and Perold (1993), p. 17.

to determine the value creation potential of a risk-management action within a bank. Since we will find that RAROC is not the measure of choice in this context from a theoretical point of view,[20] we will present the foundations for alternate approaches. We will discuss some of the already available methods in the light of practicability and their implications for risk-management decisions in banks. We will close this chapter by indicating and describing areas for further research.

RAROC AS A CAPITAL-BUDGETING TOOL IN BANKS

In this section, we will define and discuss RAROC as it is applied in the banking industry today as a current best practice approach to capital budgeting and explore how it is linked to value creation.

Definition of RAROC

According to Zaik et al., risk measurement and the determination of the amount of (risk) capital that is required to support each of the transactions of a bank (as discussed in the previous chapter) is necessary for two reasons:[21]

- For risk-management purposes to determine how much each transaction contributes to the total risk of the bank[22] and to determine the capital required by the bank as a whole.[23] Recall that internal betas recognize (only) the diversification potential within the existing bank portfolio.
- For performance evaluation purposes to determine the economic profitability of very different transactions on a comparable, risk-adjusted basis across different sources of risk.[24] The objective is to reveal the contribution of a transaction to the overall value creation of the bank in order to provide the basis for capital-budgeting and incentive compensation decisions and to identify transactions where the bank has a competitive advantage.[25]

---

[20]However, we will find that RAROC is an acceptable proxy from a practical point of view.
[21]See Zaik et al. (1996), p. 84.
[22]This contribution is measured via the volatility of the market value of the transaction or the volatility in the economic earnings as a proxy.
[23]See Zaik et al. (1996), p. 83.
[24]See Zaik et al. (1996), p. 83.
[25]See Wilson (1992), p. 112.

For the second of these two purposes, the banking industry's best practice is to employ the RAROC measure. Unfortunately, there is considerable confusion on the correct definition of RAROC. Without discussing and contrasting the details of other variants[26] of what is summarized under the umbrella RAPM (Risk-Adjusted Performance or Profitability Measures), we define RAROC as:

$$\text{RAROC} = \frac{\text{Risk} - \text{Adjusted Net Income}}{\text{Economic Capital}} \qquad (6.1)^{[27]}$$

suggesting that RAROC is a modified return on equity measure, namely the return on economic capital, where:

Risk-Adjusted Net Income[28] (in dollar terms) =
+ Expected Revenues[29] (Gross Interest Income + Other Revenues [e.g., Fees])
− Cost of Funds
− Noninterest Expenses (Direct and Indirect Expenses + Allocated Overhead)
± Other Transfer Pricing Allocations
− Expected (Credit) Losses
+ Capital Benefit[30]

and *Economic Capital* (also in dollar terms) as derived in the previous chapter being a risk measure that is completely firm specific.[31]

RAROC can be calculated at the bank level as well as at the single trans-

---

[26]For instance, RORAC (Return on Risk-Adjusted Capital) or RARORAC (Risk-Adjusted Return on Risk-Adjusted Capital), and so on. For a discussion of the differences and similarities, see, for example, Matten (1996), p. 59, Groß and Knippschild (1995), pp. 101+, Punjabi (1998), pp. 71+, Anders (2000), p. 314. However, from my point of view, all measures try to calculate a modified return on equity and just have different names, see Schröck and Windfuhr (1999), p. 145. The discussion is best summarized in the October 1998 issue of the *Journal of Lending & Credit Risk Management*, which uses the statement: "You say RAROC, I say RORAC" as a subtitle in multiple articles.

[27]See, for example, Zaik et al. (1996), p. 91, Kimball (1998), p. 36, Crouhy et al. (1999), pp. 5–6. Note that both numerator and denominator are expressed in dollar terms.

[28]For the difficulty of allocation and transfer pricing systems, see Kimball (1998), p. 41.

[29]Expected Revenues also include changes in the value.

[30]We will discuss the capital benefit in more detail in the next section.

[31]Note that the definition of risk has moved away from a market-driven definition, see Crouhy et al. (1999), p. 6.

action level, assuming that the transfer and allocation methods work correctly. As can be immediately seen, RAROC is a single-period measure.[32] Since economic capital is typically calculated at a one-year horizon,[33] the risk-adjusted net income is also determined over the same measurement period. Even though we will not discuss each of the components of the risk-adjusted net income in detail, note that the only risk adjustment in the numerator is the deduction of expected (credit) losses (as defined in the previous chapter).

Whereas some definitions of RAROC consider taxes in the risk-adjusted net income, we are only dealing with a pretax version of this RAPM measure for the following reasons:

- As we saw in the "Taxes" section of Chapter 3, taxes do not provide a strong rationale for conducting risk management at the corporate level in order to create value.[34]
- RAROC can be calculated at the transaction level, but it is very difficult, if not impossible, to determine the tax treatment at this level.
- For internationally operating banks, taxes can provide a considerable skew in the comparability of the results. Therefore, many of them use pretax RAROC numbers to evaluate business units operating under different tax codes.

Given that RAROC is a single-period measure calculated at the one-year horizon, it is also often rewritten in economic profit [35] or residual earnings form in the spirit of EVA®[36] and shareholder value concepts:[37]

---

[32]RAROC is very similar to the so-called Sharpe ratio, which is defined as (see, for example, Sharpe and Alexander (1990), pp. 749–750) $S_i = (R_i - R_f)/\sigma_i$, where S_i = Sharpe ratio for transaction i; R_i = Return of transaction i; R_f = Risk-free rate of return; σ_i = Standard deviation of the rate of return of transaction i. Assuming that risk-adjusted net income equals R_i, subtracting R_f from the RAROC numerator and assuming that economic capital equals σ_i, it is easy to show that—given that (as we will see below) the capital benefit equals the risk-free rate—some banks apply RAROC (without capital benefit) correctly in the sense that they want to maximize the Sharpe ratio in order to maximize value. Dowd (1998), pp. 143–153, discusses the problems and deficiencies of this view at length.

[33]As discussed in the previous chapter.

[34]The convexity of the tax system at the corporate level is hard to prove or believe.

[35]See Zaik et al. (1996), p. 91.

[36]For a discussion of economic value-added (EVA®) concepts in banks see Uyemura et al. (1996).

[37]Lehn and Makhija (1996) argue that EVA® is probably not as well linked to the return to shareholders as is commonly claimed.

(Risk-Adjusted Net Income) − (Cost of Economic Capital) =
= Economic Profit (6.2)

where Cost of Economic Capital = Economic Capital × Hurdle Rate
and

Hurdle Rate = Appropriate rate of return for the investment as determined, for example, by the CAPM and required by the (equity) investors = R_E^{h}.[38]

This assumes that the risk-adjusted net income is a (good) proxy for the free cash flows to the shareholders at the end of period 1[39] and that the economic capital equals the equity investment in the transaction. We will discuss the latter part of this assumption in more detail in the next section. Note that economic profits are neither accounting profits nor cash flows. They rather represent the contribution of a transaction to the value of the firm by considering the opportunity cost of the capital that finances the transaction.[40] If the economic profit is larger than zero, this value contribution is positive, otherwise negative (i.e., value is destroyed).

Given this transformation of RAROC into economic profits, it is easy to show—by rearranging the terms—that to find out whether a transaction creates or destroys value, it is sufficient to compare the calculated RAROC with the hurdle rate.[41] As long as the RAROC of a transaction exceeds the shareholders' minimum required rate of return (i.e., the cost of equity or hurdle rate), then a transaction is judged to create value for the bank.[42] Otherwise, it will destroy value.

Advantages of RAROC

One of the most obvious advantages of RAROC is that it is the only performance measure and capital-budgeting tool that reflects the bank's concern with total risk by using a risk measure (economic capital) that is—as we

---

[38]Note again that the CAPM (beta) does not consider the risk and the costs associated with default. See Crouhy et al. (1999), p. 5.

[39]Uyemura et al. (1996) suggest four adjustments to reported bank accounting earnings to transform them into a proxy for free cash flows: (1) actual charge-offs instead of loan loss provisions, (2) cash taxes rather than tax provisions, (3) exclusion of securities gains and losses, (4) consideration of nonrecurring events as an adjustment to either earnings or capital.

[40]What that opportunity cost should be will also be addressed below.

[41]See, for example, Schröck (1997), p. 154.

[42]See Zaik et al. (1996), p. 87.

determined in the last chapter—extremely relevant for banks. Additionally, RAROC (implicitly) calculates the economic profit of a transaction by including the opportunity cost of capital—which is a dramatic improvement over other traditional bank measures used to determine the value contribution of a transaction.

Moreover, many users praise the practical easiness of RAROC because it is straightforward both to implement and to communicate and can, therefore, form the basis of a bankwide risk-management culture.[43] This is also due to the fact that RAROC—before being applied—splits a bank's activities into those risks that can be managed (influenced) by a specific unit, transfer pricing all other risks out to other specialized units within the bank. This strengthens employees' performance incentives and insulates them from risks beyond their control. For instance, RAROC leaves the Credit Department with illiquid credit risk and specific operational risk[44] because it assumes that all (hedgable) interest rate and currency risk is sold to the bank's Treasury unit.[45] However, if the Treasury unit decides not to sell off these hedgable risks in liquid markets, it will be allocated (economic) capital and has to earn a fair return on it.

Furthermore, using RAROC avoids having to calculate the external beta for each transaction (in order to determine the required hurdle rate return via the CAPM). RAROC assumes that one single hurdle rate can be used bankwide for all transactions, because the amount of required economic capital correctly adjusts for risk by changing the leverage of the transaction accordingly. This assumes that a correct risk measure is used to allocate capital.[46] However, in a RAROC world, capital is allocated according to the project's internal beta[47] and not the project's systematic or priced risk in the broad market.[48] We will examine potential problems arising from this approach in the subsequent sections in more detail.

When this approach does not work correctly, a fixed hurdle rate across all businesses and transactions has two problems. It leads to the following behavior:[49]

---

[43]See, for example, Wilson (1992), p. 112.

[44]This is exactly the purpose for which RAROC was first developed at Bankers Trust; see, for example, Zaik et al. (1996), p. 84.

[45]See James (1996), p. 14, who describes this as "matched duration" funding at Bank of America.

[46]Even though the risk on an "unlevered" basis varies widely across transactions, such a measure would adjust it on a levered basis, so that the risk is the same for all activities.

[47]We have stated above that only the existing portfolio matters in that context.

[48]See James (1996), p. 12.

[49]See Brealey and Myers (1991), Chapter 5. Also see Kimball (1998), p. 38.

- High-risk projects with negative NPV are accepted
- Low-risk projects with positive NPV are rejected

Such behavior, in turn, could lead to corporate-wide underinvestment, where managers are likely to reject projects with positive NPV, which would in turn lower the manager's average RAROC.[50] In order to avoid this problem, RAROC can easily be transposed into "economic profits" (and hence dollar numbers), as indicated and defined above, because this is considered to be a proxy for the NPV rule. However, this conclusion is based on some implicit assumptions made in the RAROC approach, which we will discuss in more detail in the next section.

Assumptions of RAROC

As can be easily seen, the comparison of RAROC to a single, bankwide hurdle rate in order to determine whether a transaction adds value (or not) is based on several assumptions. In order to be able to identify, discuss, and evaluate these assumptions, we will use a RAROC model developed by Crouhy et al. (1999). We will use this model because it is based on the Merton approach, which has already been employed in the top-down estimation of economic capital and was found to be one of the most general approaches because it expresses parameters in market values rather than accounting values. Another advantage of this model is that it allows for risky debt and hence default. However, it is based—like the assumption that the comparison of RAROC and a hurdle rate can be used to determine value creation—on neoclassical assumptions. The model presented here, therefore, presumes frictionless markets and no taxes, and hence does not allow for financial distress costs to be associated with default, implying that capital-structure decisions are irrelevant.

Again, we assume that there is only one class of (zero-coupon) debt D maturing at time T with face value F and current market value $V_{D,t}$ at time t, being equal to $F/(1 + R_D)^{(T-t)}$, where R_D is the promised yield to maturity of the debt. The market value of (the) asset(s) A and equity E at time t are labeled $V_{A,t}$ and $V_{E,t}$, respectively.

Since RAROC is a single-period measure, we set T equal to a one-year horizon. As we have seen, the value of equity and debt at the end of the estimation horizon T equals:

$$V_{E,T} = \begin{cases} V_{A,T} - F & \text{, if } V_{A,T} \geq F \\ 0 & \text{, if } V_{A,T} < F \end{cases} \quad \text{and} \quad V_{D,T} = \begin{cases} F & \text{, if } V_{A,T} \geq F \\ V_{A,T} & \text{, if } V_{A,T} < F \end{cases} \quad (6.3)$$

---

[50]And hence their compensation if it is linked to their achieved RAROC.

which is similar to an option payoff. Therefore $V_{E,t}$ and $V_{D,t}$ can be expressed as:

$$V_{D,t} = \frac{F}{(1+R_f)^{(T-t)}} - p[V_{A,t}; F]$$ (6.4)

and

$$V_{E,t} = c[V_{A,t}; F]$$ (6.5)

where p and c are the values of a European call and put option on the underlying asset A with strike price F.[51]

Note that, as shown in Equation (6.4), the value of debt at time t is the value of a default-free bond with face value F discounted at the risk-free rate R_f less an insurance premium for the default risk, which is quantified by the value of the put option.[52]

We use the same assumptions for the market value of A as used previously in the top-down estimation of economic capital, and additionally assume:

$$V_{A,t} = V_{E,t} + V_{D,t}$$ (6.6)

since capital structure is irrelevant.

Therefore, the probability of default of the bank is:

$$p(default) = p[V_{A,T} \leq F] = N(-d_2),$$ (6.7)

where

$$d_2 = \frac{\ln\left(\dfrac{V_{A,0}}{F}\right) + \left(\mu_A - \dfrac{\sigma_A^2}{2}\right) \cdot T}{\sigma_A \cdot \sqrt{T}}$$ (6.8)

and $N(\cdot)$ is the cumulative standard normal probability distribution function, estimating the actual default probability.[53]

One of the underlying premises of RAROC is that the required economic capital to support a transaction (or the overall bank) is calculated to keep the probability that the bank will go into default constant (at the chosen confidence level). Therefore, d_2 in the above equation needs to be fixed.

---

[51]Both options can be priced according to the Black-Scholes option-pricing theory (OPT). However, we do not show the details of their determination here. For a discussion see, for example, Hull (1997), pp. 240–242.

[52]See Merton and Perold (1993), p. 20, and their references to the literature.

[53]As shown in the previous chapter, we therefore use μ_A instead of R_f (as the OPT would do to estimate risk-neutral probabilities).

However, as can be easily seen, in order to do so, we will need to change the capital structure (i.e., $V_{A,T}/F$ and hence D/E) as σ_A (the riskiness of the transaction) changes.

However, as we change the capital structure (D/E as plotted on the x-axis in Figure 6.1), we also change the return on equity (here denoted as R_E). Note that $D/E = 11.5$ represents an equity percentage of 8%, 15.67 represents 6%, and 24.0 represents 4%. So, in the typical areas of bank and transaction leverage ratios, we experience significant variations in the expected equity return for relatively small changes in the capital structure. This may seem to be at odds with the intuition of the M&M propositions at first sight.[54] However, we are not trying to demonstrate the irrelevance of the financing decision on the firm value here, but rather the effects when a firm is trying to fix its default probability.[55]

Because the same holds true when the correlation of the asset with the market portfolio ($\rho_{A,M}$) increases, we can plot the following table that summarizes the results (see Table 6.1)

where $E(R_A)$ = Expected return on asset (which is determined via the CAPM)

$E(R_E)$ = $E(V_{E,T})/V_{E,0} - 1$ = The expected return on equity (which is also determined via the CAPM)

$\uparrow (\downarrow)$ = Indicate an increase (decrease) in the respective measure.

So, we can conclude from the above discussion that one can either fix the default probability or $R_E{}^h$ (the hurdle rate), but not both at the same time.[56] Before we turn to the consequences of this conclusion in the next section, we will now define RAROC—using the same modeling context—so that it can be compared to a CAPM-based hurdle rate.

Let us consider a single one-year investment A of the bank. Let I be the cost of the investment for asset A, which is an NPV = 0 transaction, and $V_{A,t}$ be the market value of the investment at time t. It follows that therefore $V_{A,0} = I$. Let us further assume that economic capital EC is necessary to set up a reserve pool that is invested in risk-free bonds to fix the probability of default at the predetermined confidence level, which is a common assumption for calculating RAROC in practice.

---

[54]Note that we are using the same assumptions as they do.

[55]And hence the effects on R_E rather than on WACC, the weighted average cost of capital, or on value. Note that R_D is labeled R_D in Figure 6.1.

[56]Fixing the default probability (i.e., d_2) has an effect on the required rate of return that is of an order of magnitude less than the effect of fixing the required rate of return on the change in the default probability. See Crouhy et al. (1999), pp. 11–13.

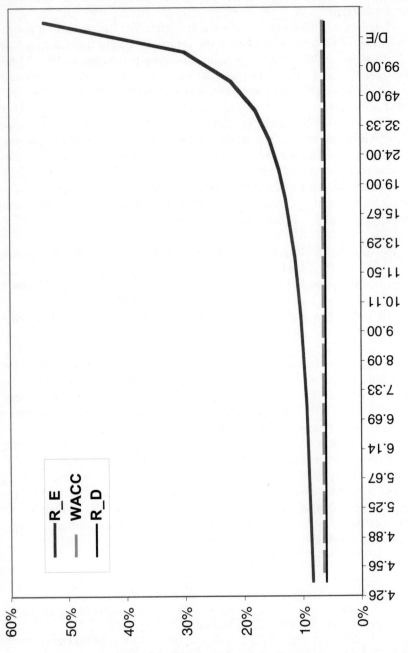

Figure 6.1   Return on equity and changing capital structure.

Table 6.1 Effects of Keeping the Default Probability Constant

σ_A	$\rho_{A,M}$	D/E	$E(R_A)$	$E(R_E)$
$\uparrow$	Const.	$\downarrow$	$\uparrow$	$\uparrow$
Const.	$\uparrow$	$\uparrow$	$\uparrow$	$\uparrow$

Therefore, in order to finance A, we need to raise funds as follows:

$$I + EC = V_{D,0} + V_{E,0} \qquad (6.9)$$

For the time being, the split between debt ($V_{D,0}$) and equity ($V_{E,0}$) financing, that is, the actual leverage of the transaction does not need to be determined. Since we invested EC at the risk-free rate, we have additional funds available in the end of the measurement horizon. Therefore, the probability of default has a slightly different definition:

$$p(default) = p[V_{A,T} \le F - EC(1 + R_f)] \qquad (6.10)$$

We assume that EC, the required amount of economic capital, is determined so that the probability of default is kept constant and that it includes all possible sources of risk, meaning that there are no misspecifications or omissions leading to an incorrect amount of EC.

Hence, we can model the value of equity at the end of the measurement horizon as:

$$V_{E,T} = V_{A,T} + EC(1 + R_f) - V_{D,T} \qquad (6.11)$$

and the expected return on equity is hence:

$$E(R_E) = \frac{E(V_{A,T}) + EC(1 + R_f) - V_{D,0}(1 + R_D)}{V_{E,0}} - 1 \qquad (6.12)$$

where R_D = (Promised) yield-to-maturity on the debt ($> R_f$).

This expression can be transformed into RAROC[57] only if the following assumptions are met:

1. $I = D_{V,0}$, that is, the investment itself is completely financed by debt, which is common practice in bank transactions.[58]

---

[57]Note that $E(V_{A,T})$ is assumed to correctly reflect the expenses and expected losses as defined in the risk-adjusted net income of the RAROC equation. We will discuss the missing costs of funds and the capital benefit shortly.
[58]For 1. and 2., see, for example, Crouhy et al. (1999), pp. 15–16.

2. $EC = V_{E,0}$, that is, economic capital is completely provided by the shareholders (at least initially).[59]

We can then derive:

$$\text{RAROC} = \frac{E(V_{A,T}) + EC(1 + R_f) - V_{D,0}(1 + R_D)}{EC} - 1$$

$$= \frac{E(V_{A,T}) - V_{D,0}(1 + R_D) + EC \cdot R_f}{EC} \tag{6.13}$$

Therefore, risk-adjusted net income is defined exactly as shown previously,[60] where $V_{D,0}(1 + R_D)$ is the cost of funds (including the repayment) and $EC \cdot R_f$ the (nominal) capital benefit,[61] which is the amount of money made on the investment of economic capital in risk-free assets until the end of the measurement period.

Only under these conditions will RAROC be an ROE measure that can be compared to a CAPM-determined hurdle rate R_E^h.

Wilson (1992) points to the same problem that RAROC is only applicable under very restrictive assumptions. He claims that RAROC—as currently defined and used—will only lead to correct results if it is applied to zero value (i.e., $V_{A,0} = 0$ and NPV = 0) self-financing (i.e., $I = V_{D,0} = 0$) portfolios. Applying the above-developed framework under these conditions, we can show that Wilson is right, but that his assumptions are only a special case of our framework.[62] It is worthwhile to note however that he is correct in stating that in his approach "the natural hurdle [...] rate [...] is the risk-free rate"[63] as we can show that RAROC reduces then to:

$$\text{RAROC} = \frac{V_{E,0}(1 + R_f)}{V_{E,0}} - 1 = R_f = R_E \tag{6.14}$$

in our framework.

---

[59]See Zaik et al. (1996), p. 84.

[60]Note that these are gross amounts and not returns expressed as dollar amounts.

[61]The expression capital benefit is introduced by Copeland et al. (1994), pp. 481–482. In our context, we need to assume either that EC determines the real capital structure and hence reduces the funding need by debt, so that the capital benefit is calculated at the interest rate of debt (following the Copeland et al. argument), or that EC is invested in a(n) (insurance) pool at the risk-free rate of return (as we do in the RAROC context).

[62]Nonetheless, Wilson (1992), p. 114, comes to the conclusion that RAROC would be biased in an opposite direction, given an incentive to invest in risk-free projects generating an infinite RAROC (which is true, because RAROC is, like the Sharpe ratio, not defined for risk-free assets).

[63]See Wilson (1992), p. 119.

The model presented above shows how RAROC has to be constructed so that it can be compared to the cost of equity capital as determined for example, by the CAPM. RAROC therefore assumes that economic capital is compensated by the market and that it is the correct risk measure. Only then are decisions based on RAROC versus $R_E{}^h$ consistent with maximizing value. However, this assumes that the riskiness of the economic capital is the same as that of the bank's equity capital[64] and that hence economic capital has to earn the same returns as the equity capital.

Given the discussion in the previous chapter and that economic capital is assumed to be invested in a reserve pool to guarantee a certain default probability, this seems unlikely to be the case. Additionally, and as pointed out for instance by Johanning, economic capital determined on a VaR basis is incompatible with the maximization of expected utility in the neoclassical world. Therefore, RAROC is not a suitable internal performance measure in all circumstances.[65]

Deficiencies of RAROC

In this section, we will discuss the deficiencies and fundamental problems of RAROC.

Deficiencies of the Generic RAROC Model   One of the advantages of RAROC mentioned previously, is that it adjusts the risk of any transaction to that of the bank's equity by changing the leverage of the transaction via a different economic capital requirement. Therefore, RAROC avoids the need to estimate the external beta of the transaction.[66] There are two problems associated with this approach.

First, the allocated capital is a cushion to absorb losses up to a prespecified confidence level and, therefore, a total risk measure.[67] The risk contributions of single transactions are based on internal betas that are calculated vis-à-vis the existing bank portfolio. Since these results are compared to externally driven hurdle rates, one has to assume that the bank portfolio is a good proxy for the market portfolio.[68] This might actually be correct, because typically we find bank betas to be around 1.0,[69] in which case one could show that the internal betas are similar (if not identical) to external

---

[64]See Crouhy et al. (1999), p. 6.
[65]See Johanning (1998), pp. 73–86. We will address this problem below.
[66]See Crouhy et al. (1999), p. 7.
[67]See Grübel et al. (1995), p. 618.
[68]As claimed by Zaik et al. (1996), p. 87.
[69]See Schmittmann et al. (1996), p. 648, for large German universal banks (not niche players).

betas.[70] However, one should keep in mind that the chosen total risk measure is different from the priced and systematic market risk. Since RAROC does not use any valuation model to derive the relative ordering of expected returns,[71] it is not able to provide a consistent relative ranking of transactions.[72]

Second, we have already shown that you can either fix the default probability or the hurdle rate, but not both at the same time.[73] Thus, the following assumption is not justified: that due to changes in the leverage, which fix the default probability, we can use a single hurdle rate across all bank transactions.[74]

In order to prove that the RAROC analysis generates reliable results with regard to value creation, one could formulate the following fundamental hypotheses:

- If we consider a zero NPV project, RAROC should always equal the (bankwide) hurdle rate $R_E{}^b$ and should, thus, indicate that the bank is indifferent vis-à-vis this transaction.
- If we consider a transaction with positive (negative) NPV, RAROC should always be larger (smaller) than the (bankwide) hurdle rate $R_E{}^b$.

However, given the above analysis, we can show that these fundamental premises do not necessarily hold true.

Let us first consider zero NPV transactions. In the above-defined model, RAROC changes even for NPV = 0 transactions with a change in the riskiness of the transactions and with changes in the correlation of the transactions to the broad market portfolio (as defined in a CAPM world). Figure 6.2 depicts the effects that are derived applying the analysis conducted by Crouhy et al. (1999).

As can be seen, RAROC increases with increases in the riskiness of a transaction. RAROC is also higher, the higher the correlation of the transaction is to the broad market portfolio. Banks applying RAROC as defined previously, therefore, tend to choose high-risk, high-correlation projects, be-

---

[70]However, this is not true in general.
[71]See Crouhy et al. (1999), p. 16.
[72]See James (1996), p. 14, and which we will see in more detail below.
[73]When the leverage is set so that it matches a fixed equity return, the prespecified default level will change with changes in the asset risk—or fixing the capital structure for the default probability results in a change of the equity return with a change in the asset risk. The same holds true for changes in the correlation. See above and Crouhy et al. (1999), p. 12.
[74]See Crouhy et al. (1999), p. 8.

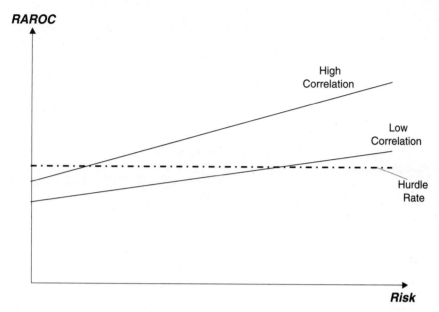

Figure 6.2 Changes in RAROC for changes in riskiness and correlation. *Note:* Results for plotting this graph are derived similarly to Crouhy et al. (1999).

cause such projects would make them "break even" earlier with the required and fixed rate of return, indicating that they create value.

Since we are considering an NPV = 0 project here, it is obvious that the implicit assumption that RAROC compensates correctly for changes in risk[75] is wrong. The bank would have to determine the beta of the transaction[76] in order to find out about the true value of the project. However, this will be impossible in practice—especially for illiquid credits. Crouhy et al. therefore suggest the calculation of an adjusted RAROC,[77] which we will not discuss here.[78]

Let us now turn to transactions with either positive or negative NPV, that is, when $I \neq V_{A,0}$. So far, there has been no need to discuss and deter-

---

[75]See Wilson (1992), p. 112.
[76]See Crouhy et al. (1999), p. 20.
[77]This adjusted RAROC corrects for the steepness of the RAROC curve for increases in riskiness, making it a constant function. However, this holds only true for NPV = 0 projects.
[78]Their model is also extremely difficult to parameterize because they suggest an "instantaneous" equity beta ($\beta_E = (V_{A,0}/V_{E,0}) \cdot N(d_1) \cdot \beta_A$) to derive the hurdle rate, with $N(d_1)$ as in the Black-Scholes OPT and β as in the CAPM.

mine what happens to the NPV in a RAROC world. This is a problem because, on the one hand—as we will show shortly—nonzero NPV projects lead to further skews in RAROC,[79] and determining the hurdle rate for each project separately does not fix this problem. On the other hand, one should keep in mind that the NPV is exactly what we are trying to find out when we are calculating RAROC, making this discussion a "circular problem."

We can depict the effects of positive and negative NPV projects on RAROC as follows (see Figure 6.3).

Given the setup of our model, it is reasonable to assume that, in our flows-to-equity[80] world, the NPV of a project flows to V_E at time T and hence eventually to economic capital EC.[81] Additionally, we assume that the correlation of the asset under consideration to the broad market portfolio does not change; we are only investigating what happens when the riskiness of the transaction changes.

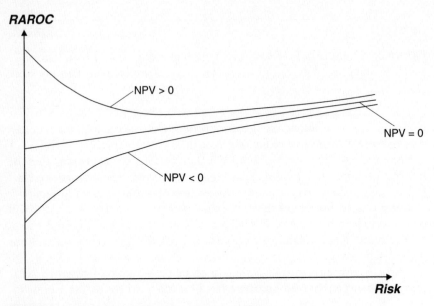

Figure 6.3   RAROC and nonzero NPV projects.
Note: Results for plotting this graph are derived similar to Crouhy et al. (1999), especially Table 4, p. 19.

---

[79]See Crouhy et al. (1999), pp. 16 and 32.
[80]Actually, RAROC is a "flows-to-economic capital" approach.
[81]However, even though a positive NPV might reduce the equity requirement in a transaction, it might not decrease the required amount of economic capital to buy the necessary asset insurance.

We have shown in Equation (6.13) that RAROC is a function of $E(V_{A,T})/EC$ and $-I(1+R_D)/EC$, assuming still that $I = V_{D,0}$, that is, the investment is fully funded by debt.

Let us first consider negative NPV projects, that is, $I > V_{A,0}$. We examine the effects of a negative NPV on these two ratios that determine RAROC. We find that the change in the first of the two ratios when increasing risk will always outweigh the change in the second ratio, making RAROC an increasing function at a decreasing rate for negative NPV projects.[82]

For positive NPV projects, that is, $I < V_{A,0}$, the change in the two ratios is more sophisticated. For low-risk projects, the change in the first ratio is smaller than in the second, making RAROC a decreasing function. For high-risk projects the reverse holds true.

This leads to the following consequences:

1. For NPV = 0 projects, there is only one point where RAROC in combination with a bankwide hurdle rate leads to the right decision rule, namely to be indifferent about the investment. This consequence has already been described. Employees will have an incentive to choose high-risk, high-correlation projects that indicate value creation where there is none (this problem area is depicted gray in Figure 6.4).

2. For NPV < 0 projects, we will at least get the answer that their RAROC is smaller than the RAROC of the same project with NPV = 0. However, unless the bankwide hurdle rate is not consistently higher than the depicted RAROC curve,[83] the bank will create an even greater incentive to choose high-risk, high-correlation projects. As is shown in Figure 6.5, the gray shaded problem area lies further out to the right.

3. For NPV > 0 projects, we will again get the answer that their RAROC is higher than for NPV ≤ 0 projects. However, for NPV-positive projects, it could happen that a large number of positive NPV projects are rejected because their RAROC is below the bankwide hurdle rate, as indicated by the gray shaded area in Figure 6.6. As also indicated in Figure 6.6, this assumes that the hurdle rate is very high. Assuming this is not the case, RAROC will correctly indicate that projects add value because they are above the hurdle rate. However, when

---

[82]Note that the change in the two ratios exactly offsets each other for NPV = 0 projects, making this function linear.

[83]This situation might be very unlikely.

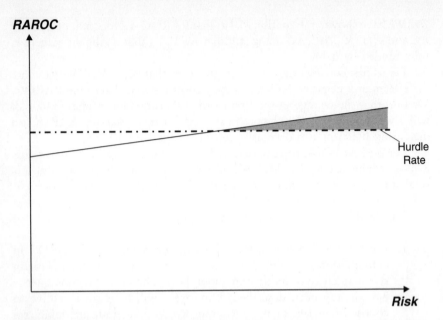

Figure 6.4   Problem areas applying the RAROC decision rule: Zero NPV projects.
Note: Results for plotting this graph are derived similar to Crouhy et al. (1999), especially Table 4, p. 19.

transforming these results into economic profits, this obviously will indicate the wrong amount of value added to the bank.[84]

We have highlighted the problem areas of applying the RAROC-decision rule in Figures 6.4 to 6.6 by shading them in gray. They reflect situations in which the bank either decides to undertake investments that are deemed to create value on a RAROC basis where there is none (or there is even value destruction; see Figure 6.5) or to reject projects that have a positive NPV, but are found to be value-destroying under the RAROC rule.[85]

A bank therefore needs to decide whether it would like to accept these often only slightly wrong incentives induced when applying a simple decision rule (i.e., RAROC in combination with a bankwide hurdle rate), or

---

[84]Even though economic profit is positive in this case, this will not reflect the correct NPV of the project and does not allow for a correct relative ranking of the projects.
[85]Note that by using the adjusted RAROC proposed by Crouhy et al. the problem areas are eliminated. But on an economic profit basis, the adjustment does not lead to correct results (as proxy for NPV) nor to a correct relative ranking.

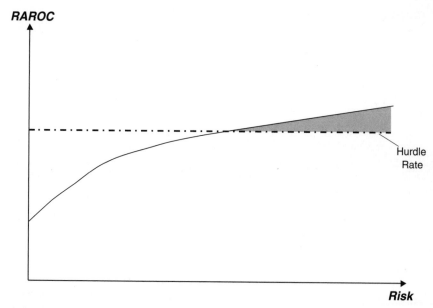

Figure 6.5 Problem areas applying the RAROC decision rule: Negative NPV projects.

Note: Results for plotting this graph are derived similar to Crouhy et al. (1999), especially Table 4, p. 19.

whether it wants to make the extra effort and estimate the required minimum hurdle rate transaction by transaction.[86]

Modifying RAROC to Address Its Pitfalls   The model that we have used to identify the deficiencies in the RAROC methodology when comparing it to a single, bankwide hurdle rate to identify value creation through risk-management activities is only a simplified version of what is used in reality. The actual best practice approaches to RAROC in banks are much more sophisticated and address the many and important pitfalls that can lead to incorrect results when implementing RAROC.

These practical approaches address pitfalls[87] ranging from the incorrect derivation[88] and differentiation[89] of the CAPM hurdle rate to the problem

---

[86]Note that this can be a difficult task when the constitution of the portfolio changes frequently.

[87]For a discussion of these pitfalls see, for example, Dermine (1998), Drzik et al. (1998a and 1998b), or Froot and Stein (1998a), pp. 75–77.

[88]For instance, the risk-free rate for calculating the CAPM hurdle rate should be consistent with the measurement horizon (here: one year) and not just a short-term (i.e., 3 months) interest rate that is readily available.

[89]See, for example, Drzik et al. (1998b), p. 67.

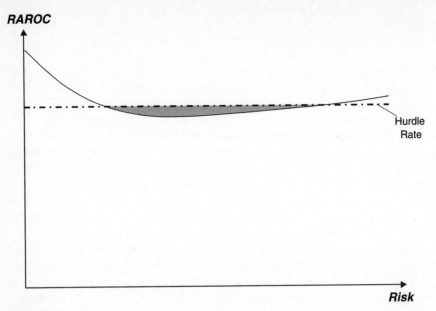

Figure 6.6   Problem areas applying the RAROC decision rule: Positive NPV projects.
Note: Results for plotting this graph are derived similar to Crouhy et al. (1999), especially Table 4, p. 19.

of how to consider diversification effects on the standalone capital requirement of a decentralized profit center.[90] Others address the difficulties with the usage of accounting data as proxies for market values[91] and the incorrect disentangling of revenues and costs down to transaction level.[92]

Another problem area addressed in practical approaches is that RAROC is—at least in its original definition—a single period measure. To calculate RAROC for multiperiod loan transactions, one needs to keep in mind to take expected (i.e., default probability weighted) net cash flows[93] and needs to address the problem of a nonflat yield curve.[94]

Given that there are sophisticated answers to all of these questions, one could assume that when RAROC is applied correctly, i.e., when one avoids

---

[90]See Dermine (1998), p. 25.
[91]See, for example, Drzik et al. (1998a), pp. 24–25, who suggest net asset value as a proxy for market value of assets by including, for example, hidden reserves and market value-adjusted book values.
[92]See for example, Kimball (1998), p. 35.
[93]For multiperiod extensions of RAROC for credits see, for example, Schröck and Windfuhr (1999).
[94]See Dermine (1998), p. 23.

all the pitfalls during its implementation, RAROC's bias is not too large and it is a directionally correct measure to identify value creation in banks (at least) for practical purposes.

However, eliminating all the pitfalls—which may only exacerbate the theoretical concerns discussed above[95]—misses the point that there are much more fundamental problems with RAROC,[96] which we will discuss in the next section.

Fundamental Problems of RAROC   Comparing RAROC to a CAPM-derived hurdle rate to determine the value created by a (risk-management) transaction (as shown in Figure 6.7) results in two fundamental problems:

- Economic capital has to be treated synonymously with equity capital provided by the shareholders, and it has to be assumed to be able to ultimately fix the actual bank capital structure.
- CAPM is a market-driven equilibrium model in which only systematic risk with a broad market portfolio counts. It is unclear why a hurdle rate derived in such a world should be compatible with a risk measure that is based on the bank's concern with the total risk of its (existing) portfolio.

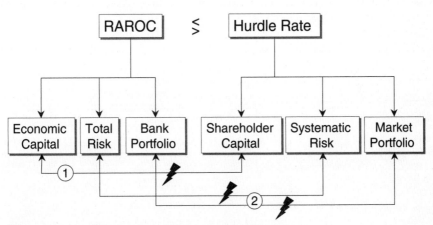

Figure 6.7   Fundamental problems with RAROC.

---

[95]Note that these theoretical concerns shown in the simplified model we have used above do not necessarily disappear in a more sophisticated world.

[96]Many authors (including myself) spent significant time on trying to fix RAROC and make it multiperiod while ignoring the real key concerns with this measure that lead to fundamental inconsistencies.

Even though these theoretical concerns have been raised in rudimentary form, for example, by Wilson (1992) and James (1996), they seem to have been ignored by the industry and in the application of the practical solutions economic capital and RAROC.[97] We will address both problem areas in turn below.

The Capital Structure Assumption of RAROC   In this section, we take a more reality-driven view and investigate what happens if the actual capital-structure decision of a bank deviates from the strict assumptions behind the above-mentioned RAROC model. This is likely to be the case as we recall that capital has two different functions in banks:[98]

- A source of funds and, therefore, a part of the working capital of a bank
- A cushion for economic risks to protect debt holders against losses

Therefore, in reality, it is likely that not all transactions are funded purely by debt (in our model above: I is not necessarily equal to $V_{D,0}$), and hence economic capital is not necessarily equal to the capital as provided by the shareholders (i.e., $EC \neq V_{E,0}$). Moreover, there are many bank transactions that do not require any up-front cash investment at all. For instance, swaps are especially designed to not require such an investment. RAROC is also intended to be applicable to many other nontraditional, fee-based transactions that do not require the investment of cash capital at all.[99] Nonetheless, all of these activities might require a certain amount of economic capital.

However, RAROC takes only economic capital into account and ignores the actual capital-structure decision taken by the bank. Only as long as no real equity cash investment is necessary[100] will RAROC lead to unbiased results.[101] In reality, though, we typically find that $V_{A,0} \neq I$ (i.e., the bank wants to create value and hence invests in positive NPV projects[102]) and that the bank is financed by both debt and equity. Hence, when trying to evaluate the economic profitability of any such transaction, not only the risk capital

---

[97]Only Johanning (1998) points out that VaR-based measures should only be used as a restriction and not as an objective function for business decisions.

[98]See Kimball (1998), p. 44.

[99]See Zaik et al. (1996), p. 83.

[100]Another case would be—however coincidental—when economic capital matches the real equity capital.

[101]As Wilson (1992), p. 116, rightly observes, therefore RAROC should only be applied to self-financing portfolios with zero value.

[102]Some of the bank's investments might be intentionally negative NPV projects (so-called loss leaders) in order to gain more profitable transactions via cross-selling.

to support the riskiness of the transaction needs to be taken into account, but also the (cash) capital.

In order to demonstrate that invested capital and economic capital can be very different and that RAROC fails to compensate invested capital and economic capital at the same time, we can create the following economic balance sheet (see Figure 6.8). As also observed by Merton and Perold (1993) and discussed in the previous chapter, accounting balance sheets disregard the provision of economic capital, unless explicit external (asset) insurance is bought and booked as an asset.

We assume that the bank invests cash capital into a transaction. Recall that the implicit (asset) insurance "economic capital" is only a fictional amount of money. It is—as is also true for the RAROC methodology described above—assumed to be kept in a separate pool that is invested in risk-free assets so that it is available for unexpected losses up to a prespecified confidence level at the end of the measurement period. The key to showing the true economic profitability is to make the implicit (asset) insurance as transparent in the calculation as an external one by booking it as an asset in the economic balance sheet.

We assume for our example that we have only one class of debt, meaning that we do not differentiate between various other debt tranches (as

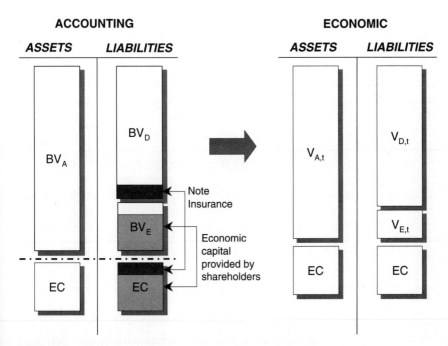

Figure 6.8 Economic balance sheet including economic capital.

discussed in the previous chapter). We further assume that this class of debt provides its own contribution to the (asset) insurance pool. The value of this "note insurance" can be determined by the value of the put option, as shown in Equation (6.4) and is equal to the amount that is necessary to insure the debt (tranche) up to a level so that it is virtually risk-free.[103] It is represented as the dark gray box in the left-hand part of Figure 6.8.

Moreover, we assume that the difference between the required amount of economic capital EC and the value of the note insurance is provided by the equity holders (as represented by the light gray shaded box in the left hand part of Figure 6.8). As can be seen immediately, the amount of invested equity capital and the amount of economic capital can differ. Note that most of the economic capital is provided by the shareholders, but contrary to the RAROC world, not necessarily all of it.

The left-hand part of Figure 6.8 depicts the accounting balance sheet view of the transaction. The book value of the asset BV_A equals the sum of the book value of debt BV_D and the book value of the equity BV_E; however, BV_D, and BV_E net of the contribution to the economic capital pool do not represent the economic value of debt and equity, nor is economic capital considered as an asset.

This is done in the economic balance sheet view—as depicted in the right-hand part of Figure 6.8. Note that the amount of required economic capital is unchanged in this world because it was already determined on an economic basis beforehand. And again, the market value of debt $(V_{D,t})$ and equity $(V_{E,t})$ add up to the market value of the transaction $(V_{A,t})$.[104] Again, $V_{E,t}$ can be very different from EC. Especially the amount of invested capital (i.e., $V_{E,0}$ at time $t = 0$) at the initiation of transaction A, does not have to equal EC. This also makes explicit the fact that economic capital cannot be required to make the equity hurdle rate—only the cash capital has to. However, this raises the question: What is the adequate return that economic capital has to earn in order to create value for the bank? We will address this question in the next section.

Before we do so, we can briefly summarize the previous points:

■ Setting economic capital equal to equity (provided by the shareholders) ignores the default risk (of other tranches) and is, therefore, only a first-order approximation[105] of reality.

---

[103]Recall from above that the value of a risky bond is the sum of a risk-free bond plus the value of the put option.

[104]However, this is not an indicator that capital structure is irrelevant.

[105]See Crouhy et al. (1999), p. 21, footnote 21.

- It is not necessary that a bank aligns its actual equity capital with economic capital, because shareholders only bear one tranche of the default risk among others.
- Economic capital is, in general, independent from the choice of the actual capital structure.[106] However, the actual capital structure does not determine the cost of total risk.

Required Hurdle Rate Return of RAROC Setting the hurdle rate in the RAROC approach is eventually a normative management action. However, it should be based on proper financial theory foundations[107] in order to indicate whether value is created or not.

Per our RAROC definition above, the hurdle rate is chosen to be consistent with the CAPM required return—either at the bank level or at the transaction level. This creates two serious problems, which are demonstrated in the following example.

We know from the discussion in the previous chapter that economic capital is a total risk measure that includes both systematic and unsystematic risks.[108] We assume for our example the following split of economic capital between the three types of risk (see Table 6.2).[109]

We know from our previous discussion that, typically, operational risk is mostly idiosyncratic or firm-specific risk. The same is true for parts of the credit portfolio since we assume that the bank does not hold a fully diversified portfolio, because it contains regional and customer-specific concentration risk. Because the market risk portfolio is rather diversified, we assume the following split between systematic and specific risk, in a CAPM sense, for our example (see Table 6.3).

Table 6.2 Split of Economic Capital among Types of Risk

Risk Type	Economic Capital (in Dollars)
Credit Risk	50
Market Risk	20
Operational Risk	30
Total	100

---

[106]As we showed in the beginning of Chapter 5, the optimal capital structure is set as a trade-off between various marginal costs and benefits.
[107]See Schmittmann et al. (1996), p. 649.
[108]See Wilson (1992), p. 116.
[109]As we have seen above, this split is not atypical for commercial banks.

Table 6.3   CAPM Hurdle Rate and Economic Capital

Types of Risk	Systematic Risk (%)	Specific Risk (%)	Systematic Risk (in Dollars)	Specific Risk (in Dollars)
Credit Risk	70%	30%	35	15
Market Risk	95%	5%	19	1
Operational Risk	10%	90%	3	27
			57	43
Total Economic Capital			100	

We now assume that—as suggested in the RAROC methodology—the required economic capital amount[110] has to earn the required CAPM return. If the risk-free rate (R_f) equaled 6%, the market risk premium $(R_M - R_f)$ was also 6%, and the bank's CAPM beta (β) was 1.0, the hurdle rate could be determined via the following equation:

$$Hurdle\ Rate = R_f + \beta \cdot (R_M - R_f) \qquad (6.15)$$
$$= 6\% + 1 \cdot 6\% = 12\%.$$

Therefore, the required return on a dollar amount would be $12\% \cdot 100 = 12$. However, we know that the market (in the CAPM sense) does not price specific risk, that is, it is only compensated at the risk-free rate. Holding economic capital for specific risk (which is necessary in our above definition) therefore should only be compensated at 6% and not 12%. Hence, the adjusted required return is: $57 \cdot 12\% + 43 \cdot 6\% = 9.42$, which is 21.5% less than what the RAROC model would require.

This example reveals two serious problems with RAROC when it is used to determine the value created by a transaction:

- The CAPM-based hurdle rate only considers systematic risk, whereas economic capital is a total risk measure.
- Economic capital is measured as the total risk contribution to the (existing) bank portfolio (internal beta). It does not (necessarily) reflect the correlation to a broad market portfolio as required by the CAPM (external beta).

---

[110]To make matters even more plausible, we could additionally assume that (coincidentally) economic capital is equal to shareholder capital.

Therefore, RAROC cannot be required to compensate for risks as the market does.[111] This is because, on the one hand, market considerations do not enter economic capital as a risk measure. On the other hand, the market ignores the cost of total risk, which is only relevant when holding risks internally and when there is a concern with financial distress costs.

Because only the market value of equity $V_{E,0}$ can be the basis for calculating the required return to shareholders,[112] merely the cash equity needs to earn the CAPM return. Nonetheless, economic capital is costly—but, in general, it has (as we saw in the previous section) nothing to do with cash capital. Since cash capital and economic capital are fed from different pools of resources for very different purposes, they should also have very different required returns.

However, in order to determine what that adequate cost of economic capital is, we cannot apply a neoclassical model (such as CAPM), where financial distress costs and the concern with total risk are not relevant. If you nonetheless try to do so, this will inevitably lead to inconsistent results.

Evaluation of RAROC as a Single-Factor Model for Capital Budgeting in Banks

The economic capital requirement is based on the economic principles that were described at the outset of our discussion of why banks try to manage risk in order to create value. It takes into account a bank's concern with total risk that makes a bank behave as if it were risk averse, and forms the denominator of RAROC equation. This is something that none of the other capital-budgeting tools in banks takes into consideration and is one of the big advantages of this modified return on equity ratio.

Even though the RAROC numerator also tries to proxy the expected free cash flows of a valuation framework, RAROC unfortunately does not show the immediate link to value creation, as is commonly assumed in the banking industry. On the one hand, RAROC is based on rigid assumptions to make it comparable to a return on equity benchmark. On the other hand, in spite of its simplicity and practicability, it is a biased measure that, additionally, has two fundamental problems:

- It is only the economic capital that matters in a RAROC context. The actually invested cash capital is ignored.

---

[111]Even if the amount of economic capital and the (risk-adjusted) returns are both calculated correctly.

[112]See Schmittmann et al. (1996), p. 649.

■ Even if the economic capital were equal to the invested cash capital—which we have shown is not necessarily the case—only the cash
capital should earn the rate of return required by the bank's shareholders. Economic capital should be linked to the costs associated
with total risk. However, these financial distress costs are determined
in turn by the actual capital structure of the bank. Both of these
concerns are ignored in the current RAROC setting.

Therefore, we can conclude that RAROC compares "apples to oranges,"
making it an unreliable predictor for value creation and the identification
where a bank has competitive advantages, because:

■ The CAPM benchmark return used in RAROC understates the true
costs of an investment, especially for illiquid bank assets. In a world
where economic capital is relevant, CAPM is not the appropriate
capital-budgeting benchmark, because "unmarketable idiosyncratic
risks will impose real costs on the firm. Capital-budgeting procedures should, therefore, take those costs into account. Consequently,
the CAPM (or any other standard asset-pricing model) will no longer
be universally valid as a capital-budgeting tool [...]."[113]
■ RAROC is a "hybrid" of single-factor models,[114] because on the one
hand it includes concerns with respect to the total risk of the (existing) portfolio, but on the other hand it compares this total risk to
components that only reflect systematic and market-driven concerns.

Hence, shareholder equity should be benchmarked against CAPM returns (as in the traditional valuation framework), and economic capital should
be viewed as a buffer against unexpected losses that is invested in risk-free
assets and that requires compensation, which should be linked to its contribution to the bank's total risk. However, both concerns cannot be captured
by a single-factor model such as RAROC. They can only be reflected in a
model using two variables. We will discuss such models in the next section.

NEW APPROACHES TO CAPITAL BUDGETING IN BANKS

As we have seen in the previous sections, whereas RAROC only considers
"internal" betas and the relevance of the bank's own portfolio, all currently
applied (neoclassical) pricing models only consider "external" betas and

---

[113]See Froot et al. (1993), p. 1650.
[114]See Froot and Stein (1998a), p. 75.

market-driven considerations. RAROC is correct in that it reflects the bank's concern with total risk and financial distress costs, because, in reality, a transaction's contribution to the overall riskiness of a bank's own portfolio is an important factor in the bank's capital-budgeting decision.[115] However, this is something that is not addressed in the neoclassical finance approaches.[116] We have also seen that single-factor models cannot reflect both concerns at the same time.

Therefore, in this section we are going to discuss the idea that traditional capital-budgeting tools and RAROC need to be expanded to include aspects that are ignored in each of these two worlds. Because, in reality, a project's true cost of capital is determined both by the project's market beta and the internal beta, we will describe and evaluate possible blends of these two factors and compare them against RAROC in its current form. We will see that these two-factor models are still subject to further research, but that they can provide a new and more detailed and integrated decision-making framework for risk-management actions. Because risk management cannot be separated from capital-budgeting and capital-structure decisions[117] in banks in such a world, we will then describe the implications of these two-factor approaches on the normative theory of risk management.

Overview of the New Approaches

Wilson (1992) was one of the first to identify the fact that there is a fundamental problem with RAROC when it is applied as a single-factor model in combination with a CAPM-based hurdle rate using only economic capital and ignoring invested (real) shareholder capital. His solution, however, is trying to fix the problem in a single-factor world. This results in the recognition of real capital, while adjusting the confidence level (α) at which economic capital needs to be calculated in order to make RAROC compatible with the neoclassical world. This (variable) adjustment of α, in turn, contradicts the bank's concern with total risk and how (and why) it decided to determine the economically required amount of capital in the first place.

Some other practitioners and academics subsequently realized that economic capital is costly, but that the CAPM-determined hurdle rate does not reflect these "total risk costs", that is, it does not consider the risk and cost associated with default.[118]

Merton and Perold (1993) provide the theoretically purest model and

---

[115]See James (1996), p. 5.
[116]See Froot/Stein (1998b), p. 60.
[117]See James (1996), p. 5.
[118]See Crouhy (1999), p. 5.

combine these two concerns into a two-factor approach. They require the invested cash capital to earn the CAPM-determined rate of return, because this is the economically correct price for the risk, as priced in capital markets. They show that the cost of risk capital[119] is driven by the agency and information costs that make financial distress costs the main rationale for conducting risk management,[120] that is, because total risk is expensive and hence external finance is costly. Since they view risk capital as the provision of (asset) insurance, as long as this (implicit) insurance is bought at the fair market price, there are no economic costs associated with it.[121]

However, due to information asymmetries and agency concerns between the various bank stakeholders, this insurance can only be obtained by paying a spread over the (actuarial) fair market value.[122] These "deadweight losses" are the economic costs of risk capital for the bank.[123] However, the problem with this approach is that, in order to determine these total risk costs, one would need to apply the theoretically correct (actuarial) model and compare its results against observable market prices to identify these costs. Obviously, this is impossible to do in practice for all the various tranches of (asset) insurance.

Froot and Stein[124] also present a two-factor model. They argue along the lines that market frictions make risk management and capital structure matter. In such a world, bank-specific risk factors should be an important element of the capital-budgeting process.[125] They conclude that a transaction's contribution to the overall variability of the bank's own portfolio will affect the transaction's hurdle rate or cost of capital in the following way:

$$Hurdle\ Rate_i = R_f + \beta_i \cdot (R_M - R_f) + \lambda \cdot \sigma_{i,P} \qquad (6.16)$$

where $\lambda = \dfrac{R_P - R_f}{\sigma_P^2}$ = Unit cost for volatility of the bank's portfolio of non-hedgable cash flows.

$\sigma_{i,P}$ = Covariance of transaction i with the bank portfolio P.

---

[119]Recall that they suggest the full-blown approach to determine risk capital and not its reduced and practical version "economic capital."

[120]These transaction and agency-related costs also provide incentives for diversification within the bank portfolio.

[121]If a bank could buy (asset) insurance at these fair terms, risk capital would not be costly, and hence the model would fall back to a CAPM solution, where the firm is indifferent vis-à-vis risk management.

[122]This is mostly due to the fact that banks are opaque institutions. See Merton and Perold (1993), p. 26.

[123]See Merton and Perold (1993), p. 25.

[124]See Froot and Stein (1998a and 1998b).

[125]See James (1996), p. 8.

Therefore, the transaction's hurdle rate reflects the priced (market) risk (as, for example, in the CAPM) plus the contribution of the project to the overall volatility of the bank's cash flows that cannot be hedged in the market. The price for the bank-specific risk will vary directly with the cost of external financing and depends on the current capital structure of the bank.[126]

The Froot and Stein model obviously comes to the somewhat extreme conclusion that a bank should hedge all tradable risks as long as they can be hedged at little or no cost in the capital markets.[127] This is because the bank's required price for bearing tradable risk will exceed the market price for risk by the contribution of a hedgable risk to the overall variability of the bank's portfolio. Hence, the only risk the bank should bear is illiquid or nontradable risk[128]—which contradicts reality. There are the following problems with this particular model:

- It is not immediately obvious that the second pricing factor in the model necessarily reflects total risk costs in the sense developed in this book.
- Froot and Stein admit that it could be extremely difficult to estimate these costs, since they cannot be observed directly in the market.[129]
- The model is very unspecific about when it falls back to one or the other single-factor solution, that is, when does it price as the market does in the neoclassical solution[130] and when does it use only the internal portfolio as the relevant universe?
- Also, the model is unspecific about the trade-off between the costs of selling hedgable risk in the market and the cost of total risk of keeping hedgable risk within the bank's portfolio.

Stulz also develops a two-factor model.[131] Like Merton and Perold, he concludes that invested cash capital should be required to make (at least) the CAPM-determined hurdle rate. Since economic capital is a total risk measure with regard to the bank's own portfolio, it should—in addition to the costs of standard capital budgeting—reflect the costs of the impact of the project on the bank's total risk.[132] If economic capital is costly, ignoring

---

[126]See James (1996), p. 7.

[127]See Proposition 1 in Froot and Stein (1998a), p. 63.

[128]Note that this is already reflected in the previous equation.

[129]See Froot and Stein (1998a), p. 77.

[130]Except for the fact when the bank holds so much capital that it does not care about total risk or the risk is clearly a liquid and marketable risk like interest rate or foreign exchange risk.

[131]See Stulz (1996, 1999, and 2000).

[132]See Stulz (1999), p. 7.

these costs will lead to a mistake in the capital-budgeting decision-making process. Hence, the value of a project for a bank is the "traditional" NPV (as determined in the neoclassical world) minus the cost of total risk.

Even though Stulz leaves open how these costs of total risk can be quantified in reality, he proves that the total risk costs can be approximated for small changes in the portfolio by a constant incremental cost of economic capital per unit of economic capital.[133] Note that these costs of total risk do not disappear, irrespective of whether we deal with risk in liquid or illiquid markets. This puts holding risk within a bank portfolio always at a disadvantage vis-à-vis the market.

We can summarize these three two-factor models as follows. All models agree that a "total risk" component in addition to the neoclassical capital-budgeting approach is necessary in a world where risk management does matter to banks in order to create value. Even though none of these approaches shows how one could exactly quantify these total risk costs in practice, the "Stulz" approach appears to be the most plausible and promising for practical purposes for the following reasons:

- It integrates a total risk measure (economic capital) that is already widely used throughout the banking industry into the new capital-budgeting decision rule.
- Despite the fact that the total risk component does not vanish in liquid markets, as, for example, in the "Froot and Stein" model,[134] it has (as we will show) the best potential to identify transactions where the bank has competitive advantages and can really create value.
- As already mentioned, neither the "Merton and Perold" model nor the "Froot and Stein" model seem appropriate for practical purposes. Both models are impractical because of the unavailability of observable market data to determine the costs of the second pricing factor. Additionally, the latter model seems inappropriate because of its unrealistic conclusion that the bank will only hold nonhedgable risk.

Evaluation of RAROC in the Light of the New Approaches

RAROC was initially judged to be a good starting point for a capital-budgeting tool in banks, because it reflects the concern with total risk. After evaluating its usage in the light of the new, two-factor models presented above, it appears that RAROC only works correctly in a directional sense

---

[133]See Stulz (2000), p. 4-23, assuming that we can determine the total cost of risk for the total amount of economic capital at the bank level.
[134]As mentioned above, the exact workings of this effect are unclear.

when it evaluates transactions that are either completely illiquid or whose hedgable risk has been completely sold off or transfer-priced out.[135] Even though these conditions are typically met in reality and, therefore, make the bias in RAROC much smaller[136] (since the missing market component does not matter in these situations), RAROC cannot claim to be a general capital-budgeting rule for all banking and risk-management purposes, as is often thought in the financial industry.

If one follows the "Stulz" model, one could be tempted to conclude that a simple expansion of the RAROC hurdle rate by a margin necessary to cover the cost of total risk would avoid the problem. Unfortunately, this does not fix the omission of the invested capital and the incorrect link to market considerations. Nonetheless, the "Stulz" model could be thought of as the two-factor expansion of the RAROC model.[137]

The liquefaction of the credit markets as well as the common usage of RAROC in other (liquid market) risk sectors require this expansion for an additional market component. Since such a component is missing in RAROC, as it is currently applied, it is not surprising that a more active and growing secondary credit market provides information on loan pricing that is significantly different from that provided by RAROC models.[138]

RAROC, however, seems unable to identify where a bank's competitive advantages are (and hence where it really creates value) or how much risk management is needed and which exact risk-management instruments should be used in order to maximize value.[139] We will see in the next section that a two-factor model might be much better suited to identify these open issues.

Implications of the New Approaches to Risk Management and Value Creation in Banks

As already indicated, we will focus the further discussion on the "Stulz" model. This two-factor model defines the required rate of return for capital-

---

[135]Note that RAROC was first developed at Bankers Trust in the 1970s to evaluate the risk-adjusted performance of (illiquid) credit transactions when only the bank's own portfolio counts; see Zaik et al. (1996), p. 84.

[136]See James (1996), p. 13, or Froot and Stein (1998a), p. 76.

[137]This is another reason why the Stulz model is so attractive for practical purposes.

[138]See Shearer et al. (1999), p. 44. However, much of this pricing is derived using neoclassical pricing models, where credits would be priced equally by all market participants irrespective of their existing portfolios. This is not the case in reality and total risk concerns do enter the pricing of traded credits.

[139]Froot and Stein (1998a), p. 57, claim that it is not clear that RAROC is the optimal technique for dealing with the sorts of capital-budgeting problems faced by financial institutions, because RAROC "is not developed under the paradigm objective to maximize shareholder value."

budgeting decisions of a transaction i as the sum of the CAPM-determined rate of return $(R_{E,i})$ on the invested shareholder capital $(V_{E,i})$ and the total risk costs. These, in turn, are the product of the required economic capital of the transaction (EC_i) and the (proportional) financial distress costs of the bank (FDC).[140] Therefore:

$$Required\ Return_i = R_{E,i} \cdot V_{E,i} + FDC \cdot EC_i \qquad (6.17)$$

Clearly, in this model, holding risk within a bank portfolio is always costly. Even though the first component of the required return is the fair market price—which is not costly in an economic sense—the second component reflects the costs associated with the contribution of the transaction to the total risk costs of the bank's portfolio, which is driven by the actual capital structure. Hence, the price for holding risk on one's own books always exceeds the costs as paid in the market.

Even though this insight might contradict conventional financial theory, it can, on the one hand, explain the interdependence of risk-management, capital-budgeting, and capital-structure decisions in a bank when total risk matters (as depicted in the left-hand part of Figure 6.9). On the other hand, this fact sheds some more light on the normative theory of risk management in banks. Let us first consider the implications of this model for the risk-management decisions of a bank.

Implications for Risk-Management Decisions   Since holding risks on the bank's own books is costly, risk management can create value because it can reduce these costs. A bank has the following options to do so:

- Reduce the risk in its own portfolio, and hence the amount of required economic capital[141] and, therefore, the total risk costs
- Reduce the cost of total risk for a given level of economic capital

The ultimate consequence of the first option would be to sell all the bank's business and invest the proceeds into risk-free assets. Note that this is something Wilson predicts as a consequence of using RAROC as a performance measure.[142] However, this would include selling risks where

---

[140]Again, we do not specify here how these costs are determined. This is an issue for further research; see the "Areas for Further Research" section later in this chapter. Here, it is a constant percentage assigned to the required amount of economic capital.

[141]See Merton and Perold (1993), p. 27.

[142]See Wilson (1992), p. 114.

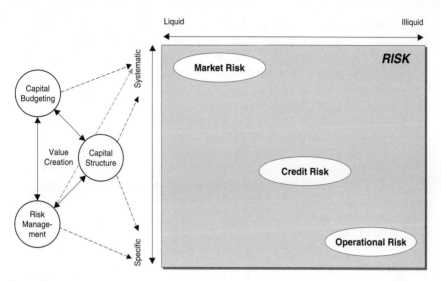

Figure 6.9 Overview of the components of a normative theory for risk management.

the bank has a competitive advantage and where it could really create value—despite the fact that it is costly for the bank to hold these risks. Therefore, this appears not to be an option for the bank.

Thus, only the second option is viable. It can be achieved in three ways:[143]

1. **Increasing actual capital:** As indicated previously, the institution's credit risk is inversely related to its available real equity capital. However, when a bank increases equity capital, the exact effects on economic capital and its associated costs must be considered. If a bank raises its equity to expand its business (at the same riskiness), this does not lower the costs of total risk. Therefore, equity would have to be invested in projects that have a negative internal beta to the existing portfolio. Neither an investment in risk-free assets nor the repayment of debt changes the bank's required economic capital.[144] But both actions change the cost of total risk, assuming that the other operations are left unchanged. However, holding equity

---

[143]See Stulz (2000), p. 4-37.
[144]See Stulz (2000), p. 4-39.

capital has an opportunity cost.[145] Therefore, holding enough equity to make risk management irrelevant is not an option for the bank.[146]

2. **Selecting projects according to their impact on total risk:** Selecting projects in order to improve the (internal) diversification of the bank's portfolio, to manage risk, is also expensive. On the one hand, as a market benchmark, one can observe that the diversification discount for conglomerates vis-à-vis a portfolio of their specialized competitors is approximately 14%.[147] On the other hand, expanding into unfamiliar sectors can be very costly, because this often adds an additional (and costly) management layer or can lead to unexpected high credit losses.[148] However, in our model, these costs have to be balanced against the cost savings in total risk costs. Note that, in contrast, Zaik et al. (1996) claim that RAROC gives the message that internal diversification pays off in any case—even beyond familiar business segments.

3. **Using derivatives to hedge and other (financial) risk-management instruments to shed risks:** Applying these risk-management instruments in liquid markets is the most cost-efficient way to reduce firm-wide risk. Therefore, a bank should evaluate the total risk contribution of a new transaction only after carrying out these hedging activities.[149] However, and as we will see in the implications below, the cost of these instruments has to be lower than the total risk costs of these transactions.

The application of this model leads us to the following practical implications for risk management in banks:

---

[145]Shareholders expect the CAPM return on equity—which is not costly in an economic sense. However, when a bank uses equity to buy back debt, this gives a windfall to the existing debt holders (making their debt safer) and therefore redistributes some of the benefits of increasing equity capital to other stakeholders. Moreover, a part of the tax shield is lost for the bank when debt is bought back. Other information asymmetries and agency costs (e.g., managerial discretion) as well as the transaction costs (of issuing new capital) also make new equity expensive. For a detailed discussion of these effects, see also Chapter 3.

[146]See Stulz (2000), p. 4-39.

[147]See Stulz (2000), p. 4-40.

[148]See, for example, Winton (2000), p. 3. Increased competition may magnify the "Winner's Curse" problem faced by a bank on the entry into a new lending area, making diversification very costly. Banks—facing greater competition—may therefore find it more attractive to specialize.

[149]Note that this is partly what RAROC does via transfer pricing.

Implication 1

The two-factor model will identify where the bank has competitive advantages and where it can really create value.

Reasoning

As long as a bank is able to expropriate extra-normal (economic) rents from informational advantages that exceed both cost components of Equation (6.17), it can actually increase the bank's value by holding these risks internally. This will most likely happen in illiquid areas (see right-hand part in Figure 6.9), because—by definition—markets are only liquid when market players have homogenous expectations and no informational advantages. Therefore, when the bank decides to hold positions in liquid market risks (where market inefficiencies are very unlikely to occur), the price needs to cover (at least) both the market costs and the total risk costs in order to create value. Otherwise, this will be a value-destroying proposition.

Implication 2

The bank should sell all risks when it does not have a competitive advantage, that is, all hedgable or noncompensated[150] risks should be sold, as long as the costs for doing so will not exceed the total risk costs.

Reasoning

As the bank will not have informational or competitive advantages that will compensate for both cost components of Equation (6.17) for all of its transactions,[151] it will destroy value by keeping these risks. Again, one needs to trade off the costs of shedding these risks against the total risk costs:

- In liquid markets these risks, most likely, trade at their fair market prices. In this case, the decision is obvious. The costs (i.e., the spreads above the fair market value) for selling off these risks are lower: the greater the volume of transactions in a given market, the lower the volatility of the underlying asset price, and the less private informa-

---

[150]See Schrand and Unal (1996), p. 1, who define compensated risks as those risks where the bank has comparative advantages with regard to their management. These risks are therefore the source of the economic profits of the firm. Hedgable risks are, on the contrary, those risks where the bank cannot extract economic rents (mostly liquid or traded risks).

[151]Note that some risks, where the bank has competitive advantages, can only be bought as a bundled package of risks, which can also contain noncompensated risks. See Schrand and Unal (1996), p. 1.

tion[152] is relevant for pricing the underlying asset.[153] Hence, the bank should sell or redistribute these liquid risks using derivative hedging instruments,[154] because the costs of doing so are almost certainly lower than the total risk costs incurred when holding these transactions in the bank's own portfolio.

■ Not all risks are traded in liquid markets. However, there are other on- and off-balance sheet[155] risk instruments available that can be applied across the whole risk spectrum.[156] Securitizations, (internal) diversification, insurance, loss prevention by process control, and so on, should be applied as long as their costs do not exceed the total risk costs of the underlying transactions.

Note that the conclusion to sell all liquid risks is similar to the result of the Froot and Stein model. However, the Stulz model allows for competitive advantages even in liquid markets, whereas the Froot and Stein model would indicate that all liquid risks should be sold off immediately without further considerations. However, speculating "on the market" in these liquid segments will require economic capital and is, therefore, costly. If the bank, nonetheless, decides to hold on to risks that it could more cheaply shed, it will destroy value.

Implication 3

Hedging specific risks and diversification of the bank's portfolio can create value even if it comes at a cost.

Reasoning

As long as the costs of, for example, diversifying credit risk and managing operational risk (which is typically highly specific risk, see right-hand part

---

[152]Therefore, it is unlikely for the bank to have a competitive advantage in these markets.
[153]See Smith (1995), p. 27.
[154]These instruments are forwards, futures, swaps, and options.
[155]See Smith (1995), p. 22. Financial risk-management products provide a more effective separation of production and risk-management activities, since they are more liquid and flexible to allow for more rapid adjustments.
[156]See Smith (1993), pp. 13+. Risk spectrum means in this context risks ranging from (firm-) specific risks, such as fires, lawsuits, the outcomes of R&D projects, of exploration and development activities, to systematic or market-wide risks, such as unexpected changes in interest or exchange rates, oil prices, or GDP. This is also depicted in the right-hand part of Figure 6.9.

in Figure 6.9[157]) are lower than the total risk costs they incur, it will pay for the bank to do so. This contradicts the conclusion of the neoclassical theory that spending time and money to eliminate firm-specific risks will destroy value in any case.[158] Note that we dealt with this issue in the "Operational Risk" section of Chapter 5 when we discussed the benefits of self-insurance (internal risk pooling) versus third-party insurance for event risks.

Implications for Capital-Budgeting Decisions   We have seen that, when total risk matters, banks can increase their value through risk management. However, this fact makes risk management inseparable from capital-budgeting decisions. On the one hand, as previously indicated, capital-budgeting decisions on transactions should only be taken after all noncompensated risks[159] have been shed via risk-management actions. On the other hand, the bank may only be able to buy a risk—where it does have a compensated informational advantage—as a part of a "risk"-bundled product.[160] However, the bank may not be able to shed the other, noncompensated risks that are also associated with that "bundled" transaction later, because the costs of doing so would exceed the total risk costs as indicated by Equation (6.17) and as described in Implication 2. However, these risks impose a real cost on the bank. Therefore, the bank cannot and should not separate risk management from the capital-budgeting decision. Applying our two-factor model with all its implications *ex ante* would prevent the bank from investing in such risks beforehand—unless the compensation of the informational advantage were to exceed the additional total risk costs imposed by the unsalable risk components of the package.

Implications for Capital-Structure Decisions   Because the actual capital structure determines the total risk costs for the bank, neither risk management nor capital-budgeting decisions can be made without considering the actual capital structure.

---

[157]Note that the three types of risk in Figure 6.9 are only schematically put into places where they are most likely to be found. Deviations might well be possible. For instance, there might be both highly illiquid or highly specific market risk, and so on.
[158]Consider, for example, a transaction that has hedgable specific risk. The traditional NPV rule does not consider such risks and, as shown previously, hedging at a cost would destroy value. However, hedging this risk, even at a cost, would make sense if the reduction in total risk costs outweighed the costs.
[159]Noncompensated risks are those risks that are cheaper to sell off than to keep internally.
[160]As an example, this might be a credit in a specialized lending area of the bank, where the bank has no specific skills, but that has sophisticated interest rate and foreign exchange features associated with it.

In our model, both real equity and total risk are costly. Decreasing the leverage of the bank (i.e., increasing the equity capital ratio) decreases the total risk costs but increases the overall equity costs. If increasing equity to decrease the cost of total risk is costly,[161] then, at the margin, the cost of total risk has to equal the cost of equity, and the capital structure has to be adjusted until equilibrium is reached.[162] However, this does not mean that economic capital and actual equity capital also have to be equal. Knowing the required amount of economic capital, therefore, does not resolve the problem of the actual capital-structure choice. Note that since increasing total risk has a significant cost that has to be taken into account in everything the bank does, higher capital ratios in banks might be less expensive than is commonly thought of—given that they can lower total risk costs. An extreme conclusion of this discussion is that if the bank held infinite (real) capital, it would be risk-neutral, as in the neoclassical world. This is something that is not reflected in RAROC because the economic capital always has to earn the CAPM-required return.

New Approaches as Foundations for a Normative Theory of Risk Management in Banks

We can draw the following conclusions from the application of the suggested two-factor model:

- Risk management can create value. There is a whole spectrum of instruments (apart from just derivatives in liquid markets) that can be used, as long as the cost of applying them is lower than the total risk costs associated with the transaction.
- As shown in the left-hand part of Figure 6.9, capital-budgeting, capital-structure, and risk-management decisions are interrelated and need to be determined simultaneously—rather than separately as in the neoclassical world.
- As also shown in Figure 6.9, when total risk matters and is costly to the bank, the world cannot be reduced to just dealing with systematic and specific risks. It is rather a question of whether risks generate—via the bank's competitive advantages—enough revenues to compensate for both market and total risk costs, so that it is worthwhile to hold them internally. Even though these competitive advantages are likely to exist in illiquid markets, where informational asymmetries prevail, they can be achieved across the whole risk spectrum (as shown in the right-hand part).

---

[161]Due to the increase in transaction and agency costs.
[162]See Stulz (1999), p. 9.

■ The bank should concentrate on these competitive advantages and should understand where they come from[163] and why they exist.[164] Risk management allows the bank to concentrate on these risks, because the capital-budgeting decision rule of the two-factor model encourages the shedding of all other risks whose revenues do not cover both cost components.[165] Only those risks without competitive advantages that have little impact on the overall firm risk, but that are expensive to eliminate, should be kept within the bank's portfolio.

These conclusions are not dramatically new—since many of them are already being practiced in the financial industry. The difference, however, is that they cannot be explained by the tools and theories that are currently available. As suggested above, two-factor models can, therefore, provide the foundations for a normative theory of risk management. Not only can this new approach explain why risk management can create value at the bank level, but also it provides much more detailed and differentiated (theoretical) arguments of what to do and which instruments can be applied in order to achieve the ultimate goal of value maximization.

Of course, all of this contradicts traditional intuition. But hedgable risks eat up a fraction of the overall available risk capacity that could be used to extract economic rents by using the bank's comparative advantages. Therefore, the pure and "naïve" implication of the neoclassical world that the bank should simply reduce risks cannot be the goal. It is rather the right "coordination" of risks that is required.[166]

The need to identify and concentrate on competitive advantages as well as the right coordination of risks is most obvious in the recent developments in the area of traditional bank lending. Loan securitizations and the "unbundling" of the traditional lending business model[167] from a "buy-and-hold" strategy to a separation of loan origination and active credit portfolio management[168] (in secondary markets) both require the expansion of RAROC

---

[163]See Stulz (1996), p. 15.

[164]Braas and Bralver (1990) point out that most foreign exchange trading desks do not make money by position taking, but rather by market making (i.e., turnover). This is something that a simple RAROC calculation would not reveal.

[165]Since our model indicates that it is typically advisable to sell off all marketable/liquid risks, implicitly the model falls back to the neoclassical solution since the bank's (quasi) risk aversion does not enter into its decision-making process in these cases.

[166]Schrand and Unal (1996) show that financial institutions hedge interest rate risks in order to be able to take on more credit risks—which is consistent with what our model has to say.

[167]See, for example, Kuritzkes (1998) and (1999).

[168]See, for example, Reading et al. (1998), p. 22.

to obtain a market component and a tool that properly identifies the informational advantages in the credit process.[169]

AREAS FOR FURTHER RESEARCH

From the discussion of capital-budgeting tools in banks, we can identify a number of areas for further research. These are:

- **Determination and usage of total risk costs:** The two-factor approach for capital budgeting in banks that was presented is an obvious area for further research. The most immediate subject is the determination of FDC, the constant percentage cost assigned to the allocated economic capital per transaction and its use for (marginal) total risk costs. Unfortunately, there are hardly any broad and international studies that estimate the "severity" (i.e., the percentage loss of assets) of bank defaults. One could use this data to calculate an "expected loss" percentage as a proxy for the total risk costs, which are the product of a bank's default probability (determined by its agency rating) and the severity (as determined in such studies). However, for example, when assuming a 30% loss of total assets[170] and a default probability of 0.03% for Deutsche Bank for the end of 1999, one would assign a cost of roughly four dollars per dollar unit of economic capital—which seems to be completely unrealistic. Alternately, one could use observable market data[171] such as the conglomerate discount (14%)[172] or data on the impact of large losses on the market capitalization of banks to calibrate the model—which, however, needs to be developed first.

- **Usage of risk-adjusted returns in the two-factor model:** The comparison of risk-adjusted returns to the required return as defined in Equation (6.17) needs further research. First, expected (credit) losses should still be deducted from net revenues.[173] Second, it was not determined what assumptions should be used in the two-factor model with regard to funding the bank's transactions. If it were still all debt-

---

[169]Note that RAROC might not be able to do so, given our earlier judgement.

[170]This would be roughly in line with the study conducted by James (1991) for the U.S. banking market.

[171]One would need to discuss whether a loss in franchise value should enter the calculations.

[172]See above.

[173]Many banks apply EL now. However, the tax treatment vis-à-vis loan loss provisions needs to be clarified.

financed, one would need to discuss the treatment of the capital benefit and the assumed investment of economic capital until the end of the measurement horizon in such a world. Third, the treatment of the NPV in transactions with nonzero NPV is as unresolved as in the RAROC calculation.[174] Fourth, it is unclear where and how the costs for running risk measurement and risk management should enter into the calculation. Last, but not least, one would need to specify the exact workings of the change in economic capital and the risk-adjusted return when adding a new transaction to an existing portfolio.[175]

- **Aggregation and allocation of economic capital:** We calculate in our framework the amount of required economic capital based on internal betas. As can be shown,[176] this approach does not leave any economic capital unallocated, and the sum of the incremental economic capital amounts will always add up to the total. However, this assumes that internal betas and the marginal economic capital amount—the amount that we found relevant for value decisions—are equal. But, internal betas can lead to different answers from marginal capital.[177] The two approaches only provide the same answers when the business mix of the portfolio already exists and is not changed in its relative size by the (new) transaction. Hence, in situations where business units grow at very different rates, the marginal risk contribution might be more appropriate and needs to be determined by a "with and without" calculation. However, this procedure potentially leaves a huge portion of the economic capital unallocated[178]—even though the error is small when only small fractions of the portfolio are considered. Therefore, there is an ongoing debate as to which procedure should be used in practice and which one best avoids a misallocation of economic capital[179] that, in turn, can lead to incorrect pricing and biased strategic moves.[180] Note that both of the presented procedures can lead to a negative economic capital allocation, which would result in a negative opportunity cost associated with total risk. A possible conclusion that using the

---

[174]An open question is, for example, whether the NPV should change the actual leverage of the transaction.

[175]See Stulz (2000), pp. 4-23+.

[176]See, for example, Stulz (2000), pp. 4-32–4-33.

[177]See Kimball (1998), p. 48.

[178]See Merton and Perold (1993), pp. 27–30.

[179]As indicated above, various weighting schemes are applied in practice.

[180]See Dermine (1998), p. 25.

marginal calculation for new business and the internal beta for existing business needs further elaboration and research.

- **Effects of the trade-off between capital structure and total risk costs:**
There is very little knowledge about the effects of changing the actual capital structure on the total risk costs and how these effects
could be modeled in a neoinstitutional world (also see first area
indicated in this list).

- **Intertemporal consequences for risk management:** Our model (and
basically also RAROC[181]) has avoided dealing with multiperiod issues so far. However, these issues are exactly the ones that are most
relevant with regard to value creation. For instance, it is unresolved
as to how the required return in the two-factor model and economic
capital would have to be determined in a multiperiod setting. If the
measurement horizon H is expanded, then the confidence level α
would be lower, because default over, for example, a five-year horizon is much more likely than over one-year horizon. At first glance,
the consequence would appear to be that the capital requirement
would, therefore, be lower. However, the bank has to hold enough
economic capital in each of the years not to default (i.e., the marginal, not the cumulative, default probability counts). Additionally,
there are many more intertemporal issues associated with risk management, such as the fact that it is unclear whether short-term optimal risk management leads to long-term value maximization. These
are subject to further research (and empirical testing, see the next
area).

- **Empirical tests:** Currently, conducting empirical tests of whether the
previously discussed capital-budgeting tools (both RAROC[182] and
the new approaches) are correlated with value creation in banks (as
indicated by their market capitalization) is very difficult because of
the lack of appropriate data. Even though the suggested top-down
procedure to estimate the required amount of economic capital
(as discussed in the "Suggestion of an Approach to Determine Economic Capital from the Top Down" section of Chapter 5) would
be a promising starting point, it needs more published or publicly
available economic capital numbers to calibrate the model. This,
however, has the caveat that currently there is no consistent reporting of economic capital numbers (consistent confidence levels and

[181]We have already referred to multiperiod expansion of RAROC. See, for example,
Brüning and Hoffjan (1997) and Schröck and Windfuhr (1999).
[182]Despite the theoretical concerns, it is still a widely used performance measure in
practice.

aggregation procedures) and that RAROC still lacks a consistent industry-wide definition, making the comparability of published results questionable. But the new Basle Accord and the increased disclosure requirements under Pillar Three will be helpful in making banks more transparent in this respect in the near future. The upside of using data at the bankwide level would be that there would be no data availability problems at the business unit level as well as no allocation and transfer-pricing problems vis-à-vis the skew at the trans-action level. Additionally, one could apply the bankwide hurdle rate (as can be easily observed in the market), avoiding the determination problems and potential skews at the business unit or transaction level. Moreover, rating agencies (such as Standard & Poor's) provide sanitized return data on an accounting basis at the bankwide level that could be easily transformed into risk-adjusted return proxies.[183]

SUMMARY

We started this chapter with a discussion of the various available capital-budgeting tools in banks and their ability both to identify the potential for value creation and to reflect the bank's concern with total risk. We, thus, identified RAROC as the most promising candidate, because it uses an adequate total risk measure (economic capital) and is linked to (traditional) shareholder value concepts via the comparison to a CAPM-determined (bankwide) hurdle rate.

Despite its advantages, we found that RAROC is based on rigid assumptions and is subject to various deficiencies. Moreover, there are fundamental theoretical concerns with RAROC when it comes to the determination of value creation:

- The comparison of RAROC to a hurdle rate that is determined in a neoclassical world is not consistent with a risk measure that is motivated by the neoinstitutional theory, where total risk counts and risk management can create value.
- The assumption that economic capital is the same as "cash" equity capital provided by shareholders is not appropriate (it is not necessarily the case, as covered in the extensive discussion in Chapter 5).

---

[183]For instance, one could take the average of the loan loss provisions of the previous five years as a proxy for expected (credit) losses, etc.

We, therefore, concluded that RAROC compares "apples to oranges" and that in order to include both the required market return and the costs associated with financial distress situations, it is best to use a two-factor model. We found that such a two-factor model could lay proper foundations for a normative theory for risk management in banks and would allow the bank to focus on its comparative advantages. However, much more research needs to be done in order to make such a model operational in practice. Therefore, RAROC might, currently, be the only practical solution to capital budgeting in banks that is communicable and implementable at all bank levels.

CHAPTER 7

Conclusion

The starting point of the discussion in this book was the observation that banks are—by their very nature—in the risk business and that they conduct risk management as an empirical fact; the combination of these factors constitutes a positive theory for risk management in banks. However, the central role of risk in the banking business is merely a necessary condition for the management of risks. Only the fact that risk management can also create value would make it a sufficient condition for doing so, assuming that value maximization is the ultimate objective of banks. Despite the fact that other stakeholders' interests are both diverse and strong (e.g., to ensure a bank's safety and survival, as required by regulators and depositors), we found this to be the case.

Therefore, the focus of this book was to examine risk management at the corporate level in the light of the sufficient condition, that is, as to establish whether and how risk management can be used as a device to increase the value of banks (and not for other purposes).

However, we found that there is very little known from a theoretical point of view on where and how a bank can create value by practicing risk management. Also, there is only anecdotal and only weak or inconclusive (because of limitations in available data) empirical evidence for a link between risk management and value creation. Hence, the intention of this book was to diminish the discrepancy between theory and practice by exploring whether there is also a normative theory for risk management that offers more detailed instructions of how to achieve value creation, and to examine how this compares to what is already done in practice.

We first examined financial theory to see whether it offers rationales for conducting risk management at the bank level to enhance value and, in order to derive the conditions under which risk management can do so (which was the first goal of this book).

We found that the neoclassical finance theory offers no foundation for conducting corporate risk management in order to create value. Under the strict assumptions of this theory, risk management is irrelevant, unnecessary, and can even be harmful, because investors could replicate or reverse all of a bank's risk-management actions at no (extra) cost. Incurring higher costs for conducting risk management at the bank level would, therefore, be a value-destroying proposition. We also found that in the neoclassical world capital-budgeting, capital-structure, and risk-management decisions can be separated, and the application of the traditional valuation framework (DCF-approach) is justified, since only the systematic risk to a broad market portfolio counts.

However, since under the strict assumptions of the neoclassical theory there would be no reason for banks to exist, we also explored the neoinstitutional finance theory as it relaxes many of these unrealistic assumptions. Here, we were able to find manifold reasons why risk management at the corporate level can increase the value of a bank. This is so because risk management can now decrease the present value of the agency costs of equity (allowing banks to increase their leverage without increasing the probability of default) and debt (using risk management as an equity substitute) as well as those of transaction costs. Risk management can thus reduce the expected payments to the various stakeholders of a firm.

We identified the likelihood of default as the central component among the reasons for conducting risk management. It builds the foundation for practically all of the rationales for corporate risk management in the neoinstitutional world. However, its most compelling manifestation is its ability to address the direct and indirect (transaction) costs that are associated with financial distress situations—particularly when viewed from a cost-benefit perspective, because value gains seem to be most profound when a firm tries to avoid these costs via risk management. This is especially true for banks, since the central role of (relative) creditworthiness in the provision of financial services and the potential loss of their franchise value lead to high default costs and to high costs for (unexpected) external financing (which is most costly in situations when it is needed most). Both of these costs cause banks to behave as if they were risk averse, even though they are not in and of themselves, and (since these costs are higher for banks than for other firms) to conduct relatively more risk management.

Therefore, firms, and especially banks, are trying to avoid financial distress situations or are trying to decrease the likelihood of their occurrence by using risk management. Since these "lower-tail outcomes" can be caused by both systematic and (firm-) specific risks, banks do worry about total risk, and the composition of their existing bank portfolio matters when they make capital-budgeting decisions. Actions aimed at addressing both of these issues can be observed in reality, but are unexplained in the neoclassical world. In a world where these two concerns matter, risk management could indeed increase the bank value by reducing total risk and the costs associated with it.

However, these total risk costs can also be influenced by the actual capital structure. Given that banks hold risks on their books, increasing financial leverage also increases the probability of incurring the costs of financial distress. Therefore, holding equity capital commensurate with the risks on the bank's books is sensible from both an economic and a regulatory point of view and can thus be considered as an alternate form of risk management. Additionally, when risk management can create value, it can also influence capital-budgeting decisions. Therefore, capital-structure, capital-budgeting, and risk-management decisions cannot be separated, and the traditional valuation framework might not be applicable in such a world.

Even though the neoinstitutional theory provides the rationale for conducting risk management at the bank level in order to increase value, we concluded that it only forms the basis for the design of a comprehensive risk-management approach for banks and, hence, for a normative theory (whose derivation was the second goal of this book). It is only a partial solution to our initial problem, because it does not provide detailed instructions on which risk-management instruments should be used and to what degree, and how value creation should be measured in such a world.

The prevention of (costly) financial distress situations requires an adequate total risk measure, because (especially in a non-normal world) neither systematic nor specific risk captures the concern with lower-tail outcomes well. We have derived such an appropriate risk measure for the bank's concerns in a value creation context. We found that "risk capital" is—from a theoretical point of view—the relevant and correct measure both for quantifying total risk and to determine the economically required amount of capital in banks, because it considers the concerns of all bank stakeholder groups. Risk capital splits up the bank's overall default risk into various tranches and makes them default free by buying (implicit) asset insurance from the various stakeholder groups so that each group bears that part of the default risk it wants to bear.

However, since the required negotiation process among the various stakeholders appeared to be extremely complex, we identified the shortcut measure "economic capital" as the only feasible practical proxy. It concentrates the concern with lower-tail outcomes on a single critical threshold level where a bank run would be triggered. This similarity to the value at risk concept might be the reason why economic capital has developed as the standard, best-practice approach at leading institutions in the financial industry.

We subsequently presented various ways how economic capital can be determined for banks in a valuation context. We first developed and discussed a detailed methodology to estimate the required economic capital in a consistent bottom-up way, differentiated by the three types of risk typically faced by banks (market, credit, and operational risk). We thereby determined the contribution of a transaction to the overall risk of the bank's existing portfolio. We also introduced a new top-down approach, which is a variant of the Merton default model, to be able to check the aggregated results from this bottom-up procedure. Applying this (theoretical) top-down model to a real-life example, we found that the results are coherent given the few observable data points.

We then returned to the question of how we can measure the value creation potential of a bank's risk-management transaction in a world where total risk matters. We briefly discussed the traditional capital-budgeting tools in banks and concluded that they are not suitable measures in such a world. Computing a project's NPV using the CAPM and accepting all positive NPV projects is not the right solution for a bank that is concerned with lower-tail outcomes and hence economic capital. Because of this and because, when a bank evaluates a project, the cost of the project's impact on the total risk of the bank needs to be taken into account, banks developed the practical heuristic RAROC as a capital-budgeting tool. Because the denominator of this modified return-on-equity ratio uses the required economic capital amount, it takes into account both the concern with total risk and the risk contribution of a transaction to the bank's existing portfolio. In order to determine whether a transaction creates value, RAROC is compared to a CAPM-determined (bankwide) equity hurdle rate, in a manner similar to the EVA®-approach, as a single-period variant of the traditional valuation framework.

However, when we closely examined this risk-adjusted performance measure, we found that in order to make RAROC comparable to such an equity return, one has to accept a set of (implicit) assumptions. For instance, even though economic capital is a fictional amount of money, RAROC assumes that it is the same as "cash" equity capital provided by the shareholders, that the bank holds exactly this amount of equity in reality, and that all cash flows will flow to it as well. We showed upon further investigation that even if one accepts these (rigid) assumptions, the standard RAROC approach is biased and may lead to accepting negative NPV projects when this is inadvisable.

Moreover, we identified the fact that there are many more fundamental theoretical concerns with RAROC when it comes to the determination of value creation. RAROC compares a risk measure that has its foundations in the neoinstitutional finance theory with a hurdle rate that was derived in the neoclassical world under very different assumptions. Whereas RAROC only considers the risk contribution to the total risk of the bank's existing portfolio, the neoclassical theory is only concerned with the systematic risk of a broad market portfolio. Obviously, this discrepancy leads to inconsistent results.

Additionally, in a world where total risk matters, a capital-budgeting tool needs to include a component that compensates for both the market price of risk (i.e., the required market return) as well as a component that reflects the contribution of a transaction to the total risk of the bank's existing portfolio. We concluded that, because RAROC mixes these two components into a single-factor model, RAROC is inappropriate for capturing both of these effects and hence is not an adequate capital-budgeting tool for banks from a theoretical point of view. Such an evaluation of RAROC in the light of the prior theoretical discussion was the third goal of this book. Unfortunately, it contradicts what is done in practice, where RAROC is used as an acceptable proxy to indicate value creation from a practical point of view.

We saw, therefore, that two-factor models are better suited to capture both of the (pricing) components described above. We presented the foundations for these alternate approaches and discussed some of the already available methods in the light of their practicability and their implications for risk-management decisions in banks. We concluded that these two-factor models are better tools to identify whether a bank should hold a transaction on its own books and whether it can really create value by doing so. We found that these two-factor models allow for much more detailed instructions on what banks should do exactly and which risk-management actions can enhance value, because they consider the cost of total risk. They can thus form the foundation for a normative theory of risk management in banks (the development of which was the fourth and last goal of this book) and will allow banks to focus on their comparative advantages.

We, therefore, concluded that when total risk counts and is costly, banks can indeed increase their value (and that of a transaction) through risk management by decreasing (the contribution to) total risk. The new (decision) rules deduced from the two-factor models could replace what banks have been doing intuitively for a long time and what is an observable phenomenon in real life. It, however, requires the joint and endogenous determination of risk-management, capital-budgeting, and capital-structure decisions—as we have already anticipated in our theoretical discussion.

The difficulty with these new two-factor models is that the NPV criterion can then no longer be the universally valid capital-budgeting decision tool, contradicting the principles that have been used in corporate finance over the past twenty-five years. This book provides only the foundation for applying this new paradigm. Much more research needs to be done in order to parameterize such a model and make it operational, communicable, and implementable in practice. Until this is the case, banks may want to apply RAROC because it is currently the only practicable solution to capital-budgeting problems in banks, but they need to be aware that they are applying a biased tool that delivers only directionally correct answers.

references

Aguais, Scott D., and Anthony M. Santomero (1997) "Incorporating New Fixed Income Approaches into Commercial Loan Valuation," working paper 98-06, Financial Institutions Center, The Wharton School, University of Pennsylvania.

Aït-Sahalia, Yacine, and Andrew W. Lo (1998) "Nonparametric Risk Management and Implied Risk Aversion," working paper, January 1998.

Albrecht, Thomas (1998) "Die Vereinbarkeit der Value-at-Risk-Methode in Banken mit anteilseignerorientierter Unternehmensführung," *ZfB Zeitschrift für Betriebswirtschaft*, Volume 68, Number 3, pp. 259–273.

Alexander, Carol (Editor) (1997) *The Handbook of Risk Management and Analysis*, New York: John Wiley & Sons, Inc.

Allen, Franklin, and Anthony M. Santomero (1996) "The Theory of Financial Intermediation," working paper 96-32, Financial Institutions Center, The Wharton School, University of Pennsylvania.

Allen, Franklin, and Anthony M. Santomero (1997) "The Theory of Financial Intermediation," *Journal of Banking and Finance*, Volume 21, pp. 1461–1485.

Anders, Ulrich (2000) "RaRoC—ein Begriff, viel Verwirrung," *Die Bank*, Issue 5/2000, pp. 314–317.

Arnsfeld, Torsten (1999) "Der marginale Value-at-Risk," *Die Bank*, Issue 5/99, pp. 353–355.

Artzner, Philippe, Freddy Delbaen, Jean-Marc Eber, and David Heath (1997) "Thinking Coherently," *Risk Magazine*, Volume 10, Number 11, November 1997, pp. 68–71.

Artzner, Philippe, Freddy Delbaen, Jean-Marc Eber, and David Heath (1999) "Coherent Measures of Risk," *Mathematical Finance*, Volume 9, Number 3, July 1999, pp. 203–228.

Asarnow, Elliot, and David Edwards (1995) "Measuring Loss on Defaulted Bank Loans: A 24-Year Study,"*The Journal of Commercial Lending*, March 1995, pp. 11–23.

Asquith, Paul, and David Mullins (1986) "Equity Issues and Offering Dilution," *Journal of Financial Economics*, Volume 15, pp. 61+.

Bamberg, Günter, and Franz Baur (1991) *Statistik*, Seventh Edition, Munich: Oldenbourg.

Bamberg, Günter, and Adolf G. Coenenberg (1992) *Betriebswirtschaftliche Entscheidungslehre*, Seventh Edition, Munich: Vahlen.

Bangia, Anil, Francis X. Diebold, Til Schuermann, and John D. Stroughair (1999) "Modeling Liquidity Risk, with Implications for Traditional Market Risk Measurement and Management," working paper 99-06, The Wharton School, Financial Institutions Center, University of Pennsylvania, December 1998.

Basak, Suleyman, and Alexander Shapiro (1999) "Value-at-Risk Based Risk Management: Optimal Policies and Asset Prices," working paper, June 1999.

Basle Committee on Banking Supervision (1988) "International Convergence of Capital Measurement and Capital Standards," available at www.bis.org, July 1988.

Basle Committee on Banking Supervision (1998) "Operational Risk Management," Basle, available at www.bis.org, September 1998.

Basle Committee on Banking Supervision (1999) "A New Capital Adequacy Framework," available at www.bis.org, June 1999.

Basle Committee on Banking Supervision (2001) "Overview of The New Basel Capital Accord—Consultative Document," available at www.bis.org, January 2001.

Beeck, Helmut, Lutz Johanning, and Bernd Rudolph (1997) "Value-at-Risk-Limitstrukturen zur Steuerung und Begrenzung von Marktrisiken im Aktienbereich," CFS working paper 97/02.

Benninga, Simon, and Oded Sarig (1998) "Bank Valuation," working paper, New York Institute of Finance, July 1998.

Berger, Allen N., and S.M. Davies (1994) "The Information Content of Bank Examinations," Board of Governors of the Federal Reserve Finance and Economics Discussion Series (FEDS) Paper 94-20, July 1994.

Berger, Allen N., Richard J. Herring, and Giorgio P. Szegö (1995a) "The Role of Capital in Financial Institutions," working paper 95-01, Financial Institutions Center, The Wharton School, University of Pennsylvania.

Berger, Allen N., Richard J. Herring, and Giorgio P. Szegö (1995b) "The Role of Capital in Financial Institutions," *Journal of Banking & Finance*, Volume 19 (June), pp. 393–430.

Bernstein, Peter L. (1996) *Against the Gods—The Remarkable Story of Risk*, New York: John Wiley & Sons, Inc.

Bhat, Narayan (1984) *Elements of Applied Stochastic Processes*, Second Edition, New York: John Wiley & Sons Inc.

Black, Fischer, and Myron Scholes (1972) "The Valuation of Option Contracts and a Test of Market Efficiency," *Journal of Finance*, Volume XXVII, May 1972, pp. 349–417.

Blanden, Michael (1999) "Consolidation Continues," *The Banker*, July 1999, pp. 88–210.

Block, J.R., and T.J. Gallagher (1986) "The Use of Interest Rate Futures and Options by Corporate Financial Managers," *Financial Management*, Volume 15, Autumn 1986, pp. 73–78.

Bodnar, G.M., G.S. Hayt, and R.C. Marston (1996) "1995 Wharton Survey of Derivatives Usage by U.S. Non-Financial Firms," *Financial Management*, Volume 25, Number 4, pp. 113–133.

Bodnar, G.M., G.S. Hayt, and R.C. Marston (1998) "1998 Wharton Survey of Financial Risk Management by U.S. Non-Financial Firms," *Financial Management*, Volume 27, Number 4, pp. 70–91.

Bodnar, Gordon M., and Günther Gebhardt (1998) "Derivatives Usage in Risk Management by U.S. and German Non-Financial Firms: A Comparative Survey," CFS working paper 98/17.

Booth, J.R., R.L. Smith, and Richard Stolz (1984) "The Use of Interest Rate Futures by Financial Institutions," *Journal of Bank Research*, Volume 15, Spring 1984, pp. 15–20.

Braas, Albéric, and Charles N. Bralver (1990) "An Analysis of Trading Profits: How Most Trading Rooms Really Make Money," *Journal of Applied Corporate Finance*, Volume 2, Number 4, Winter 1990, pp. 85–90.

Bralver, Charles N., and Andrew Kuritzkes (1993) "Risk Adjusted Performance Measurement in the Trading Room," *Journal of Applied Corporate Finance*, Volume 6, Number 3, Fall 1993, pp. 104–108.

Brand, Leo, and Reza Bahar (1999) *Special Report—Ratings Performance 1999*, Standard & Poor's, New York.

Brealey, Richard A., and Stewart C. Myers (1991) *Principles of Corporate Finance*, Fourth Edition, New York: McGraw-Hill, Inc.

Breeden, Douglas, and S. Viswanathan (1996) "Why Do Firms Hedge? An Asymmetric Information Model," working paper, Duke University.

Brüning, Jan-Bernd, and Andreas Hoffjan (1997) "Gesamtbanksteuerung mit Risk-Return-Kennzahlen," *Die Bank*, Issue 6/1997, pp. 362–369.

Buhr, Reinhard (2000) "Messung von Betriebsrisiken—ein methodischer Ansatz," *Die Bank*, 03/2000, pp. 202–206.

Bundesbank (2000) *Statistical Appendix, Monatsbericht*, Dezember 2000, Frankfurt: Deutsche Bundesbank.

Burrough, Bryan, and John Helyar (1990) *Barbarians at the Gate—The Fall of RJR Nabisco*, New York: Harper & Row, Inc.

Byrd, John, Robert Parrino, and Gunnar Pritsch (1998) "Stockholder-Manager Conflicts and Firm Value," *Financial Analysts Journal*, May/June 1998, pp. 14–30.

Carlstrom, C.T., and K.A. Samolyk (1995) "Loan Sales as a Response to Market-Based Capital Requirements," *Journal of Banking & Finance*, Volume 19 (June), pp. 627–646.

Carty, Lea V., and Dana Lieberman (1996) "Defaulted Bank Loan Recoveries," Moody's Investor Service, Special Report, November 1996, pp. 1–9.

Choi, Jongmoo Jay, Elyas Elyasiani, and Anthony Saunders (1996) "Derivative Exposure and the Interest Rate and Exchange Rate Risk of U.S. Banks," working paper presented at The Wharton Financial Institutions Center Conference "Risk Management in Banking", October 13–15, 1996.

Christoffersen, Peter F., Francis X. Diebold, and Til Schuermann (1998) "Horizon Problems and Extreme Events in Financial Risk Management," working paper 98-16, The Wharton School, Financial Institutions Center, University of Pennsylvania, April 1998.

Clarke, Roger (1985) *Industrial Economics*, Oxford: Blackwell Publishers.

Cooper, Lisa (1999) "The Struggle to Define and Measure Goes On," *Operational Risk Special Report, Risk Magazine*, July 1999, pp. 6–7.

Copeland, Thomas E. (1994) "Why Value Value?" *The McKinsey Quarterly*, Number 4, pp. 97–109.

Copeland, Thomas E., Joshi, and Queen (1996) "How to Evaluate Corporate FX Risk Management Programmes," working paper, McKinsey & Co.

Copeland, Thomas E., Tim Koller, and Jack Murrin (1994) *Valuation— Measuring and Managing the Value of Companies*, Second Edition, New York: John Wiley & Sons, Inc.

Copeland, Thomas E., and J. Fred Weston (1988) *Financial Theory and Corporate Policy*, Third Edition, Reading, MA: Addison-Wesley Publishing Company.

Cordell, Lawrence R., and Kathleen Kuester King (1995) "A Market Evaluation of the Risk-Based Capital Standards for the U.S. Financial System," *Journal of Banking & Finance*, Volume 19 (June), pp. 531–562.

Cremonino, Andrea, and Marco Giorgino (1998) "A VAR Model as Risk Management Tool and Risk Adjusted Performance Measures," working paper, Department of Economics and Production, Politecnico di Milano.

Crouhy, Michel, and Robert Mark (1998) "A Comparative Analysis of Current Credit Risk Models," working paper, Canadian Imperial Bank of Commerce, October 1998.

Crouhy, Michel, Stuart M. Turnbull, and Lee M. Wakeman (1999) "Measuring Risk-Adjusted Performance," *Journal of Risk*, Volume 2, Number 1, Fall 1999, pp. 5–35.

CSFP (1997) *CreditRisk+—A Credit Risk Management Framework*, Credit Suisse Financial Products.

Culp, Christopher L., and Merton H. Miller (1995) "Hedging in the Theory of Corporate Finance," *Journal of Applied Corporate Finance*, Volume 7, Number 4, Winter 1995, pp. 63+.

Culp, Christopher L., and Merton H. Miller (1998) "Value at Risk: Uses and Abuses," *Journal of Applied Corporate Finance*, Volume 10, Number 4, Winter 1998, pp. 26–38.

Damodaran, Aswath (1997) *Corporate Finance—Theory and Practice*, New York: John Wiley & Sons, Inc.

Davis, Donald, and Kevin Lee (1997) "A Practical Approach to Capital Structure for Banks," *Journal of Applied Corporate Finance*, Volume 10, Number 1, Spring 1997, pp. 33–43.

DeMarzo, Peter, and Darrel Duffie (1991) "Corporate Financial Hedging with Proprietary Information," *Journal of Economic Theory*, Volume 53, pp. 261–286.

DeMarzo, Peter, and Darrel Duffie (1992) "Corporate Incentives for Hedging and Hedge Accounting," working paper, Northwestern University.

Dermine, Jean (1998) "Pitfalls in the Application of RAROC in Loan Management," *The Arbitrageur*, Volume 1, Number 1, pp. 21–27.

DeStefano, Michel T., and Virginia L. Manzer (1999) *Financial Institutions Criteria*, New York: Standard & Poor's.

Deutsche Bank (1999) *Annual Report, Risk Report*, pp. 123–139.

Dewenter, Kathryn L., and Alan C. Hess (1997) "Risk and Returns in Relationship and Transactional Banks: Evidence from Banks' Returns in Germany, Japan, the U.K., and the U.S.," working paper 97-23, Financial Institutions Center, The Wharton School, University of Pennsylvania.

Diamond, Douglas (1984) "Financial Intermediation and Delegated Monitoring," *Review of Economic Studies*, Volume 51, pp. 393–414.

Diamond, Douglas W., and Raghuram G. Rajan (1999) "A Theory of Bank Capital," working paper, University of Chicago, Revised: April 1999.

Diebold, Francis X., Til Schuermann, and John D. Stroughair (1998) "Pitfalls and Opportunities in the Use of Extreme Value Theory in Risk Management," working paper 98-10, The Wharton School, Financial Institutions Center, University of Pennsylvania, March 1998.

Dixit, Avinash K., and Robert S. Pindyck (1994) *Investment under Uncertainty*, Princeton: Princeton University Press.

Dolde, Walter (1993) "The Trajectory of Corporate Financial Risk Management," *Journal of Applied Corporate Finance*, Volume 6, Number 3, Fall 1993, pp. 33–41.

Dowd, Kevin (1998) *Beyond Value At Risk—The New Science Of Risk Management*, Chichester: John Wiley & Sons Ltd.

Dowd, Kevin (1999) "Financial Risk Management," *Journal of Portfolio Management*, July/August 1999, pp. 65–71.

Drzik, John, Marc Intrater, and Peter Nakada (1997) "Managing the Hidden Hedge Funds within Banks," Enterprise-Wide Risk Management Supplement, *Risk Magazine*, November 1997, pp. 1–3.

Drzik, John, Peter Nakada, and Til Schuermann (1998a) "Risk, Capital, and Value Measurement in Financial Institutions—Part I: The Debtholder's Perspective," *The Journal of Lending & Credit Risk Management*, September 1998, pp. 22–27.

Drzik, John, Peter Nakada, and Til Schuermann (1998b) "Risk, Capital, and Value Measurement in Financial Institutions—Part II: The Shareholder's Perspective," *The Journal of Lending & Credit Risk Management*, November 1998, pp. 64–69.

Eales, Robert, and Edmund Bosworth (1998) "Severity of Loss in the Event of Default in Small Business and Larger Consumer Loans," *The Journal of Lending & Credit Risk Management*, May 1998, pp. 58–65.

Eckbo, B.E. (1986) "Valuation Effects of Corporate Debt Offerings," *Journal of Financial Economics*, Volume 15, January–February 1986, pp. 119–151.

Economist (1992) "Survey on World Banking," May 2, 1992, pp. 3–50.

Economist (1993) "A Comedy of Errors," in: "International Banking Survey," April 10th, 1993, pp. 3–42.

Economist (1996) "Corporate Risk Management," February 10, 1996.

Embrechts, P., C. Klüppelberg, and T. Mikosch (1997) *Modeling Extremal Events for Insurance and Finance*, Berlin: Springer.

Embrechts, P., S. Resnick, and G. Samorodnitsky (1998) "Living on the Edge," *Risk Magazine*, Volume 11, Number 1, January 1998, pp. 96–100.

FAZ (2000) "Cobra hält trotz des Commerzbank-Kursverfalls an Hofmann fest," *Frankfurter Allgemeine Zeitung*, September 4, 2000, Number 205, p. 23.

Fenn, George W., Mitch Post, and Steven A. Sharpe (1997) "Does Corporate Risk Management Create Shareholder Value?—A Survey of Economic Theory and Evidence," in: *Financial Risk and the Corporate Treasury: New Developments in Strategy and Control*, London: Risk Publications, pp. 13–31.

Fishburn, P.C. (1977) "Mean-Risk Analysis with Risk Associated with Below-Target Returns," *American Economic Review*, Volume 67, pp. 116–126.

Fisher, Irving (1965) *The Theory of Interest*, New York: Kelley, Reprint of the 1930 Edition.

Fitch IBCA (1998) *Bank Rating Methodology*, April 1998, Fitch IBCA.

Friedrich, Stephan A., Heinz K. Stahl, and Hans H. Hinterhuber (2000) "Erfolgreiche Unternehmen sind für Ihre Stakeholder da," *Frankfurter Allgemeine Zeitung*, Number 145, June 26, 2000, p. 31.

Froot, Kenneth A., David S. Scharfstein, and Jeremy C. Stein (1993) "Risk Management: Coordinating Corporate Investment and Financing Policies," *Journal of Finance*, Volume XLVIII, Number 5, December 1993, pp. 1629–1658.

Froot, Kenneth A., David S. Scharfstein, and Jeremy C. Stein (1994) "A Framework for Risk Management," *Harvard Business Review*, November–December 1994, pp. 91–102.

Froot, Kenneth A., and Jeremy C. Stein (1998a) "Risk Management, Capital Budgeting, and Capital Structure Policy for Financial Institutions: An Integrated Approach," *Journal of Financial Economics*, Volume 47, pp. 55–82.

Froot, Kenneth A., and Jeremy C. Stein (1998b) "A New Approach to Capital Budgeting for Financial Institutions," *Journal of Applied Corporate Finance*, Volume 11, Number 2, Summer 1998, pp. 59–69.

Garman, M.B., and J.A. Ohlson (1981) "Valuation of Risky Assets in Arbitrage-Free Economics with Transaction Costs," *Journal of Financial Economics*, Volume 9, pp. 271–280.

Garside, Thomas (1998) "Credit Portfolio Models—Selection, Customisation and Applications," presented at AIC Conferences on October 29, 1998.

Garside, Thomas, Henry Stott, and Gunther Strothe (1999) "Portfoliomanagement des Kreditrisikos," in: *Handbuch Informationstechnologie in Banken*, 1999, XXXII, Jürgen Moormann and Thomas Fischer (editors), Wiesbaden: Gabler, pp. 186–207.

Géczy, Christopher C., Bernadette A. Minton, and Catherine Schrand (1999) "Choices Among Alternative Risk Management Strategies: Evidence from the Natural Gas Industry," working paper, November 1999.

Géczy, Christopher C., Bernadette A. Minton, and Catherine Schrand (1995) "Why Firms Use Derivatives: Distinguishing Among Existing Theories," working paper, September 1995.

Gesetz zur Kontrolle und Transparenz im Unternehmensbereich (KonTraG) (1998).

Glaeser, Betsy (1996) "Save a Place for VaR," *Risk Magazine*, Volume 9, Number 12, December 1996, pp. 17–18.

Glaum, Martin, and Gerhart Förschle (2000) *Finanzwirtschaftliches Risikomanagement deutscher Industrie- und Handelsunternehmen—Industriestudie*, PwC Deutsche Revision Aktiengesellschaft Wirtschaftsprüfungsgesellschaft (editors), Frankfurt am Main: Fachverlag Moderne Wirtschaft.

Graham, John R., and Daniel A. Rogers (1999) "Is Corporate Hedging Consistent with Value Maximization?—An Empirical Analysis," working paper.

Graham, John R., and Clifford W. Smith, Jr. (1996) "Tax Incentives to Hedge," unpublished working paper, University of Rochester.

Graman, Mark (1996) "Improving on VaR," *Risk Magazine*, Volume 9, Number 5, May 1996, pp. 61–63.

Gramlich, Dieter, Benjamin Tobias Peylo, and Martin Staaden (1999) "Effiziente Portefeuilles im μ-/VaR-Raum," *Die Bank*, Issue 6/99, pp. 422–425.

Greene, William H. (1993) *Econometric Analysis*, Second Edition, London: Prentice Hall International Inc.

Groß, Hermann, and Martin Knippschild (1995) "Risikocontrolling in der

Deutschen Bank AG," in: *Risikomanagement in Kreditinstituten*, B. Rolfes, H. Schierenbeck, and S. Schüller (editors), Frankfurt: Fritz Knapp Verlag, pp. 69–109.

Grübel, Oswald, Jaakko Kärki, and Cecilia Reyes (1995) "Wirtschaftliche Rentabilitätsrechnung von Handelsaktivitäten," in: *Handbuch Bankcontrolling*, Henner Schierenbeck and Hubertus Moser (editors), Wiesbaden: Gabler, pp. 611–636.

Guldimann, Till M., Peter Zangari, Jacques Longerstaey, John Matero, and Scott Howard (1995) "RiskMetrics™—Technical Document," Third Edition, New York: J.P. Morgan.

Gup, Benton E. (1998) *Bank Failures in the Major Trading Countries of the World—Causes and Remedies*, Westport: Quorum Books.

Gupton, Greg M., Christopher C. Finger, and Mickey Bhatia (1997) "CreditMetrics™ Technical Document," J.P. Morgan & Co. Incorporated.

Guthoff, Anja, Andreas Pfingsten, and Juliane Wolf (1996) "On the Compatibility of Value at Risk, Other Risk Concepts, and Expected Utility Maximization," in: *Geld, Finanzwirtschaft, Banken und Versicherungen*, Christian Hipp et al. (editors), Karlsruhe: VVW, pp. 591–614.

Guthoff, Anja, Andreas Pfingsten, and Juliane Wolf (1998) "Der Einfluß einer Begrenzung des Value at Risk oder des Lower Partial Moment One auf die Risikoübernahme," in: *Credit Risk und Value-at-Risk Alternativen*, Andreas Oehler (editor), Stuttgart: Schäffer-Poeschel, pp. 111–153.

Harker, Patrick T., and A. Zenios Stavros (1998) "What Drives the Performance of Financial Institutions?" working paper 98-21, Financial Institutions Center, The Wharton School, University of Pennsylvania.

Hartmann-Wendels, Thomas, Andreas Pfingsten, and Martin Weber (1998) *Bankbetriebslehre*, Berlin: Springer.

Haubenstock, Michael J. (1998) "Linking RAROC to Strategic Planning," *The Journal of Lending & Credit Risk Management*, October 1998, pp. 26–31.

Haubenstock, Michael, and Arun Aggarwal (1997) "Risk Optimisation— Applying Risk-Adjusted Performance Measurement to Increase Shareholder Value," in: *Risk Management for Financial Institutions—Advances in Measurement and Control*, London: Risk Publications, pp. 175–189.

Haubenstock, Mike, and Frank Morisano (1997) "Beyond Loss Avoidance to Strategic Risk Management," *Banking Strategies*, Volume 73, Number 4, July/August 1997, pp. 61–63.

Hille, Christian T., Christoph Burmester, and Matthias Otto (2000) "Modelle zur risikoadjustierten Kapitalallokation," *Die Bank*, Issue 3/2000, pp. 190–195.

Hirschbeck, Thomas (1998) *Management von Handelsrisiken in Banken— Konzeptionen zur Erfassung und Steuerung der Marktpreis- und Kredit-*

risiken aus Handelsgeschäften vor dem Hintergrund betriebswirtschaftlicher und aufsichtsrechtlicher Anforderungen, Reihe: Finanzierung, Steuern, Wirtschaftsprüfung, Volume 31, Köln: Botermann & Botermann.

Homestake (1990) *Annual Report 1990.*

Hommel, Ulrich, and Gunnar Pritsch (1998) "Notwendigkeit des unternehmerischen Risikomangements aus Shareholder-Value-Sicht," in: *Handbuch Corporate Finance,* 6, A. K. Achleitner and G. F. Thoma (editors). Ergänzungslieferung, Köln, pp. 1–21.

Hull, John C. (1997) *Options, Futures, and Other Derivatives,* Third Edition, Upper Saddle River, NJ: Prentice-Hall.

Jackson, Patricia, David J. Maude, and William Perraudin (1998) "Bank Capital and Value at Risk," working paper, The Bank of England, ISSN 1368-5562.

Jagtiani, J., A. Saunders, and G.F. Udell (1995) "The Effect of Bank Capital Requirements on Bank Off-Balance Sheet Financial Innovations," *Journal of Banking & Finance,* Volume 19 (June), pp. 647–658.

James, Christopher M. (1987) "Some Evidence on the Uniqueness of Bank Loans," *Journal of Financial Economics,* December 1987, pp. 217–235.

James, Christopher M. (1991) "The Losses Realized in Bank Failures," *Journal of Finance,* Volume XLVI, Number 4, September 1991, pp. 1223–1242.

James, Christopher M. (1996) "RAROC Based Capital Budgeting and Performance Evaluation: A Case Study of Bank Capital Allocation," working paper 96-40, Financial Institutions Center, The Wharton School, University of Pennsylvania.

Jensen, Michael C. (1986) "Agency Costs of Free Cash Flow, Corporate Finance, and Takeovers," *The American Economic Review,* Volume 76, Number 2, pp. 323–329.

Jensen, Michael C. (1993) "The Modern Industrial Revolution, Exit, and the Failure of Internal Control Systems," *The Journal of Finance,* Volume XLVIII, Number 3, July 1993, pp. 831–880.

Jensen, Michael C., and William H. Meckling (1976) "Theory of the Firm: Managerial Behavior, Agency Costs and Ownership Structure," *Journal of Financial Economics,* Volume 3, pp. 305–360.

Jensen, Michael C., and William H. Meckling (1991) "Specific and General Knowledge, and Organizational Structure," in: *Main Currents in Contract Economics,* Lars Werin and Hans Wijkander (editors), Oxford: Blackwell, pp. 251–274.

Johanning, Lutz (1998) *Value-at-Risk zur Markrisikosteuerung und Eigenkapitalallokation,* Reihe: Risikomanagement und Finanzcontrolling, Volume 1, Bernd Rudolph (editor), Bad Soden: Uhlenbruch.

Johnson, Hazel J. (1996) *The Bank Valuation Handbook—A Market-Based Approach to Valuing A Bank,* Second Edition, Chicago: Irwin.

Johnson, Shane A. (1998) "The Effect of Bank Debt on Optimal Capital Structure," *Financial Management*, Volume 27, Number 1, pp. 47–56.

Jorion, Philippe (1997) *Value at Risk - The Benchmark for Controlling Market Risk*, Chicago: Irwin.

Kealhofer, Stephen (1995) "Managing Default Risk in Portfolios of Derivatives," *Derivative Credit Risk—Advances in Measurement and Management*, London: Risk Publications, pp. 49–63.

Kennedy, Christopher (1999) "Shareholder Value in europäischen Banken," *Die Bank*, Issue 4/99, pp. 224–227.

Kim, Daesik, and Anthony Santomero (1988) "Risk in Banking and Capital Regulation," *Journal of Finance*, Volume XLIII, Number 5, December 1988, pp. 1219–1233.

Kimball, Ralph C. (1998) "Economic Profit and Performance Measurement in Banking," *New England Economic Review*, July/August 1998, pp. 35–53.

Krahnen, Jan P., Christian Rieck, and Erik Theissen (1997) "Messung individueller Risikoeinstellungen," CFS working paper, Institut für Kapitalmarktforschung an der Universität Frankfurt, October 28, 1997.

Kümmel, Axel Tibor (1993) *Bewertung von Kreditinstituten nach dem Shareholder Value-Ansatz—Unter besonderer Berücksichtigung des Zinsänderungsrisikos*, Johann Heinrich von Stein (editor), Studienreihe der Stiftung Kreditwirtschaft an der Universität Hohenheim, Ludwigsburg/Berlin: Verlag Wissenschaft & Praxis.

Kuritzkes, Andrew (1998) "Transforming Portfolio Management," *Banking Strategies*, July/August 1998, without page numbers.

Kuritzkes, Andrew (1999) "SPI Part One: How to unlock shareholder value in wholesale banking? Unbundle the business," *EIU (Economist Intelligence Unit) Strategic Finance*, June to August 1999, pp. 71–81.

Lam, James (1999) "The Wheel of Misfortune," available at www.erisks.com.

Lam, James, and Greg Cameron (1999) "Measuring and Managing Operational Risk within an Integrated Risk Framework—Putting Theory into Practice," in: *Operational Risk and Financial Institutions*, London: Risk Publications, pp. 81–94.

Lehn, Kenneth, and Anil Makhija (1996) "EVA and MVA as Performance Measures and Signals for Strategic Change," working paper, University of Pittsburgh, Katz Graduate School of Business; also in *Strategy and Leadership*, May/June 1996, pp. 34–38.

Lessard, Don (1990) "Global Competition and Corporate Finance in the 1990s," *Journal of Applied Corporate Finance*, Volume 1, pp. 59–72.

Linsmeier, Thomas J., and Neil D. Pearson (1996) "Risk Measurement: An Introduction to Value at Risk," working paper, University of Illinois at Urbana-Champaign, July 1996.

Lintner, J. (1965) "The Valuation of Risky Assets and the Selection of Risky

Investments in Stock Portfolios and Capital Budgets," *Review of Economics and Statistics*, Volume 47, pp. 13–37.

Lister, Michael (1997) *Risikoadjustierte Ergebnismessung und Risikokapitalallokation*, Frankfurt am Main: Fritz Knapp Verlag.

Mark, Robert M. (1995) "Integrated Credit Risk Measurement," in: *Derivative Credit Risk - Advances in Measurement and Management*, London: Risk Publications, pp. 109–139.

Mark, Robert M. (1997) "Optimal Firm-Wide Risk Management: The Whole Company Approach," in: *Risk Management for Financial Institutions—Advances in Measurement and Control*, London: Risk Publications, pp. 145–174.

Markowitz, Harry M. (1952) "Portfolio Selection," *Journal of Finance*, Volume VII, pp. 77+.

Markowitz, Harry M. (1959) *Portfolio Selection—Efficient Diversification of Investment*, New Haven, CT: Yale University Press.

Mason, Scott P. (1995) "The Allocation of Risk," working paper 95-060, Harvard Business School.

Matten, Chris (1996) *Managing Bank Capital—Capital Allocation and Performance Measurement*, Chichester: John Wiley & Sons, Inc.

Mayers, D., and Clifford W. Smith, Jr. (1987) "Corporate Insurance and the Underinvestment Problem," *Journal of Risk and Insurance*, Volume 54, pp.45–54.

Mayers, D., and Clifford W. Smith, Jr. (1990) "On the Corporate Demand for Insurance: Evidence from Reinsurance Market," *Journal of Business*, Volume 63, pp. 19–40.

McNeil, A.J. (1998) "History Repeating," *Risk Magazine*, Volume 11, Number 1 January 1998, p. 99.

McNeil, A.J., and T. Saladin (1997) "The Perks over Thresholds Method for Estimating High Quantiles of Loss Distributions," working paper, ETH Zurich.

Mello, A.S., and J.E. Parsons (1995) "Funding Risk and Hedge Valuation," working paper, University of Wisconsin-Madison.

Mello, A.S., J.E. Parsons, and A.J. Triantis (1995) "An Integrated Model of Multinational Flexibility and Financial Hedging," *Journal of International Economics*, 1995, pp. 27–51.

Merton, Robert C. (1989) "On the Application of the Continuous-Time Theory of Finance to Financial Intermediation and Insurance," *The Geneva Papers on Risk and Insurance*, Volume 14, July 1989, pp. 225–262.

Merton, Robert C. (1995a) "Financial Innovation and the Management and Regulation of Financial Institutions," *Journal of Banking & Finance*, Volume 19 (June), pp. 461–481.

Merton, Robert C. (1995b) "A Functional Perspective of Financial Intermediation," *Financial Management*, Volume 24, Number 2, Summer 1995, pp. 23+.

Merton, Robert C., and Zvi Bodie (1992) "On the Management of Financial Guarantees," *Financial Management*, Volume 21, Number 4, Winter 1992, pp. 86–109.

Merton, Robert C., and André F. Perold (1993) "Theory of Risk Capital in Financial Firms," *Journal of Applied Corporate Finance*, Volume 6, Number 3, Fall 1993, pp. 16–32.

Meybom, Peter, and Michael Reinhart (1999) "Länderrisikosteuerung mittels kapitalmarktinduzierter Bewertung," *Die Bank*, Issue 8/99, pp. 568–572.

Mian, Shehzad L. (1996) "Evidence on Corporate Hedging Policy," *Journal of Financial and Quantitative Analysis*, Volume 31, Number 3, pp. 419+.

Miller, Merton H. (1995) "Do the M&M Propositions Apply to Banks?" *Journal of Banking & Finance*, Volume 19, pp. 483–489.

Miller, William D. (1995) *Commercial Bank Valuation*, New York: John Wiley & Sons, Inc.

Mindestanforderungen an das Betreiben von Handelsgeschäften (1995).

Mitra, Amitava (1993) *Fundamentals of Quality Control and Improvement*, New York: Macmillan.

Modigliani, Franco, and Merton H. Miller (1958) "The Cost of Capital, Corporation Finance, and the Theory of Investment," *American Economic Review*, Volume 48, pp. 261–297.

Modigliani, Franco, and Leah Modigliani (1997) "Risk-Adjusted Performance—How to Measure It and Why," *The Journal of Portfolio Management*, Winter 1997, pp. 45–54.

Moody's Investor Services (1997) *Rating Migration and Credit Quality Correlation—1920—1996*, Global Credit Research, July 1997.

Morisano, Frank (1998) "Managing Capital Resources Efficiently to Optimize Shareholder Value," *The Journal of Lending & Credit Risk Management*, September 1998, pp. 28–32.

Mossin, J. (1966) "Equilibrium in a Capital Asset Market," *Econometrica*, Volume 34, pp. 768–783.

Mudge, Dan (2000) "A Simple Consistency," *Risk Magazine*, March 2000, p. 61.

Myers, Stewart C. (1984) "The Capital Structure Puzzle," *Journal of Finance*, Volume XXXIX, July 1984, pp. 575–582.

Myers, Stewart C., and Nicholas Majluf (1984) "Corporate Financing and Investment Decisions When Firms Have Information That Investors Do Not Have," *Journal of Financial Economics*, Volume 13, June 1984, pp. 187–222.

Myers, Stewart C., and Richard S. Ruback (1993) "Discounting Rules for Risky Assets," working paper MIT-CEEPR 93-001WP, Massachusetts

Institute of Technology—Center for Energy and Environmental Policy Research, January 1993.

Myers, W. (1977) "Determinants of Corporate Borrowing," *Journal of Financial Economics*, Volume 5, pp. 147–175.

Nance, Deane R., Clifford W. Smith, Jr., and Charles W. Smithson (1993) "On the Determinants of Corporate Hedging," *The Journal of Finance*, Volume XLVIII, Number 1, pp. 267–284.

Obst, Georg, and Otto Hintner (1991) *Geld-, Bank- und Börsenwesen: Ein Handbuch*, 38th Edition, Norbert Kloten and Johann Heinrich von Stein (editors), Stuttgart: Poeschel.

Oliver Wyman Report (2000) "BIS II: A Step in the Right Direction," Volume 9, Number 3, New York: Oliver, Wyman & Company.

Ong, Michael K. (1999) *Internal Credit Risk Models—Capital Allocation and Performance Measurement*, London: Risk Publications.

Opler, Tim C., Michael Saron, and Sheridan Titman (1997) "Designing Capital Structure to Create Shareholder Value," *Journal of Applied Corporate Finance*, Volume 10, Number 1, Spring 1997, pp. 21–32.

Perridon, Louis, and Manfred Steiner (1995) *Finanzwirtschaft der Unternehmung*, Eighth Edition, Munich: Vahlen.

Pfingsten, Andreas, and Gerhard Schröck (2000) "Bedeutung und Methodik von Krediteinstufungsmodellen im Bankwesen," in *Kreditrisikomanagement—Portfoliomodelle und Derivate*, Andreas Oehler (editor), Stuttgart: Schäffer-Poeschel, pp. 1–23.

Pritsch, Gunnar, and Ulrich Hommel (1997) "Hedging im Sinne des Aktionärs—Ökonomische Erklärungsansätze für das unternehmerische Risikomanagement," *DBW*, Volume 57, 1997, pp. 672–693.

Punjabi, Sanjeev (1998) "Many Happy Returns," *Risk Magazine*, Volume 11, Number 6, June 1998, pp. 71–76.

Punjabi, Sanjeev, and Oliver Dunsche (1998) "Effective Risk-Adjusted Performance Measurement for Greater Shareholder Value," *The Journal of Lending & Credit Risk Management*, October 1998, pp. 18–23.

Raposo, Clara C. (1999) "Corporate Hedging: What Have We Learned So Far?" *Derivatives Quarterly*, Volume 5, Number 3, Spring 1999, pp. 41–51.

Rawls, S. Waite III, and Charles W. Smithson (1989) "The Evolution of Risk Management Products," *Journal of Applied Corporate Finance*, Winter 1989, pp. 18–26.

Reading, Ronald D., Alden L. Toevs, and Robert J. Zizka (1998) "Winning the Credit Cycle Game," *The Journal of Lending & Credit Risk Management*, March 1998, pp. 16–24.

Reiss, R.D., and M. Thomas (1997) *Statistical Analysis of Extreme Values*, Basel: Birkhauser Verlag.

Reyniers, Paul (1991) *Risk Adjusted Profitability Measurement in Banks—Volume 1: Concepts and Applications*, London: Price Waterhouse.

Risk Magazine (1997) "The Decade of Risk," *Risk Magazine*, Volume 10, Number 12, December 1997.

Rolfes, Bernd (1999) *Gesamtbanksteuerung*, Stuttgart: Schäffer-Poeschel.

Ross, S.A. (1976) "The Arbitrage Theory of Capital Asset Pricing," *Journal of Economic Theory*, Volume 13, December 1976, pp. 343–362.

Schierenbeck, Henner (1997) *Ertragsorientiertes Bankmanagement, Band 2: Risiko-Controlling und Bilanzstruktur-Management*, Fifth Edition, Wiesbaden: Gabler, especially pp. 470–495.

Schierenbeck, Henner (1998) "Shareholder Value-Management im Konzept Ertragsorientierter Banksteuerung," *Die Bank*, Issue 1/98, pp. 13–17.

Schierenbeck, Henner, and Michael Lister (1997) "Integrierte Risikomessung und Risikoallokation," *Die Bank*, Issue 8/97, pp. 492–499.

Schierenbeck, Henner, and Michael Lister (1997) "Verfahren zur Risikoallokation," *Schweizer Bank*, Issue 97/10, pp. 61–62.

Schmidt, Reinhard H., and Eva Terberger (1997) *Grundzüge der Investitions- und Finanzierungstheorie*, Fourth Edition, Wiesbaden: Gabler.

Schmittmann, Stefan, Hans-Gert Penzel, and Norman Gehrke (1996) "Integration des Shareholder Value in die Gesamtbanksteuerung," *Die Bank*, 11/96, pp. 648–653.

Scholtens, Bert, and Dick van Wensveen (2000) "A Critique on the Theory of Financial Intermediation," *Journal of Banking & Finance*, Volume 24, Number 8, August 2000, pp. 1243–1251.

Schrand, Catherine, and Haluk Unal (1996) "Hedging and Coordinated Risk Management: Evidence from Thrift Conversions," working paper 96-05, Financial Institutions Center, The Wharton School, University of Pennsylvania.

Schröck, Gerhard (1997) *Risiko- und Wertmanagement in Banken—Der Einsatz risikobereinigter Rentabilitätskennzahlen*, Wiesbaden: Deutscher Universitätsverlag, Gabler.

Schröck, Gerhard, and Marc Windfuhr (1999) "Calculation of Risk-Adjusted Performance Measures in Credit Markets," in: *Elektronische Dienstleistungswirtschaft und Financial Engineering—2. Internationale FAN-Tagung 1999*, Manfred Steiner, Thomas Dittmar, and Christian Willinsky (editors), Münster: Schüling Verlag, pp. 139–151.

Schröder, Michael (1996) "Value at Risk—Proposals on a Generalization," discussion paper No. 96-12, Zentrum für Europäische Wirtschaftsforschung (ZEW), May 1996.

Schuster, Leo (2000) *Shareholder Value Management in Banks*, Houndmills: MacMillan Press Ltd.

Sharpe, William F. (1964) "Capital Asset Prices—A Theory of Market Equilibrium under Conditions of Risk," *Journal of Finance*, Volume IXX, pp. 425–442.

Sharpe, William F. (1994) "The Sharpe Ratio," *The Journal of Portfolio Management*, Fall 1994, pp. 49–58.

Sharpe, William F., and Gordon J. Alexander (1990) *Investments*, Fourth Edition, Englewood Cliffs, NJ: Prentice-Hall.

Shearer, Angus T., Robert D. Christensen, and Brooks Brady (1999) "Profitability Measures and Market Reality: The Paradox of Commercial Lending Competition," *Commercial Lending Review*, Volume 14, Number 3, Summer 1999, pp. 35–44.

Shearer, Angus T., and Lawrence R. Forest, Jr. (1998) "Improving Quantification of Risk-Adjusted Performance Within Financial Institutions," *Commercial Lending Review*, Volume 13, Number 3, Summer 1998, pp. 48–57.

Shimko, David, and Brett Humphreys (1998) "Voting on Value," *Risk Magazine*, December 1998, p. 33.

Simons, Katerina (1998) "Risk-Adjusted Performance of Mutual Funds," *New England Economic Review*, September/October 1998, pp. 33–48.

Smith, Clifford W., Jr. (1993) "Risk Management and Banking: The Principles," *Finanzmarkt und Portfolio Management*, Volume 7, Number 1, pp. 12–23.

Smith, Clifford W., Jr. (1995) "Corporate Risk Management: Theory and Practice," *The Journal of Derivatives*, Summer 1995, pp. 21–30.

Smith, Clifford W., Jr., and René M. Stulz (1985) "The Determinants of Firm's Hedging Policies," *Journal of Financial and Quantitative Analysis*, Volume 20, No. 4, December 1985, pp. 391–405.

Smithson, Charles W. (1997) "Capital Budgeting," *Risk Magazine*, Volume 10, Number 6, June 1997, pp. 40–41.

Smithson, Charles W. (1998) "Questions Regarding the Use of Financial Price Risk Management by Industrial Companies," working paper, CIBC World Markets, October 1998.

Smithson, Charles W., Clifford W. Smith, Jr., and D. Sykes Wilford (1990) *Managing Financial Risk—A Guide to Derivative Products, Financial Engineering, and Value Maximization*, First Edition, Chicago: Irwin.

Smithson, Charles W., Clifford W. Smith, Jr., and D. Sykes Wilford (1995) *Managing Financial Risk—A Guide to Derivative Products, Financial Engineering, and Value Maximization*, Second Edition, Chicago: Irwin.

Stahl, Gerhard, and Uwe Traber (2000) "Backtesting in Action," in: *Kreditrisikomanagement—Portfoliomodelle und Derivate*, Andreas Oehler (editor), Stuttgart: Schäffer-Poeschl, pp. 85–106.

Standard & Poor's (1997) *Ratings Performance 1996: Stability and Transition*, Special Report, February 1997.

Starr, Michael, Glen Grabelsky, Timothy Comiskey, Ian Jaffe, and Glen Potolsky (1999) *Understanding U.S. Bank Failures—A Look at the Past*, FitchIBCA Financial Institutions, United States Special Report, December 9, 1999.

Steiner, Manfred, and Christoph Bruns (1995) *Wertpapiermanagement*, Fourth Edition, Stuttgart: Schäffer-Poeschel.

Steiner, Manfred, Thomas Hirschbeck, and Christian Willinsky (1998) "Risikobereinigte Rentabilitätskennzahlen im Controlling von Kreditinstituten und ihr Zusammenhang mit der Portfoliotheorie—Eine vergleichende Analyse unter der Annahme normalverteilter Renditen," in: *Informationssysteme in der Finanzwirtschaft*, C. Weinhardt, H. Meyer zu Selhausen, and M. Morlock (editors), Berlin: Springer, pp. 361–384.

Steiner, Manfred, and Martin Wallmeier (1999) "Unternehmensbewertung mit Discounted Cash Flow-Methoden und dem Economic Value Added-Konzept," *FinanzBetrieb*, Issue 5/1999, pp. 1–10.

Stewart, G. Bennet (1991) *The Quest for Value—A Guide for Senior Managers*, New York: HarperCollins, Inc.

Stiglitz, Joseph E. (1969) "A Re-Examination of the Modigliani-Miller Theorem," *American Economic Review*, Volume 59, pp. 784–793.

Stoughton, Neal M., and Josef Zechner (1999) "Optimal Capital Allocation Using RAROC™ and EVA®," working paper, UC Irvine/University of Vienna, January 1999.

Strutz, Eric (1993) *Wertmanagement von Banken*, Dissertation der Hochschule St. Gallen, Bern: Verlag Paul Haupt.

Stulz, René M. (1984) "Optimal Hedging Policies," *Journal of Financial and Quantitative Analysis*, Volume 19, June 1984, pp. 127–140.

Stulz, René M. (1996) "Rethinking Risk Management," *Journal of Applied Corporate Finance*, Volume 9, Number 3, Fall 1996, pp. 8–24.

Stulz, René M. (1999) "What's wrong with modern capital budgeting?" Address delivered at the Eastern Finance Association meeting, Miami Beach, April 1999.

Stulz, René M. (2002) "Derivatives, Risk Management, and Financial Engineering," Southwestern College Publishing, forthcoming, available at www.cob.ohio-state.edu/fin/faculty/stulz.

Theodore, Samuel S., Christopher T. Mahoney, and Gregory W. Bauer (1999) "Rating Methodology—Bank Credit Risk (An Analytical Framework for Banks in Developed Markets)," *Global Credit Research*, April 1999, New York: Moody's Investor Service.

Tufano, Peter (1996) "Who Manages Risk? An Empirical Examination of Risk Management Practices in the Gold Mining Industry," *The Journal of Finance*, Volume LI, Number 4, September 1996, pp. 1097–1137.

Tufano, Peter (1998) "Agency Costs of Corporate Risk Management," *Financial Management*, Volume 27, Number 1, Spring 1998, pp. 67–77.

Uyemura, Dennis G., Charles C. Kantor, and Justin M. Pettit (1996) "EVA® for Banks: Value Creation, Risk Management, and Profitability Measurement," *Journal of Applied Corporate Finance*, Volume 9, Number 2, Summer 1996, pp. 94–113.

Wall, L.D., and John Pringle (1989) "Alternative Explanations for Interest Rate Swaps—An Empirical Analysis," *Financial Management*, Volume 18, pp. 59–73.

Weiss, L.A. (1990) "Bankruptcy Resolution," *Journal of Financial Economics*, Volume 27, October 1990, pp. 285–314.

Williams, Deborah (1999) "Risk Technology Spending: An Update," *Risk Management Research Brief*, Meridian Research, Inc., June 1999.

Williamson, O.E. (1985) *The Economic Institutions of Capitalism*, New York: Free Press.

Wills, Simon, Susan Hinko, Michael Haubenstock, Kathleen Leibfried, Andrea Pozzi, and Nicholas Hayes (1999) *Operational Risk—The Next Frontier*, British Bankers' Association/International Swaps and Derivatives Association (ISDA)/ Pricewaterhouse Coopers/RMA, ISBN 1-57070-301-9.

Wilson, Thomas C. (1992) "RAROC Remodelled," *Risk Magazine*, Volume 5, Number 8, September 1992, pp. 112–119.

Wilson, Thomas C. (1996) "Calculating Risk Capital," in: *The Handbook of Risk Management and Analysis*, Carol Alexander (editor), Chichester: John Wiley & Sons Ltd., pp. 193–232.

Wilson, Thomas C. (1997a) "Portfolio Credit Risk I," *Risk Magazine*, September 1997, pp. 111–117.

Wilson, Thomas C. (1997b) "Portfolio Credit Risk II," *Risk Magazine*, October 1997, pp. 56–61.

Winton, Andrew (2000) "Don't Put All Your Eggs in One Basket?—Diversification and Specialization in Lending," working paper 00-16, Financial Institutions Center, The Wharton School, University of Pennsylvania, also presented at "Competition Among Banks: Good or Bad?" conference in Frankfurt, April 6–8, 2000.

Wittrock, Carsten (1995) *Messung und Analyse der Performance von Wertpapierportfolios—Eine theoretische und empirische Untersuchung*, Bad Soden: Uhlenbruch.

Zaik, Edward, John Walter, Gabriela Kelling, and Christopher James (1996) "RAROC at Bank of America: From Theory to Practice," *Journal of Applied Corporate Finance*, Volume 9, Number 2, Summer 1996, pp. 83–93.

index

Accounting:
  fair value, 149
  policy, 33
  view. *See* Point of view, accounting
Acquisition(s), 150
Actions, legal, 156, 197
Activist shareholder groups, 10
Activities, off-balance sheet, 149, 160, 239
Adjusted present value (APV), 106, 116
Advances:
  in methodology, 56
  in technology, 56
Advantage(s):
  comparative, of (capital) markets, 111–112
  competitive, 7, 41–43, 47, 61, 85, 112, 115, 134, 136, 242, 268, 272–278, 280–281
  information(al), 28, 99, 145, 149, 277, 279, 282
Adverse selection, 76, 81, 87
Agency conflicts. *See* Conflicts of interest
Agency costs, 6, 75, 79, 81, 85–86, 94–95, 112–113, 139, 276, 280
  of debt, 75–76, 79, 82, 91, 94, 123, 125, 288
  of equity, 75, 79, 82–83, 86, 89–90, 99, 123, 125, 288
  of free cash flow, 82, 126
  of managerial discretion, 97, 276
Agency problem(s). *See* Conflicts of interest
Agency theory, 75, 87
Agents, 61, 75, 81, 86–87, 113
Airlines, troubled, 109
Alignment of interests, 22, 75, 85, 93, 125, 150, 156
ALM function. *See* Asset-liability management function
Analogue(s), market, 208
Analyst community, 10, 115
Anecdotal evidence, 4, 15, 22, 28, 39, 46, 73, 74, 101, 220, 235
Approach:
  accounting-driven, 239
  actuarial, 199
  analogue, 70, 203, 208
  analytical, 182, 186
  best practice, 130, 159, 163, 199, 210, 235, 242, 259, 289
  bottom-up, 150, 164, 170–171, 185, 199, 212–213, 216, 219–220, 231, 235, 290
  historical accounting-based, for business risk, 206, 209
  Merton, 219–221, 227, 247, 290
  Monte Carlo simulation, for business risk, 207–209
  parametric, 189–190
  regulatory, one-size-fits-all, 159, 163

Approach *(continued)*
  top-down, 162, 170, 199, 215–216,
    219–231, 235, 238, 284, 290
  value, 2, 14, 16, 186, 215
  with and without, 212, 283
APV. *See* Adjusted present value
Arbitrage, 33, 59, 64, 68
  Pricing Theory (APT), 71
  regulatory, 162
Arrow-Debreu world, 62
Asset(s):
  gross, 154
  illiquid bank or credit, 185, 214–
    215, 255, 268, 273
  net, 154–155, 160–163, 216, 260
  off-balance sheet, 165, 226
  on-balance sheet, 149, 165, 186, 226
  risk-free, 59, 69, 84, 228, 252, 263,
    268, 274–275
  risk-weighted, 139, 148, 240
Asset insurance, 161, 163, 256, 263,
    264, 270, 289
Asset-liability management function.
    See Treasury function
Asset-liability management, 157
Asset size bucket, 138–139
Asset substitution, 76, 79, 91, 93–94,
    108, 114, 125
Assumptions, implicit, 237, 241, 247,
    255, 290
Asymmetric information, 28, 75–81,
    87, 97, 114, 149
Asymmetry, behavioral, 46
Availability of external funds, limited,
    77, 105, 108

Backtesting, 190, 192
Bail out, 110
Balance sheet:
  accounting, 146, 263–264
  economic, 157, 263–264
  liquid, 163
  policy, 207
Balanced stakeholder approach, 21
Bank(s), 1, 29, 56, 113, 122, 166,
    220, 240, 273, 281
  as opaque institutions, 4, 16, 45,
    122, 145, 270

  commercial, 143, 265
  ensuring long-term survival of, 3,
    30, 33, 287
  functions of, 29
  illiquid, 144
  solvent, 122, 159, 163, 187, 192,
    195, 207
  universal, 253
Bank analyst(s), 4, 15
Bank charter, withdrawal of, 110, 112
Bank customer(s), 3, 90, 109, 122,
    141, 156
Bank default, 22–23, 225, 282
Bank failure(s), risk of, 23, 110, 122,
    144–145
Bank for International Settlements
    (BIS), 138, 194, 239
Banking (industry) index, 16–17, 34, 36
Banking industry, 1, 22, 34, 37–38,
    152, 159, 163, 240, 242, 267,
    272
Banking system:
  fragility of, 3, 110
  safety, stability, and soundness of,
    22, 142, 144
Bank performance, 4, 18, 48, 147, 239
Bank portfolio:
  as proxy for market portfolio, 253
  existing, 136, 210, 253, 266, 288
Bank run(s), 3, 23, 135, 144, 146,
    152–159, 163, 166, 169, 197,
    219, 222, 226, 236, 238, 289
Bankruptcy, 3, 30, 83, 107–109, 142,
    191
  court, 108, 177
Bank safety, 140–141
Bank stakeholder(s), 22–23, 30, 105,
    135, 137, 150, 162, 270, 289
Barings, 57, 86
Barrier(s):
  absorbing, 195
  entry, 197
Basle Accord from 1988 (Basle I), 3, 226
  market risk amendment, 191
Basle I. *See* Basle Accord from 1988
Basle II. *See* New Basle Accord
Benchmark return. *See* Rate of return,
    required

Benchmarking, 14, 209
Bernoulli, 60, 172, 177
Best practice, 130, 210, 238
Beta:
   CAPM, 245, 266
   external, 37, 246, 253–254, 266, 268
   instantaneous equity, 255
   internal, 185, 213, 242, 246, 253,
      266, 268–269, 275, 283–284
   market, 36, 168, 230, 253, 269
   of transaction, 255
Bid-ask spread, 124
BIS. *See* Bank for International
   Settlements
Black-Scholes, 131, 221–223, 227,
   248, 255
Bond holder(s):
   credit sensitive, 23, 142
   junior, 142, 151, 156, 158–161, 219
   senior, 142, 147, 151–152, 156–
      159
   external, 142
Bond, zero-coupon, 222, 247
Bonus, 85, 89
Book capital. *See* Capital, book
Book value, 110–111, 120, 149, 160–
   161, 222–227, 230–231, 260,
   264
Break even, 255
Brownian motion, geometric, 221
Business disruption, 162, 197, 216
Business risk. *See* Risk, business
   capital. *See* Capital, economic, (for)
   business
Business unit, 1, 15, 26–27, 164, 177,
   187, 193, 195, 205–209, 213,
   244, 283, 285

CAD. *See* Capital Adequacy Directive,
   European
Call option. *See* Option(s), call
Capacity, 94, 126, 130, 153
Capital adequacy, 159–161
Capital allocation, 7, 191, 205, 283
Capital:
   as buffer function of, 134, 141,
      145, 150, 159, 169, 211, 253,
      262, 268

   as cushion. *See* Capital, buffer
      function of
   as substitute for risk management,
      112, 123, 126, 140, 236
   available, 139, 145, 162
Capital base, 157, 195, 208
Capital benefit, 243–244, 251–252, 283
Capital, book, 4, 139, 146–147, 161,
   194, 219
Capital concepts, 146
Capital, economic, 5–7, 137, 156,
   158, 160, 164, 169
   aggregation across risk types, 210–
      213
   as adequate risk measure, in banks,
      164, 166, 236–237
   as proxy or shortcut for risk
      capital, 160, 163, 237
   as theoretical construct, 159, 164
   as total risk measure, 170, 185,
      214, 219, 253, 265–266, 272,
      285
   for business risk, 205–210
   for credit risk, 170–186
   for event risk, 199–205
   for market risk, 186–196
   for operational risk, 196–210
   VaR-based, 219, 236
Capital:
   excess, 150, 162
   human, 84, 86, 89
   invested, 263–264, 273
   real, 6, 192, 252, 269, 280
Capital, regulatory, 4, 142, 144–147,
   151, 154, 160, 162–163, 194,
   209, 239–240
Capital, requirement, 5, 139, 145–
   146, 150, 153, 158, 162, 165–
   166, 192, 211–212, 242, 284
   economic, 139, 143–145, 161–163,
      175, 193, 212–216, 235–236,
      253, 267
   marginal or incremental, 212, 236
   regulatory, 142–145, 164, 194, 209,
      239
   standalone, 260
Capital, risk, 5, 26, 137, 146, 151,
   153–154, 262, 270, 289

Capital:
  Tier-1, 139, 146–148, 161, 219
  Tier-2, 139, 146–148, 156, 161, 226
Capital, unallocated, 212, 283
Capital Adequacy Directive, European (CAD), 3, 147
Capital Asset Pricing Model (CAPM), 2, 15, 25, 34, 59, 62, 67, 71, 129, 134, 219, 230, 238, 240, 245–246, 249, 253–255, 261, 265–266, 268, 290
Capital budgeting, 72, 133–136, 239, 242, 267–268, 275
  new approaches, 268, 273–274
  decision rule, new, 272
  decision(s), 2–5, 27, 62–63, 72, 123
  principle(s) or procedure(s), 133–134
  tool(s), 134–135, 239, 242, 245, 267–269, 282, 284–285, 290–291
Capital Market Line (CML), 43
Capital market. *See* Market
Capital measurement, 146
Capital multiplier, 182, 185, 204
Capital structure, 4, 12, 27, 72, 95, 115, 133, 135–138, 261, 264, 284, 289
  actual, 265, 268, 274, 279–280, 284
  choice, 133, 140–141, 280
  decision(s), 4, 133–134, 247–248, 262, 269, 274, 279
  optimal, 66, 126, 130, 265
Capitalization. *See* Capital base
Cash capital, 154, 160–162, 262–264, 267–271
Cash flows:
  operating, 61, 94, 97, 107, 109
  risk profile of, 1, 12, 14, 59, 62
  stabilization of, 101
  time structure of, 1, 12, 14, 59, 62
  volatility of, 32, 107. *See also* Volatility of (free) cash flows
Catastrophe, natural, 196
Chain reaction, 144
Chapter 11, 107

Charge-off(s), 57, 245
Circular problem, 256
Claim(s):
  fixed, 81, 93, 95, 107
  junior, 147
  residual, 81, 149
  senior, 146
Claim holder(s). *See* Stakeholder(s)
  residual, 142, 152, 155–156
Clientele, 24, 70–71
CML. *See* Capital Market Line
Cohort, 174
Collateral, 32, 76, 100, 109, 142, 172, 174–175
Company(ies):
  as risk-neutral agents, 61, 100, 219, 280,
  ensuring long-term survival of, 13, 33, 55, 132
  industrial *See also* Corporation(s), industrial
Compensation, 83, 85, 89, 242, 247, 268, 279
  incentive, 86, 242
  managerial, 85
  pecuniary, 210
  performance-based, 85, 90
Competition, 1, 132, 206, 276
Competitive advantage(s). *See* Advantages, comparative
Concentration. *See also* Lumpiness
  in credit portfolios, 140–141, 145, 182
  index, 91
  ratio, 91
Concerns, with bottom-up approach, 212
Conditions:
  economic, 32, 77, 172, 208, 221
  for coherent risk measures, 213
Confidence interval. *See* Confidence level
Confidence level, 5, 74, 154, 159–160, 166, 168–170, 175, 182–185, 187–192, 194–195, 202, 204, 206, 211, 215–217, 248, 251, 253, 263, 269, 284

Conflicts of interest, 77, 81, 102, 104
  between (old and new)
    shareholders, 75, 81
  between managers and outside
    investors, 97
  between managers and
    shareholders, 12, 81–83
  between shareholders and bond
    holders, 12, 81, 91, 94, 97
Consolidation, in banking industry, 18
Consumption, 11, 13, 69, 82, 195
  on the job, 82
  stream, 69
  time pattern of, 11
Continental Illinois, 147, 157
Contract, default-free, 122
Contractual arrangements, (ex ante),
  75, 90
Contribution:
  incremental or marginal, 170, 179–
    180, 182, 187, 189, 283
  total, 135, 176, 180, 266, 290–291
  to value creation, 242, 245
Control:
  internal, 196
  questions, 44
  sample, 37–38
Coordination:
  of investment and financing, 79, 95,
    97, 104, 114, 125
  of risks, 281
Core capability or competency, 29,
  72–73, 86
Corporate
  objective. *See* Firm objective
    function
  raiders, 10
Corporation(s), industrial, 1, 15, 21,
  23, 73, 100, 104, 107, 130,
  132, 166, 237, 239, 241
Correlation, 10, 26, 102, 131, 134,
  170, 178–179, 185–186, 193,
  195, 203, 208, 210, 212, 235,
  254, 255, 257
  asset, 181, 249, 256
  between types of risk, 211, 213, 220
  country default, 182

  default, 181–182
  matrix, 189–190, 209, 211
  of joint movement in credit quality,
    181
  with existing bank portfolio, 136,
    253, 266
Cost(s):
  allocation of, 16, 241
  bankruptcy, 80, 106, 111–112, 130,
    139
  direct, 99, 107, 110, 126
  fixed, 73, 107, 113, 197, 205–207
  indirect, 99, 104, 108–112, 126
  marginal, 39, 46, 63, 73, 98, 126, 265
  observable, 201
  of (holding economic) capital, 240,
    245–246, 272, 276
  of borrowing, 32
  of contracting, 76, 90, 123
  of default (direct and indirect), 59,
    68, 76–77, 98, 107, 111, 245,
    247, 288
  of ensuring a stable risk profile, 105
  of financial distress, 79, 99, 105–
    108, 111–112, 123, 125, 132–
    134, 137, 141, 143, 155, 156,
    219, 267–270, 274, 286
  of funds, 243, 252
  of investment, 251
  of issuance, 79, 99, 105, 114
  of risk management, 26, 78–79,
    105, 113, 124, 140
  of stock price reaction, 79, 91, 98
  of total risk, 133–137, 238, 265–
    269, 271–280, 282, 284, 289,
    291
  rigid, 205–206
  social, 12–14, 110, 144–145
  variable, 206–209
Cost base, fixed, 205–206
Cost basis, historical, 149
Cost-benefit analysis, 124, 132, 202
Counterparty, 171, 173–175, 182,
  185
Covariance, of returns, 2–3, 24, 36,
  62, 145, 180, 270
Covenants, 12, 76, 93–94, 97, 108

Credit:
  derivatives, 178, 237
  enhancement, 153
  exposure, 110, 130, 149, 170, 174
  illiquid, 16, 214–215, 246, 255,
      268, 273
  markets, liquefaction of, 273
  migration, unexpected, 170, 176
Creditors:
  subordinated, 147
  uninsured, 143–144, 151–154, 158
Credit portfolio management, active,
      281
Credit quality, 141–142, 145, 157,
      165, 170–173, 181, 185–186
Credit rating, 5, 125, 157, 159–162,
      169, 172, 209
  senior debt, 169, 220, 229, 233
  target, 5, 157, 159, 162
Credit risk. See Risk, credit
Creditworthiness (of financial
      institutions), 105, 122–123,
      166
Crisis:
  country risk, 239
  financial, 18, 37, 110
  Russian, 110, 130, 149
  Savings & Loan, 144
  Southeast Asian, 18
Cross-selling, 262
Currency, common, for risk, 26, 237
Customers, credit sensitive, 109, 142,
      153, 160
Cycle, economic, 172, 206–208

Deadweight:
  costs, 95
  losses, 101, 270
Debt:
  convertible, 93, 148
  overhang, 95
  ratio, 94, 122, 126, 130, 182
  risky, 247
  senior, 147, 157, 159–160, 162–
      163, 187, 216, 220, 229, 233,
      236
  service, 106
  subordinated, 147, 156, 161, 226
  uninsured, 147, 151, 156, 158
Debt capacity, 94, 126, 130
Debt holder(s):
  junior, 152, 156, 159–161, 219
  rational, 93
  senior, 152
  subordinated, 147
Decision-making process, 4, 39, 72,
      100, 134, 272, 281
Decision, marginal, 212
Default:
  economic, 151–152, 156
  intra-year, 195
  regulatory, 151
Default cost(s). See also Cost(s), of
      financial distress
Default point (DP), 80–81, 106–107,
      151, 220, 224, 226–227, 230
Default risk, 3, 23, 68, 71, 83, 93,
      122, 134, 142, 153, 155, 170,
      220, 248, 264–265, 289
Degree of certainty, prespecified. See
      Confidence level
Delegation of decision/control power,
      86
Deposit(s), 2, 15, 23, 29, 79, 104,
      110, 141–142, 163, 165, 219,
      223
  insured, 123, 144, 146, 151–153,
      158, 226
  uninsured, 147, 151–152, 158
Deposit insurance, 23, 110, 142, 146–
      147, 151–152, 158
Deregulation, 157
Derivative(s), 23, 31, 38, 40–41, 46–
      47, 56, 63, 69, 73, 113, 122,
      125, 131, 170, 174, 186, 237,
      276, 278, 280
Derivative instrument(s). See
      Derivative(s)
Disaster(s), 165, 195–198
Disclosure, 41, 44–45, 115, 220, 285
Discounted cash flow (DCF), 1, 12,
      14, 71, 134, 288
  value framework, 136. See also
      Valuation framework

Discretion, managerial, 82, 97, 276
Disintermediation, 29
Distance to default, (normalized),
     225–226, 229, 233–234
Distribution:
  (net) asset (value), 23, 80, 150,
     158–159, 162, 216, 220, 224
  cut-off point, 204
  earnings, 215
  economic return, 215
  empirical, 190, 195, 225
  extreme tail, 158
  firm value, 80
  gains and losses, 166, 214
  loss, 182, 185, 202
  moment(s) of a, 217
  skewed, 151, 202, 204
  tail of, 158, 183–184
  value (change), 150, 158–159
Distribution (function):
  beta, 184–185, 204
  binomial, 177, 184
  lognormal, 221, 225
  non-normal, 151
  normal, 168, 177, 183, 189–190,
     223, 225, 228–229, 233, 248
  uniform, 177
Diversification, 26, 28, 40–42, 56, 60,
     62, 65–66, 69, 71, 74, 86, 103,
     122, 136, 141, 157, 159, 176,
     178, 182, 185, 200, 209, 212–
     213, 142, 260, 270, 276, 278
Divesting, 1, 7
Dividend:
  decision(s), 12, 14
  policy, 63, 121
Doctrine, "too-big-to-fail", 110, 123,
     142, 147, 230
Domino effect(s), 22
DP. *See* Default point
Drift rate, 221
Due diligence, 41

Earning(s), 31–32, 38–39, 61, 70–71,
     87, 89, 120, 149, 157, 192–
     193, 215, 239, 245
  economic, 120, 242

pretax, 120
  residual, 244
Economic Value Added (EVA®), in
     banks, 244, 290
Economy, local or regional, 140
EL. *See* Loss(es), expected
Empire building, 82
Empirical, evidence, on link between
     risk management and value
     creation, 6, 9, 43, 46–48, 55,
     287
Engineering, financial 44
Entity:
  approach, 14–15
  value, 15
Environment:
  business, 208
  competitive, 157, 207–208
  economic, 131, 216
  financial, 56
  market, 157
  operating, 157
Equilibrium, 76, 132, 155, 261, 280
Equity:
  approach, 2, 240, 256
  as scarce resource, 239
  investment, 105, 245
Estimation horizon or period, 172–
     174, 186
Eurobonds, sovereign, 175
EVA®. *See* Economic Value Added
Evaluation, risk-neutral, 223, 225, 228
Event(s):
  downside, 151
  extreme, 195
  non-credit-risk, 196
  nonmarket, 196
  nonrecurring, 245
Event loss database, 202
Event risk. *See* Risk, event
Event studies, 47
EVT. *See* Extreme value theory
Examination process, regulatory, 145,
     214
Existence
  of banks, 72, 79, 114, 138, 199
  of firms, 72

Expectations:
  homogeneous, 59, 277
  tail conditional, 218–219
Expected Default Frequency (EDF),
      172. *See also* Probability of
      default (PD)
Expected losses (EL). *See* Loss(es),
      expected
Expense(s):
  allocation of, 241
  direct, 243
  indirect, 243
  non-interest, 209, 243
  rigid, 205,
  variable, 205
Exposure, 26, 28, 38, 44, 46, 63, 70,
      74, 77, 83, 85, 88, 96, 102–
      103, 110–111, 114–115, 120,
      123, 130, 135–136, 149, 166,
      170, 172–174, 176–177, 179,
      198–200, 210, 237
Externalities, 22, 75, 144
Extreme value theory (EVT), 183,
      194–195, 218

Failure, 42, 56, 110, 122, 150, 173,
      196–197, 204
FDIC. *See* Federal Deposit Insurance
      Corporation
Federal Deposit Insurance
      Corporation (FDIC), 110, 143–
      144
Fee(s), 124, 197, 243
Finance theory
  conventional, 274
  neoclassical, 2, 5–6, 21, 33–34, 39,
      58, 67, 70–72, 136, 138, 240,
      253, 269, 272, 279–281, 287–
      288
    and risk management, 61–64. *See
      also* Risk management
      irrelevance proposition
    as partial solution, 74, 289
    assumptions of, 2, 4, 58–60, 129,
      247, 290
    corollaries with regard to risk
      management, 61

discrepancies to practice, 72
relaxation of the assumptions of,
      75–79
neoinstitutional, and risk
      management, 74, 123, 129,
      132, 136, 285, 288–289
  incentive-based approaches, 75
  transaction-cost-based approach,
      76
Financial distress, 30, 80, 82, 90,
      104–111, 123, 164, 166, 269,
      288
  costs. *See* Cost(s) of financial distress
Financial:
  institution(s). *See* Bank(s)
  intermediation, 2. *See also*
      Intermediation
  leverage. *See* Leverage
  policy, 42, 62, 135
  risk business, 3, 29, 48, 287
  system. *See* Banking system
Financing:
  decisions, irrelevance of, 61, 249
  default-free, 154
  opportunities, changing, 103
Firm(s):
  closely held, 82, 84, 89, 130
  widely held, 24, 60, 78, 130
Firm objective function, 9, 27, 100
  characteristics of, 13
  concave, 85, 87, 91, 100, 112
Firm value:
  after financial distress costs, 106
  after-tax, 116
  before financial distress costs, 106
  maximization of, 11, 33, 56
Fisher separation, 11
Flexibility, as source for value
      creation, 68
Flows-to-entity approach. *See* Entity,
      approach
Flows-to-equity approach. *See* Equity,
      approach
Fluctuations, economic, 64
Forward(s), 40, 56, 118, 278
Framework:
  capital-budgeting, 238

EL/UL, 215
value. *See* Valuation framework
Franchise value, 110, 132, 196, 282, 288
Fraud, 57, 196–197, 200, 204
Free cash flows, 1, 2, 12, 14–15, 142, 221, 245, 267
  to shareholders, 240, 245
  volatility of, 31, 82
Froot and Stein model. *See* Model, two-factor
Funding, 157, 246, 252, 282
  external, 77, 94, 97–100, 104–105, 108, 114
  internal, 97–102, 104, 125
Funds, 23, 28, 32, 60, 79, 82, 105, 133, 146, 150, 152, 154, 160, 194, 219, 232, 243, 251, 252, 262
Future(s), 40, 56, 278

Gain, 85, 93, 125, 130, 132, 151, 158, 166, 168, 194, 206, 208, 214–215, 245, 288
Gains trading, 149
Gamble, fair, 59
Gini-coefficient, 91
Goal(s):
  corporate, 27
  delegated, 26
  financial, 13
  nonfinancial, 13
  primary, of risk management, 31, 39
Goal variable, choice of, 31
Going concern value, lost, 110
Goodwill, 110, 148
Governance (system), corporate, 157, 196
Grossing up, 213
Growth:
  asset, 230
  equity, 230
  opportunities, 14, 22, 104, 131
  options, 97
Guarantee, 70, 115, 122, 125, 142, 155–156, 159–160, 169, 253
  government, 158

Guidelines, 3, 25–26, 45, 145, 148, 182, 197, 198, 200, 237

Hedge:
  built-in or natural, 102, 132
  funds, hidden, 132
  instruments, 27
  ratio, 46, 102–103, 131
Hedging. *See also* Risk management
  by small companies, 60
  complete, 38–39, 43, 46–47, 74, 102, 130
  earnings, 32, 120
  full. *See* Hedging, complete
  linear, 103–104
  negative, 46, 103
  overhedging, 46, 102–103
  selective, 28, 38, 47, 130
  strategy, 28, 32, 45–46, 63, 102, 104
  underhedging, 46, 103
  value, 32
Horizon:
  one-year, 171–172, 177, 186–187, 192–193, 196, 201, 214–215, 235–237, 244, 247, 259, 284
  time, 111, 185, 187–188, 195–196, 201, 208, 214–215, 237
Hurdle rate (of return), 5, 7, 21, 241, 245, 247, 249, 255–256, 259–260, 264–265, 270, 273, 290. *See also* Rate of return, required
  bankwide, 247, 254, 257–259, 285, 290
  CAPM, 246, 249, 252, 254, 259–260, 266, 269, 271
  single, 247, 254
Hypothesis, 37, 78, 121, 215, 241, 254

Identically and independently distributed (iid), 191, 193
iid. *See* Identically and independently distributed (iid)
Impossibility of raising external funds, 108

Incentive(s), 22, 33, 45, 75–76, 81–
82, 84–85, 86–90, 93–94, 106,
114, 120, 122–123, 138, 146–
147, 196, 209, 213–214, 239,
242, 246, 252, 257–258, 270
management, 77, 83, 87, 95, 108,
241
pecuniary, 214
Income:
after-tax, 118–119
fee-based, 141, 197
non-interest, 140
pretax, 116–118, 120
stream, 11, 25, 31, 60, 84
Index:
fund, 42
performance, 37–38
Industry:
analyst(s), 56
expert(s), 56
Information:
asymmetric, 28, 75–77, 79, 81, 87,
97–98, 114, 134, 149, 270,
276, 280
asymmetries. *See* Information,
asymmetric
complete, 14, 59
insiders, 81
outsiders, 81
Input:
equity related, 231
liability related, 231
Insolvency, 89, 111, 156
Insulation from risks beyond control,
89, 246
Insurance:
actuarial, for event risk, 40
as risk management approach, 41,
60, 122, 200–201, 278–279
catastrophe 201
external or third party, 42, 122,
200, 279
note, 263–264
self or internal, 42, 200, 201, 279
pool, 152, 161, 171, 252, 264
premium(s), 152, 155, 238, 248
Interbank market, 144

Interdependency, of capital budgeting,
capital structure, and risk
management, 98, 133, 269,
274, 280
Interest income, gross, 243
Intermediaries, 62, 72–73, 113–114,
136,
Intermediation (financial), 2, 28–29,
79, 145
Intervention:
government, 123, 142, 147
management, 195, 214–215
regulatory, 150, 158, 162, 219
Investment(s):
firm-specific, 82
non-value maximizing, 63
risk-free, 153, 155, 163
value-enhancing, 32
Investment horizon, 100
Investment opportunities, (lucrative),
94, 98–99, 102–103, 105
changing or stochastic, 77, 102
nonstochastic or fixed, 59, 77, 101–
102
Investment policy, 81, 93
Investment projects, 93–94, 97, 100,
102
Investor(s):
activism, 10
community, 10
institutional, 10
not well-diversified, 65, 69
well-diversified, 24, 60, 130

Key competency, 136
KMV, 220
Knowledge, internal, 236

Lending:
business model, unbundling, 281
guidelines, 182, 237
policy, 182
Leptokurtosis. *See* Tail(s), fat
Level of confidence. *See* Confidence
level
Leverage, 1, 14, 47, 57, 75–76, 80, 86,
122, 138–139, 147, 229, 234

at the transaction level, 249–254
constant, 97
decrease in, 156, 280
effects of changes in, 140, 246, 283
excessive, 95, 99, 146
increase in, 96, 123, 126, 130,
    288–289
optimal, 138. *See also* Capital
    structure, optimal
Liability(ies):
(default-free) customer, 154
fixed, 154
junior, 156–157
limited, 101, 121, 149, 221
off-balance sheet, 165, 226–227,
    231
on-balance sheet, 149, 165, 226
Liability holder(s), 3, 122, 141
Liability management, 2, 15
Likelihood of bank default, 22–23,
    42, 82
Likelihood of default, 79, 81, 89–90,
    125, 132, 288. *See also*
    Probability of default
central role of, 80
Limit setting. *See* Risk, limiting
Liquidation, 107, 191, 215
Liquidity, 3, 28, 109, 157, 165, 186,
    191, 197, 230
Loan loss reserves, 140, 148, 161,
    171. *See also* Reserves, loan
    loss
Loan(s), 25, 42, 79, 113, 145, 149,
    170, 174, 176, 179–180, 186,
    260
pricing, 171, 273
secured, 175, 177
unsecured, 177
Loan origination, 281
Loan portfolio, 140, 161, 176, 181,
    186
Loss(es):
actual, 174
actuarial 152. *See also* Loss(es),
    expected or credit
credit, 5, 169, 171, 175–176, 184,
    239, 243–244, 276, 282, 285

economic, 152, 170
expected (credit), 5, 74, 145, 150–
    151, 158, 161, 171–173, 175–
    176, 178–179, 182, 198, 201–
    203, 210, 217, 243, 251, 263,
    268
expected, due to event risk, 203
maximum, 168
residual, 81, 153
unexpected, 5, 74, 145, 150, 175–
    183, 185, 198, 202–203, 263,
    268
    contribution, 171, 175, 178–180,
        182–183
    standalone, 171, 176
Loss given default (LGD), 111, 172
Loss in the event of default (LIED).
    See Loss given default (LGD)
Loss leader, 262
Loss prevention by process control,
    278
Loss rate (LR), 172–179, 198
Loss volatility, 180, 215
Lottery ticket, 168
Lower partial moment (LPM), 217–218
Lower-tail outcome(s), 23, 30, 33, 39,
    112, 132, 135, 168, 225, 288–
    290
Loyalty, 89
LR. *See* Loss rate (LR)
Lumpiness, 185, 202. *See also*
    Concentration

M&A. *See* Mergers and acquisitions
M&M:
assumptions of, 59, 63, 68, 71, 78,
    102, 138
capital structure irrelevance
    proposition, 64
proposition I, turning upside down,
    78–79
proposition(s), 59, 83, 98, 129,
    138, 249
risk class, 2, 72
Management
action, normative, 265
incentive structure, 77

Managers, poorly diversified, 83
Margins:
  narrow, 15, 241
  pressure on, 239
Market(s):
  (highly) liquid, 28, 43, 47, 186,
    191, 246, 272, 276–278, 280
  complete, 2, 58, 61–62, 64, 66–67,
    72, 74, 97
  efficient, 2, 11, 14, 28, 47
  frictionless, 58–59, 61, 247
  illiquid, 42, 134, 272, 280
  imperfect(ions), 12–13, 28, 74, 79,
    97–98, 101, 114, 116, 121,
    125, 129, 135, 137
  information-efficient, 59
  perfect, 2, 12, 14, 28, 58, 62, 98,
    134
  spot, 40–41
Market capitalization, 2, 16, 18, 149,
    219, 240, 282, 284
Market conditions, adverse, 186, 193
Market crash, 195
Market discipline, 143, 216
Market expectation(s), 47
Market for corporate control, 1, 10, 81
Market imperfections, other, 79, 116,
    121
Market index, broad (M). *See* Market
    portfolio, broad
Market index. *See* Market portfolio,
    broad
Market inefficiencies, 78, 121, 123,
    125, 277
Market making, 281
Market model. *See* Model, market
Market participant(s), 3, 28–29, 41,
    47, 56, 58–59, 61, 63, 72, 74,
    76, 136, 156–157, 178, 273,
    277
Market participation, 73
Market players. *See* Market
    participants
Market portfolio, broad, 5, 16–18,
    34, 36, 136, 168, 195, 210,
    237, 246, 254, 256, 261, 266,
    288, 290

Market price:
  of risk, 271, 291
  fair, 62, 70, 124, 132, 270, 274,
    277
Market risk. *See* Risk, market
Market terms, fair, 67, 69, 97, 270
Market theory, neoclassical, 11
Market value:
  fair, 41, 149, 270, 277
  of assets, 110, 148–149, 151, 220,
    222, 226–227, 231, 247, 248,
    260
  of debt, 14–15, 81, 91, 93, 222,
    247, 264
  (of) firm, 76, 91, 121, 130, 221
  of equity, 14, 81, 149, 156, 161,
    220, 222, 227, 231, 236, 267
  of liabilities, 15, 149, 151, 156, 226
Market-to-book ratio, 104
Mark to market, 120, 149, 166, 186,
    241
Markov, 174, 195
Matched duration, 246
Matrix:
  migration. *See* Migration matrix
  transition. *See* Transition matrix
Maturity, 15, 28, 45, 147, 165, 172,
    222–223, 226, 228, 247
Measure(s):
  accounting-based, 149, 164
  economic, 10, 161
  of dispersion, 24
  of total risk, 6, 135, 237, 289
Measurement:
  period, 167, 185, 214, 237, 244,
    252, 263
  process, 210
Mergers and acquisitions (M&A), 10,
    18
Merton and Perold model. *See* Model,
    two-factor
Metallgesellschaft, 86, 114
Method(s):
  allocation, 244
  transfer, 244
Migration, 170, 176, 178
  matrix, 174

Misperception of the riskiness of a firm, 55, 121
Model(s):
  internal, 191
  macroeconomic (simulation), 208, 211, 216
  single factor, 267–269, 291
  two-factor:
    Froot and Stein, 270–272, 278
    Merton and Perold, 269–270, 272
    Stulz, 271–273, 278
Model, market, 37, 230
Modigliani and Miller. *See* M&M
Money, patient, 146–147
Monitoring, 42–43, 73, 76, 81, 89–90, 94, 114, 122, 124, 140, 147, 168, 195
Monopoly, 112
Moody's (Investor Service), 157, 173–174, 220
Moral hazard, 41, 76, 81, 83, 87, 146
Motivation, 34, 74, 89, 144
Multidimensionality, 132

Negotiation process, 155, 157, 159, 163, 289
Neoclassical (finance) world. *See* Finance theory, neoclassical
Neoinstitutional economics and finance theory. *See* Finance theory, neoinstitutional
Net income, risk-adjusted, 243–245, 251–252
Net position, 26
Net present value (NPV), 11–12, 21, 84, 238
  criterion or rule, 11, 14, 22, 134, 247, 279, 291
  of wealth, maximization of, 11
New Basle Accord (Basle II), 3, 7, 146, 159, 209, 216, 240
  Pillar Three, 285
Noise, reduction of, 88–89
Notional amount, 45
NPV. *See also* Net present value

NPV projects:
  accepting negative, 82, 93, 247, 262, 290
  forgo positive, 95–97, 99, 108, 247
  negative, 82, 121, 133, 254, 257, 259
  positive, 98, 104, 124, 133, 238, 254, 257, 260, 290
  postpone positive, 104
Numerical procedure(s), 182, 185–186

Objective, interim, 13
Objective function, 29, 113, 262
  concave, 85, 87, 91, 100, 112–113, 120
  firm's. *See* Firm objective function
  for risk management, 29
  value maximization as, 1, 13, 27
  VaR as an, 262
Obligations, short-term, 226
Oliver, Wyman & Company, 111, 210, 220
Operational Risk. *See* Risk, operational
Operations:
  back office, 197
  bank's business, 1–2, 15, 148, 156
  changes in, 63, 65, 68–69, 71, 130
  discontinuation of bank, 156
  international, 26, 55, 244
Option(s), 33, 40, 56, 63, 85–86, 93, 103, 190, 278
  call, 93, 222, 227–228
    European, 222, 227, 248
  delta of, 45, 228
  put, 93, 149, 161, 222, 248, 264
    European, 248
  real, 2, 11
  underlying of, 45, 222, 227, 248
Option payoff, 248
Option premium, 124
Option (pricing) theory, 220–221, 225–226, 248
Outcome(s), stochastic, 24
Overhead, allocated, 243
Overhedging, 46, 102–103

Overinvestment, 75, 79, 82, 86, 125
Owner-managers, 140
Ownership:
  concentration, 82, 91–92, 127
  line of equally distributed, 91

P&L. *See* Profit and loss account
Package, bundled, 277, 279
Parameterization, 175, 255
Participation (cost), 29, 73, 80, 93,
  114–115
Payment, system, 144
Payoff (structure), 63, 85–86, 89,
  154, 168
PD(s). *See* Probability of default
Pecking order theory, 32, 105
Peer group, 140, 162
Perception, (market), 13, 44, 216
  of managerial talent, 87
Performance:
  evaluation, 27, 242
  incentives, 85, 89, 246
  measurement, 25, 210, 238
  measures, 4, 89, 239–241, 253,
    274, 284
Period:
  estimation. *See* Estimation period
  holding, 188, 191, 193, 214–215.
    See also Estimation horizon
  liquidation, 193, 215
  measurement. *See* Measurement
    period
Perspective. *See* Point of view
Point of view:
  accounting, 155, 264
  bond (or debt) holder, 23, 147
  customer, 122
  economic, 7, 10, 78, 137, 144–145,
    150, 154, 168, 193, 264
  empirical, 91
  insider, 150
  integrated, 4, 26
  regulatory, 23, 33, 81, 137, 144–
    145, 147–148, 150–151, 154,
    161, 163, 192, 236, 289
  risk-based, risk-oriented, or risk-
    related, 146, 150, 159–160, 240
  shareholder, 23, 86, 114

  stakeholder, 33–34, 145, 147, 150,
    153,
  theoretical, 21, 34, 43, 137, 146,
    236, 240, 242, 287, 289, 291
Portfolio:
  composition, 28, 122, 288
  constitution, 72, 74, 134, 259
  diversification. *See* Diversification
  investment strategy, 63
  perspective, 27, 34
  self-financing, 252, 262
  theory (modern), 9, 62, 64, 178, 180
  unexpected loss, 179
  well-diversified, 64, 66, 68–69, 178
Position(s):
  non-linear, 189–190
  short, 189, 228
  trading. *See* Trading position
Preferences, nonfinancial, 59, 75
Present value (PV), 2, 11–12, 39, 65,
  111, 131, 221
  of agency costs:
    of debt, 123, 288
    of equity, 123, 129, 288
  of bank equity, 2, 240
  of expected financial distress costs,
    106, 111–112, 123
  of tax payments, 116, 120–121,
    123, 125
  of transaction costs, 129
Price-setting, 59
Price takers, 58
Pricing factor, second, 271–272
Principal(s), 75, 81, 83, 85–87, 90,
  141, 173
Principal-agent:
  conflict, 83
  problems, 90
  relationship, 85
Private sector, 145
Probability of bank default. *See*
  Likelihood of bank default
Probability of default, 43, 76, 80–82,
  84, 94–95, 104, 107, 109, 111,
  120, 123, 125–126, 147, 160,
  172–174, 176, 179, 216, 220,
  224–226, 229, 234, 236, 251,
  288

actual, 225–226, 248
cumulative, 284
fixed, 249, 254
forward, 174
implied, 220, 223, 233–234
marginal, 174
multiperiod, 174
risk-neutral, 225–226, 229, 248
Procedure, iterative, 228, 230–233
Process:
  agency rating, 205
  controlling, 27, 41, 278
  implementation, 27
  planning, 27
  Wiener, 221, 225
  work-out, 177
Product:
  life cycle, 206
  risk-bundled, 279
Profit(s):
  accounting, 245
  economic, 238–239, 244–247, 258,
    277
Profitability, economic, 239, 241–242,
  262–263
Profit and loss account (P&L), 25,
  207–208, 214–215, 238
Profit, center, decentralized, 260
Prompt corrective action, 150
Property rights (theory), 75–76
Proposition, value-destroying, 33, 71,
  277, 288
Provisions, 5, 148, 245, 285. *See also*
  Reserves, loan loss
Proxy battle(s), 12
Put option. *See* Option(s), put
PV. *See* Present value

Quantile, 167, 188–189, 207–208,
  218

Ranking, relative, 254, 258
RAPM. *See* Risk-adjusted
  performance measures
RAROC. *See* Risk-adjusted return on
  capital
RARORAC. *See* Risk-adjusted return
  on risk-adjusted capital

Rate of return:
  appropriate, 1, 21, 241, 245
  CAPM-determined, 270, 274
  expected, 60, 223
  required, 5, 21, 62, 77, 245, 249,
    255, 268, 273
  risk-free, 244, 252
  standard deviation or volatility of,
    36, 228, 244
Rate, risk-free, 155, 222–223, 225,
  228–231, 233, 244, 248, 251–
  252, 259, 266
Rating:
  analysis, 157
  borrower or counterparty, 171–173
  public or external agency, 156–157,
    159, 163, 220, 223, 225, 233
Rationale(s) for risk management. *See*
  Risk management, rationale
  for
Rationality, limited, 76
Reallocation, 213, 235
Recapitalization, 2, 132, 195
Recovery rate, 172–173, 176
Redistribution, 12, 72, 99, 155, 276,
  278
Refinancing, 141, 223
Regulation, 5, 7, 22, 58, 74, 105,
  123, 139, 143, 147, 157, 197
Regulators, 22, 33, 55, 81, 142–146,
  149, 151, 154, 158, 191, 236,
  287
Regulatory:
  capital. *See* Capital, regulatory
  requirements, 3–4, 25, 33, 56, 130,
    145, 146, 162, 164, 194
  rules. *See* Regulatory requirements
  safety net, 142
Rent(s), economic, 277, 281
Reorganization, 107
Repayment, 141–142, 158, 252, 275
Repercussion(s), systemic, 3
Reporting cycle, 214, 223
Reputation (loss of) 84, 88, 109–110,
  157
Reserve(s):
  disclosed, 148
  hidden, 161, 260

Reserve(s) *(continued)*
  loan loss, 140, 148, 161, 171, 202
  undisclosed, 148
Reserve pool, 251, 253
Resource(s), allocation of, 62, 75
Restriction:
  binding, 144, 160, 162, 164, 198,
    239–240
  transfer, 26, 171
Restructuring, 1, 7, 10, 15, 151
  of debt obligations, 173
Return(s):
  expected or mean, 25, 27, 60, 62,
    64, 108, 142, 151–152, 158,
    168–169, 186–189, 192–193,
    195–196, 223, 229, 249, 251,
    254
  geometric daily, 194
  weighted average asset, 234, 236
Return on:
  assets (ROA), 4, 151, 223, 230,
    239, 249
  economic capital, 241, 243
  equity (ROE), 4–5, 32, 39, 228,
    239–241, 243, 249–252, 267,
    276, 290
  invested (equity) capital, 240
  regulatory capital, 240
  risk-adjusted capital (RORAC), 243
Revenues, 109, 152, 197, 205–208,
    239, 241, 260, 280–282
  buffer function of, 161, 169
  expected, 161, 205, 207, 243
  marginal, 63
  other, 243
Review cycle, 171, 214
Risk(s):
  (firm-) specific risk. *See* Risk(s),
    specific
  bad, 136
  compensated, 27, 70, 134, 141–
    142, 166, 267, 277
  continuous, 25–26, 196, 197
  discontinuous, 25, 166
  downside, 23, 147, 168, 178, 219
  enterprise-level, 29
  financial, 3, 34, 41, 60, 100, 166,
    196, 216

  foreign exchange, 56, 165, 186,
    271
  good, 136
  hedgable, 246, 271, 273, 277, 279,
    281
  idiosyncratic, 133, 265, 268
  illiquid, 41, 135, 214, 246, 271,
    273, 275, 279
  interest rate, 114, 165, 186, 209,
    246, 271, 281
  liquid, 134, 165, 271, 273, 275,
    277–278, 292
  macroeconomic, 166, 215, 235
  market (-wide), 24, 34, 64, 278
  marketable, 32, 134, 271, 281
  nonhedgable, 133, 272
  nonmarketable or unmarketable,
    133, 135, 268
  nonsystematic or unsystematic. *See*
    Risk(s), specific
  perceived, 14, 121
  political, 56, 165
  specific, 24, 26, 34, 36–40, 42, 49,
    60, 62–74, 82–84, 89–90, 103,
    111–114, 133–135, 166, 168–
    169, 210, 243, 265–266, 270–
    271, 278–280, 288–289
  systematic, 2–3, 5, 24, 34, 36–38,
    40, 49, 60, 62–77, 89, 112,
    133, 135–136, 168, 240, 254,
    266, 275, 288, 290
  total, 3, 5, 36, 62, 74, 84, 113,
    132–137, 141, 151, 161, 164,
    166, 168, 170, 187, 192, 194,
    219, 236–238, 240, 242, 245,
    261, 265, 267–274, 276, 279–
    280, 283, 285, 288–291
  tradable, 271
Risk absorption, 43, 150
Risk-adjusted performance measures
    (RAPM), 5, 7, 131, 241, 243–
    244, 290
Risk-adjusted return on capital
    (RAROC), 5, 7, 136, 241, 242
  adjusted, 255, 258
  advantages of, 245–247
  as acceptable proxy, 242, 247, 258,
    267, 289, 291

as biased measure, 252, 267, 273, 290–291
as capital-budgeting tool, 6, 242, 245, 267–269, 284–285, 290–291
as flows-to-economic capital approach, 256
as modified return on equity ratio, 5, 241, 243, 267, 290
as performance measure, 241, 253, 274, 284, 290
as single factor model, 267–269, 291
as single period measure, 244, 247, 260, 290
assumptions of, 247–253
decision rule, 257–260
deficiencies of, 253–267
definition of, 242–245
fundamental problems, 253, 261–262
in practice, 6, 246, 259–262, 286, 290–291
multiperiod, 260–261, 284
pretax, 244
transformation into economic profits, 244–247, 258
Risk-adjusted return on risk-adjusted capital (RARORAC), 243
Risk allocation, 29, 122
Risk analysis, 9
Risk appetite, 162
Risk, as (negative) deviation from an expected outcome, 24, 111, 168–169, 185
Risk, as raison d'être for existence of banks, 9
Risk, as uncertainty of outcomes, 3, 11, 24–25, 32, 142, 175–176
Risk, asset-liability. *See* Risk, balance sheet
Risk-averse. *See* Risk, aversion.
Risk, aversion, 55
    individual, 60, 71, 85, 89
    managerial, 78, 83–85
    quasi, 132, 134, 281
    stakeholder, 83, 89
Risk, balance sheet, 165
Risk, bankruptcy, 3–4, 23, 28, 138

Risk bearing:
    outside the firm, 23, 60, 64, 72, 74, 77, 83, 89, 112, 136, 161, 178, 271
    within the firm, 29, 64, 74, 111, 124, 134, 136, 271–272, 274, 281, 289
Risk, beyond control, 89, 246
Risk, bundling and unbundling of, 29, 40, 277
Risk, business, 12, 141, 165–166, 196–197, 199, 205–209
Risk capacity, 121, 136, 281
Risk capital. *See* Capital, risk
Risk, categories of, 24, 165, 197, 204–205
Risk, characteristics of, 11, 176, 202
Risk component, 38, 88, 186, 272
Risk concentration, 3, 140–141, 145, 159, 182
Risk contribution, 5, 37, 170, 176, 182, 185, 237, 253, 266, 276, 283, 290
Risk, control(ling), 27, 198
Risk cost(s), standard, 171
Risk, country. *See* Risk, transfer
Risk, covariance. *See* Risk, systematic
Risk, credit, 32, 141, 145, 157, 159, 165–166, 170–186, 195, 198–199, 201–205, 209, 211, 239, 246, 265–266, 275, 278, 281, 290
Risk, definition of, 24, 243
Risk dimension, 31, 34, 136
Risk, eliminating, 38, 40–42, 46, 62, 64–66, 70–71, 178, 279, 281
Risk, event, 25–26, 40, 165–166, 196–197, 199–205, 209, 216, 279
Risk exposure(s), 26, 28, 44, 46, 63, 88, 114–115, 135, 166, 237
Risk factor(s), 21, 26, 28, 34, 39, 63, 77, 96, 102–103, 121, 132, 186, 188, 190, 195, 198, 216, 270
Risk, legal, 157, 165, 197
Risk, limiting, 7, 27, 150, 170, 187, 190, 193, 212

Risk, liquidity, 3, 165
Risk management:
  active, 27–28, 42, 193
  activities, 9, 78, 82, 88, 126, 131,
    239, 259, 278
    as purely financial transactions,
      63
  and value creation, 6, 9, 30, 43, 58,
    74, 287
  approach(es), 3, 39–42, 124, 289
  as (distinct) process, steps, 26
  as black box, 56
  as empirical fact, 287
  as not experiencing negative events,
    56
  as organizational unit, 25, 28
  as strategic weapon, 55
  as substitute to equity/capital, 4,
    112, 123, 126
  as substitute to publication of
    internal information, 115
  at the bank or firm level, 57–58,
    66, 71, 73, 78, 115, 121, 124,
    129, 137, 287–289. *See also*
    Risk management, corporate
  at the level of individual investors,
    9, 58, 60, 64, 66, 69
  benefits of, 30, 81–82, 90, 96, 121
  by asset allocation, 60, 68–69, 103
  by diversification, 42, 60, 62, 65,
    103
  central role of, in banks, 30, 42, 48
  concern with, 29, 100, 123
  condition for:
    necessary but not sufficient, 56,
      116, 287
    sufficient, 56, 58, 287
  corporate, 39, 43–44, 55, 57–58,
    61, 65–66, 69–71, 90, 120,
    123–124, 129, 134, 244, 287–
    288
    benefits, 79, 81
    dimension, 65
    incentive for, 84
    on behalf of the investor(s), 60
    rationale for, 6, 78, 112
  culture, 246

decision(s), 2, 5, 61, 71, 77, 85,
    236, 274, 280, 288–289, 291
definition of, 25
degree of, 142, 166
discrepancy between theory and
    practice, 6, 287, 290
efficiency of, 2
forms of, 137, 150, 289
function(s), 3, 26, 138, 140
goal(s) of, 9, 27, 31–34, 38–39, 74,
    120, 166
home-made, 64, 77, 112, 121
in banks, 3, 5–6, 9, 23, 28, 30–31,
    39, 48, 55, 104, 122–123, 274,
    276, 280, 286–287, 291
in practice, 3, 6, 34, 44, 55–56, 72,
    91, 198, 251, 287
instruments, 9, 38, 42–46, 66–67,
    150, 273, 276, 278, 289
irrelevance (proposition), 57, 63–
    72, 74, 77, 136, 276, 288
mechanics, 131
normative theory for, 6, 48, 57, 73,
    129, 269, 274–275, 280–281,
    286–287, 289, 291
objective of, 30, 77
positive theory for, 3, 5, 48, 55,
    287
proposition(s), 130
rationale for, 30, 58, 72, 78, 81,
    84, 100, 105
redundancy of, 61, 72, 104
replication of, 2, 37, 57, 61, 64, 69,
    72, 74, 121, 288
reversing, 2, 57, 68, 288
scenario(s), 65–71
set of actions, 39–42
skills, superior, 42, 73
strategy, 31–32, 38–39, 46, 48, 70,
    88, 91, 103, 116, 120, 129,
    131–132, 136
subjective view of, 73
techniques, state-of-the-art, 47, 130
through changes in operations, 65,
    68–69, 71, 130
through financial instruments, 56,
    61, 65–66, 69, 140

to increase transparency of management capabilities, 87–88

to make external finance redundant, 61, 104

to protect value, 77, 105

to reduce agency costs, 81–82, 90, 94, 97, 123, 126, 288,

to speculate, 32, 45–46, 56

ways to conduct, 31, 39–40, 43, 48

Risk, market, 25–26, 157, 159, 165–170, 178, 185–197, 209–215, 246, 254, 265–266, 271–277, 279, 290

Risk, model, 211, 220

Risk neutrality, 61, 100, 223, 225, 228

Risk, operational, 141, 157, 165, 170, 186, 196–211, 214, 220, 246, 265–266, 275, 278–279, 290

Risk, outsourcing of, 199–200

Risk pooling, 3, 42, 200, 279

Risk, position. *See* Risk, market

Risk preference(s), 100, 114, 223

problem, 79, 82–84, 86, 88–91, 125

Risk premium, 60, 83, 93, 111–112, 230, 233, 266

Risk professional, 141

Risk profile, 21, 27, 29, 33, 59, 62, 70, 72–73, 76, 79, 84, 90, 93, 105, 114–115, 122, 125, 141, 157, 163, 184, 202

Risk, regulatory, 165

Risk, residual. *See* Risk, operational

Risk-return perspective, 9, 27

Risk, self-insurance of, 200–201, 279

Risk-shifting, 93–94. *See also* Asset substitution

Risk spectrum, 278, 280

Risk, systemic, 3, 22, 110, 144

Risk, taking. *See* Risk, bearing

Risk, total:

concern with, 237–238, 240, 245, 267, 269, 272, 285, 290

cost of, 137, 238, 265, 267, 271–275, 280, 291

Risk trading, 29, 157

Risk transfer, 29, 43, 56, 80

Risk, transfer, 171, 196, 206

Risk transparency, 115

Risk, types (of), 6, 26, 41, 88, 150, 164–166, 169–170, 175, 186–187, 192, 196, 199, 210–211, 213–216, 220, 265–266

correlation between, 211, 213, 235, 237–238, 265, 279, 289

Risk variable, 103, 131

ROA. *See* Return on assets

ROE. *See* Return on equity

S&P. *See* Standard & Poor's

Safety level, required, 160

Safety net, 139, 142–144, 146

Savings, 15, 22–23, 90, 108, 116, 142, 151–152, 158, 163

Scenario test, 195

Scrutiny of external markets, 104

Securitization, 40, 153, 162, 178, 278, 281

Security Market Line (SML), 34, 67–68

Semivariance, 24, 217

Seniority of claim(s), 142, 155, 222

Sensitivity, 18, 23, 46, 135

analysis, 235

Separation of ownership and decision/control power, 75

Severity, 102, 172, 210, 217–219, 282

Shareholder(s):

as option holder(s), 33, 93, 149, 161

as residual claimants, 22, 93, 95

well-diversified, 60, 64, 111

Shareholder-bond holder conflict. *See* Conflicts of interest, between shareholders and bond holders

Shareholder clientele(s), 70

Shareholder-manager conflict. *See* Conflicts of interest, between managers and shareholders

Shareholder pressure, increased, 1, 240

Shareholder value approach, 14

Sharpe ratio, 244, 252
Shocks, unexpected, 141, 150
Short-selling, 58
Sigma, three, 200–201
Signaling, 33, 87
　cost(s), 99
　effect of dividends, 121
　management capabilities, 83
　management quality, 86–87
Simulation:
　historical, 190
　Monte Carlo, 173–174, 182, 185,
　　　190, 199, 204, 207–209
SML. *See* Security Market Line
Solvency of banks, 122, 159, 169,
　　　187, 191–192, 207–208
　target, 169, 185, 187, 191, 208–
　　　209
Source(s):
　of funds, 32, 98, 146, 219, 262
　of risk, marketable, 32
Specific knowledge, 42, 109, 113,
　　　136, 149
Specificity of transactions, 76
Speculation, 32, 38, 46, 86
Spread(s):
　above risk-free rate, 230, 233
　of sovereign Eurobonds, 175
Square-root-of-time rule, 192
Stakeholder(s), 3, 12, 21–23, 33–34,
　　　39–41, 55, 76, 79, 82–84, 89–
　　　90, 100, 105, 109, 112–114,
　　　122, 124–125, 135, 137, 141–
　　　145, 152–163, 166, 219, 238,
　　　276, 287–289
　value framework, 136
　value maximization, 135
Standard & Poor's, 157, 173, 220,
　　　233–234, 285
Standard asset pricing model, 71, 268
Standard deviation, 24, 175–176,
　　　188, 191, 204, 244
Statement, financial, 45, 214, 226–227
Stochastic dominance, first and second
　　　order, 218
Strategy:
　business or corporate, 131–132, 196

buy-and-hold, 281
　portfolio, 63, 131
　trading, 131
Stress-testing, 190
Strike price, 222, 248
Stulz model. *See* Model, two-factor
Sunk cost(s), 113, 124
Survey data, 44–46, 73
Swap(s), 40, 56, 153, 174, 262, 278
Syndication, 162
Synthesis of interests, 156
System, closed, 230

Tail(s), fat, 184, 190, 195
Takeover(s), hostile, 1, 10, 12, 138
Target(s), strategic, 26
Tax(es), 33, 58, 76, 78–79, 116, 134,
　　　140, 214, 244–245, 247, 282
　benefit(s), 80, 91, 116, 139
　　marginal, 139
　burden, reduction of, 33
　code, 118–119, 244
　credit, 118
　liabilities, 117, 120, 125
　loss carry forward, 117–120
　neutral, 59
　preference item, 118–120
　provisions, 245
　rate:
　　average, 116
　　marginal, 116, 119–120
　schedule:
　　concave, 119
　　convex, 77, 116–120, 125, 244
　　linear, 117
　　non-linear, 118, 120
　shield, 86, 94, 97, 121, 276
Termination of failed banks, orderly,
　　　110
Test, empirical, 284
Threshold level (critical), 151, 156–
　　　160, 163, 166, 169, 188, 206–
　　　208, 216, 220, 227, 289
Time horizon, 111, 185, 187, 195–
　　　196, 201, 208, 214–215,
　　　237
Time of default, 172, 174

Time value of money, 241
Tobin's q, 104
Total quality management (TQM), 200
TQM. *See* Total quality management (TQM)
Trade-off(s), 43, 60, 79, 131, 135, 138–139, 145, 265, 271, 284
Trade relationship(s), 75–76
Trading:
  book, 186, 215
  loss(es), 57
  portfolio, 165, 186
  position, 186, 215
  unit, 188, 195
Tranche(s):
  deposit insurance, 153, 157–158
  deposits and savings, 151–152, 158
  equity, 152, 264
  expected loss, 152
  insurance, 157, 159, 200, 270
  insured depositors, 153
  junior (uninsured) debt, 152, 155, 160–161, 219, 263
  of credit default swap, 153
  of credit securitization, 153
  of losses, 152–153, 157, 159–160, 219, 289
  senior (uninsured) debt, 157–158, 169, 216, 263
  shareholder, 152, 265
  stakeholder, 151
Transaction:
  costs, 6, 11, 14, 28, 46, 58, 62, 68, 71, 73, 76–79, 81, 84–85, 99, 105, 288
  level, 15, 21, 37, 125, 164, 170, 183, 211, 220, 244, 260, 265, 285
  shedding, 213
Transfer pricing, 16, 206, 241, 243, 246, 273, 276, 285
Transfer risk. *See* Risk, transfer
Transformation function of banks, 3, 28
Transition matrix, 174
Treasury function, 186, 246

UL. *See* Loss(es), unexpected
ULC. *See* Loss(es), unexpected, contribution
Uncertainty, 3, 11, 24–25, 75, 87, 142, 158, 175–176, 220
Underhedging, 46, 103
Underinvestment, 76, 79, 91, 94–99, 101, 104, 108–109, 125, 247
Underwriting standard, 41
Unexpected Loss Contribution (ULC). *See* Loss(es), unexpected, contribution
Unexpected losses. *See* Loss(es), unexpected
Utility, maximization, 11, 13, 59, 75, 77–78, 218–219, 253

Valuation framework:
  multiperiod, 1, 14
  traditional, 1, 4–5, 7, 14, 63, 134, 136, 240, 268, 272, 285, 288–290
Valuation model, 254
Value:
  expected, 60, 64, 80, 84, 107, 112, 117–118, 126, 151, 155, 173, 202–203, 206–207, 217, 220–221
  intrinsic, 161
  market, sanitized, 227, 231
  perception of, 13, 55
  true, 13, 99, 111, 228, 255
  unexpected changes in, 26, 96, 164
Value additivity, 222
Value at risk (VaR), 5, 74, 166–169, 218, 237, 289
  and economic capital, 192–194, 219–220, 236, 253
  annual, 192, 215
  approach, 190, 198, 201, 213, 217
  as basis for a common currency, 168, 237
  as total risk measure, 187, 192, 194, 236
  for credit risk, 215
  daily, 187, 191–195, 215
  including liquidity risk, 191

Value at risk (VaR) *(continued)*
  limit(ing using), 187, 190, 213
  limitations of and concerns with,
    194–196, 217, 262
  marginal, 189
  for market, 159, 187–196
  not coherent, 213
  for operational risk, 198, 201
  portfolio, 189, 213
  regulatory approach, 74, 159, 191–
    192, 194
  standalone or transaction, 189,
    212–213
Value-based management, 15
Value-destroying businesses, 1, 258
Value contribution, 245–246
Value creation, 2, 4–7, 9–10, 15, 29–
    30, 43, 48, 58, 61, 63, 67, 69,
    71–72, 116, 124–125, 129,
    136, 138–139, 145, 164, 200,
    214, 237–238, 240–242, 247,
    254, 259, 261, 267–268, 284–
    285, 287, 289–291
Value destruction, 39, 64, 66, 68, 71,
    91, 138, 144–145, 245, 277–
    279
Value framework for banks, 2, 6, 14–
    23, 30, 240, 267–268, 290
Value maximization, 1, 6, 9–10, 12–
    14, 18, 21–22, 27–30, 33, 43,
    48, 63, 78, 95, 135, 239, 281,
    284, 287
Value measurement, 238
VaR. *See* Value at risk
Variable, binomial or Bernoulli, 172,
    177

Variance, 24, 80, 84, 93, 106, 176–
    177, 180, 184, 191, 221, 232
Volatility, 24, 36, 56, 62, 71, 73, 85–
    87, 120, 131, 141, 149, 156, 162,
    168, 179, 182, 189, 193–194,
    205–207, 209, 215, 233, 242
  implied, 228
  of (free) cash flows, 31–32, 47, 82,
    84, 93, 100, 107, 112, 142,
    270–271
  of (market or firm) value, 32–33,
    73, 94, 113
  of (operating) income, 31, 60, 117–
    118, 125
  of assets, 221, 223, 229, 277
  reduction of, through risk
    management, 31–32, 47
  stock-price, 131

WACC. *See* Weighted average cost(s)
    of capital
Warranties, 90, 109
Weighted average cost(s) of capital, 1,
    14, 230, 233, 249–250
Wheel of misfortune, 56–57, 113, 197
Windfall to debt holders, 276
Window dressing, 226, 241
Work effort, 89
Working capital, 154, 262

Yield-to-maturity, promised, 251

Zero NPV:
  proposition, 72
  transaction, 42–43, 251–252, 254–
    255, 257–258